Subway Beats

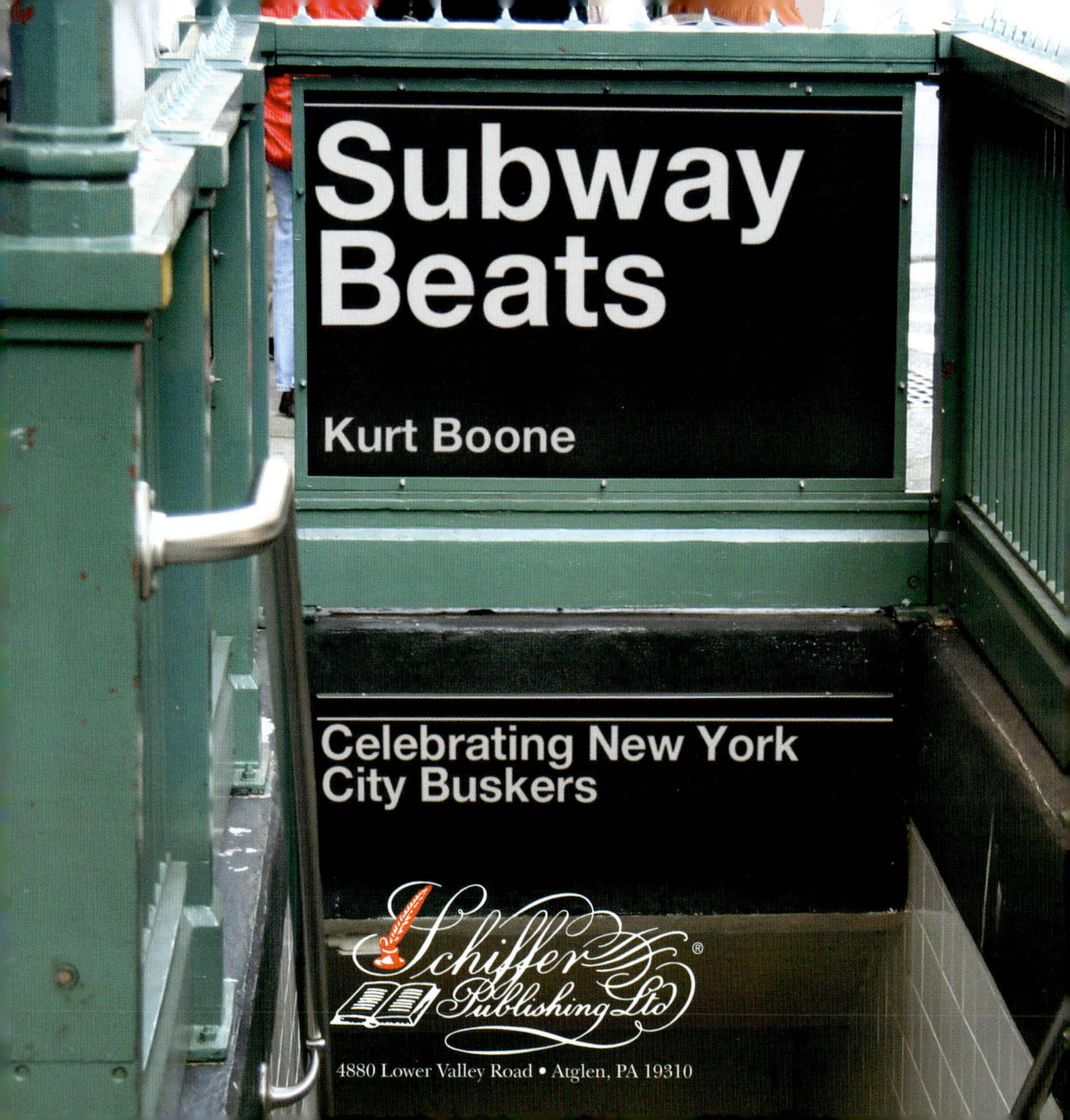

Subway Beats

Kurt Boone

Celebrating New York City Buskers

Schiffer Publishing Ltd®
4880 Lower Valley Road • Atglen, PA 19310

Library of Congress Control Number: 2016943380

Cover & Interior designed by Matthew Goodman
Type set in Helvetica

ISBN: 978-0-7643-5182-2
Printed in China

Published by Schiffer Publishing, Ltd.
4880 Lower Valley Road
Atglen, PA 19310
Phone: (610) 593-1777; Fax: (610) 593-2002
E-mail: Info@schifferbooks.com
Web: www.schifferbooks.com

Contents

Music in the Tunnels

The auditions
Musicians come far
and wide to America
Bringing with them the
sounds of home.
World music is an understatement;
tradition is a better word.
Name your instrument, for
I see them all in Subway Beats.
There is a message
in the music.
New York City is the symbolic
people's capital of the world.
"Humans of New York" you could say.
I love the Empire State.
Sing your song.
I could listen to musicians
performing in the subway all day long.

Acknowledgments

I would like to thank the Boone family for their continuous support of my work, my editor of many years, Denise Hidalgo of APlus Office on Call, Inc.™, and the MTA Music Program.

I discovered the world of subway performers working as a foot messenger in New York City for over fifteen years. Currently I am still working as a courier, but not in the traditional sense: delivering groceries and food for Uber Eats™ and Instacart™ is not exactly messenger work, but it pays the bills. It is with the knowledge of those fifteen years as a courier, riding the trains all over the five boroughs of New York City—and occasionally riding the ferry across to Staten Island to deliver a package—that I learned about and listened to hundreds of subway performers. For the last three years, with a Canon digital point-and-shoot camera in hand, I could photograph what I was seeing on the streets and under ground as I made messenger pickups and deliveries around the city.

As a writer, I have always drawn on my experience to write poems and essays about messenger life, and I love photography and using photos to tell my messenger stories. I approached photographers about my thought to capture my messenger life in photographs and they loved the idea. I also had skills in self-publishing books and I helped photographers do their own photo books. I never thought of shooting photographs myself. I thought I was too clumsy and would not be able to hold a camera still. My friend and mentor Bob Gore, a professional photographer, gave me a point-and-shoot camera as a gift. Bob told me to go ahead and shoot and not worry about the quality of the photo. He also mentioned I would not be able to do much with a point-and-shoot camera unless I was very close to the subject. Another tip he gave me about photography is if I was the only person who captured a moment with my camera then my photograph would become valuable, because I would be the only one who captured the image at

i

Introduction

that moment. So that made me think of my environment and the people I interact with every day on the streets; what if I took pictures of what I saw on those streets, since those would be unique photos expressing my viewpoint?

Toward the end of 2013 I was working for the EBay Innovation Center in New York City; EBay™ had an app they were testing called *EBay Now*, an e-commerce mobile application that included same-day delivery. In 2012, I was the first courier in New York City to do a test run for *EBay Now*, an honor I was quite proud of. By that point, my fifteen years as a foot messenger had made me a master of the city subway system, a subway system that carries millions of commuters around the city's five boroughs. At one time when I was working at Mobile Messenger Service™ I was riding twenty-three different lines every week, picking up and dropping off packages. My expertise in this arena made me a prime candidate for testing a same-day delivery app. In doing my messenger work, I must confess that for many years I never paid the subway musicians any mind. I thought of riding the subway as my job and nothing else. The MTA musicians program, now called MTA Music, was part of a gritty underground economy in New York City. The MTA has its own police department rules and regulations, including auditioning and registering performers on the subways, as I learned later.

Near the end of 2013 and my *EBay Now* job, I began to see that the app was not working very well and soon I would be out of a job. But more importantly, I told myself I needed to take something from the subway system to remember it and to show people that I rode all over the subway system for fifteen-plus years (going on eighteen years as of now). I asked myself what could I take from the system that would be cool and make me happy?

You do not make much money doing messenger work, so many messengers come up with ways to take from the city streets we traverse, including graffiti art, fashion, photography, urban cycling, or street running. I knew I did not want to take a real subway sign or collect unique pieces from all the subway stations.

As I took a long hard look at my experience under ground, thinking about it over several days, I thought why don't I take pictures of the subway performers? I saw more and more of them were performing as part of the MTA Music program. I felt I would be happy if I took pictures of fifty different artists, which I thought was a lot. Photographing subway musicians would also be a good story to talk about and solid proof that I rode the subway system all over the city for many years. It wouldn't be a pension or mean anything, but it was a good and fun story to tell about MTA Transit.

Once I started my journey to photograph subway performers, I quickly learned the cultural diversity of subway performing artists mirrors that of New York City. When I saw this in the pictures I took the freelance writer and self-published author in me came out, so I came up with this cool title for a book and blog called *Subway Beats*. I was sure the *Subway Beats* Internet domain would be taken already, but to my surprise and joy it was not; eureka, I had just struck gold! This was a New York City story waiting to be told in photographs.

I started the project with an *EBay Now* fully loaded iPhone™ camera, but I thought I would need a better point-and-shoot camera, so I took some of the bonus money from working with *EBay Now* that was in Best Buy™ points and bought a Canon Power Shot 2500. I still don't know much about shooting pictures, but the Canon Power Shot has an auto-focus feature that helped me a lot and inspired me to take even more pictures of the street scenes I encountered.

Within a few months I had photographed fifty different artists. It was exciting to photograph some of the most popular ones I had seen doing messenger work over many years, like the "Saw Lady," "Maestro Moses Josiah," and the "Ebony Hillbillies." Some of the spots where the subway musicians perform are dark and lighting was very bad, but I didn't want to use flash too much, as that could disturb the artists.

Once I passed the fifty-artist mark I started photographing bands and ensembles, focusing on the different instruments they were playing; for example, in the "Underground Horns" most of the artists use some kind of horn. I photographed Heth and Jed, who actually wrote a memoir about subway performing called *Buskers*. You will see pictures of many artists where I was unable to get the performer's name, but for each artist I photographed I indicate the station where I took the picture and describe the instrument they used. In most cases the instrument is obvious, but in some cases they are not. I also started doing research on MTA subway performers, especially those having the *MTA Music Under New York* designation. I learned there were auditions for the coveted banner.

My hope is this book amazes you as much as seeing these incredible performers made me believe that New York City is truly a city of the people of the world.

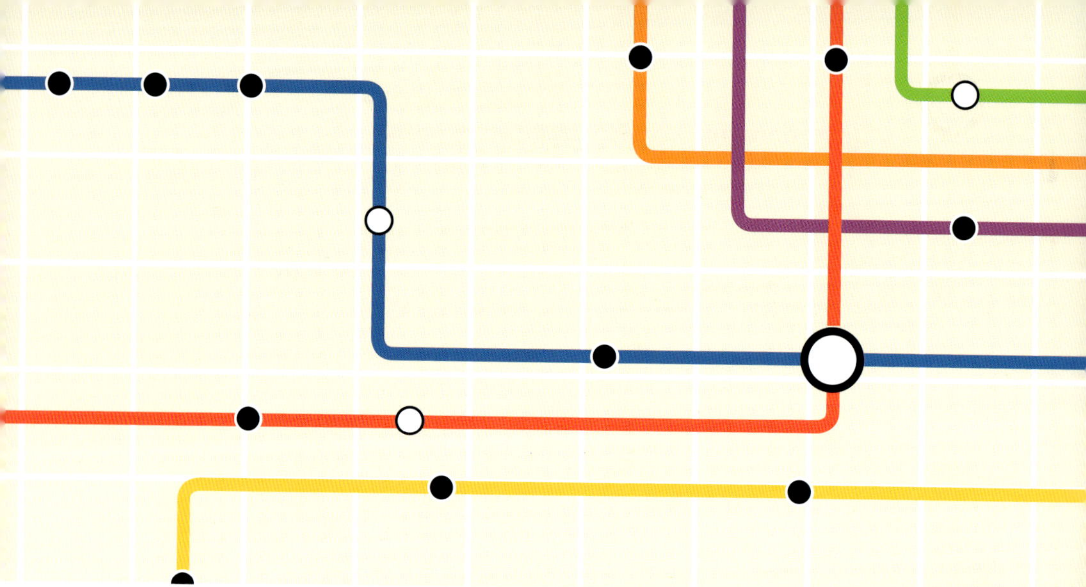

I started getting excited about my good fortune to photograph subway performers, and to become more familiar with this world, I called the MTA Music Under New York office to get a press pass and take photographs of their audition event. As I entered the Grand Central Station area where the auditions were being held I grabbed a press kit from the MTA staff. Preparing to photograph the musicians who were auditioning, I realized my photo equipment was inadequate; the lighting in Grand Central Terminal was poor for the type of camera I had. The other photographers and camera operators came with professional equipment, since most of them worked for major media outlets and were experienced photographers.

The auditions started around 9:00 a.m., with exciting New York City favorite poet and founder of the Bowery Poetry Club Bob Holman as host. The media kit listed each artist in order of their performance and provided a little background information on the MTA Music program. According to the MTA press kit there are over 350 artists in MTA Music who give over 7,500 performances per year in approximately thirty approved locations throughout the MTA transit system.

I have attended two MTA auditions; alas, the photos from the first one were not good enough to

1

Chapter 1

The Auditions

be published. The second time I went to the auditions in 2015, I was able to get better photos that are included. Both times I thought the talent pool and cultural diversity of the artists was amazing, and to see world music performed right in front of me by people who now lived and worked in New York City was truly unique.

The MTA Music auditions are open to the public. The judges who select the next group of musicians to enter the prestigious MTA Music program are experts in music and the performing arts; they are also familiar with the subway system and understand the cultural diversity of New York City. Judges are responsible for selecting twenty new artists from a field of seventy performers (chosen from nearly 200 original submissions). Those twenty that are selected will receive the official banner designating them as members of the *MTA Music Under New York* program. The judges use criteria including quality, variety, appropriateness, and volume to determine whether an artist qualifies to be in the MTA Music program.

In all, it was great to be up close and see the *MTA Music Under New York* audition live; a real treat as a "professional" subway rider and native New Yorker.

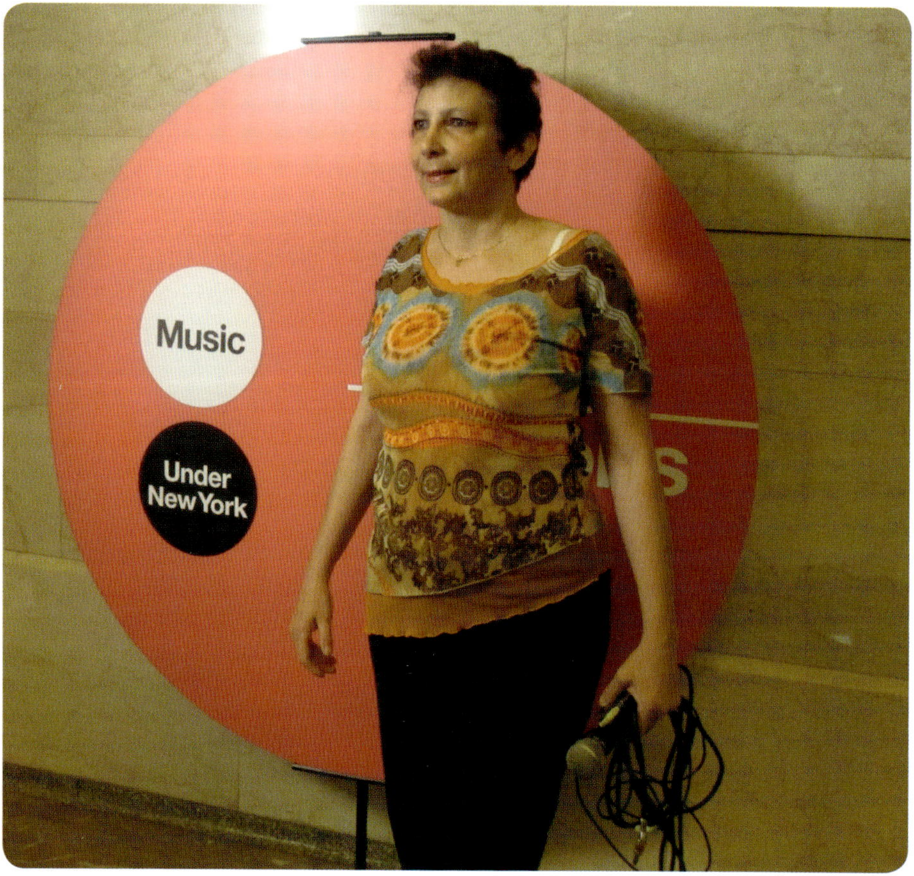

Sylvie Boisel, cabaret singer.

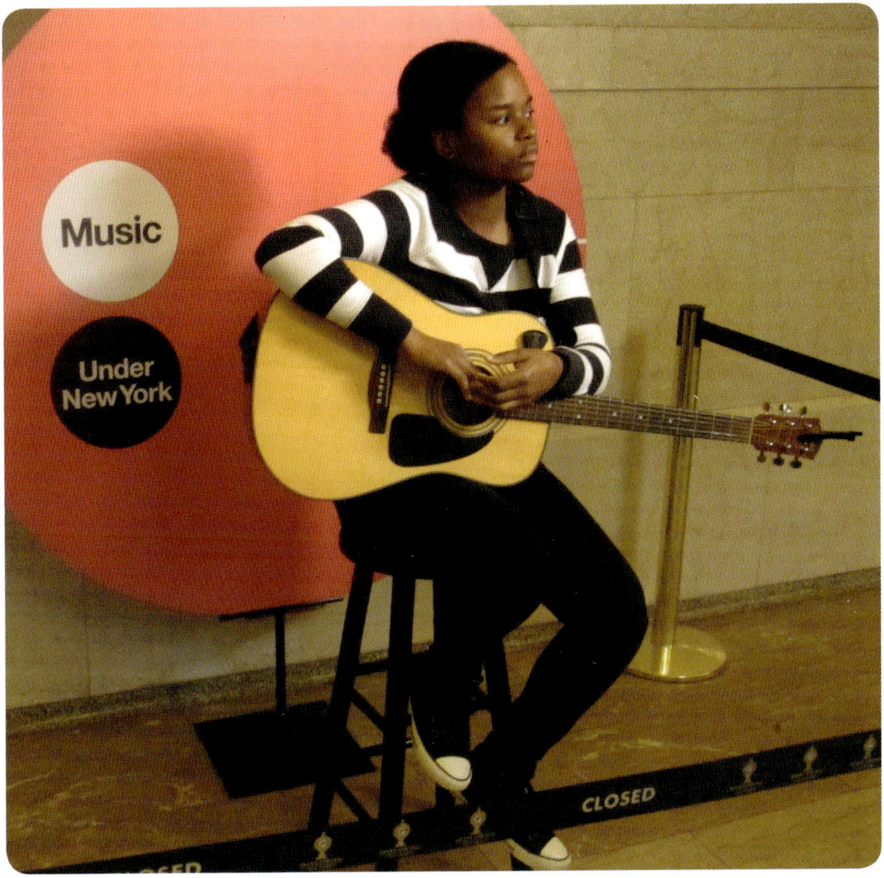

Opal EL, folk singer.

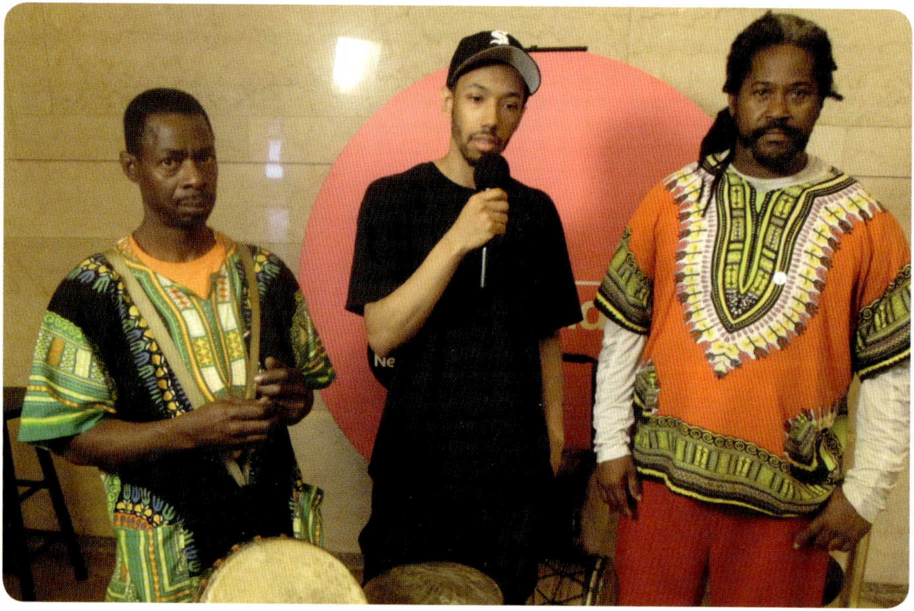

Lost In Rhythm, world afro percussion.

Bellatonic, jazz and pop band.

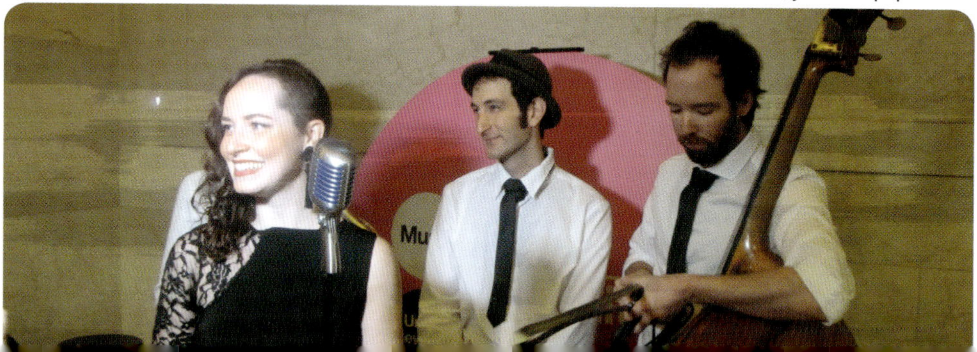

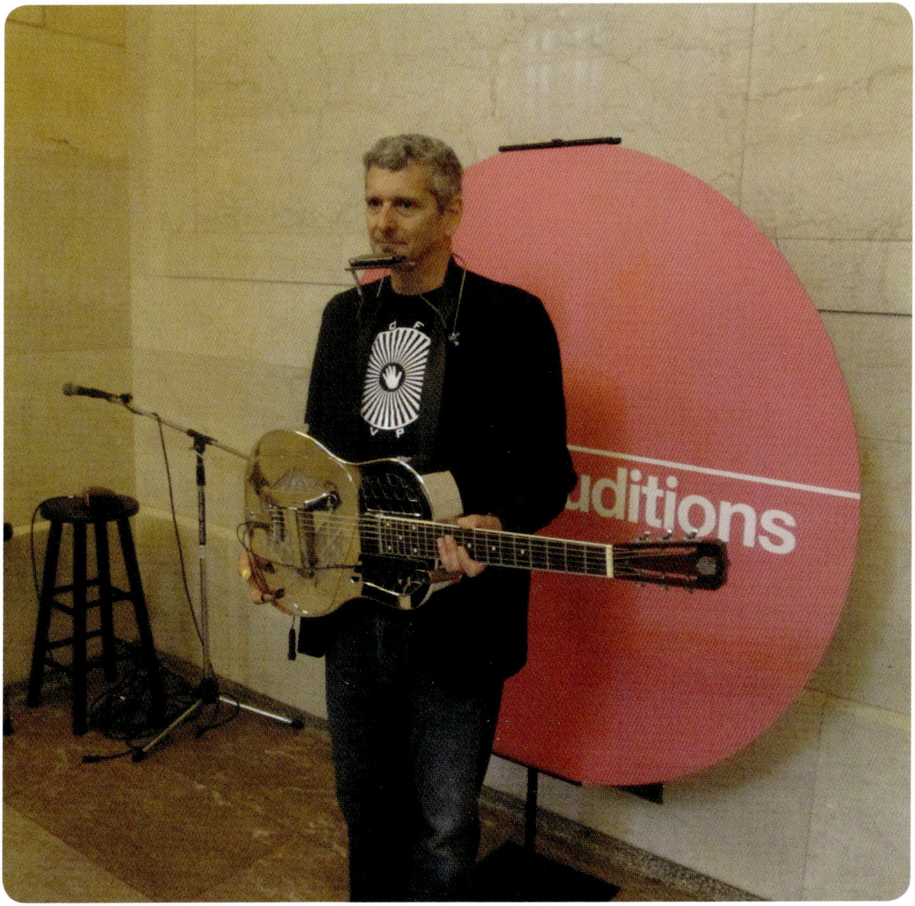

Mark Nomad, blues guitar player and singer.

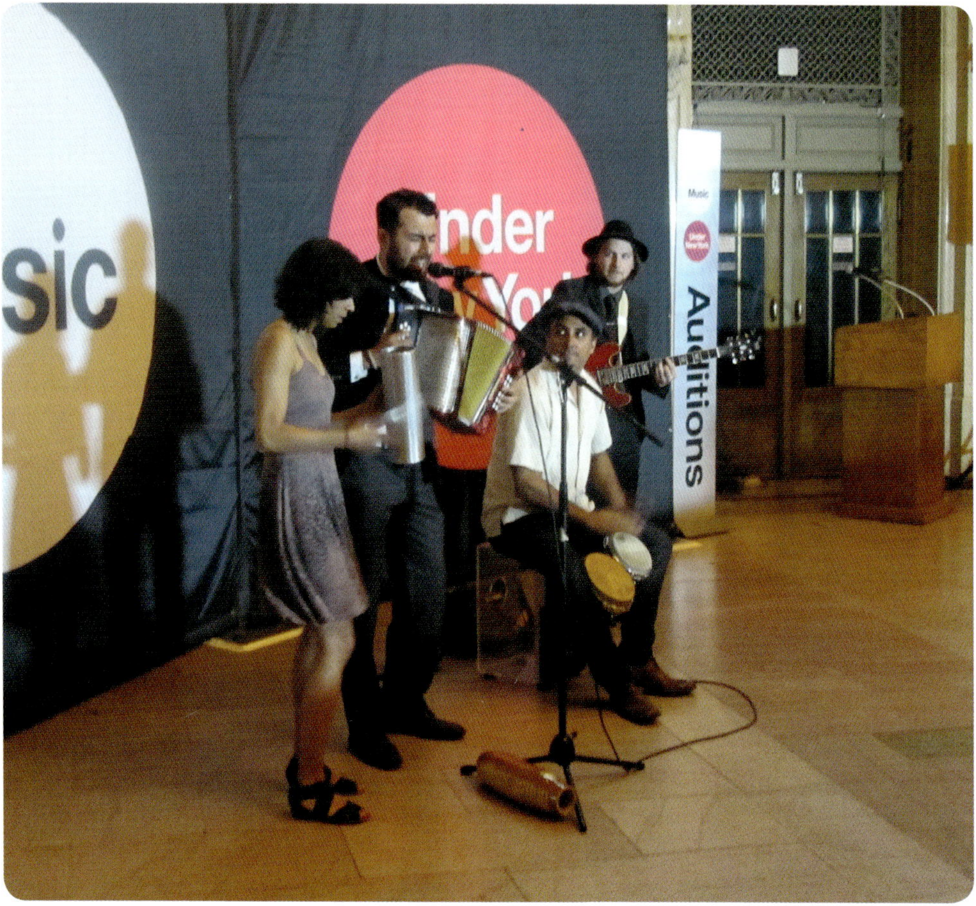

Yotoco, Latin, funk, and jazz band.

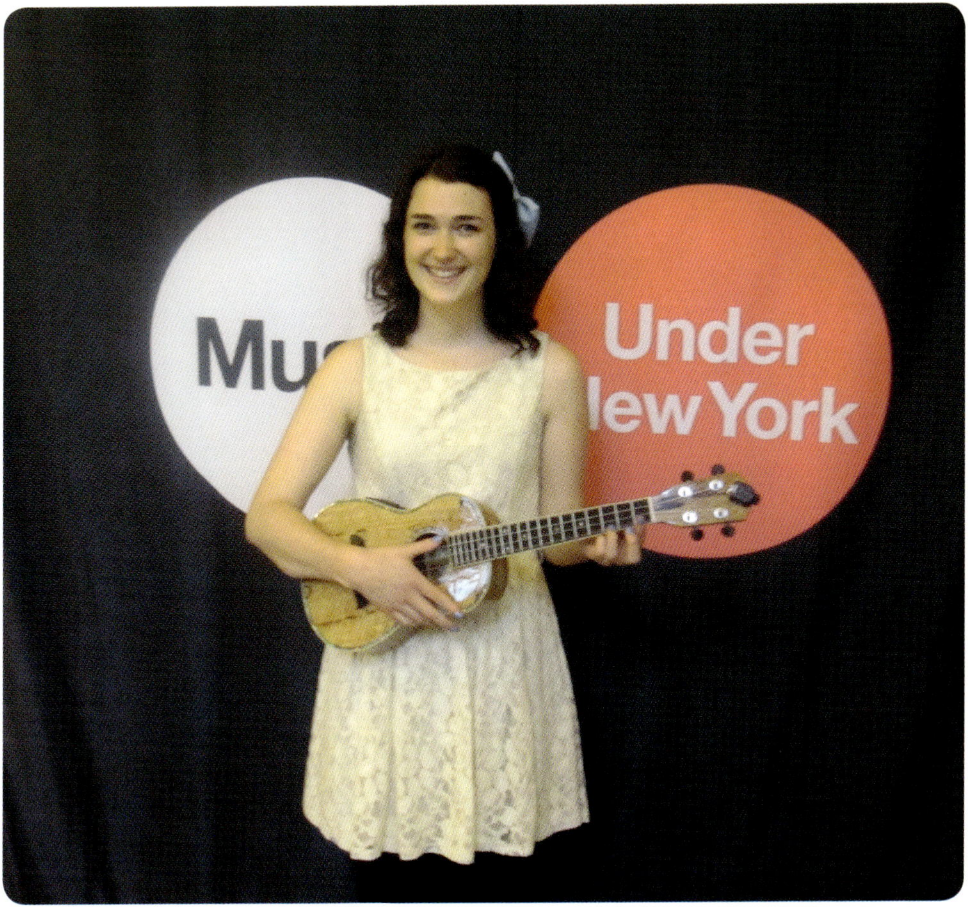

Jill Sargeant, ukulele player and folk singer.

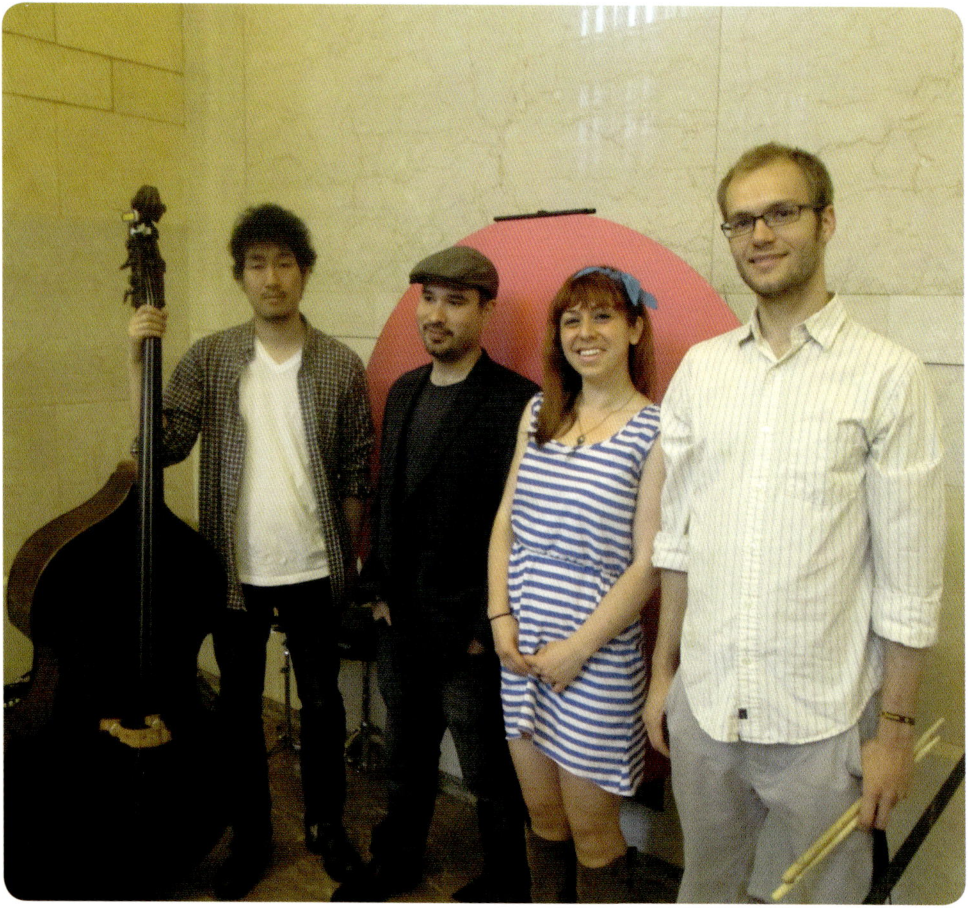

The Blue Dahlia, French reggae and jazz band.

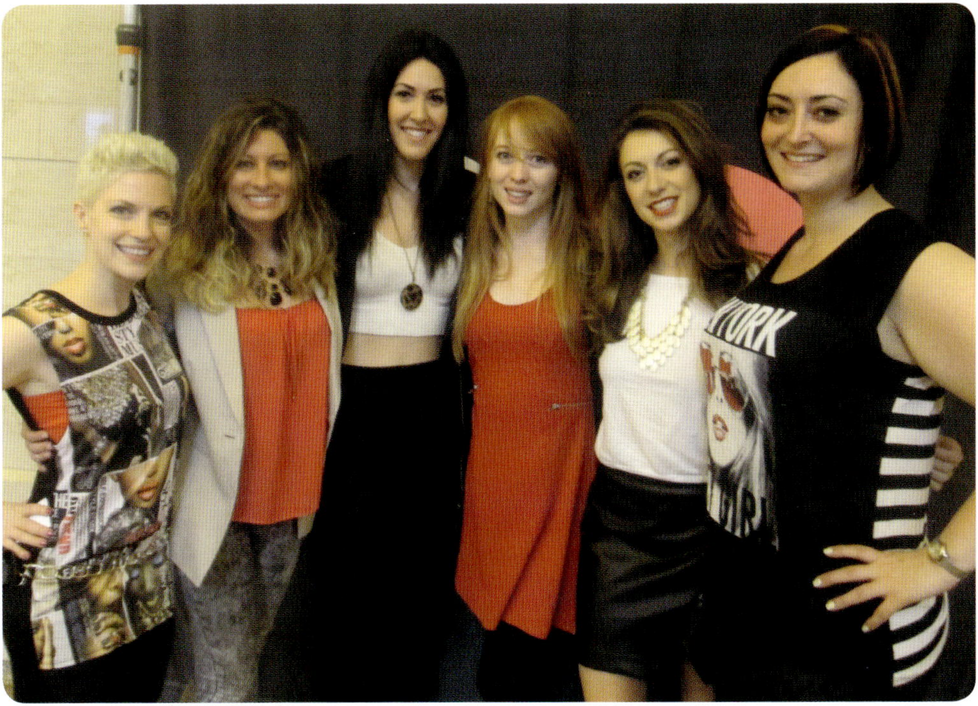

Stiletta, female acapella.

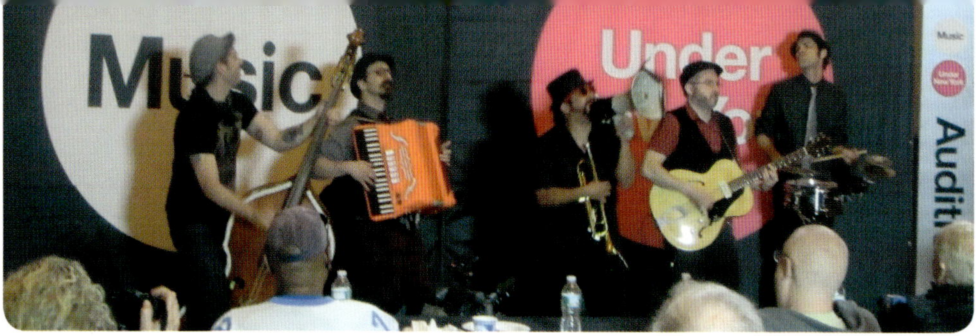

The Sunnyside Social Club, New Orleans jazz band.

Banjo.

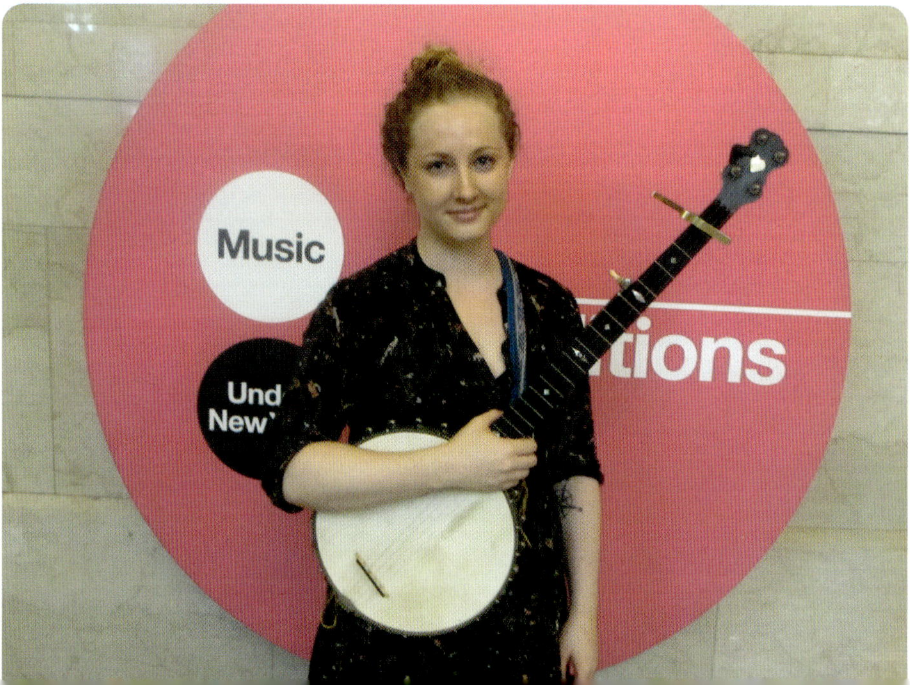

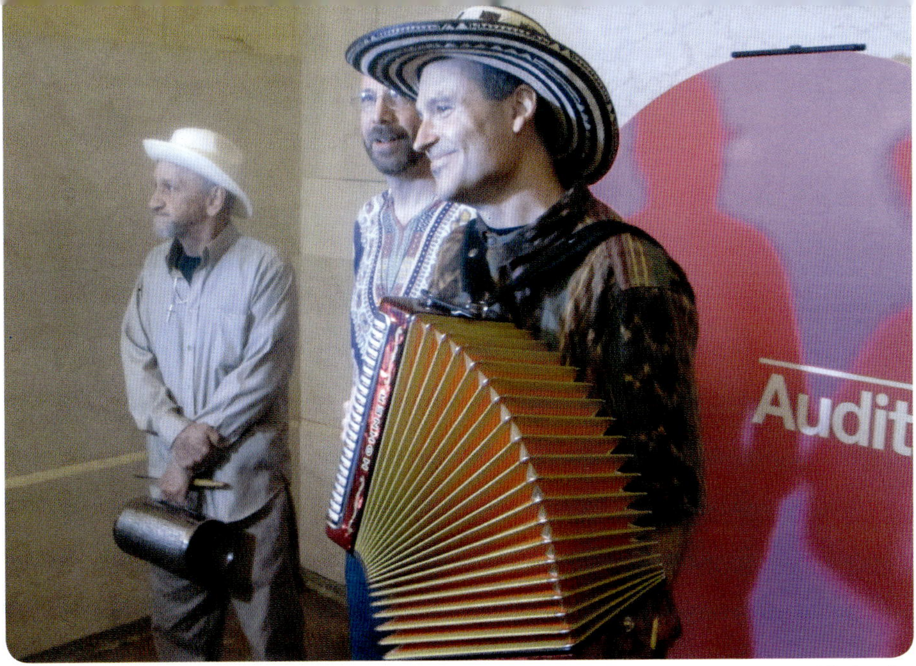

Viva Vallenato Accordion Band, Latin cumbia band.

A violinist in front of the judges.

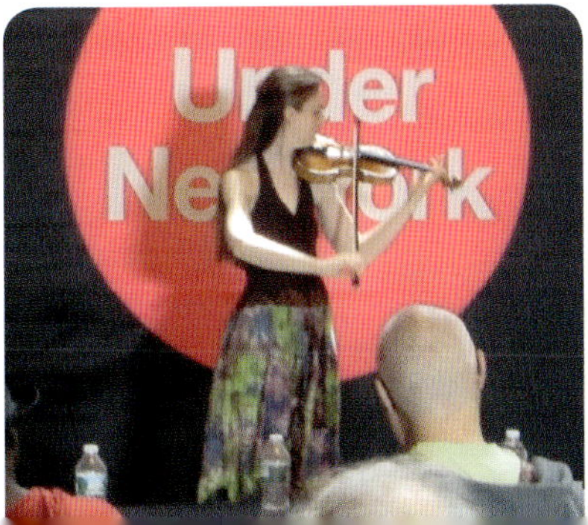

The Wisterians, French waltzes and American standards.

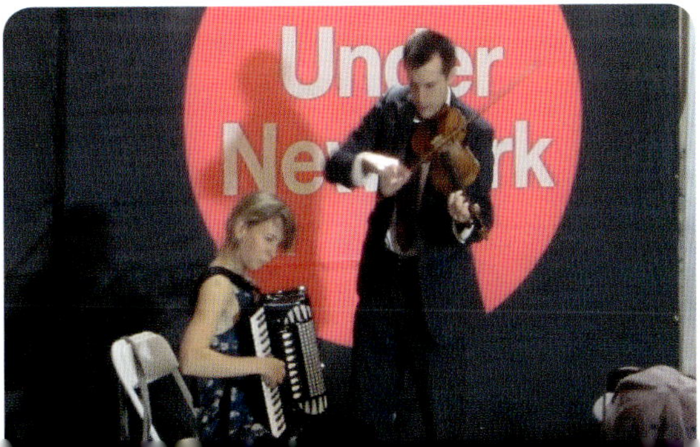

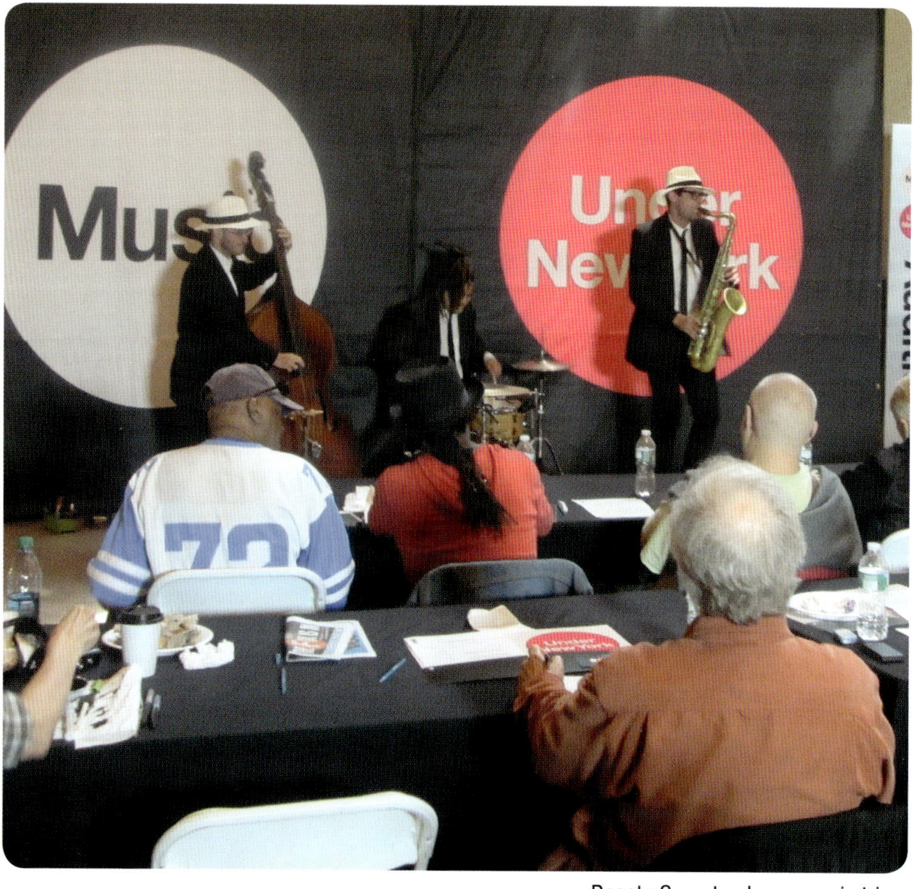

Receta Secreta, dance music trio.

Grand Central Terminal

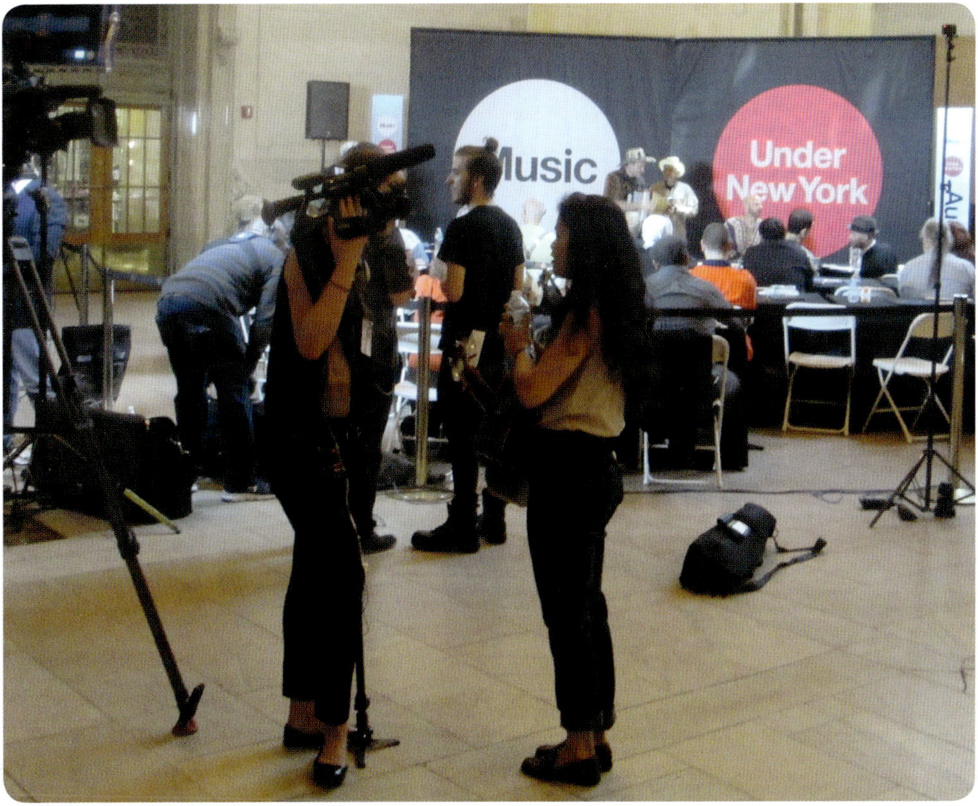

View of the audition stage in Vanderbilt Hall.

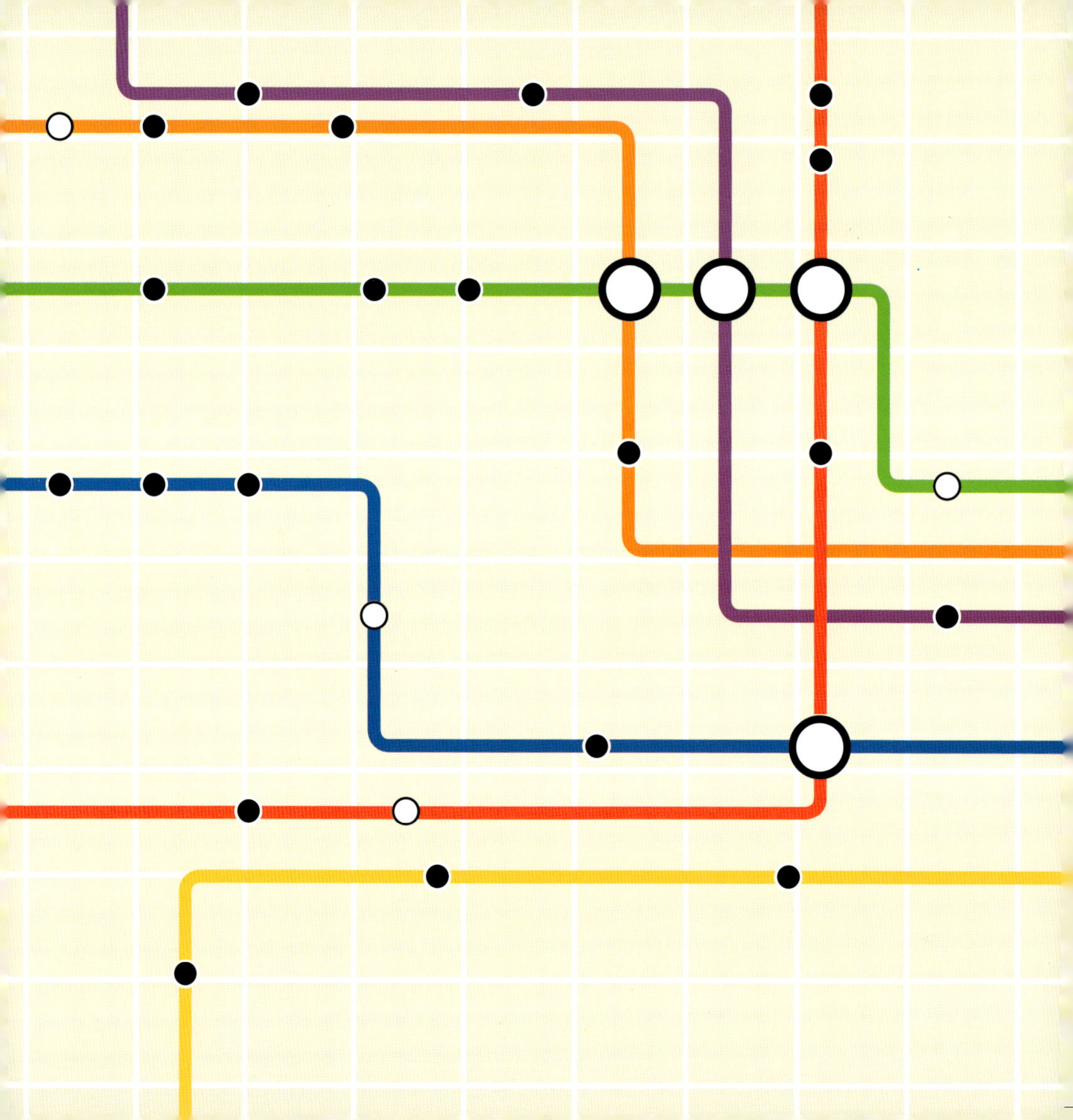

Chapter 2

World Music

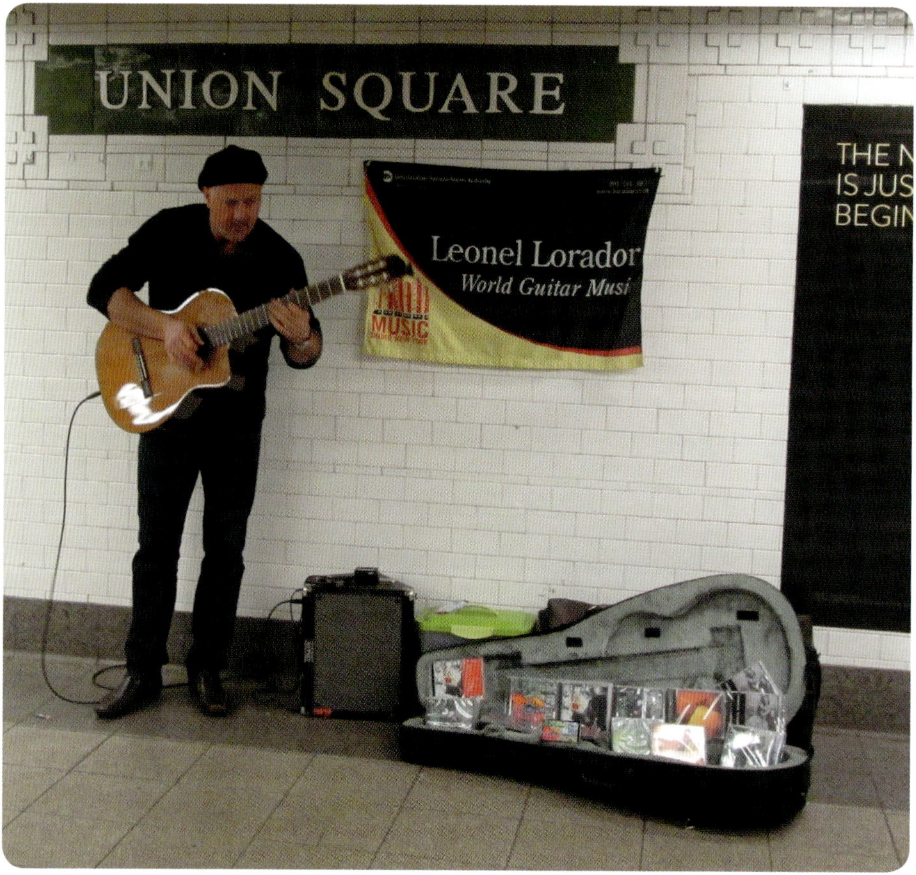

Leonel Lorador, world guitar music.

Union Square Station

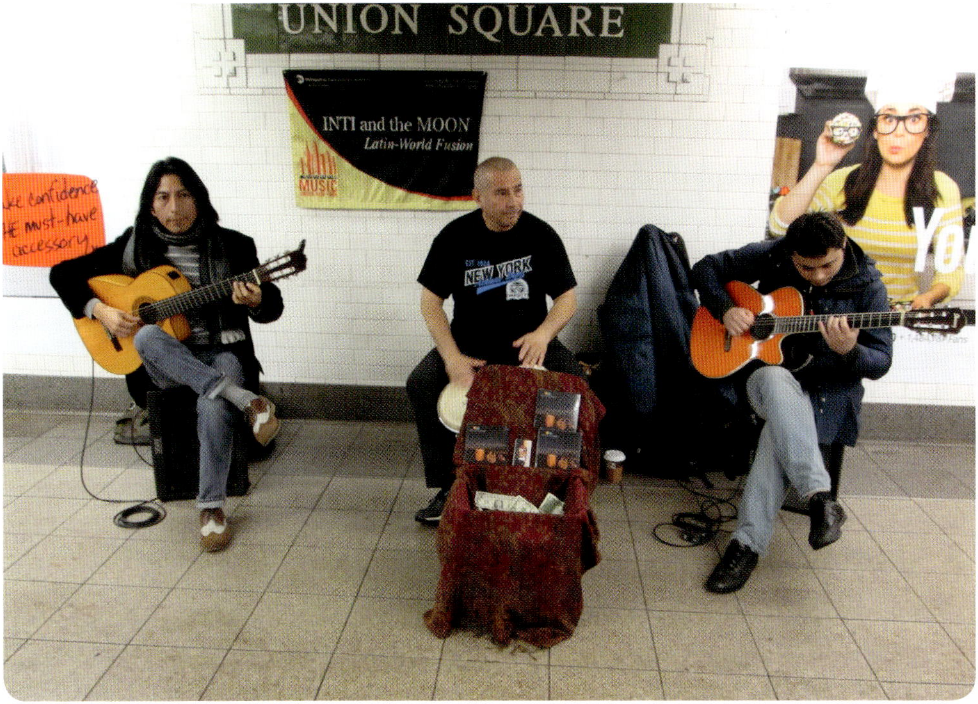

Inti and the Moon, Latin-world fusion.

Union Square Station

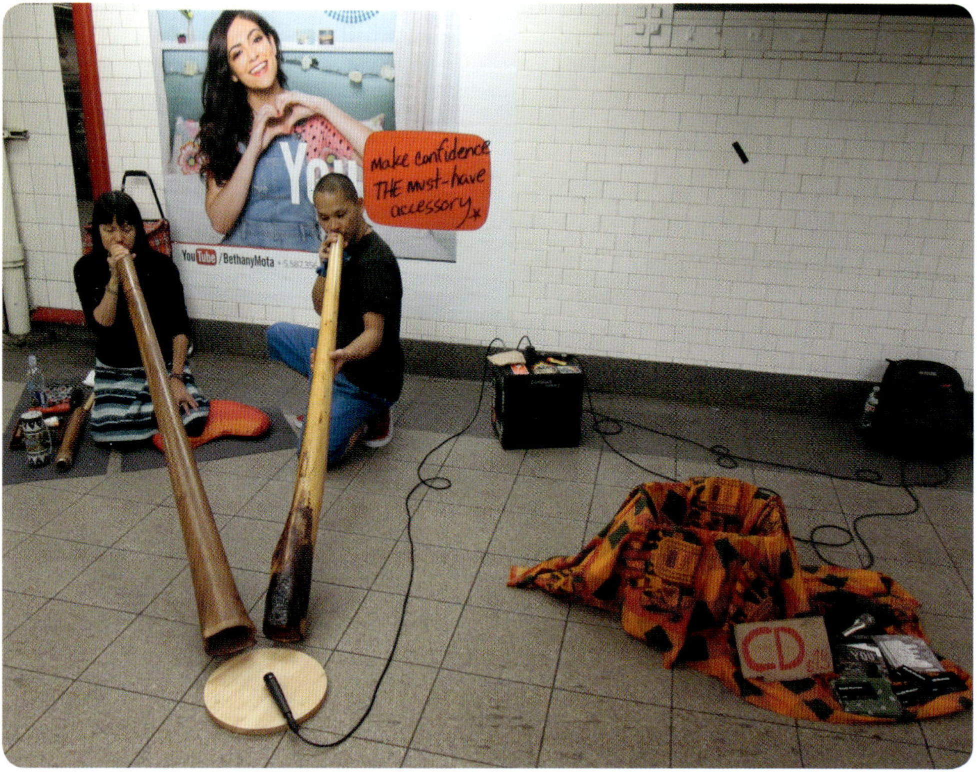

Mouth Muzician, Japanese beat boxer.

Union Square Station

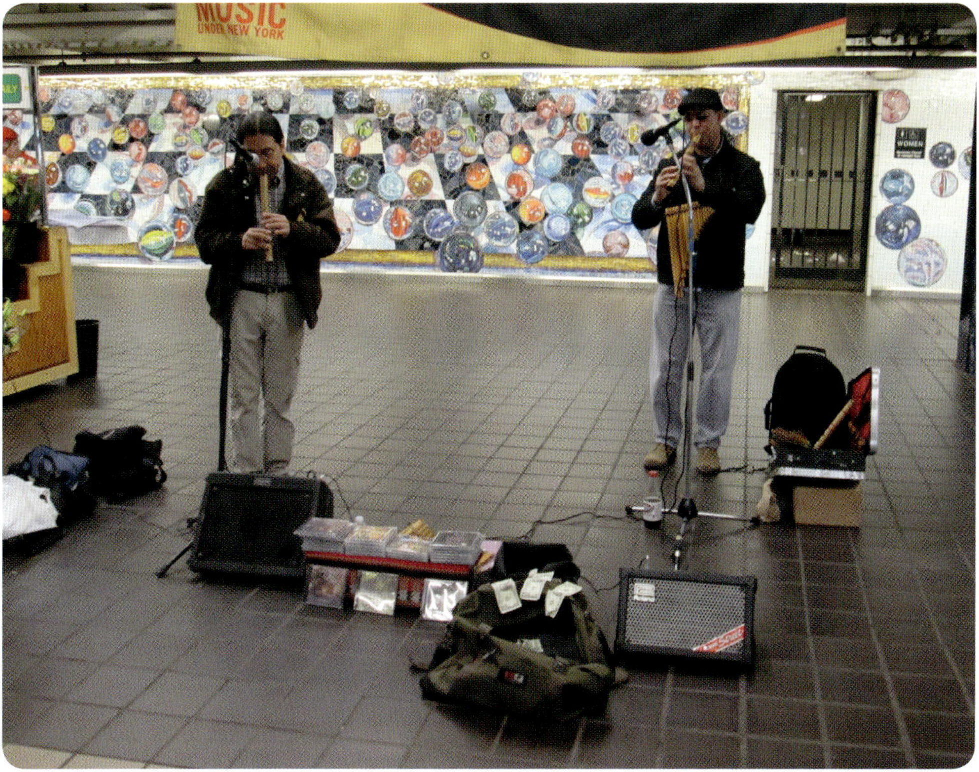

Andes Fusion, Andean and world sounds.

Port Authority Terminal/42nd Street Station

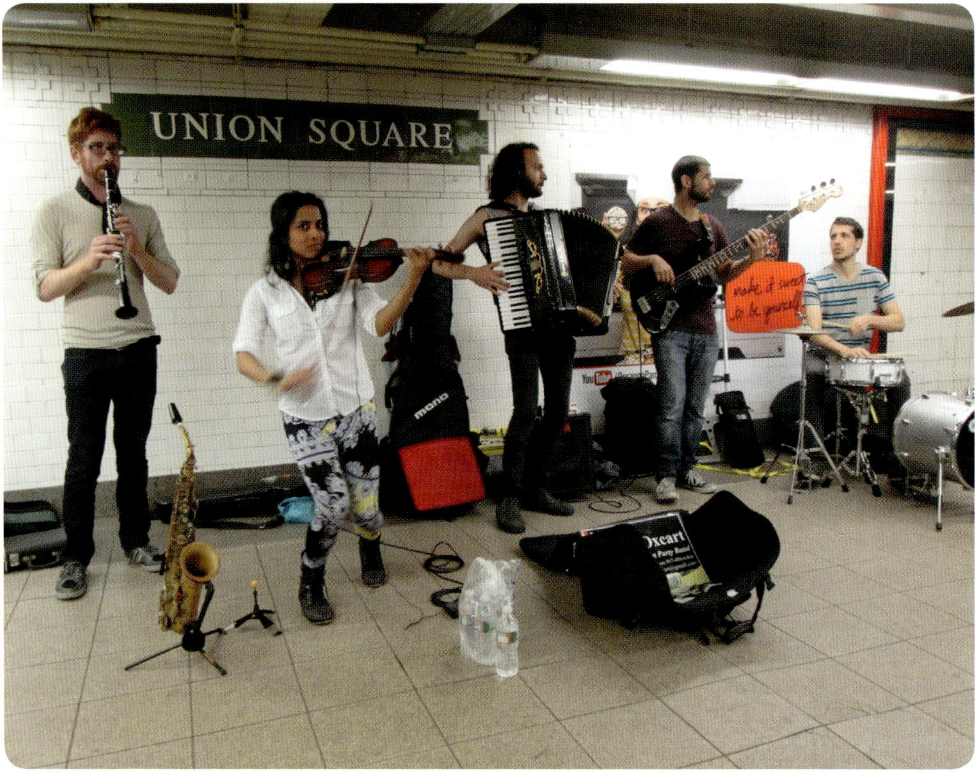

Tipsy Oxcart, Balkan party band.

Union Square Station/14th Street

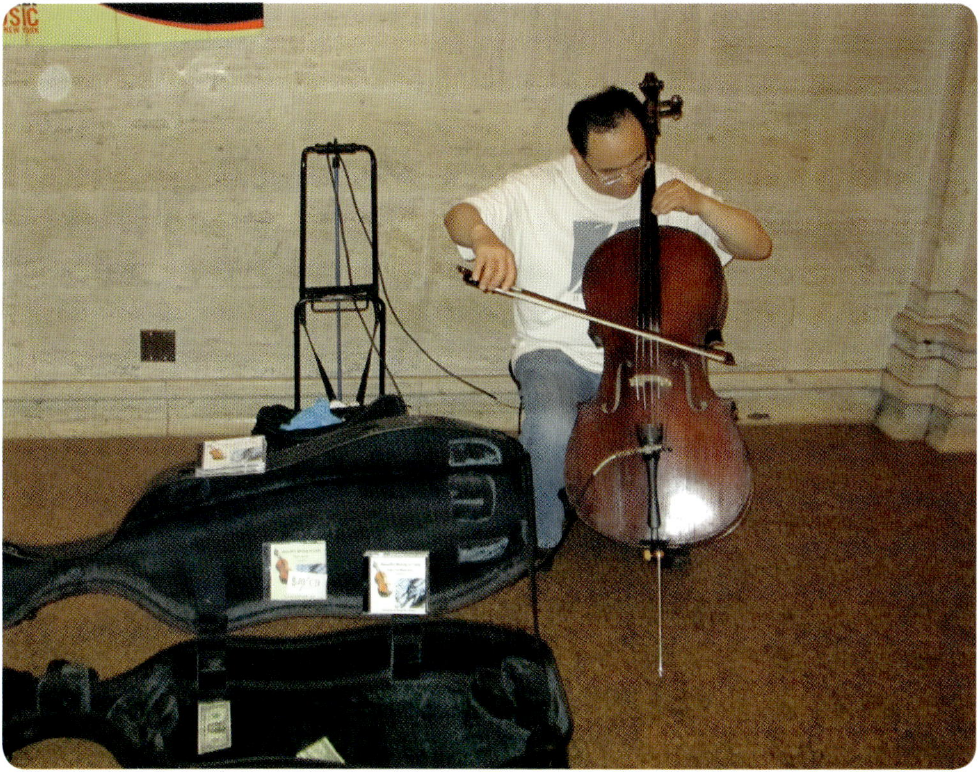

Ming Jun Zheng, classic cello.

Grand Central Station

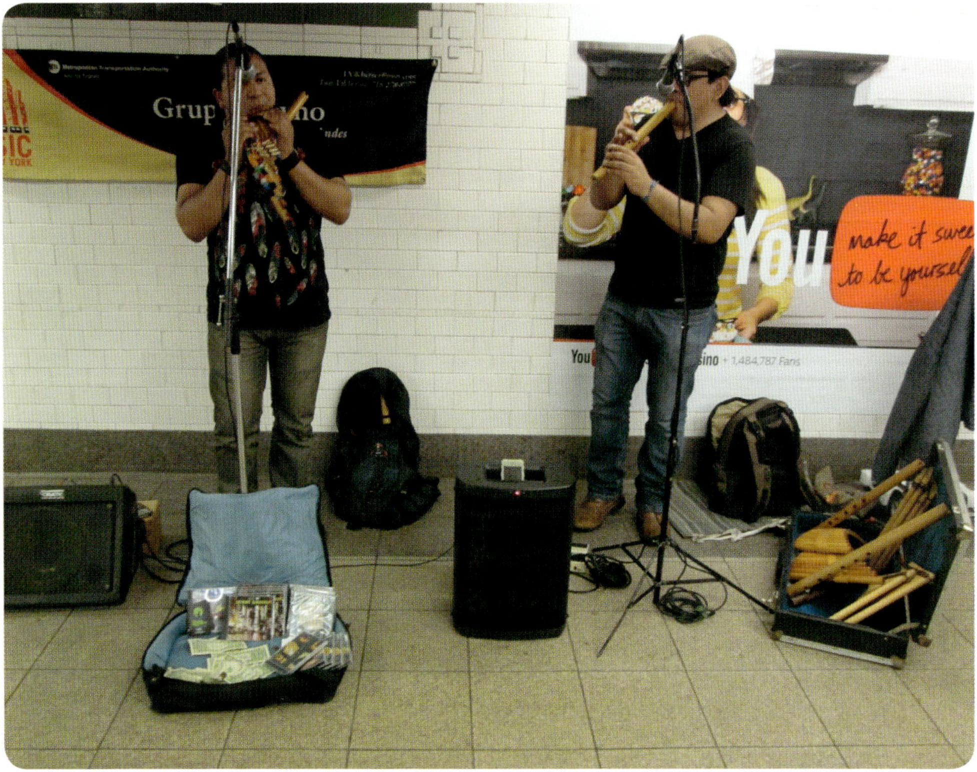

Grupo Wayno, music of the Andes.

Union Square Station

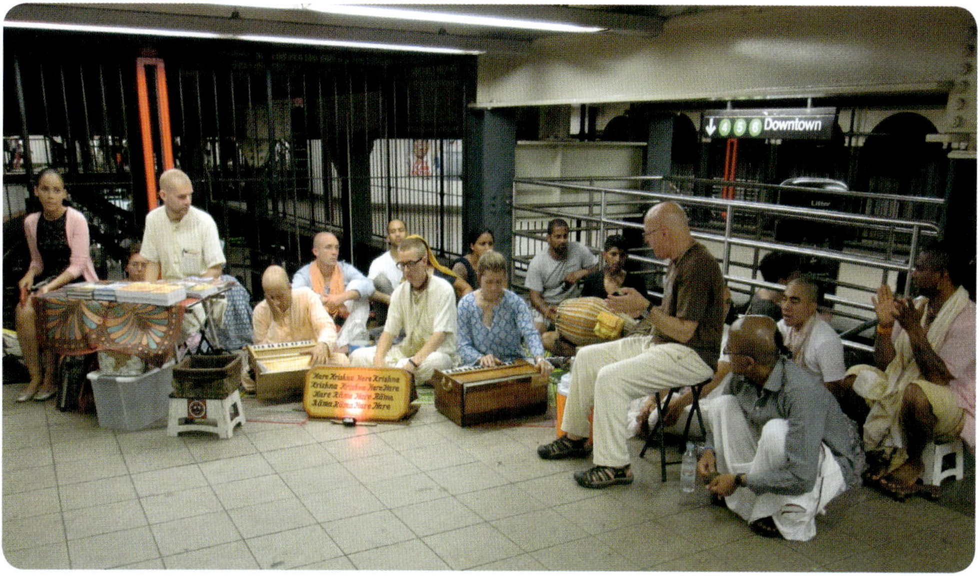

Hare Krishna.

Union Square Station

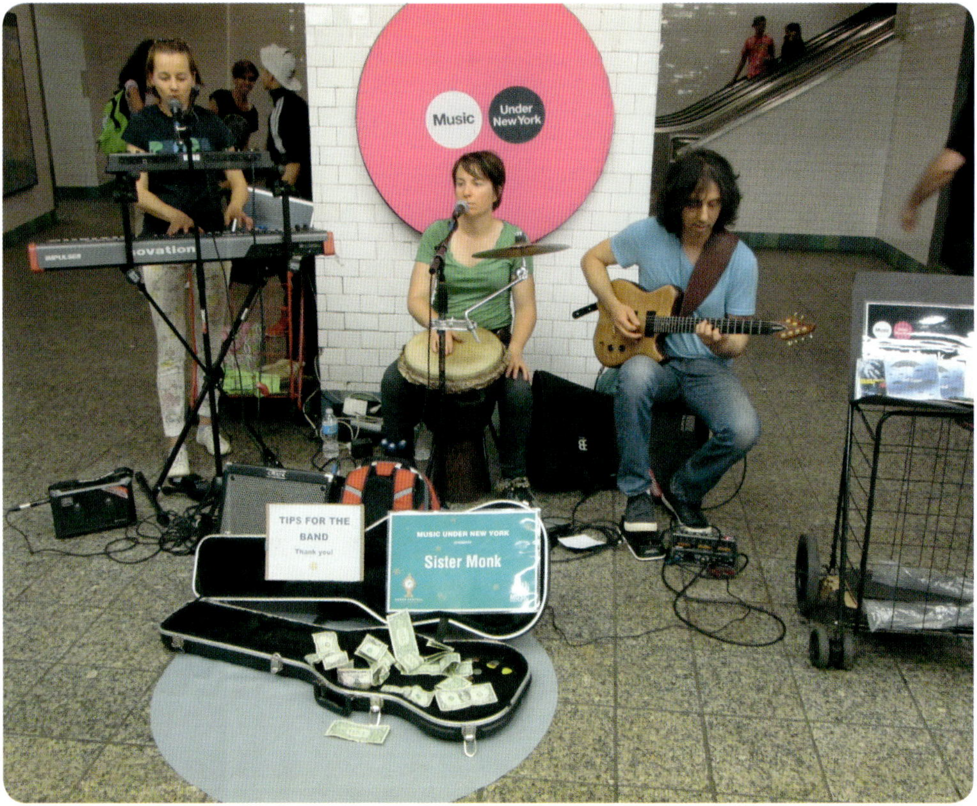

Sister Monk.

Times Square Station

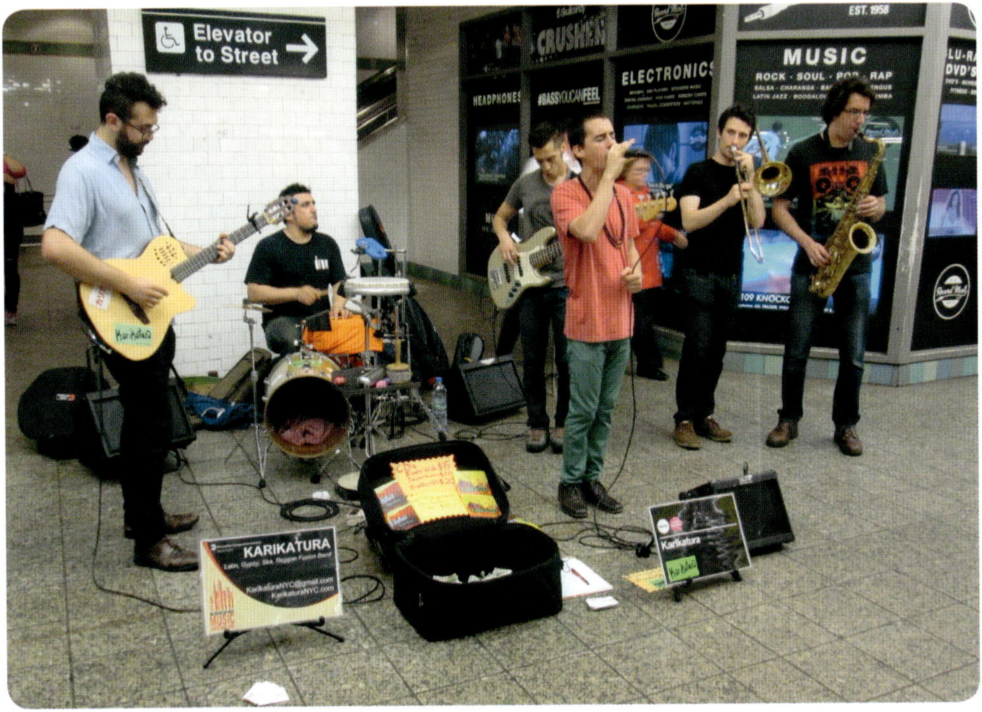

Karikatura, Latin, gypsy, ska, reggae fusion band.

Times Square Station

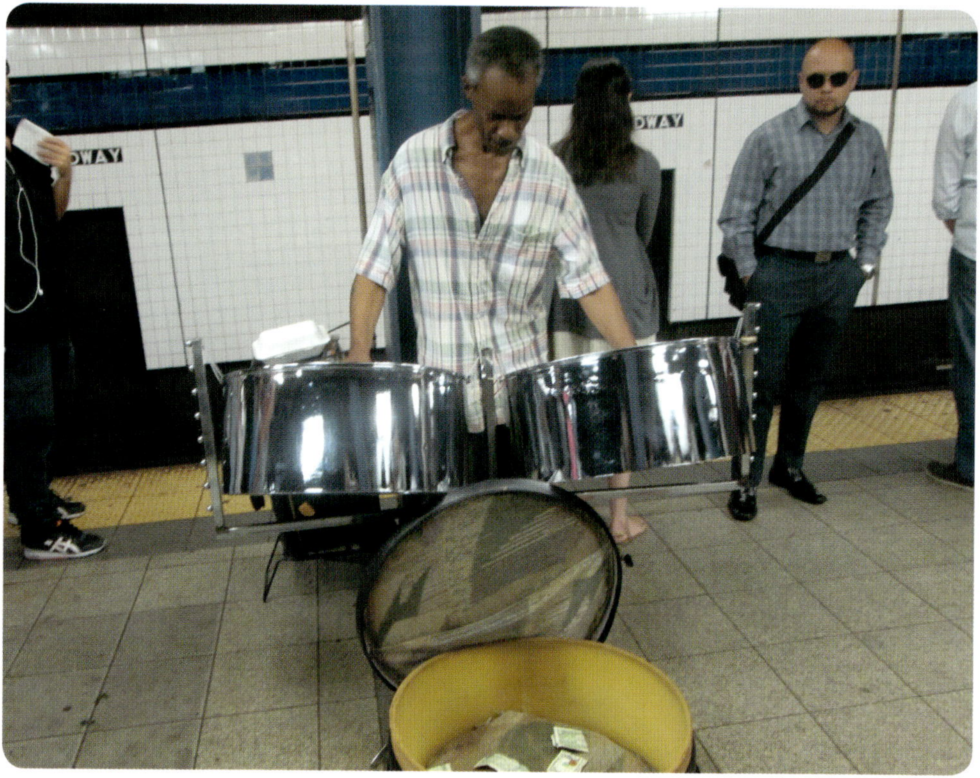

Steel drummer performer.

Broadway Lafayette Station

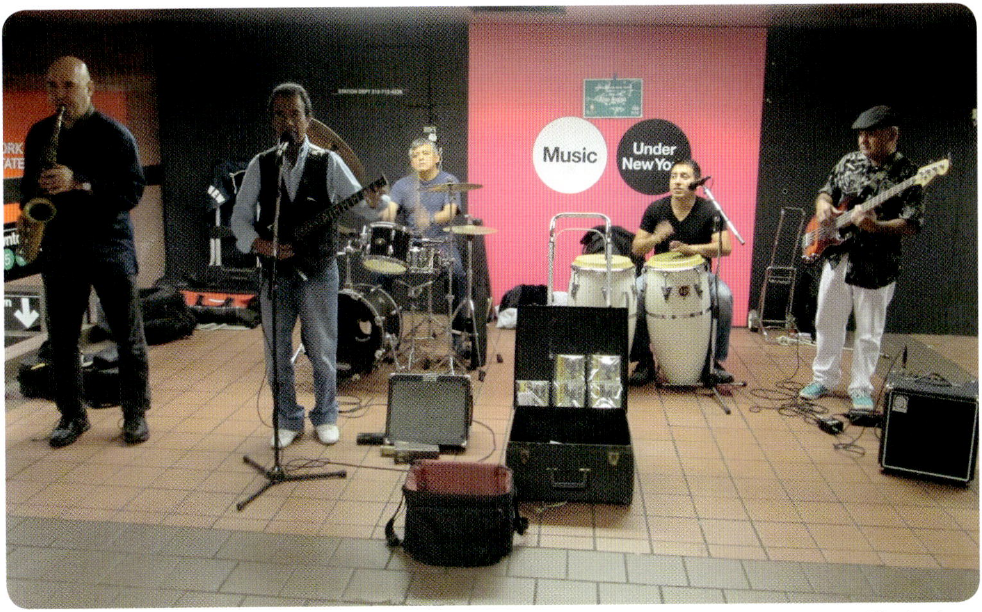

Afro Andes.

Grand Central Station

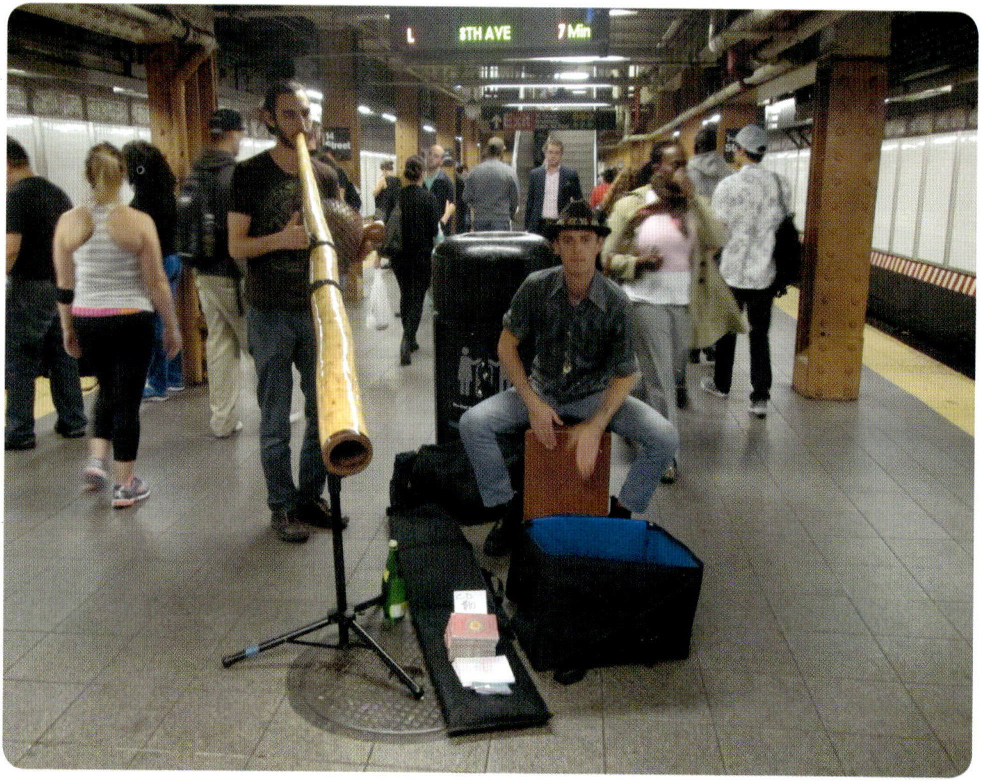

Didge Project.

14th - Street Union Square Station

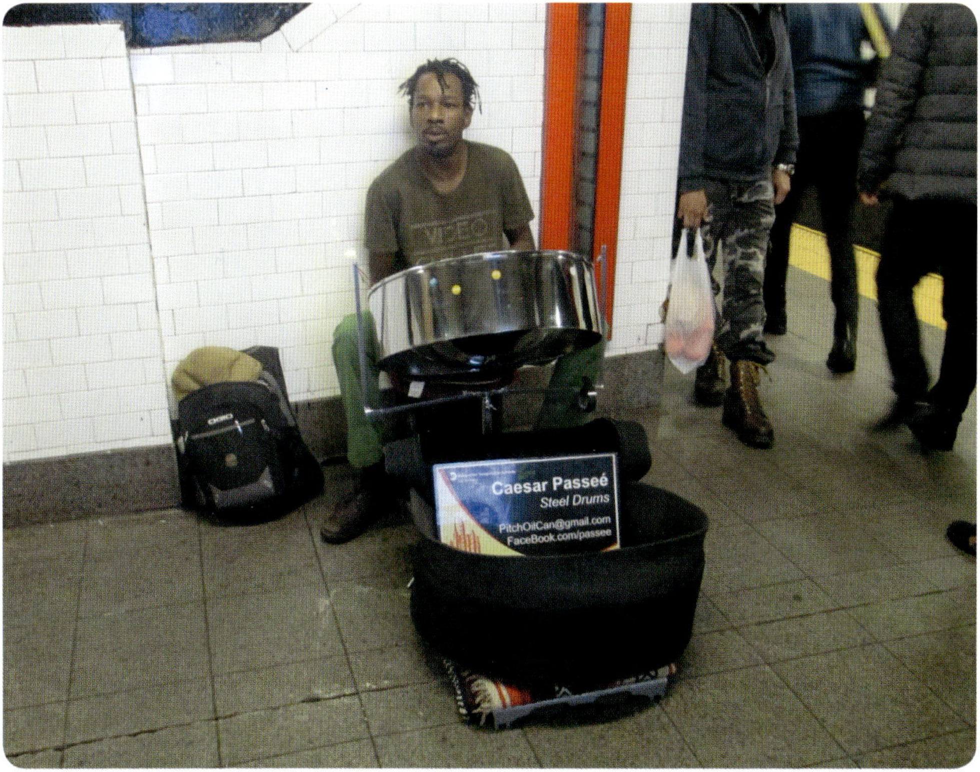

Caesar Passeé, steel drums.

14th - Street Union Square Station

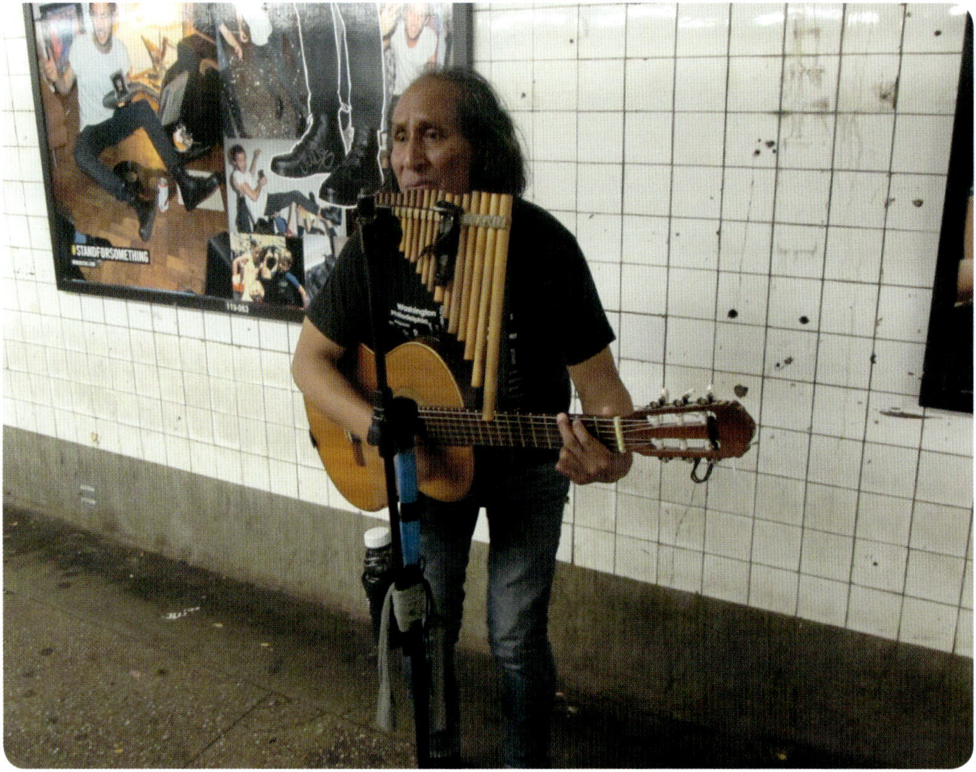

Folk guitar and pan pipe performer.

1st Avenue Station

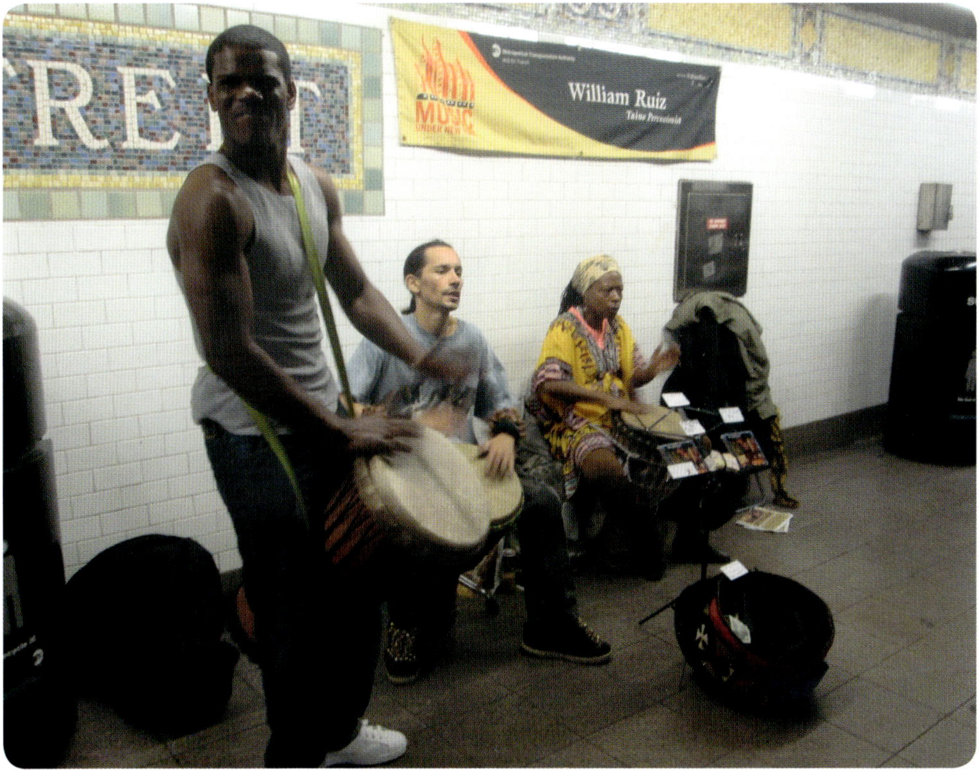

William Ruiz, Tiano log drummer.

59th Street and Lexington Avenue Station

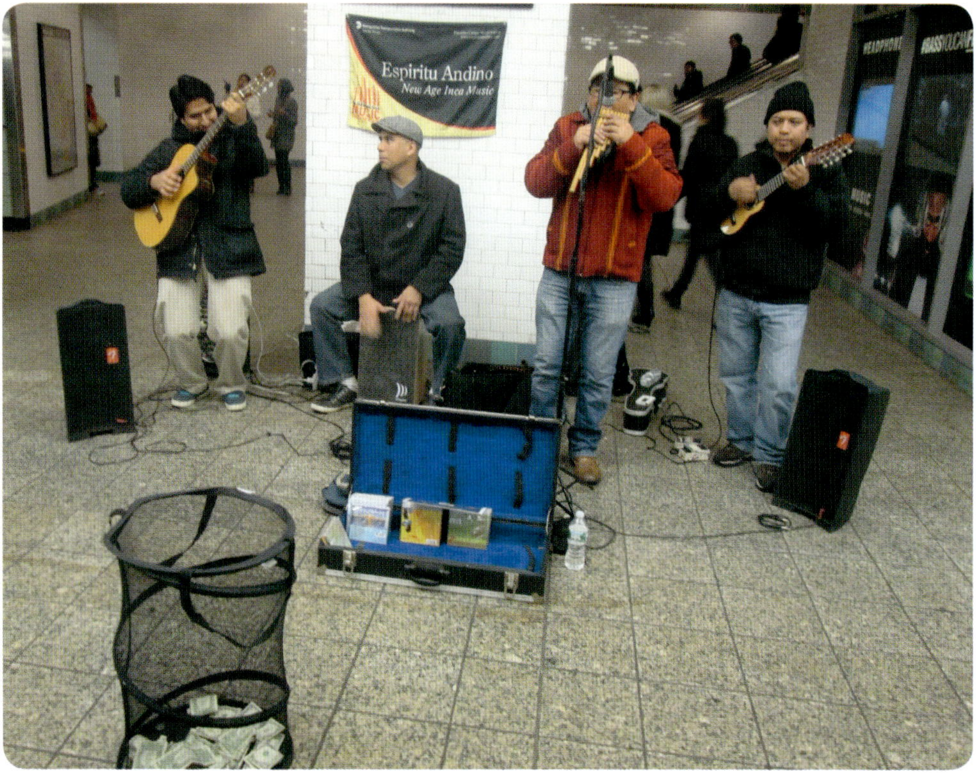

Espiritu Andino, new age Inca music.

Times Square Station

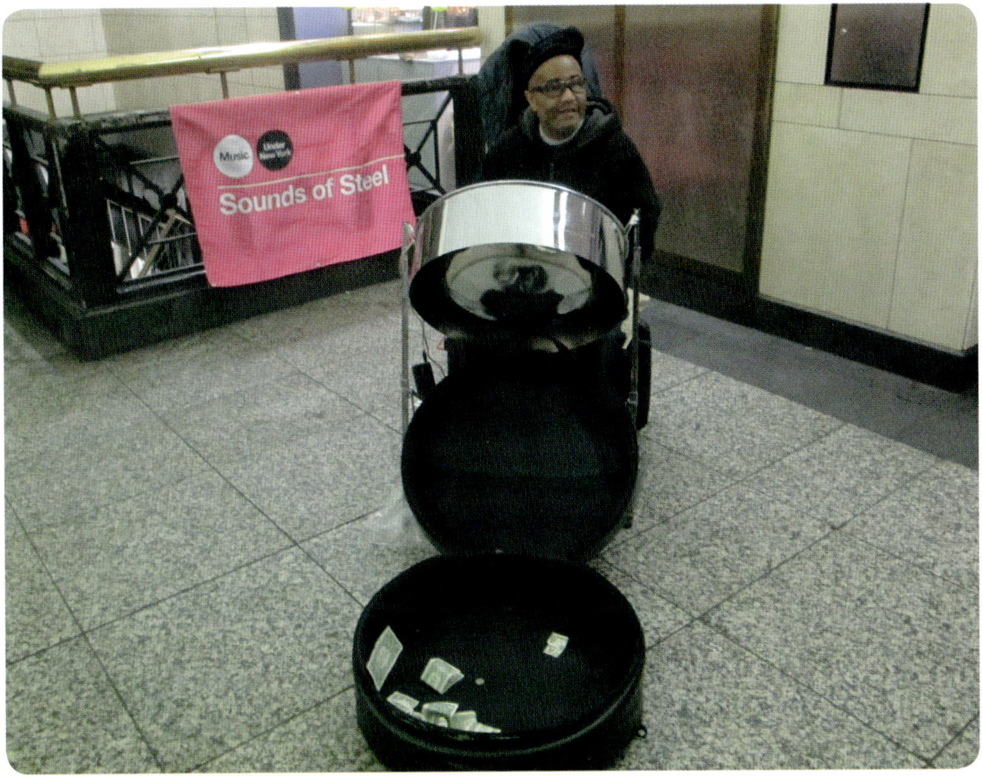

Sounds of Steel.

34th Street - Penn Station

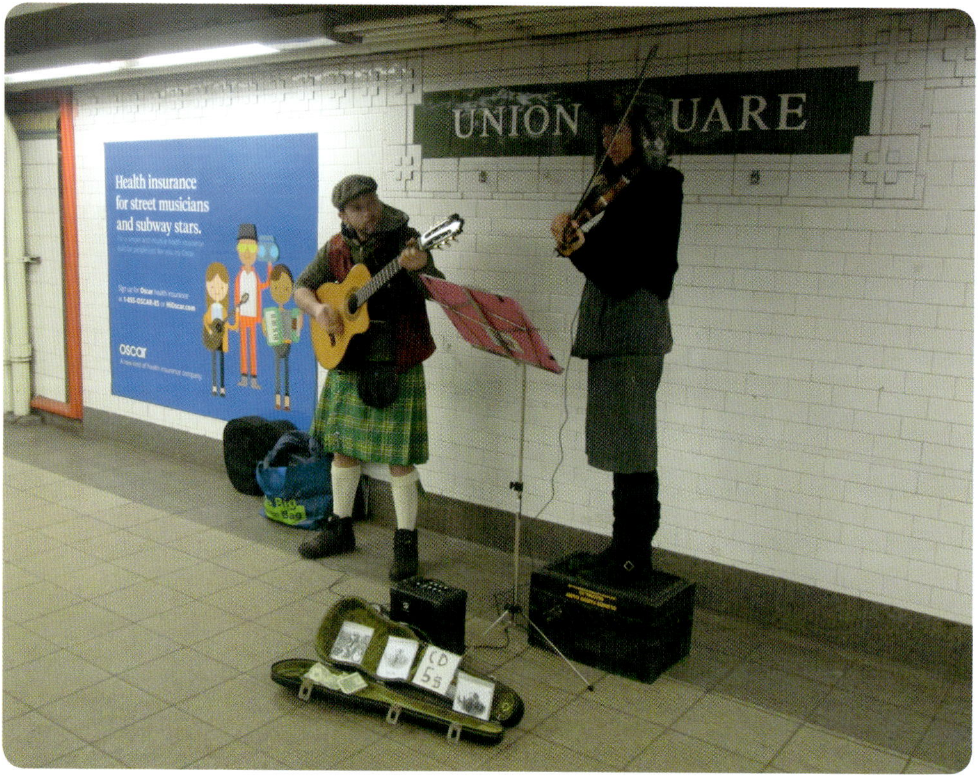

Folk guitar and violin.

Union Square Station

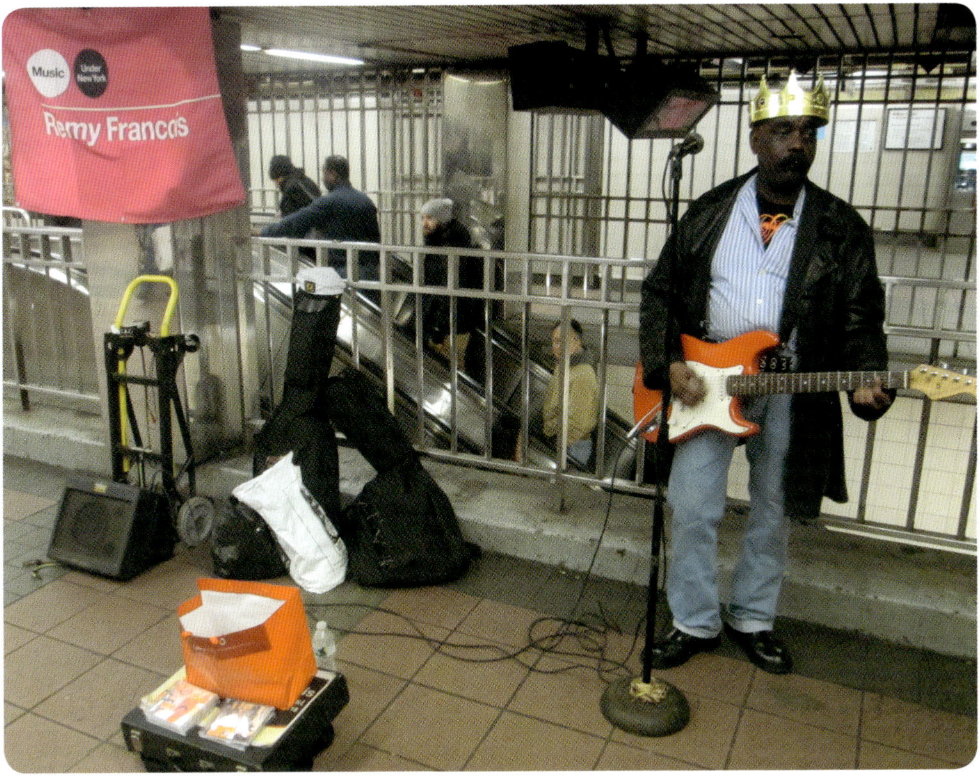

Remy Francois.

34th - Street/Herald Square Station

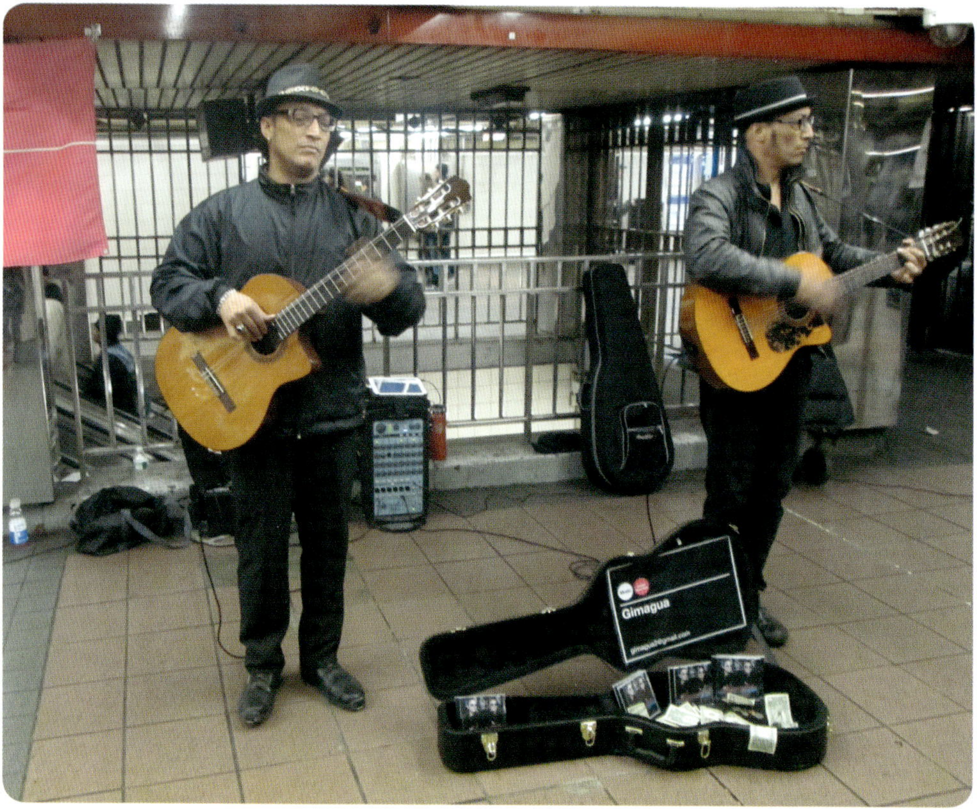

Gimagua.

34th - Street Herald Square Station

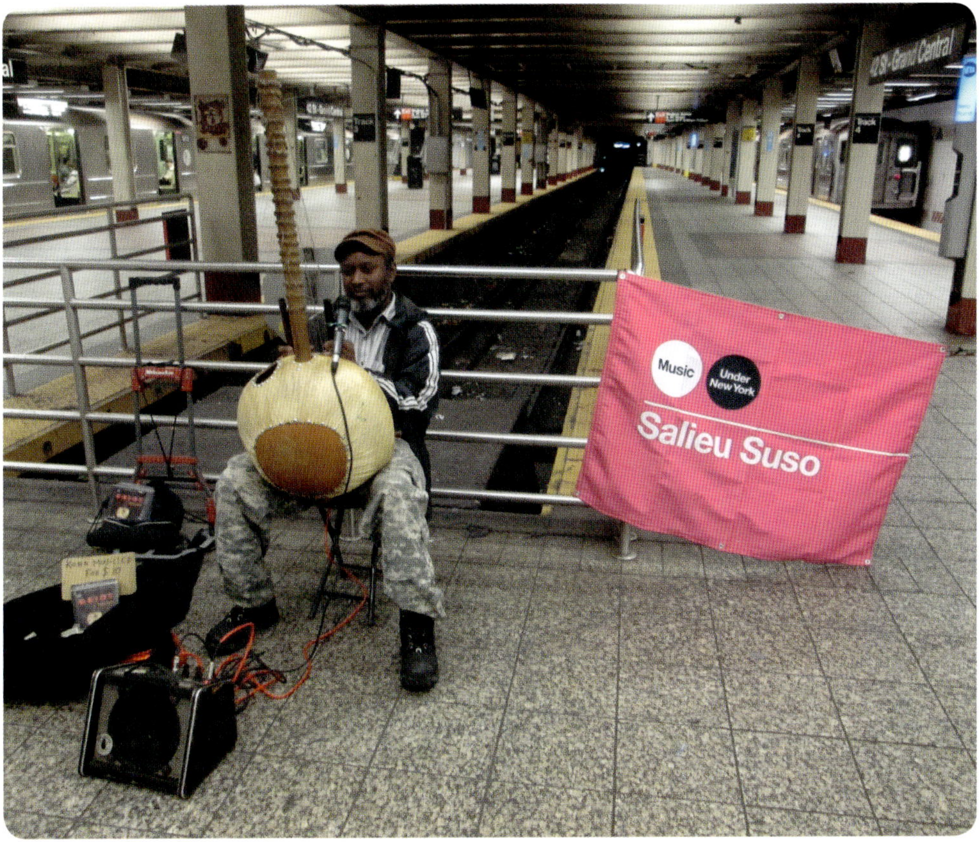

Salieu Suso.

42nd Street - Grand Central Station

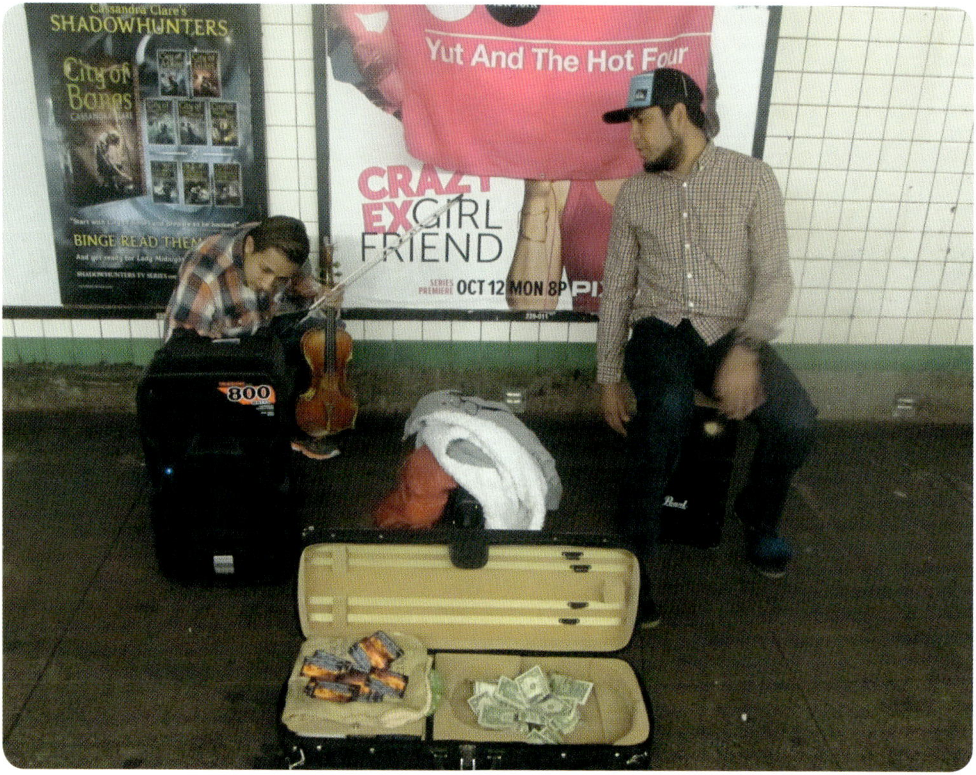

Yut and The Hot Four.

23rd Street and 6th Avenue Station

Delancey Street Station

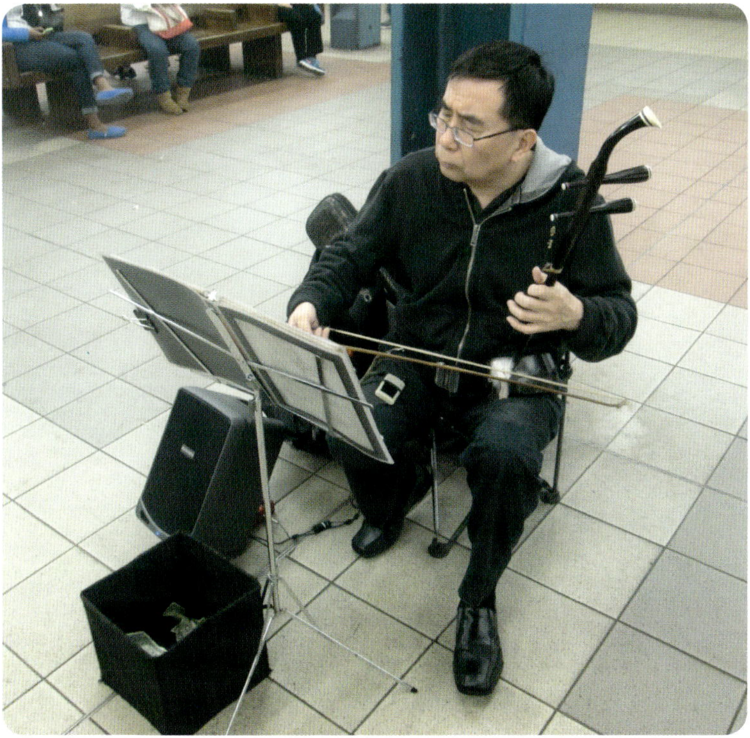

Minhao Lu.

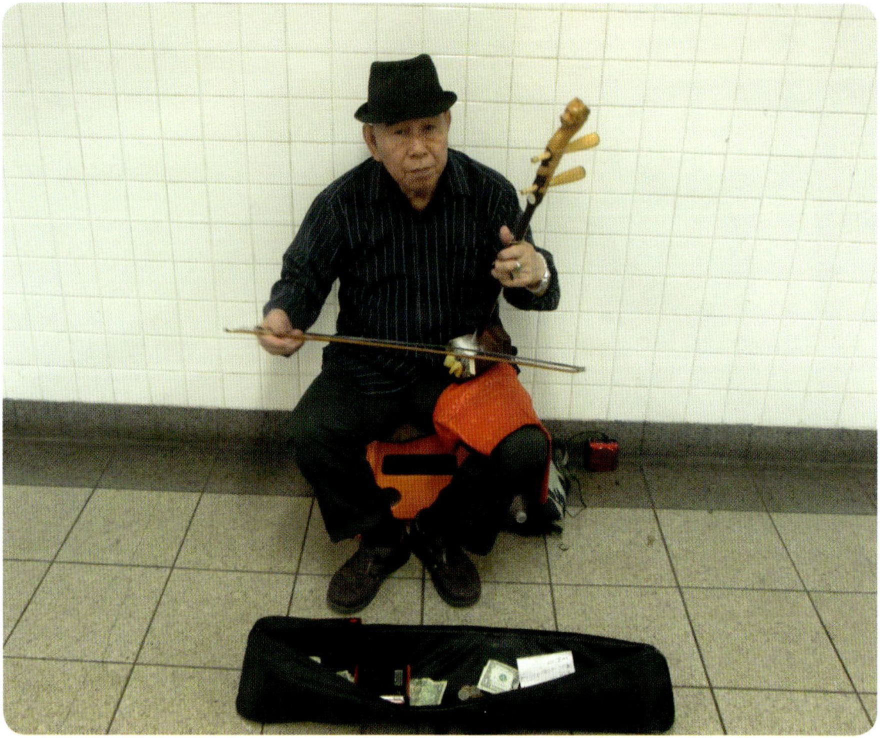

Chinese bowed string.

Canal Street Station

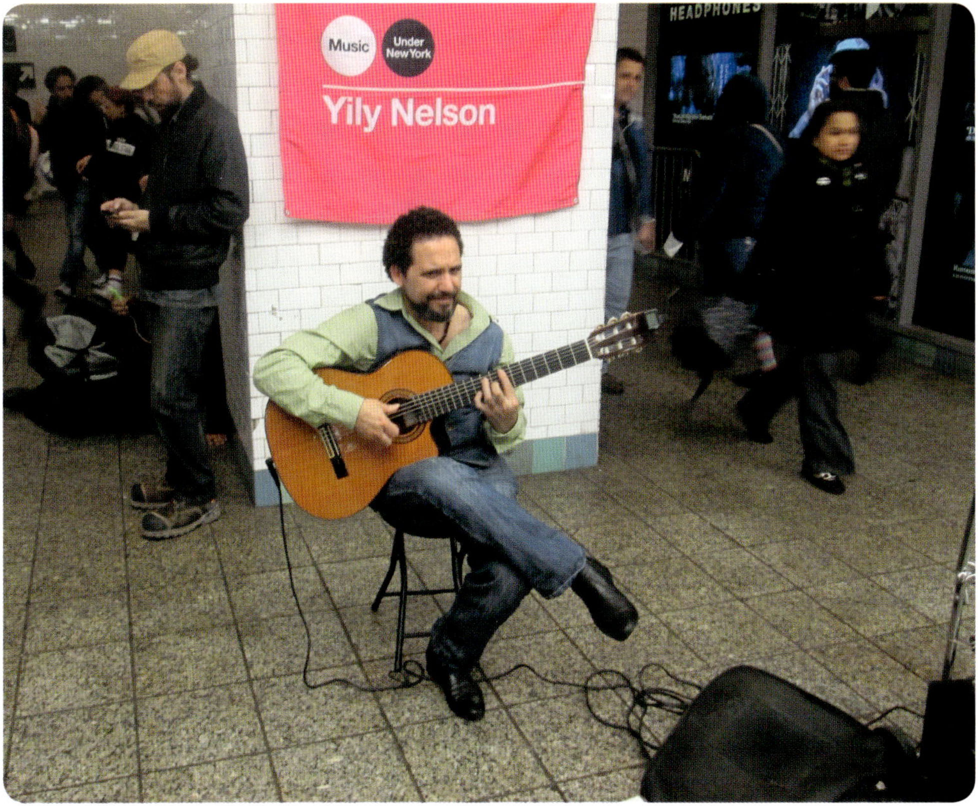

Yily Nelson, Dominican guitar.

Times Square Station

Grand Central Terminal

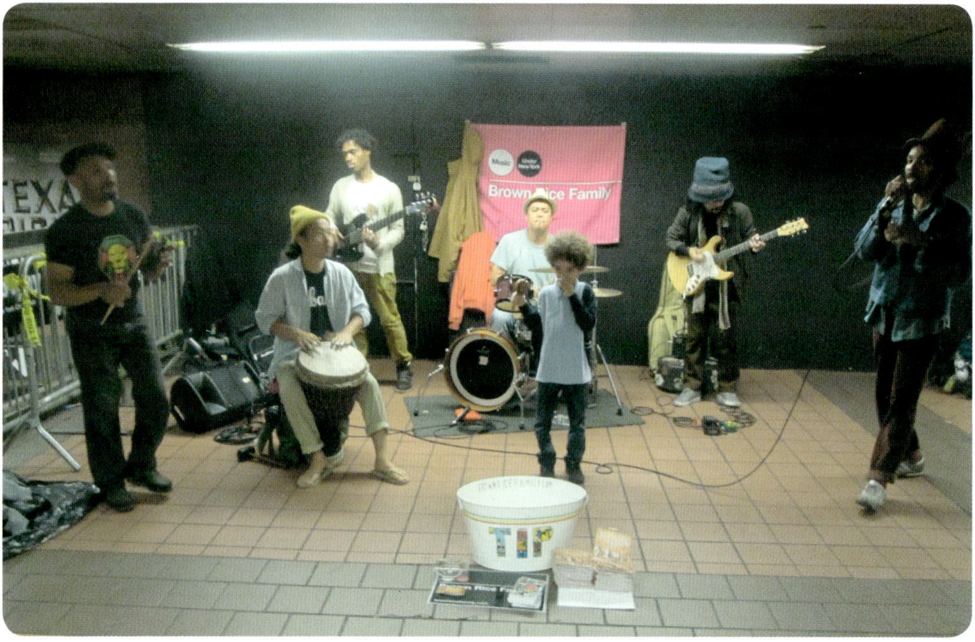

Brown Rice Family.

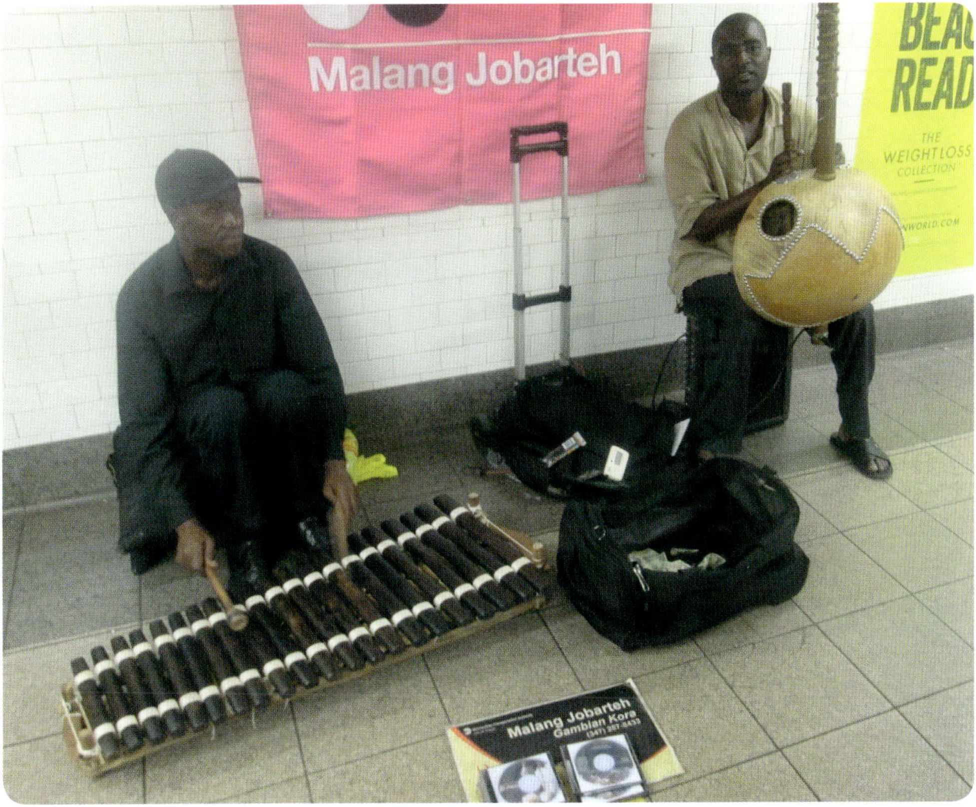

Malang Jobarteh, Gambian kora.

Union Square Station

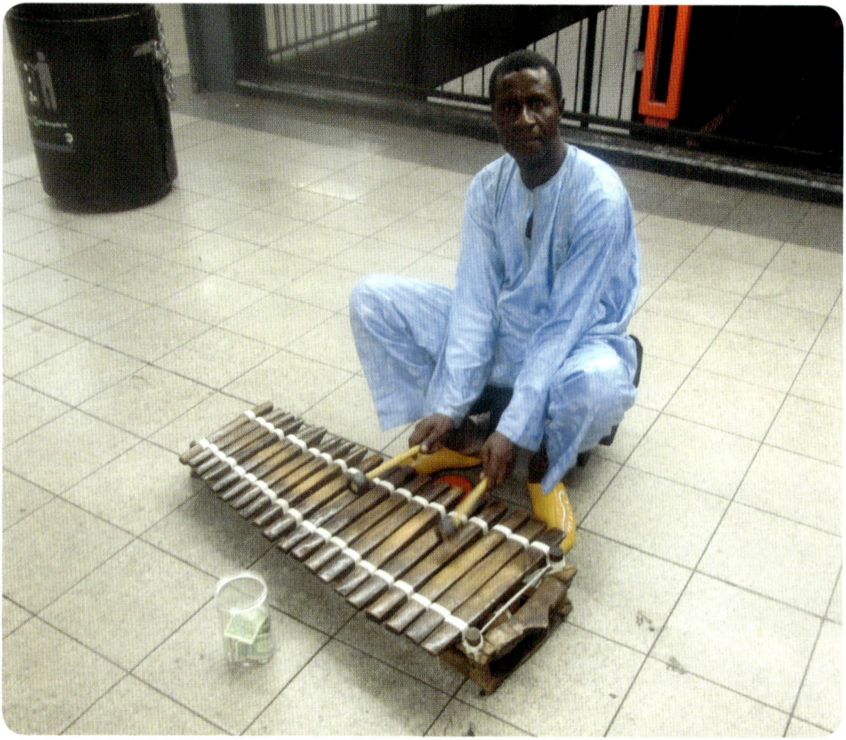

African balophon.

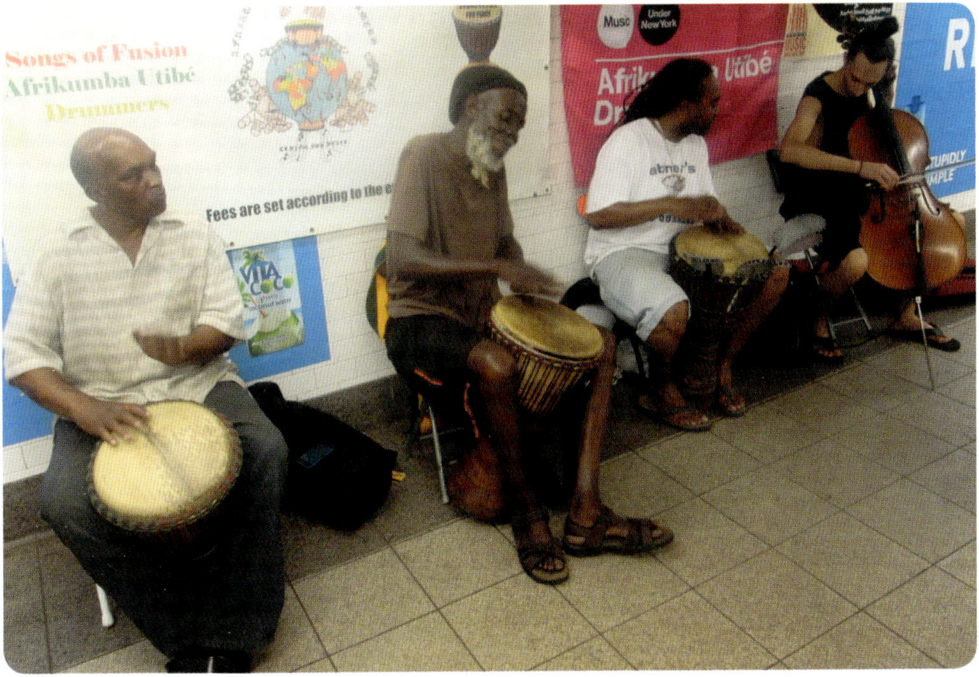

Afrikumba Utibe drummers.

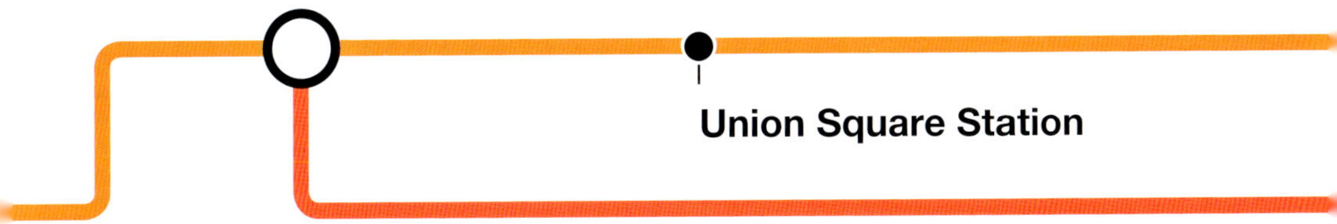

Union Square Station

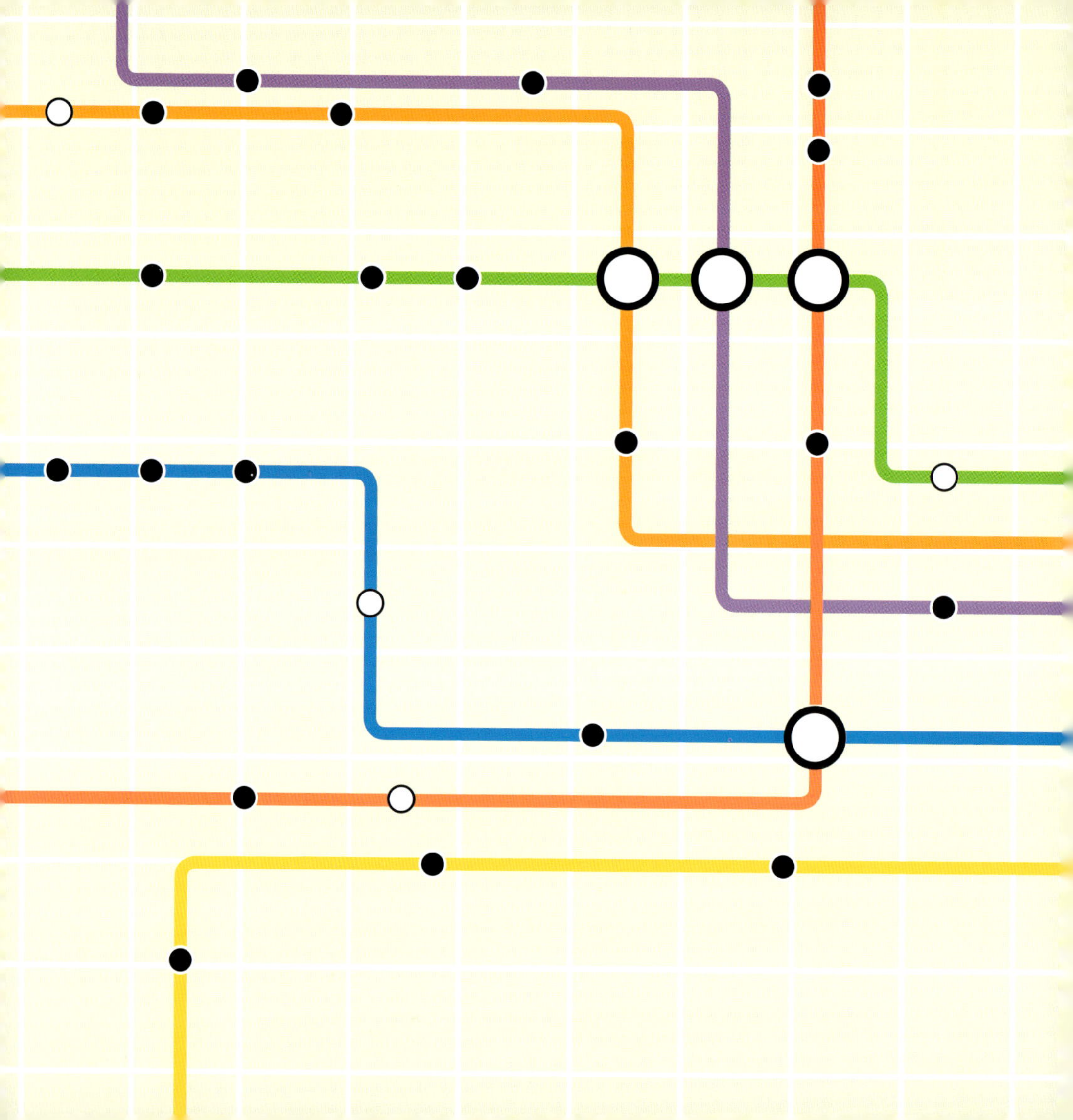

Chapter 3

Unique Artists and Dancers

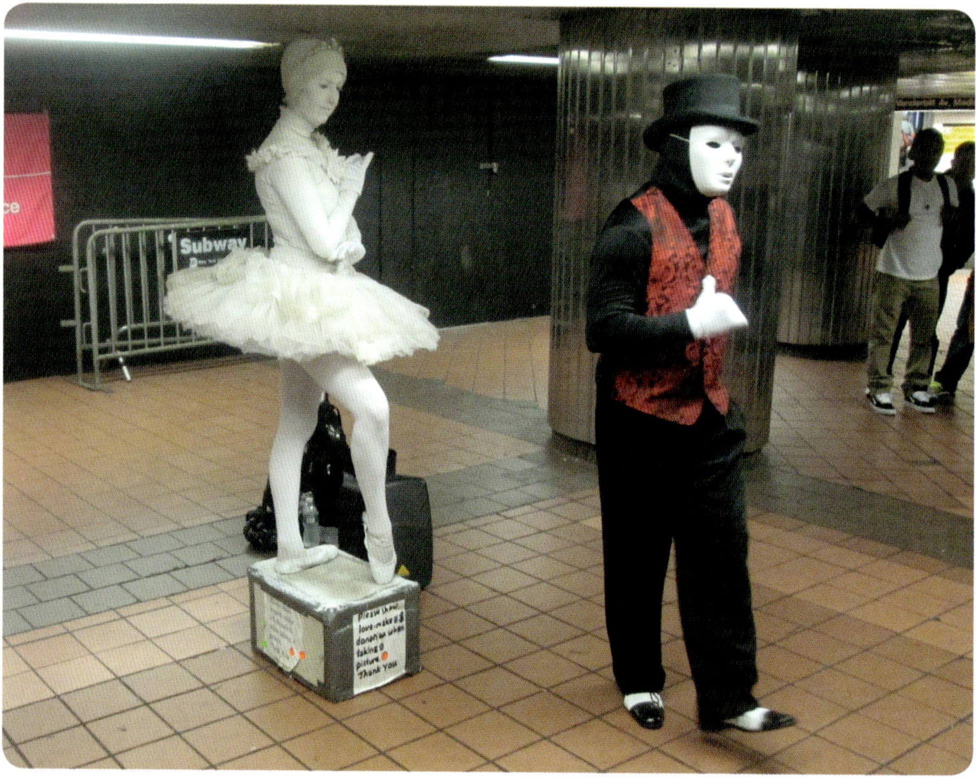

Roger G & Unique Force

Grand Central Station

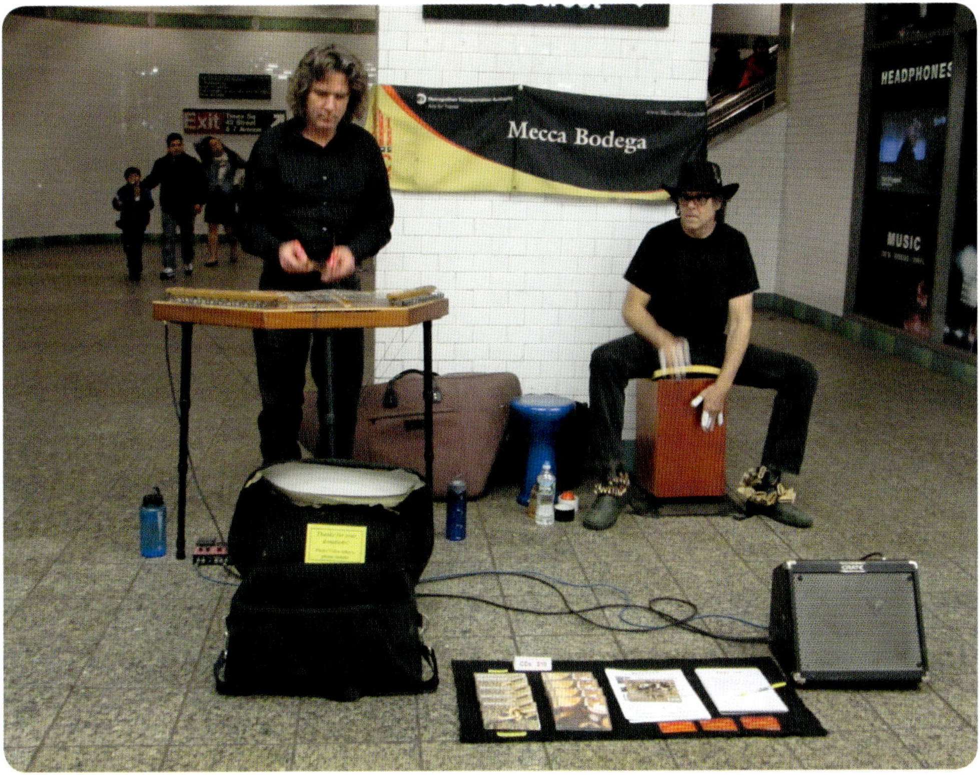

Mecca Bodega, hammer dulcimer and percussion.

Times Square Station

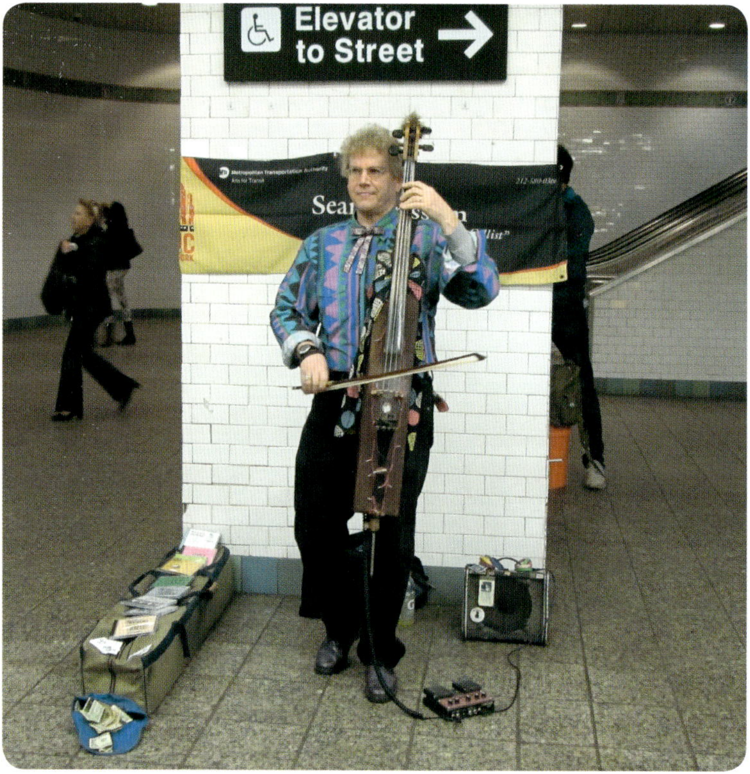

Sean Grissom, the "Cajun Cellist."

Times Square Station

42nd Street - Grand Central Station

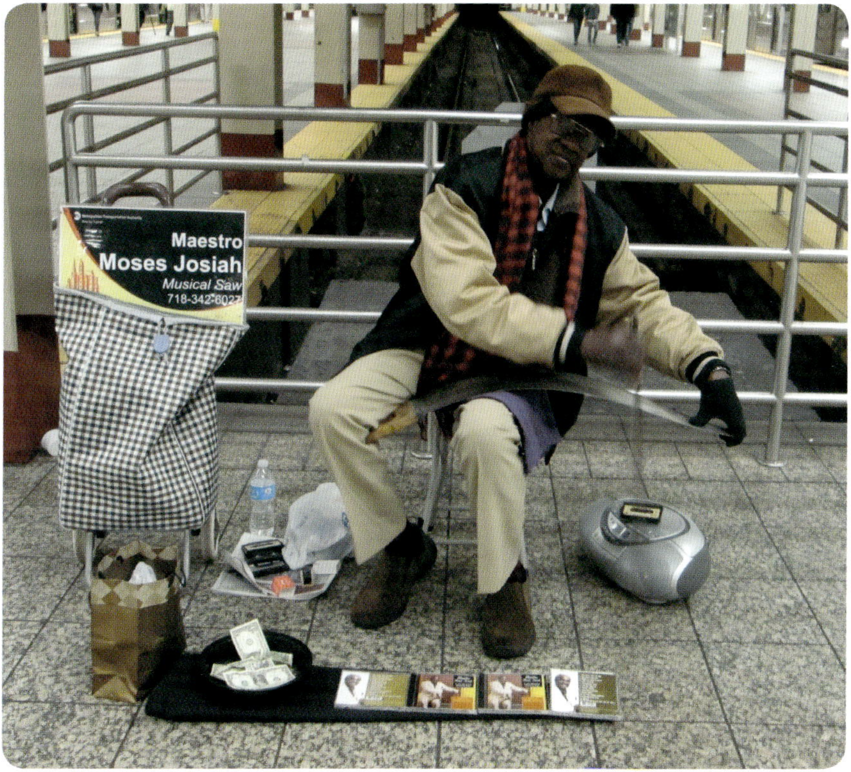

Maestro Moses Josiah, musical saw.

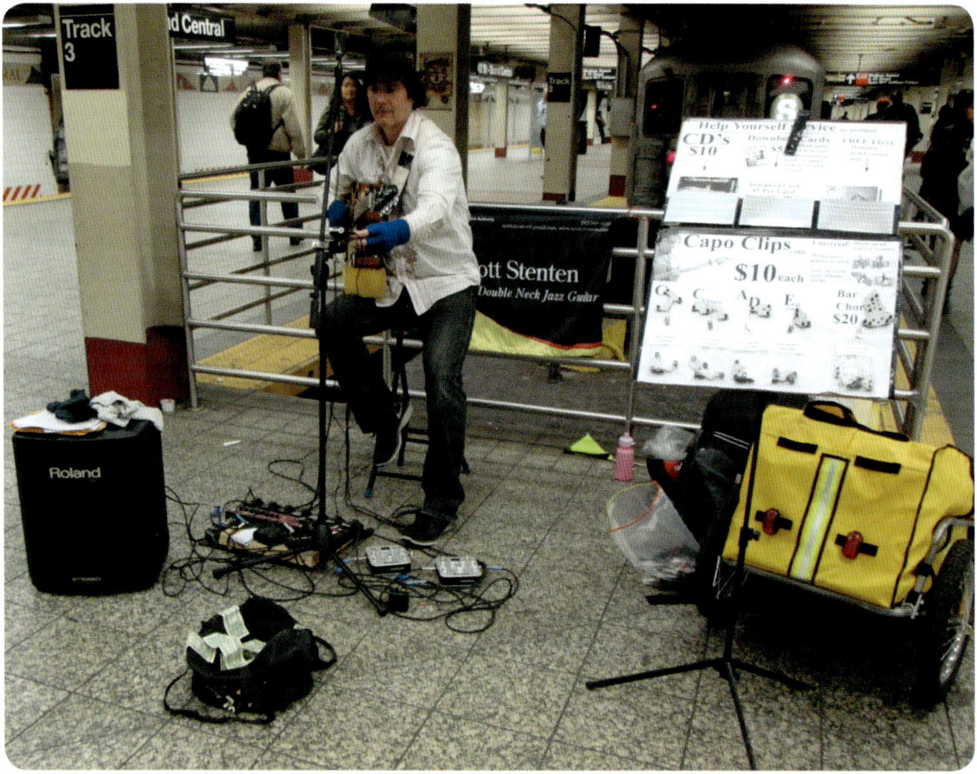

Scott Stenten, double neck jazz guitar.

42nd Street - Grand Central Station

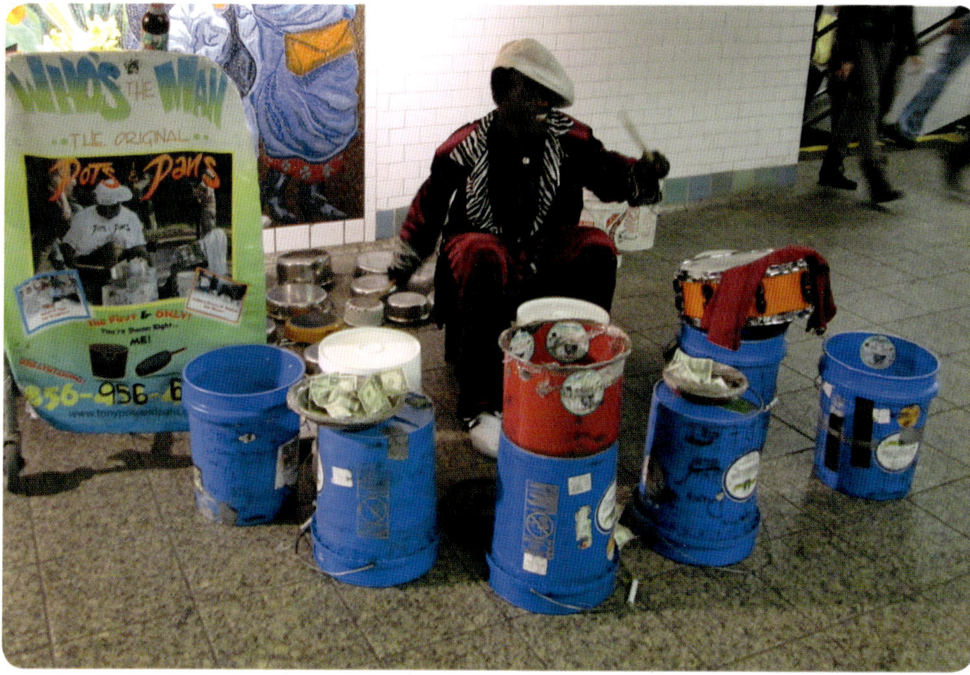

Tony "Pots and Pans," percussionist.

Times Square Station

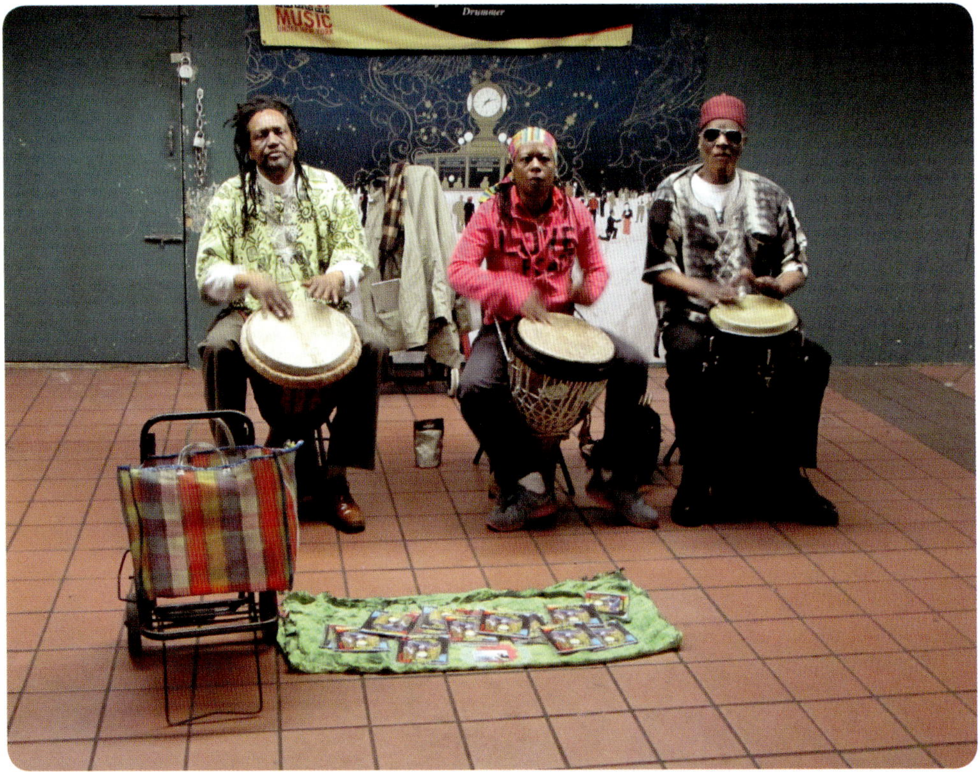

Tyrone Owuso Slater, djembe drummer.

Grand Central Station

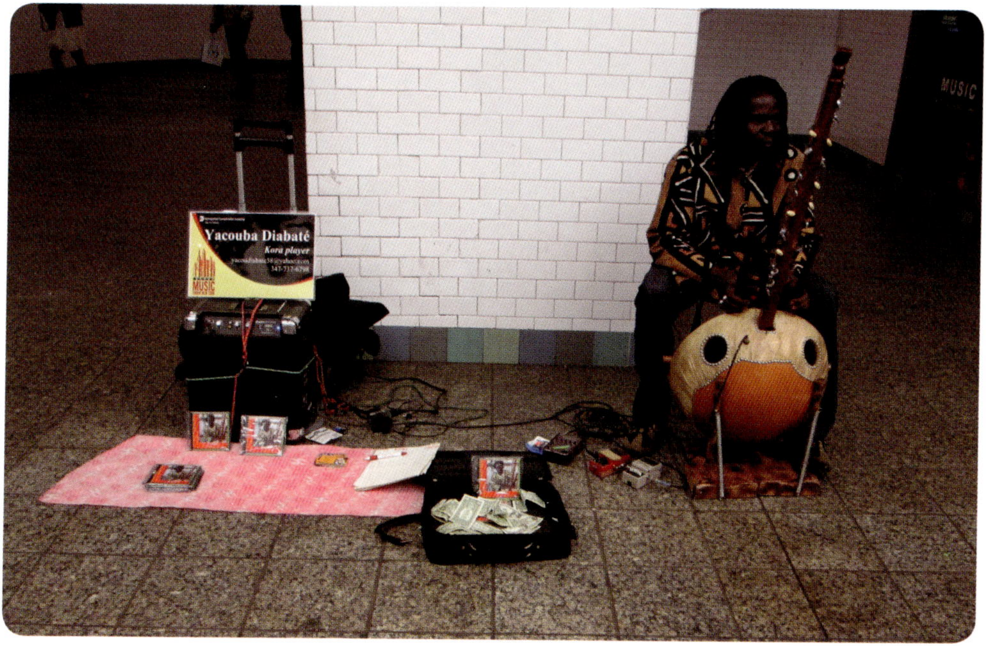

Yacouba Diabate, kora.

Times Square Station

34th Street - Penn Station

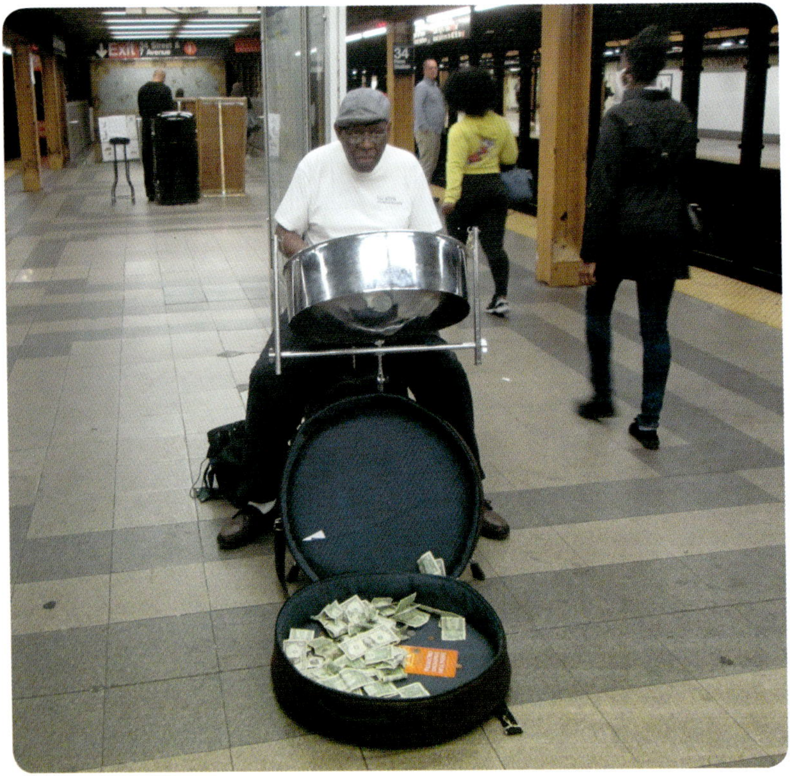

Steel drum.

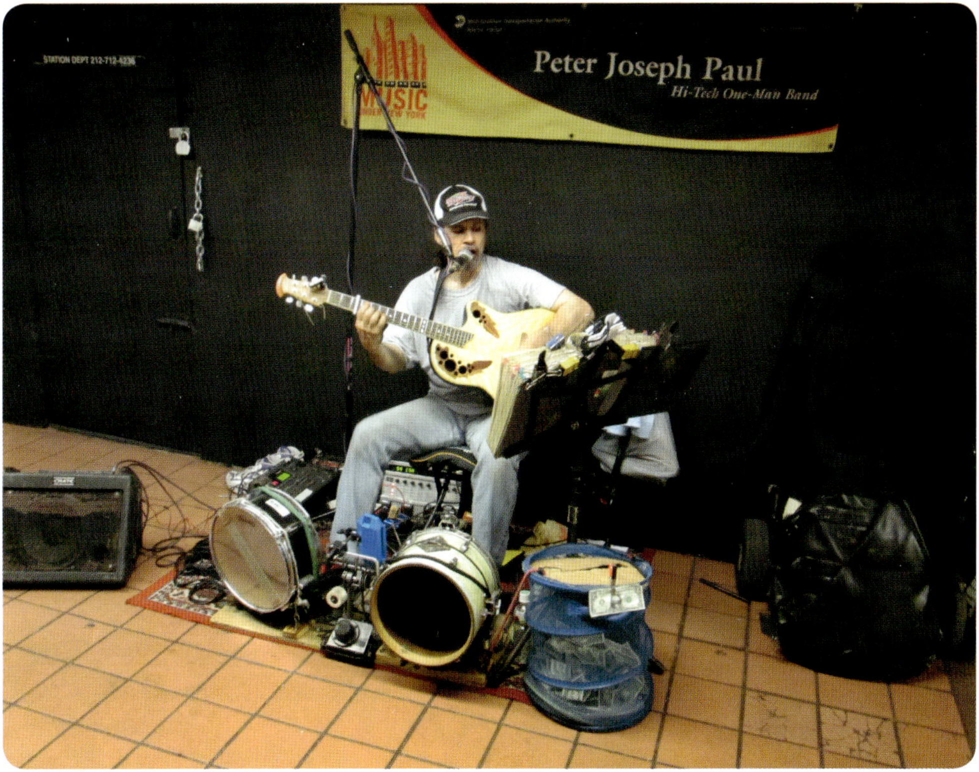

Peter Joseph Paul, Hi-Tech One-Man Band

Grand Central Station

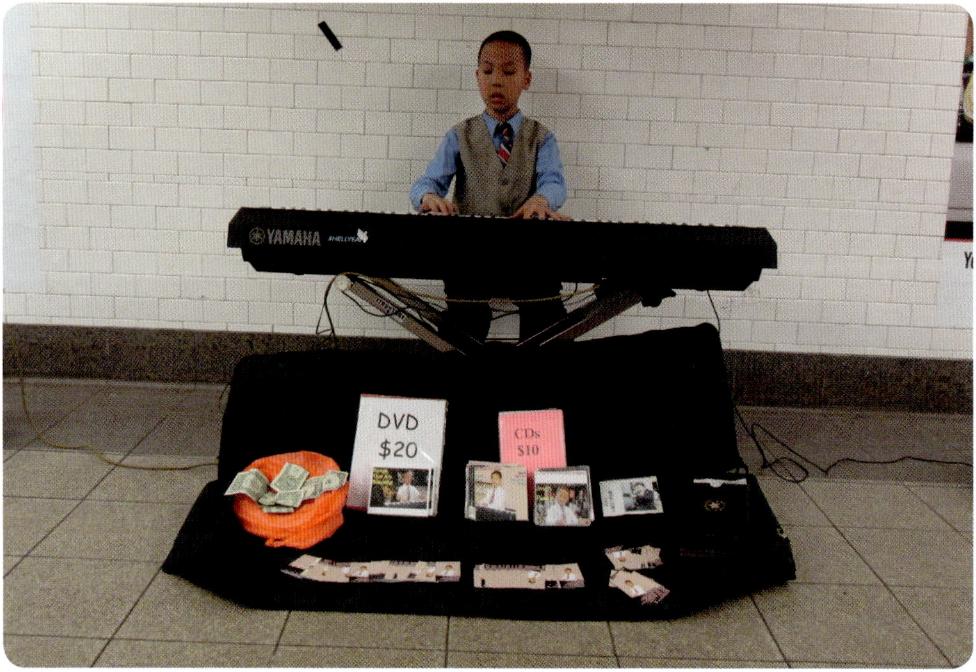

Jason Ruan, piano.

Union Square Station

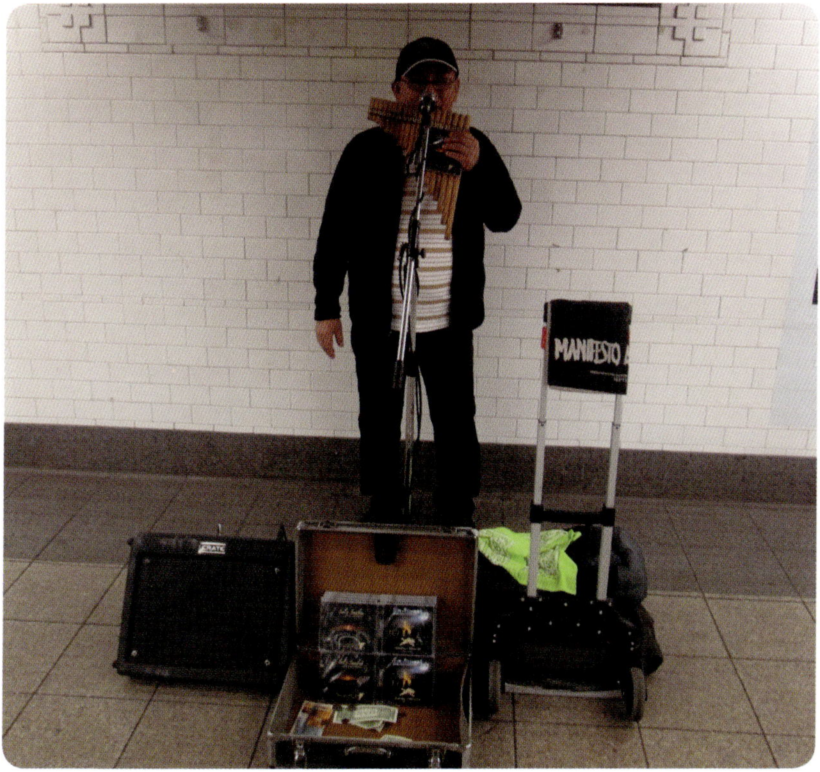

Manifesto, pan pipes player.

Union Square Station

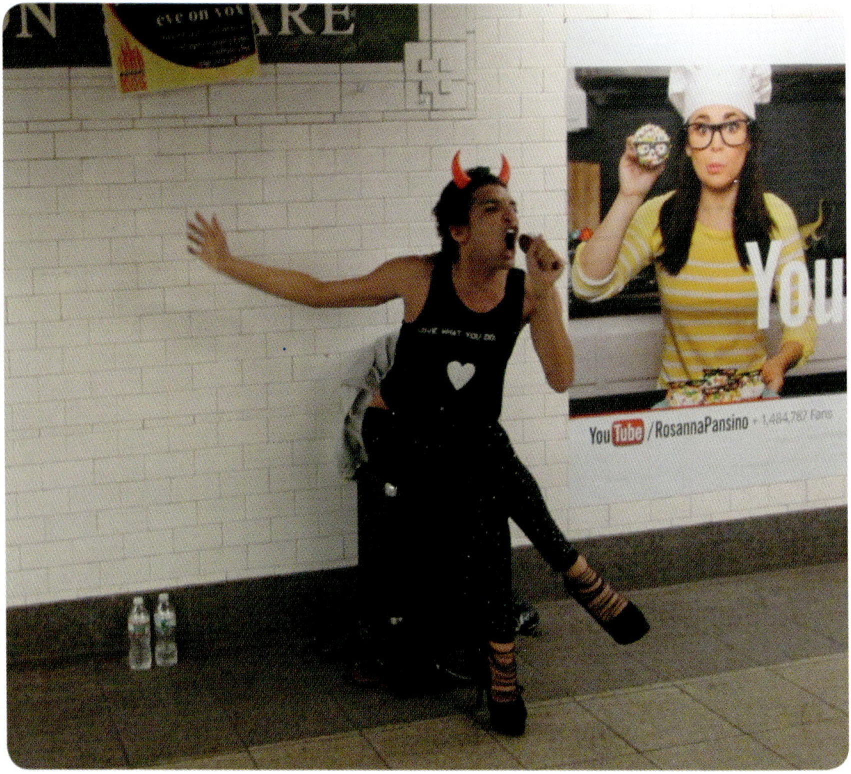

Eve on Vox, American soul singer.

Union Square Station

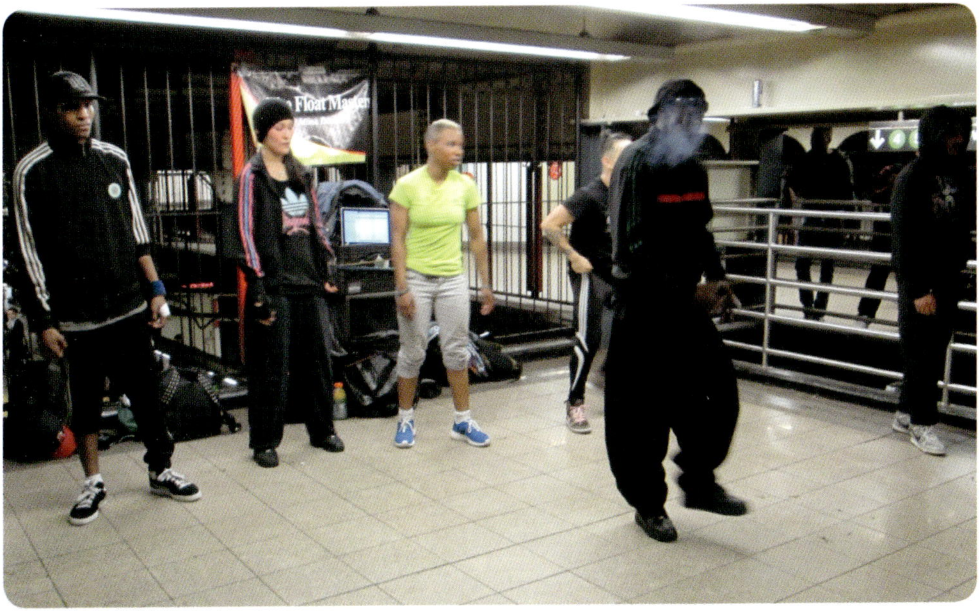

The Float Masters.

Union Square Station

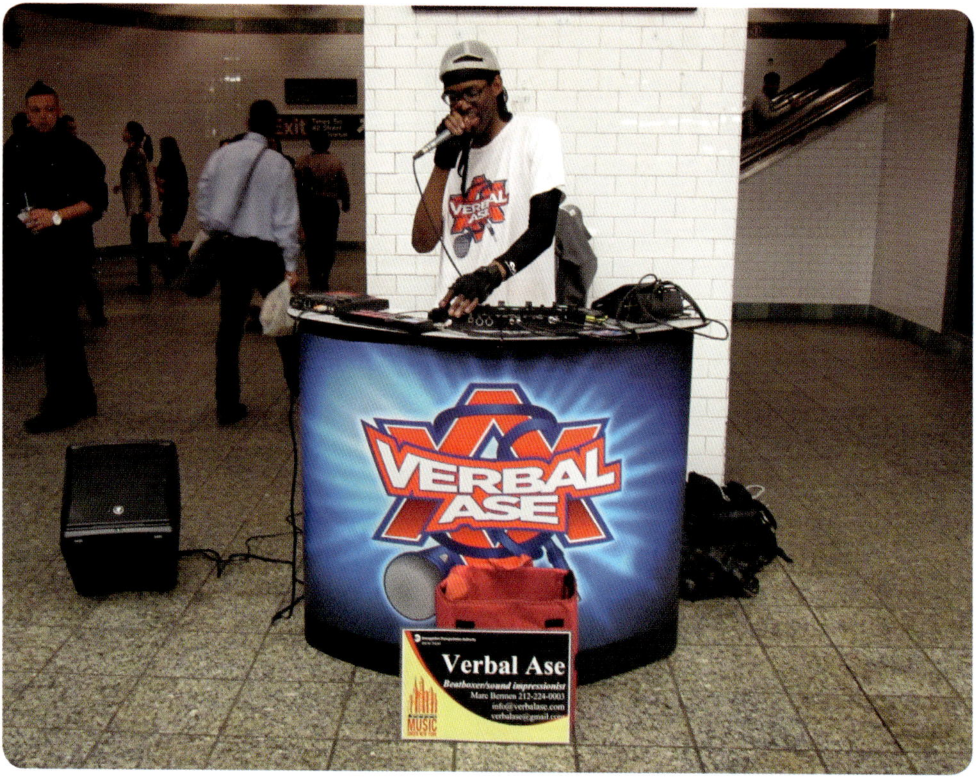

Verbal Ase, beat box vocal impressions.

Times Square Station

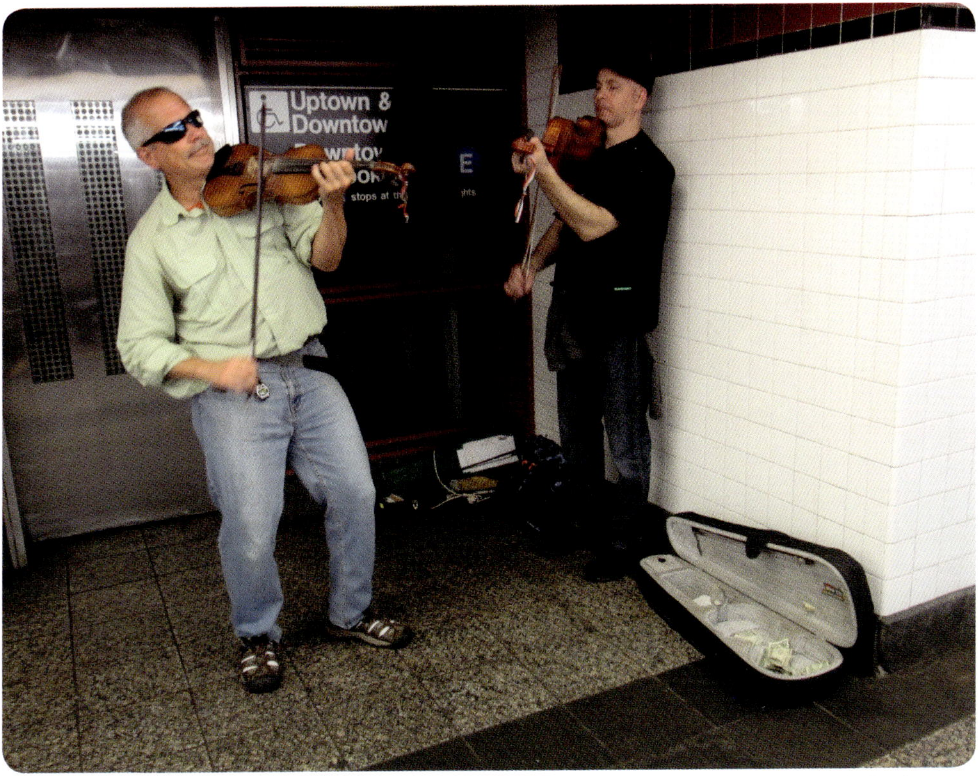

Two violin players.

34th Street - Penn Station

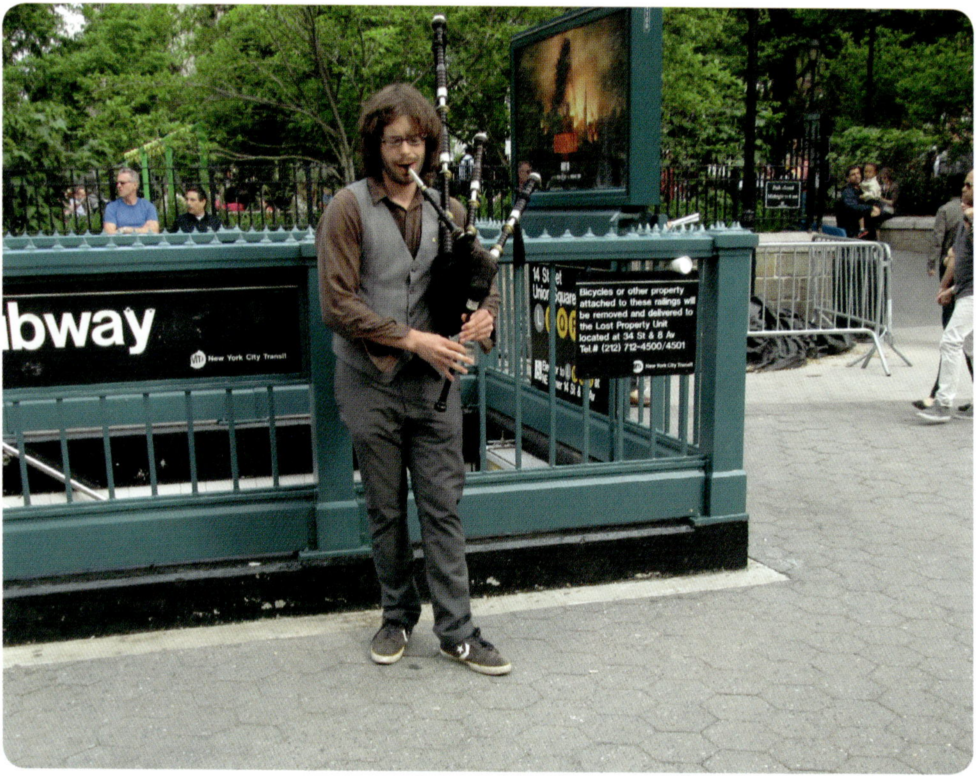

Irish bagpipes.

Union Square Station

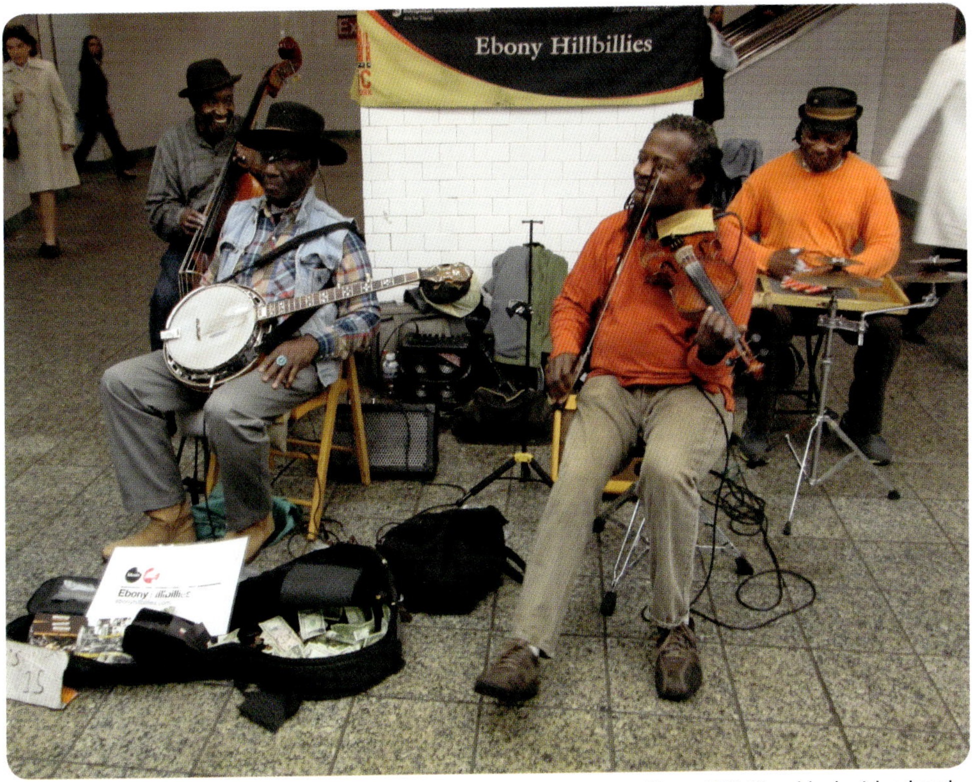

Ebony Hillbillies, black string band.

Times Square Station

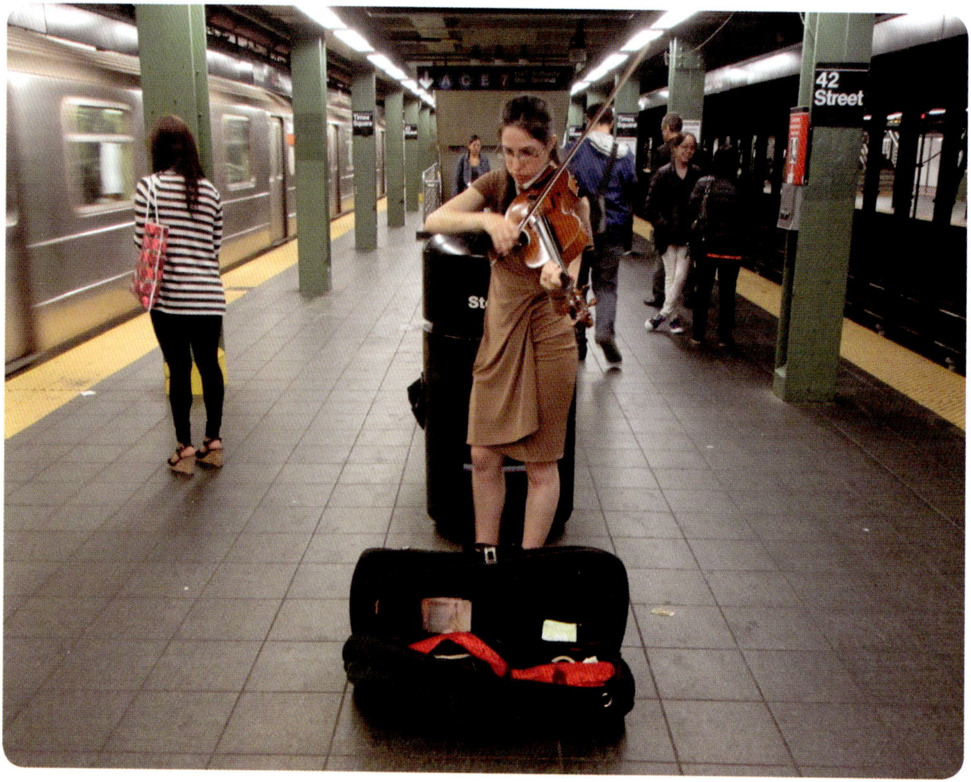

Violin.

42nd Street - Times Square Platform

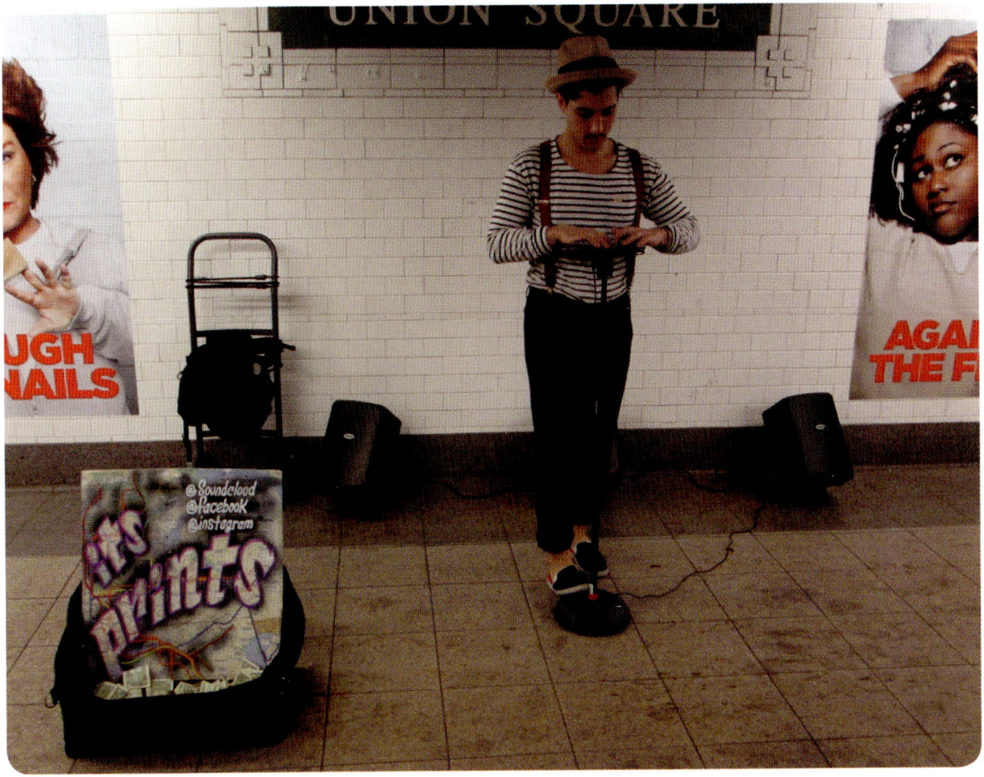

Its Prints, digital music and EDM performer.

Union Square Station

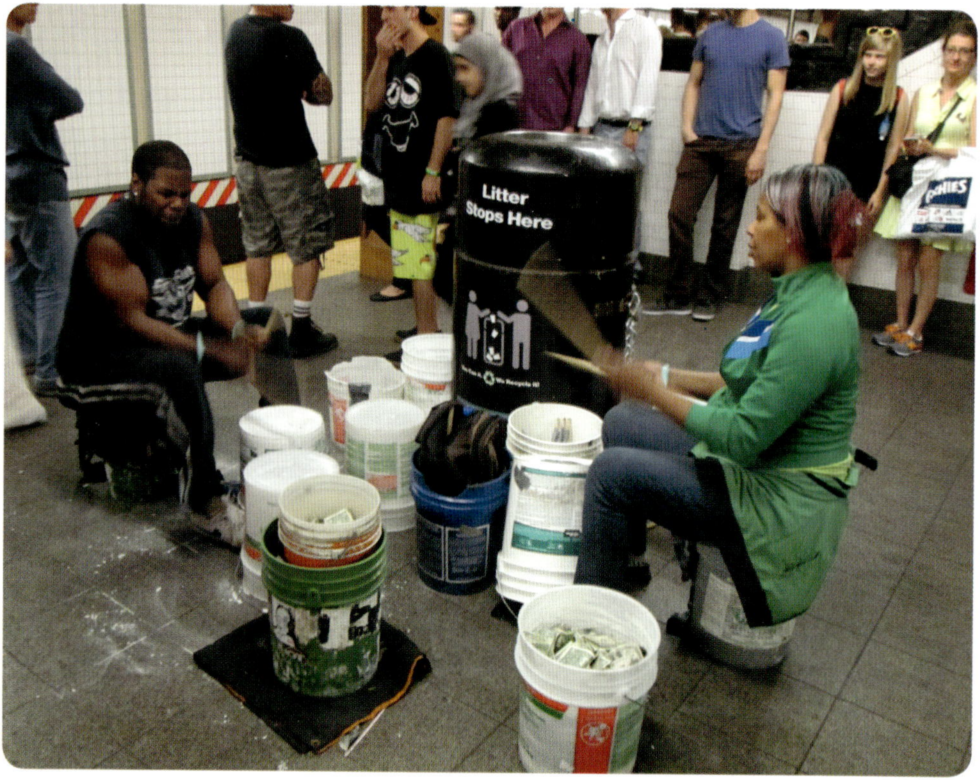

Larry Wright and Sonia Wright, bucket drummers.

L Train Platform - Union Square Station

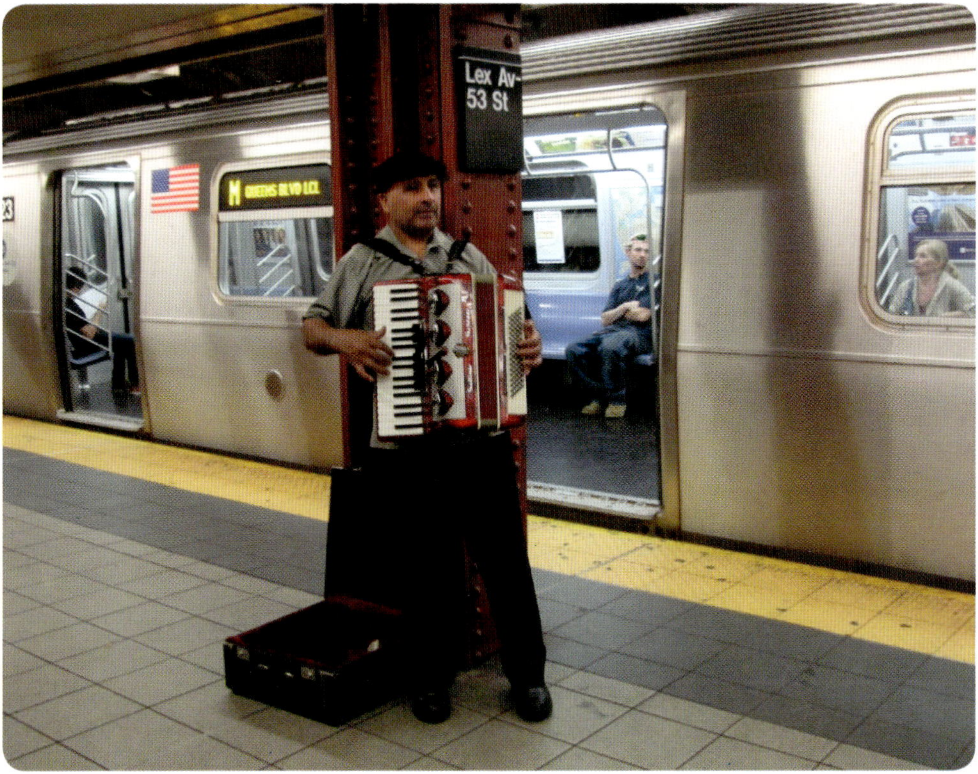

Accordion.

Lexington Avenue and 53rd Street Station Platform

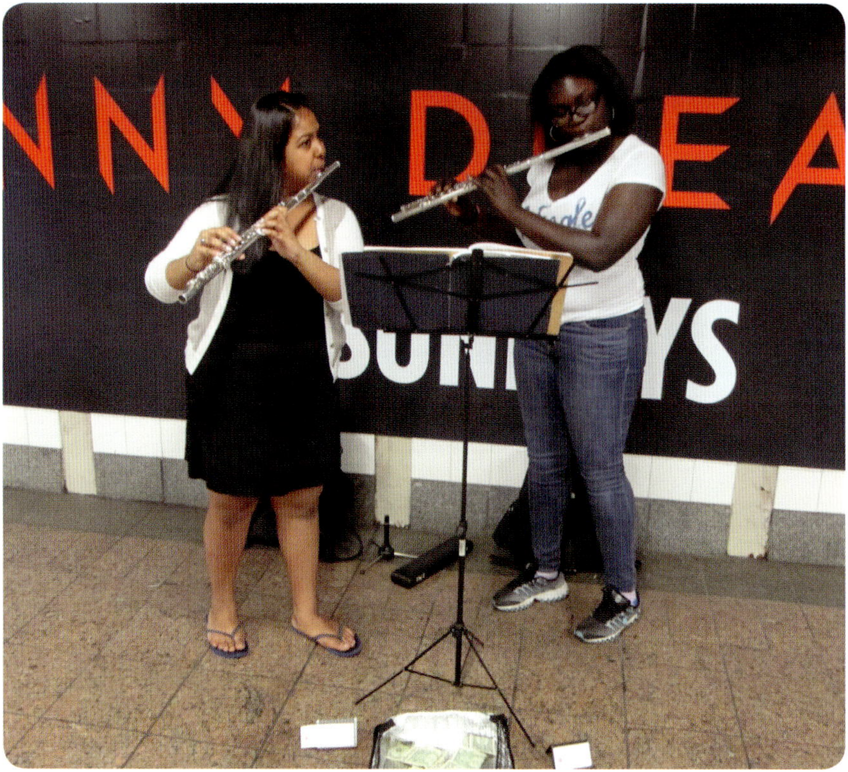

Dynamic Flute Duo: Christine Dookie and Maguette Ndiaye

Grand Central Station - Shuttle Walkway

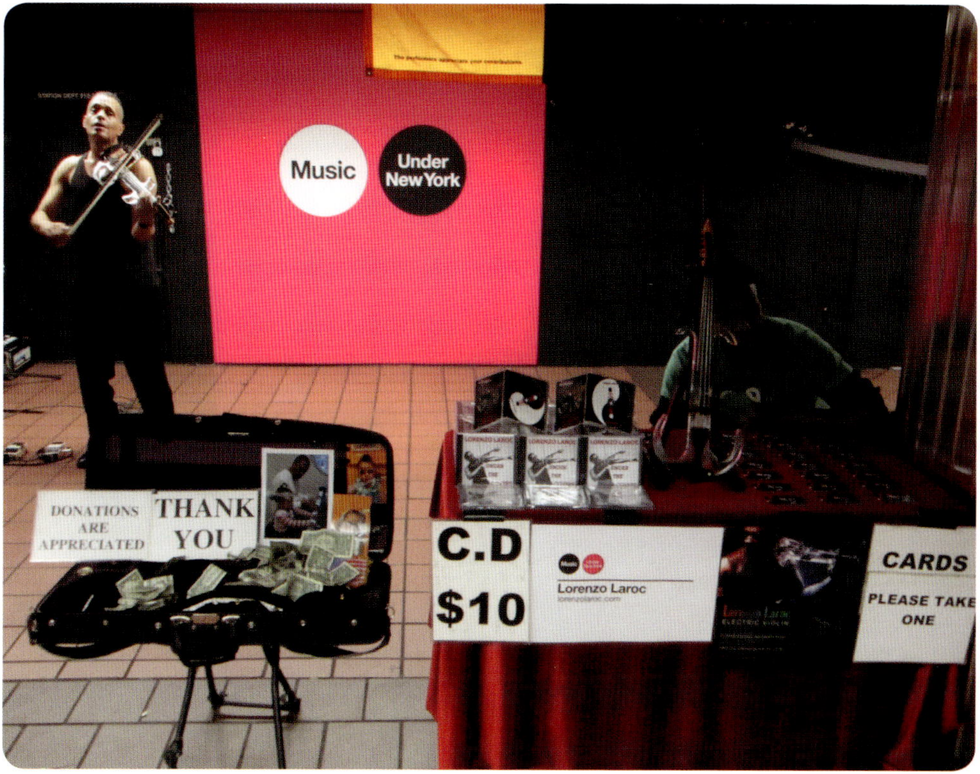

Lorenzo Laroc, electric violin

Grand Central Station

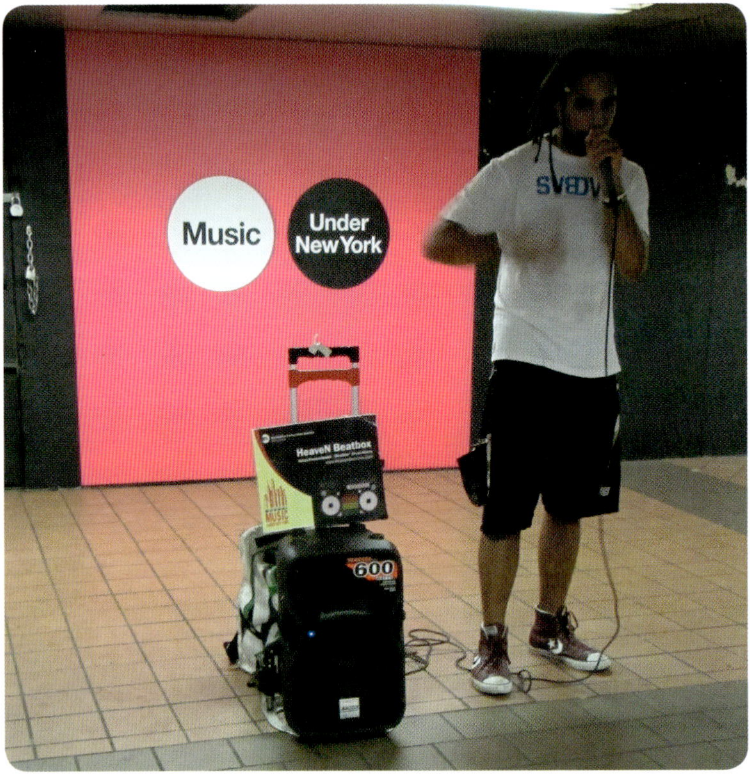

Heaven Beat Box, vocal percussionist.

Grand Central Station

West 4th Street Station

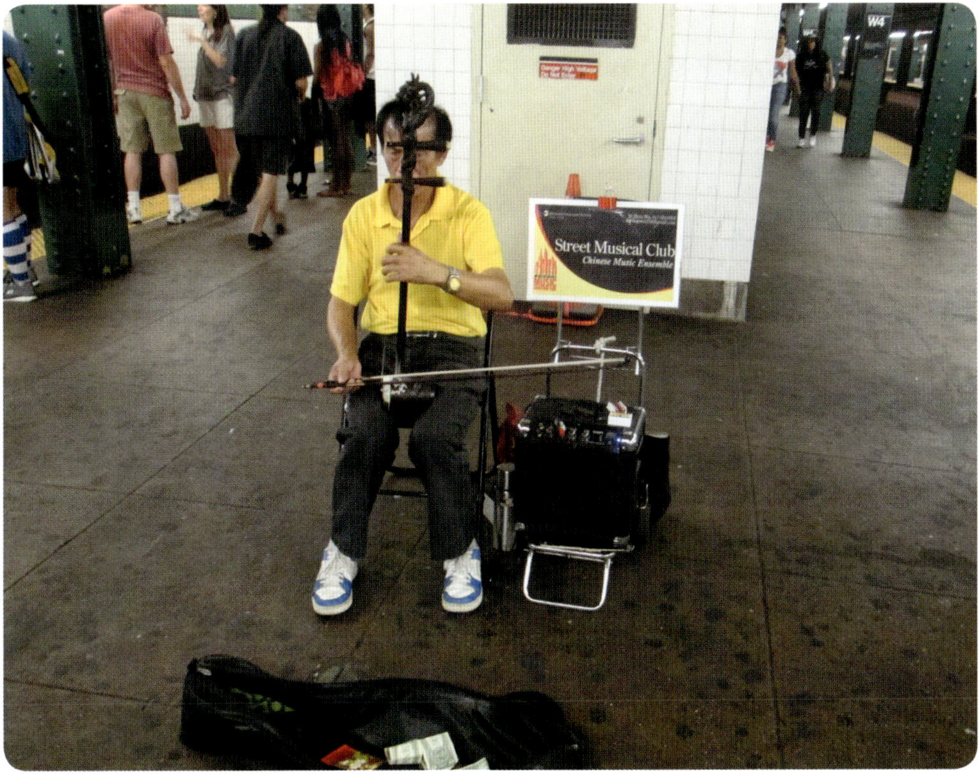

Member of Street Musical Club, Chinese music ensemble.

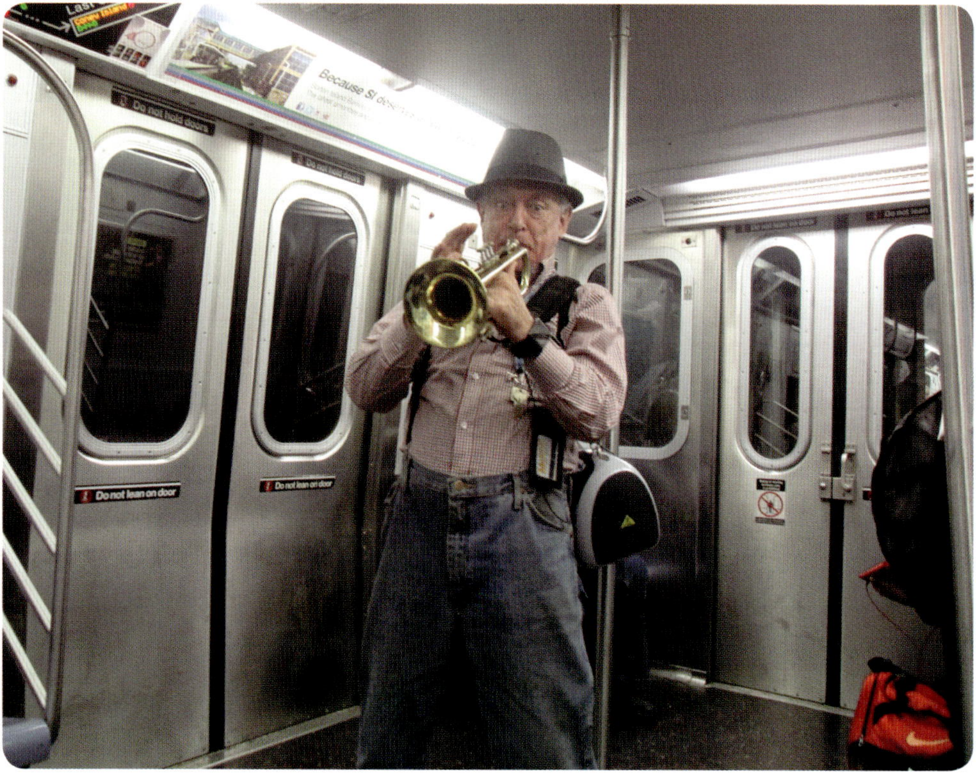

Trumpet player on the train.

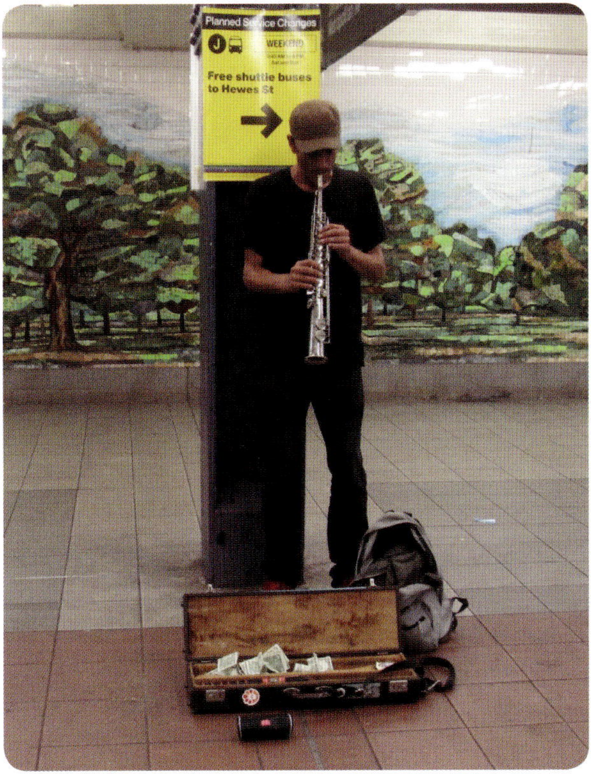

Flute.

Delancey Street Station

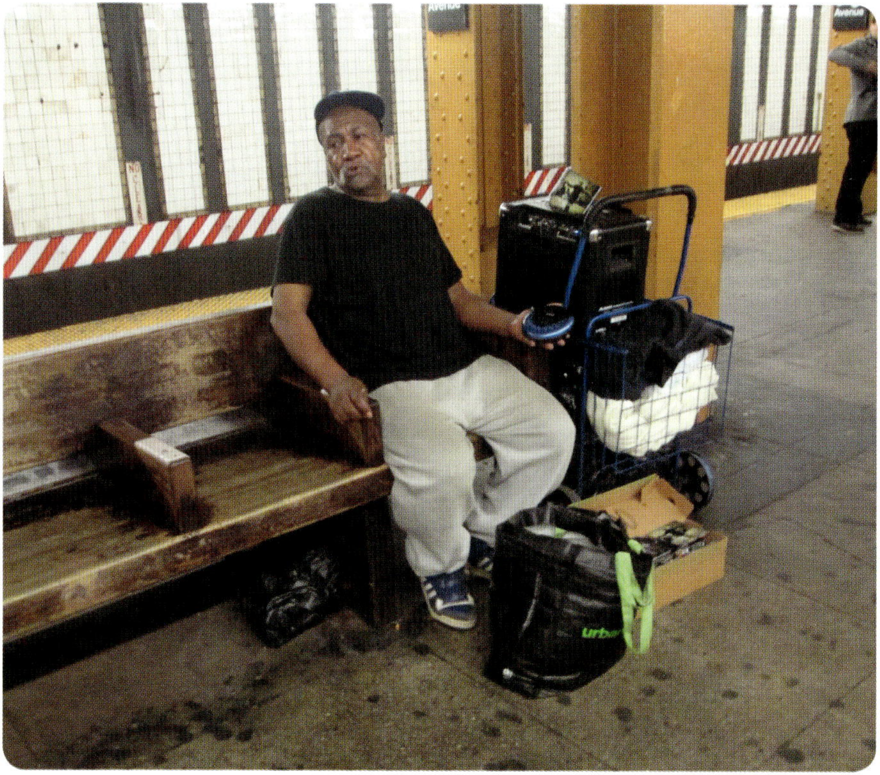

Gee Chee Dan, singer.

L Train Platform - 6th Avenue Station

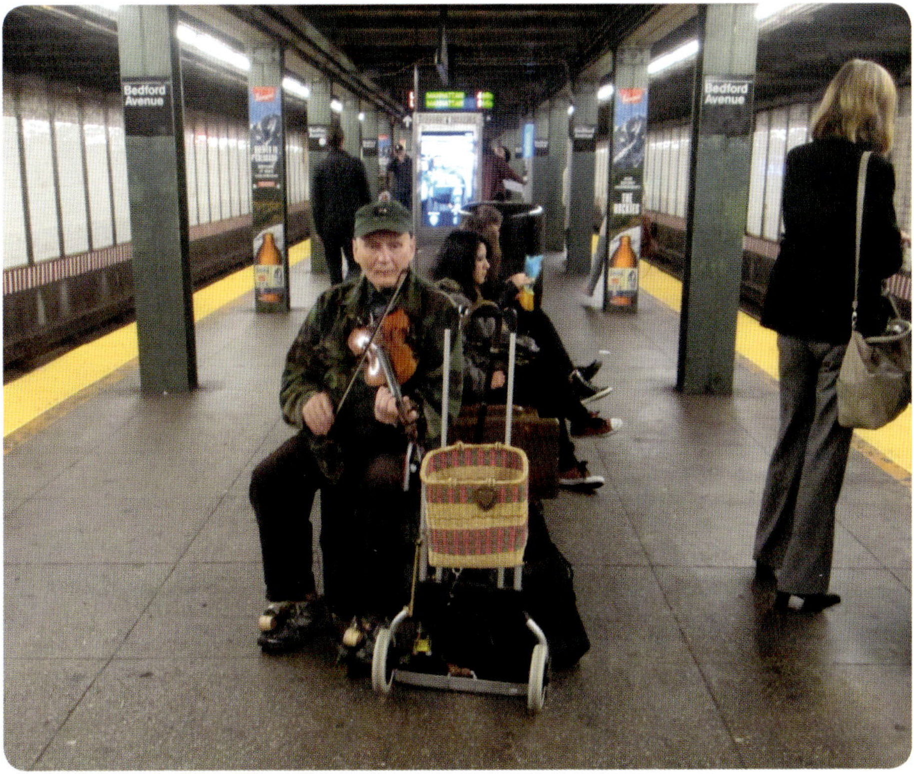

Edek Szala, violin.

Bedford Avenue Station

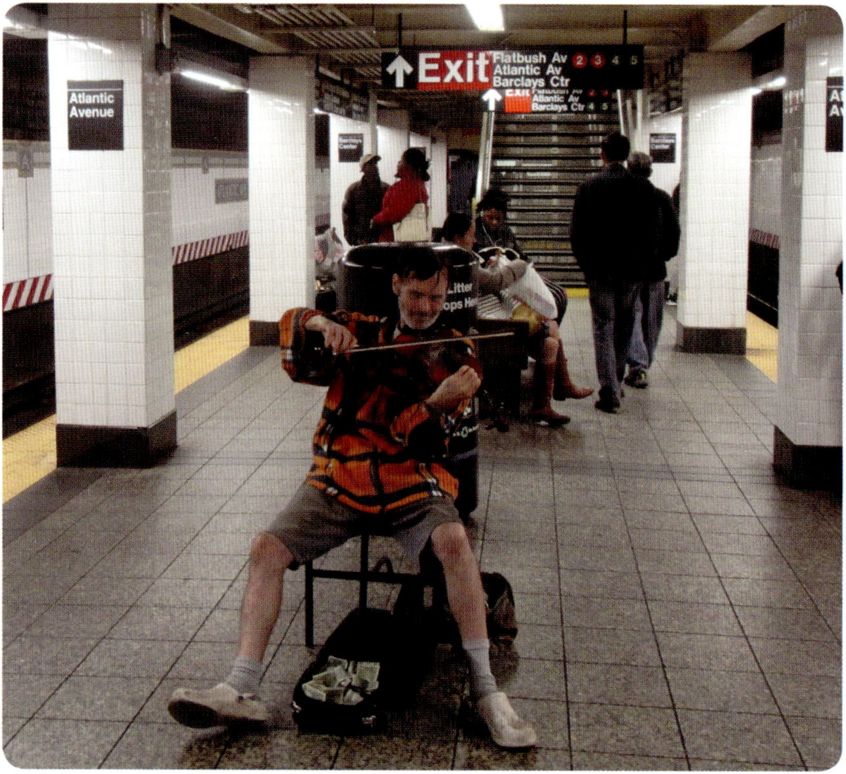

Violin.

Atlantic Avenue Station

14th Street Station - 6th Avenue Line

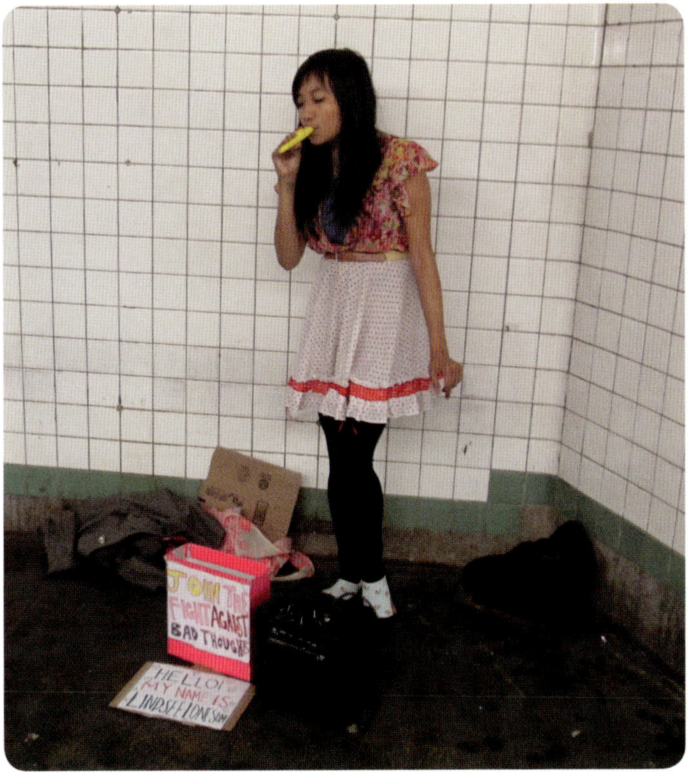

Lindsee Lone Sam

Union Square Station

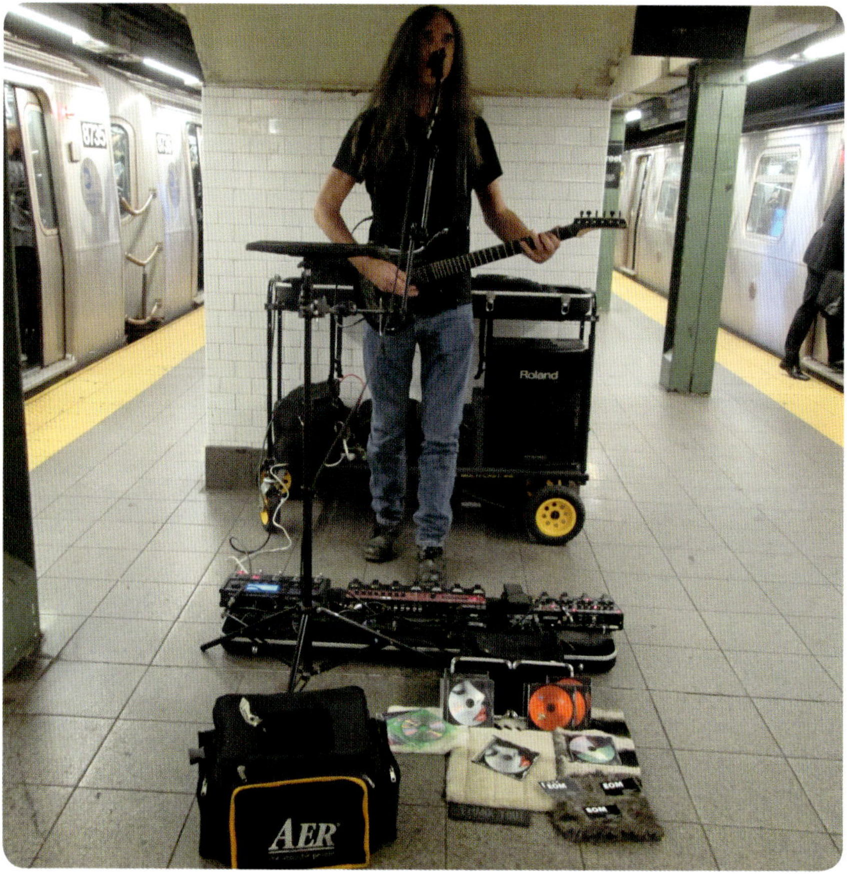

Electric guitar.

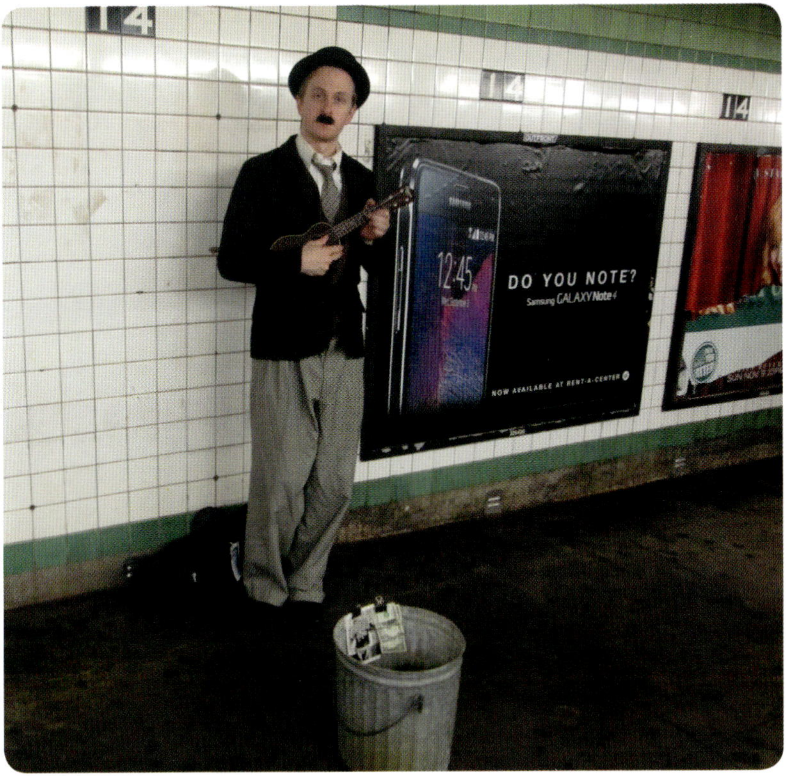

Ukulele.

14th Street Station - 6th Avenue Line

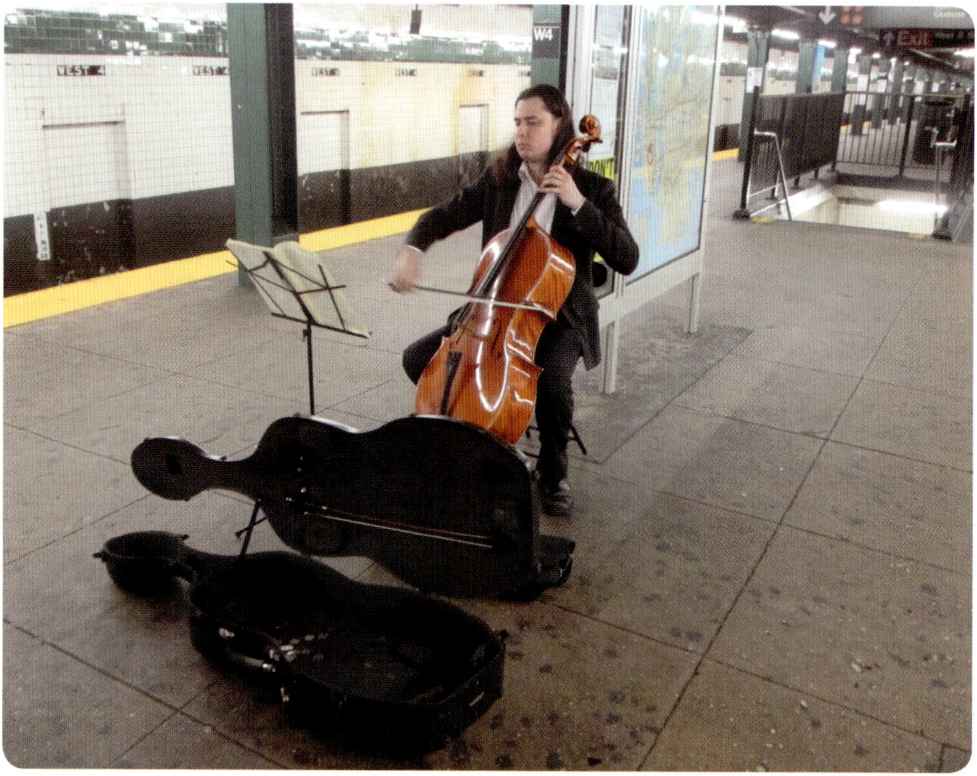

Chris "Hitchcock" Chorney, cello.

West 4th Street Station

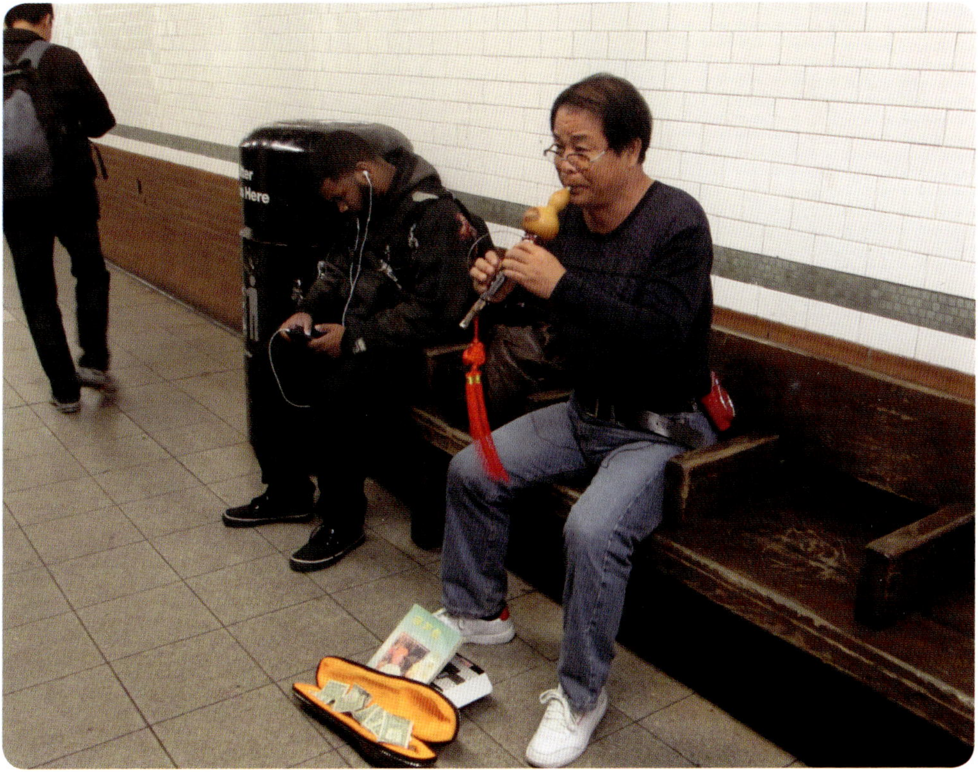

Chinese flute.

Canal Street Station

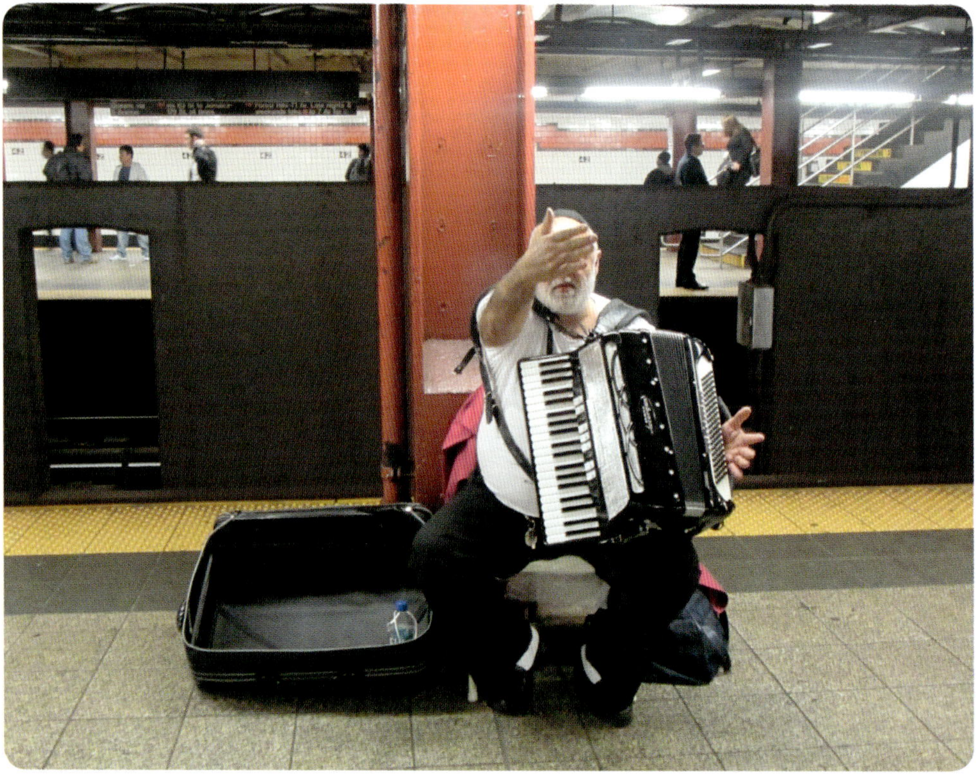

Accordion.

42nd Street Station - 6th Avenue Line

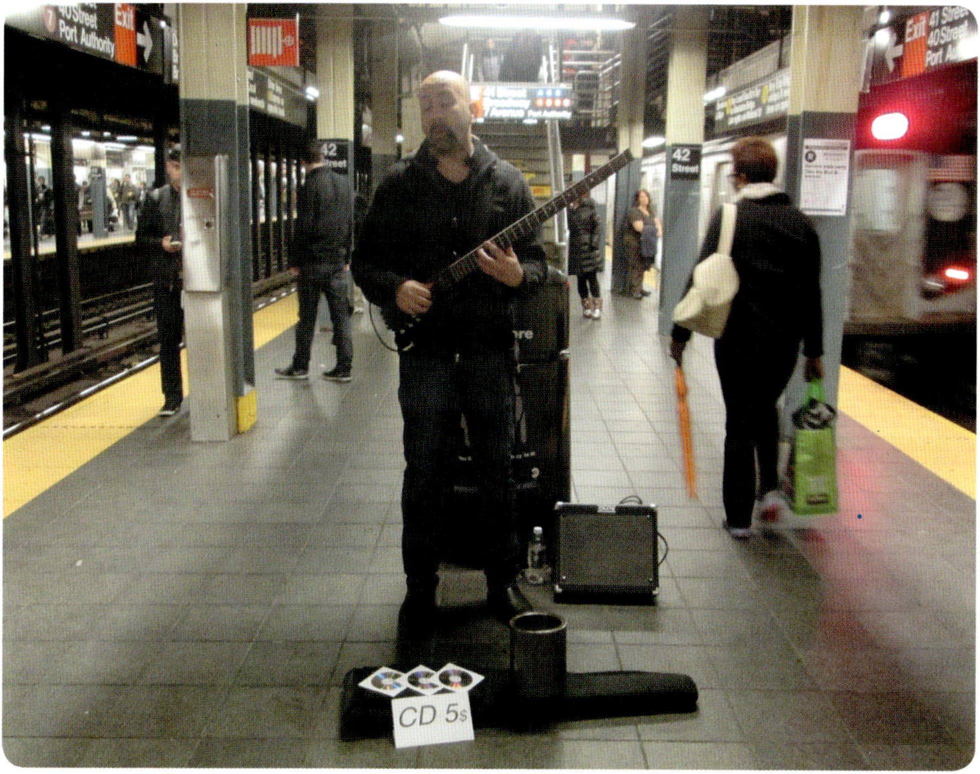

Gonzalo Silva, non-head electric guitar.

42nd Street - Times Square Station

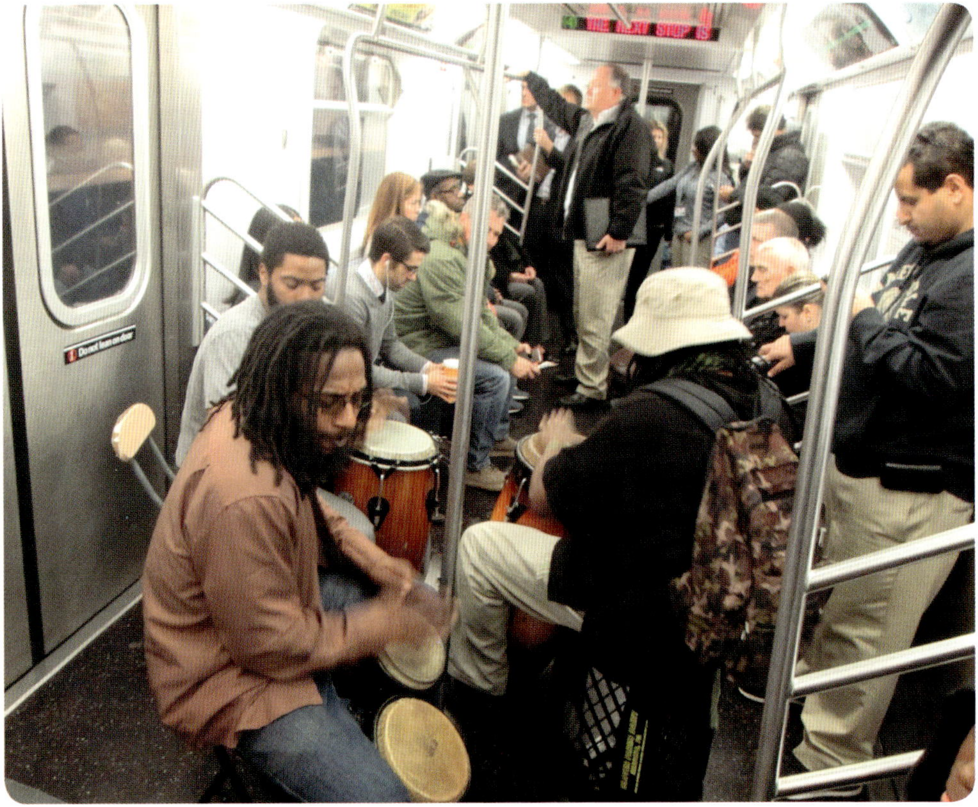

Fresh 2 Life

Playing on 4 Train

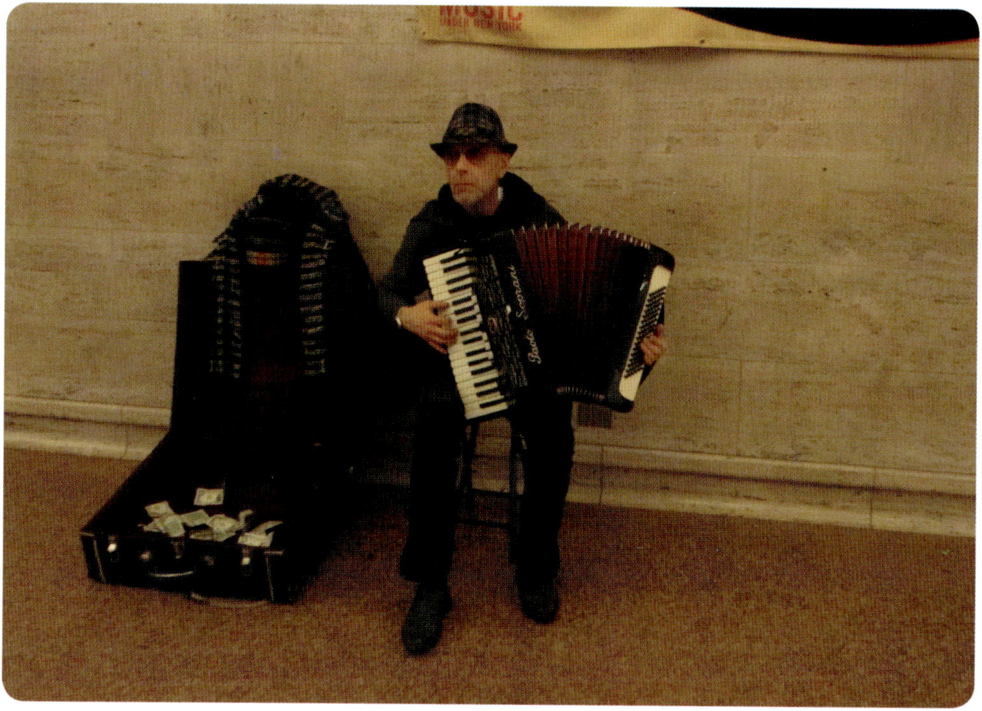

Yuriy Zak, accordionist.

Grand Central Terminal

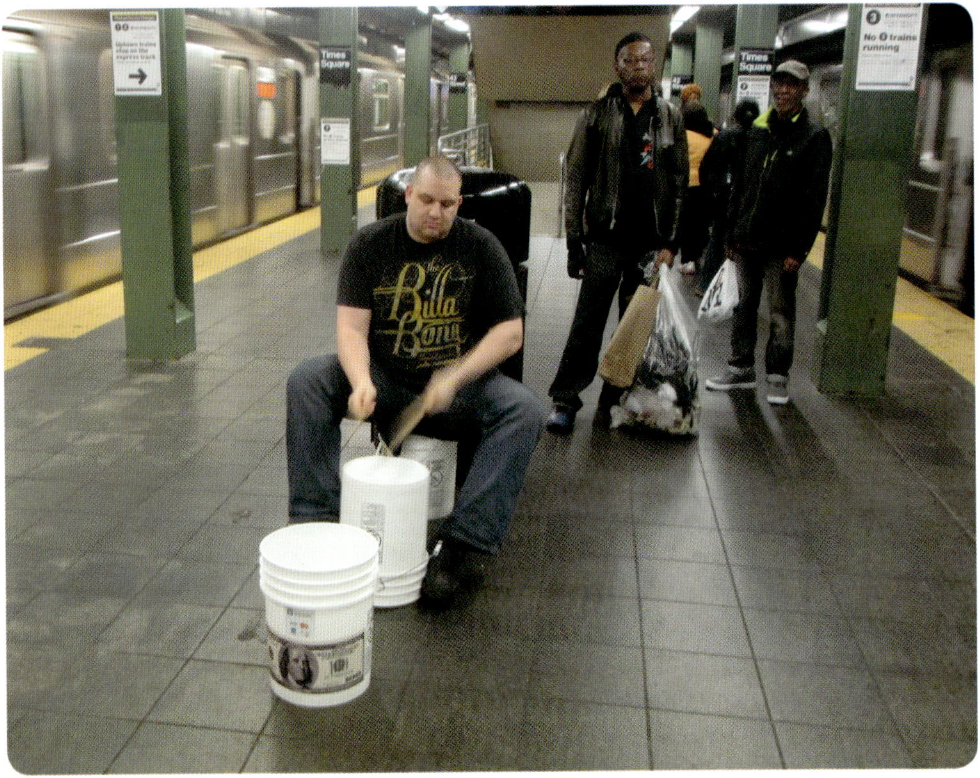

Bucket drummer.

42nd Street - Times Square Station

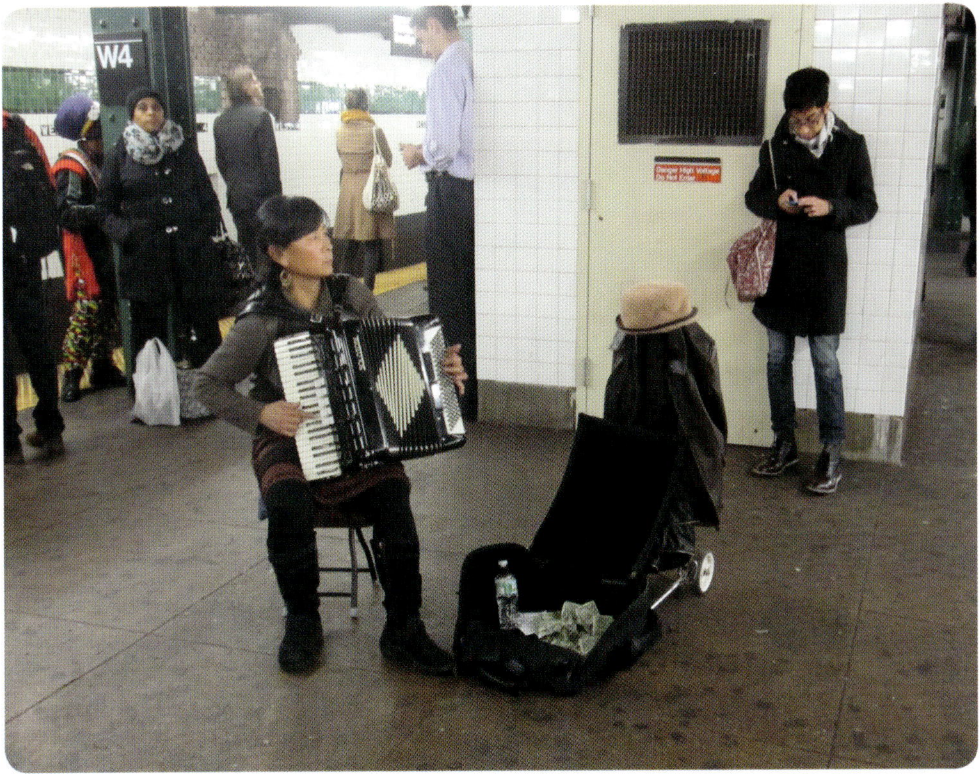

Accordion.

West 4th Street Station

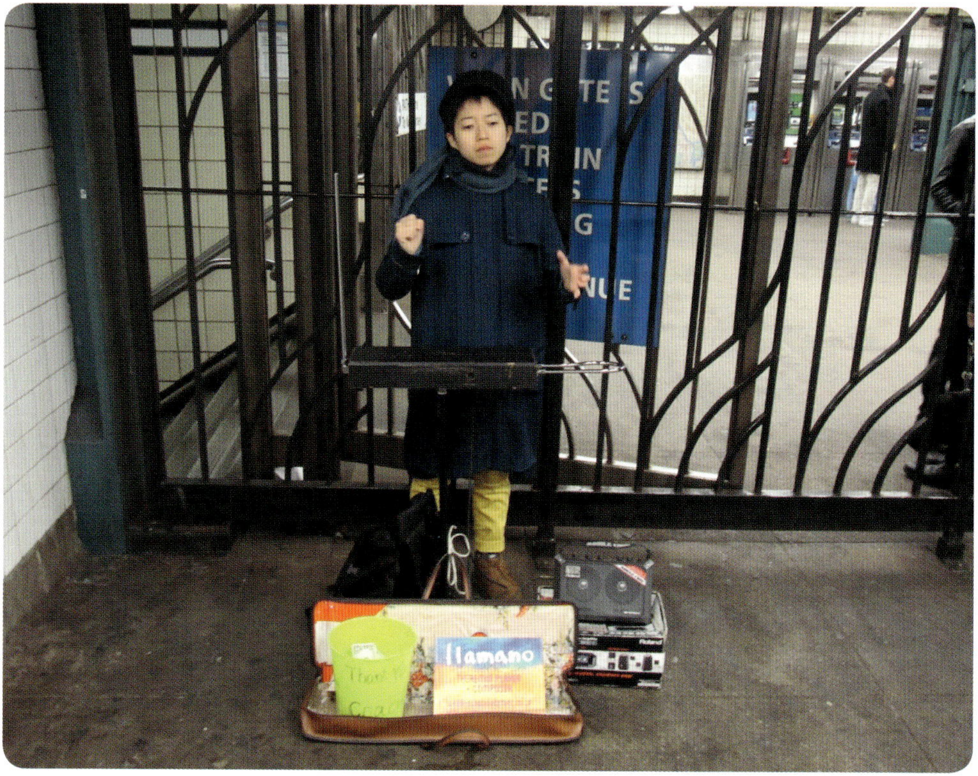

Llamano, theremin.

14th Street Station - 6th Avenue Line

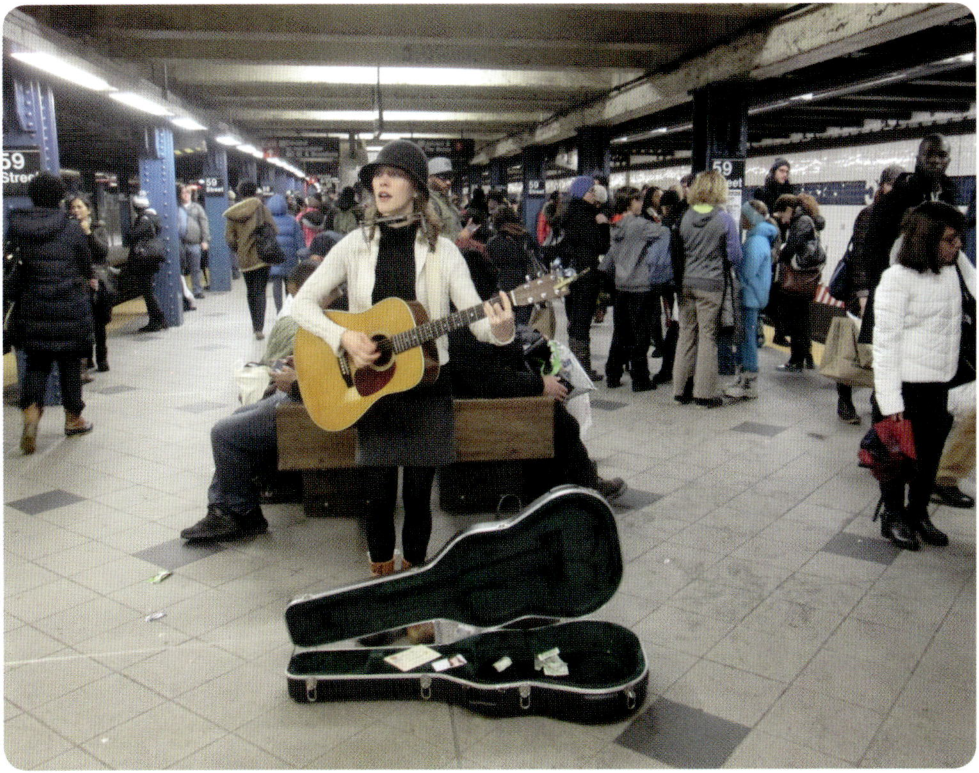

Brittany Brook, singer.

59th Street - Columbus Circle Station

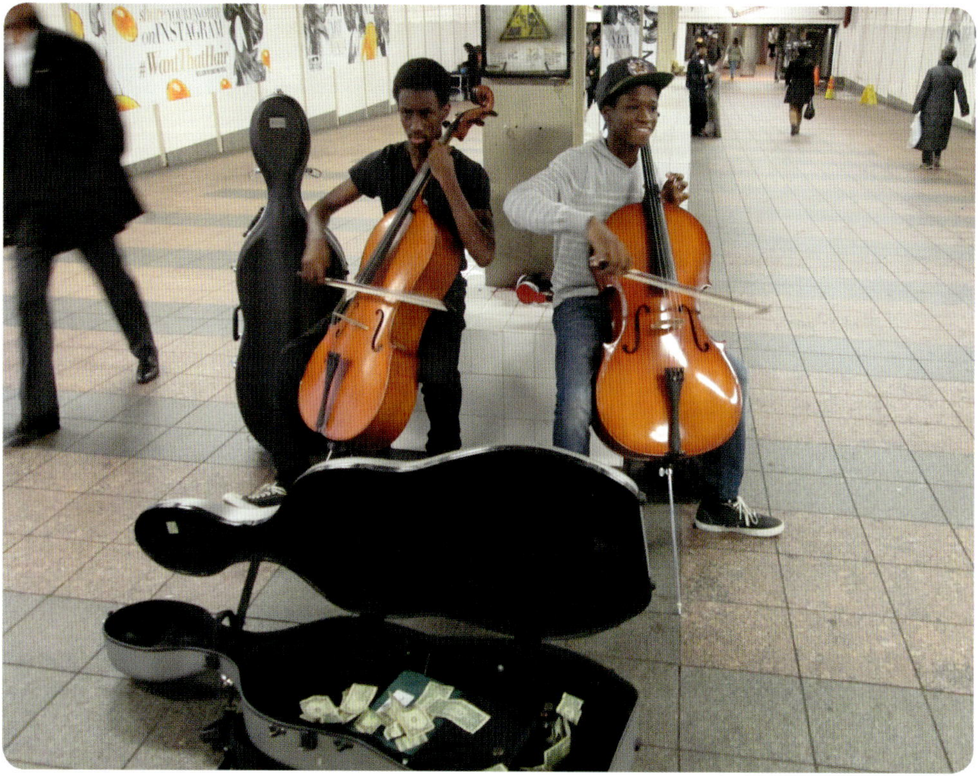

Cello X

Grand Central Station - Shuttle Walkway

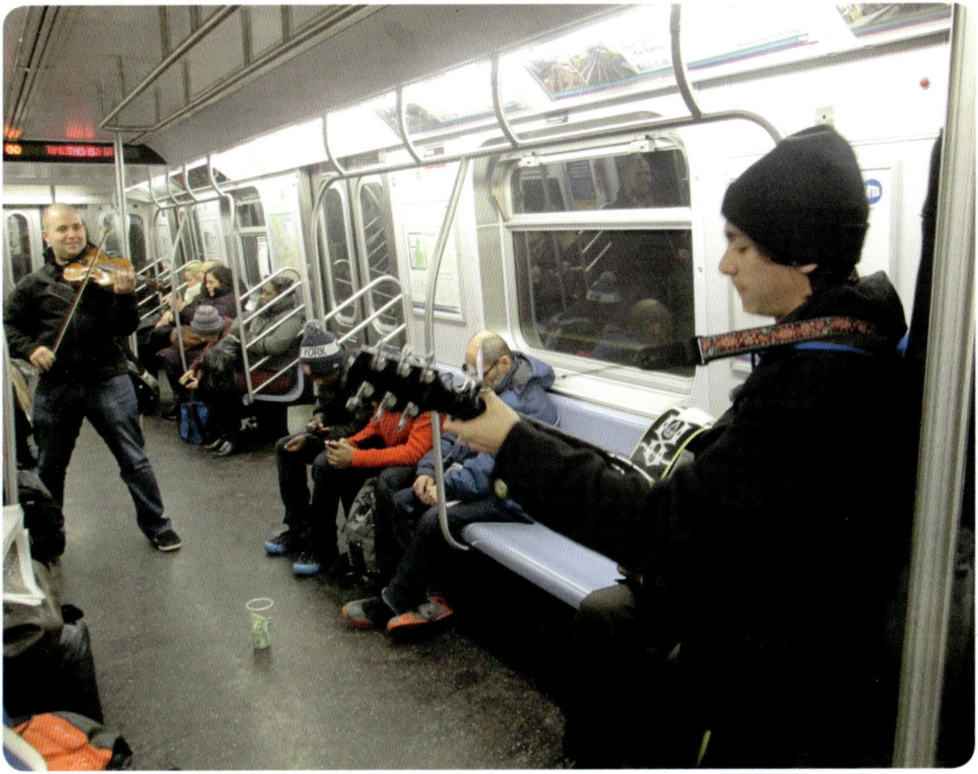
Violin and folk guitar.

Performing on N Train

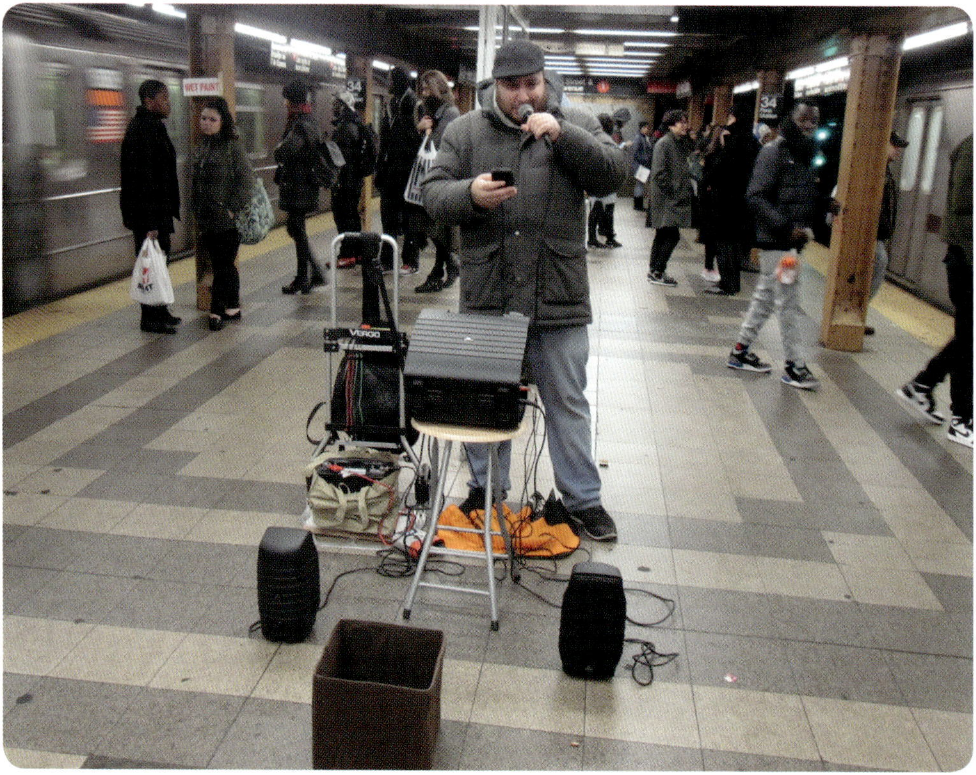

Unique singer.

34th Street - Penn Station

Times Square Station

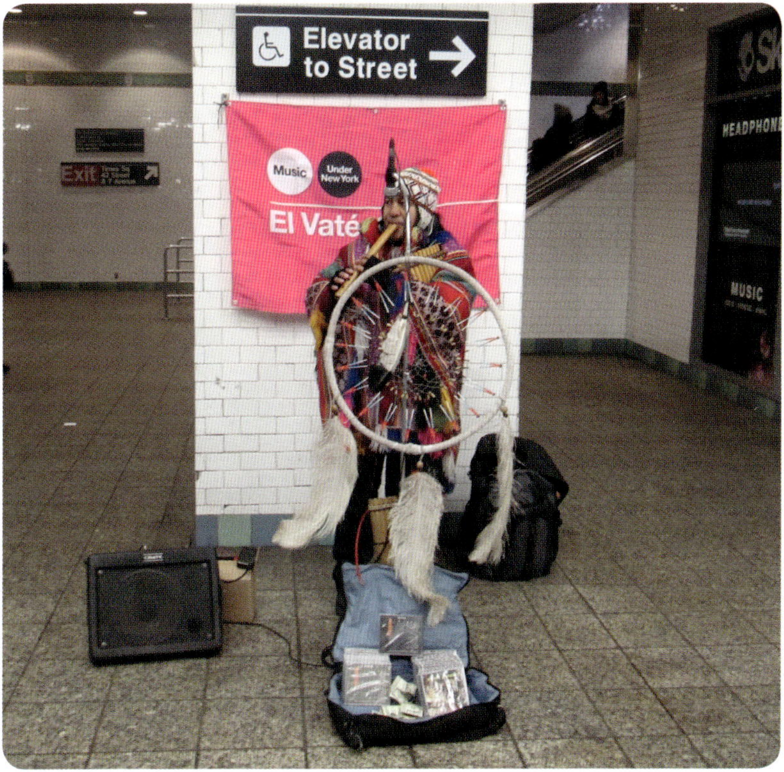

El Vaté

Fifth Avenue - 53rd Street Station

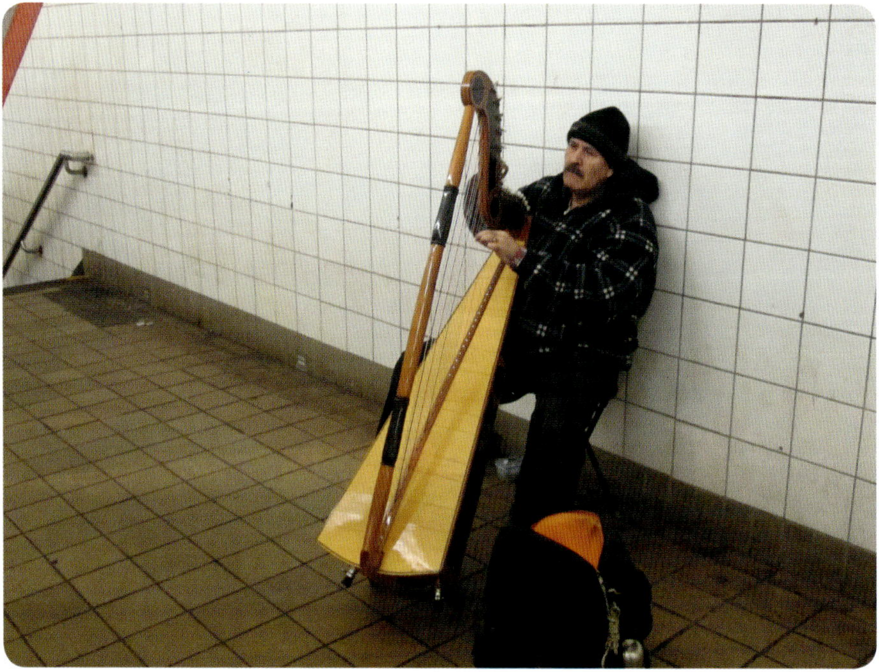

Harp.

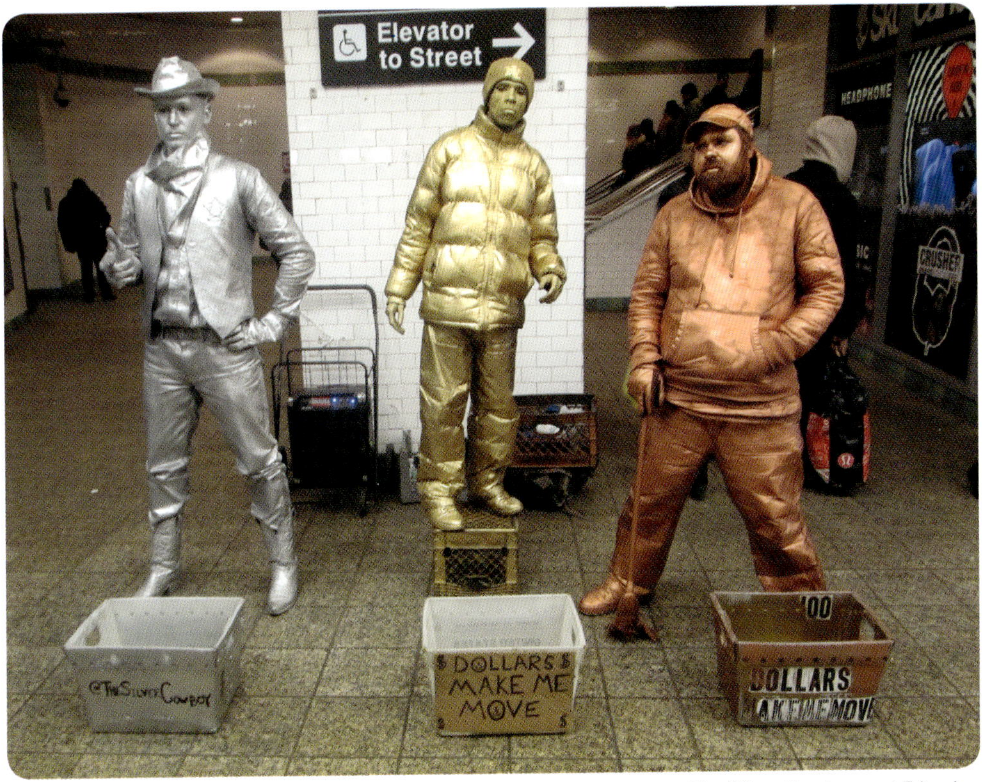

The Silver Cowboy and Friends

Times Square Station

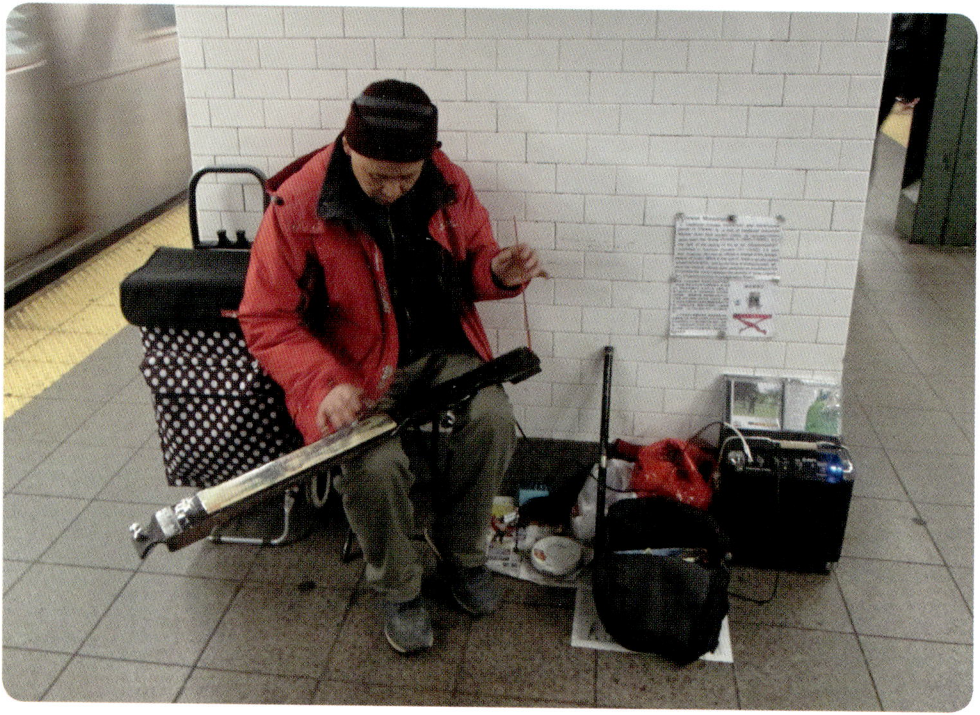

Chinese monochord.

Union Square Station

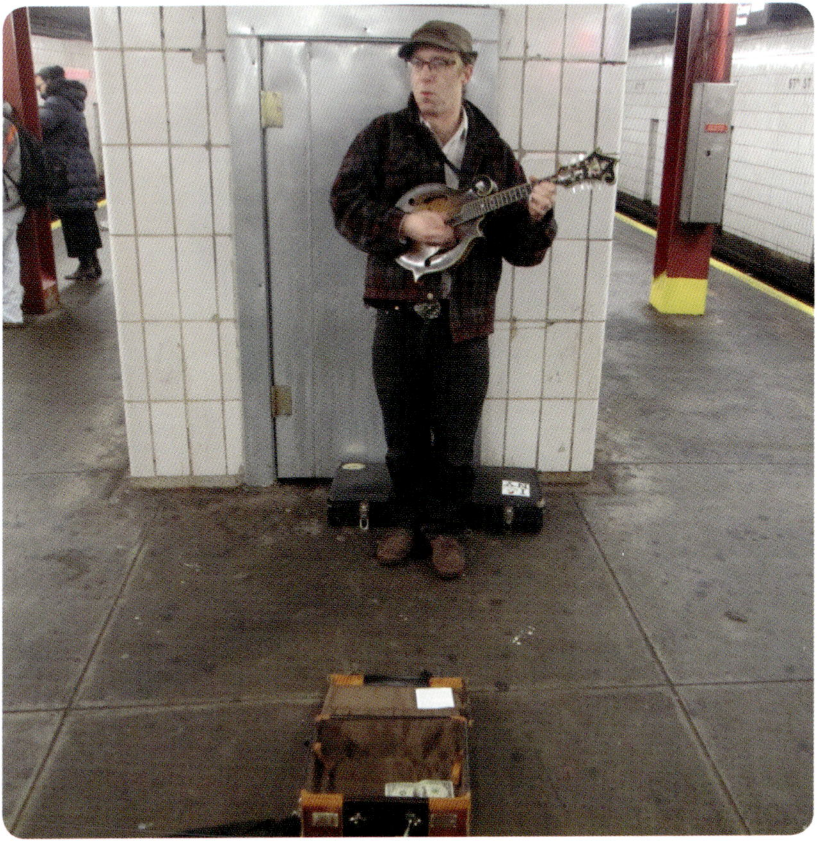

Ukulele.

57th Street Station

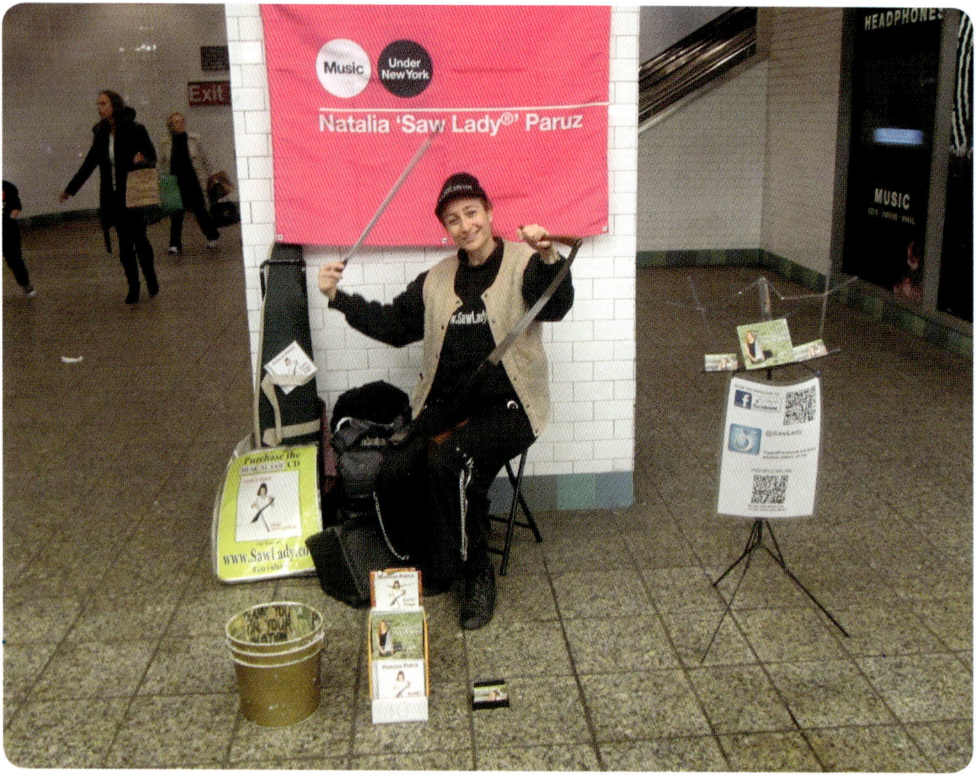

Natalia "Saw Lady" Paruz

Times Square Station

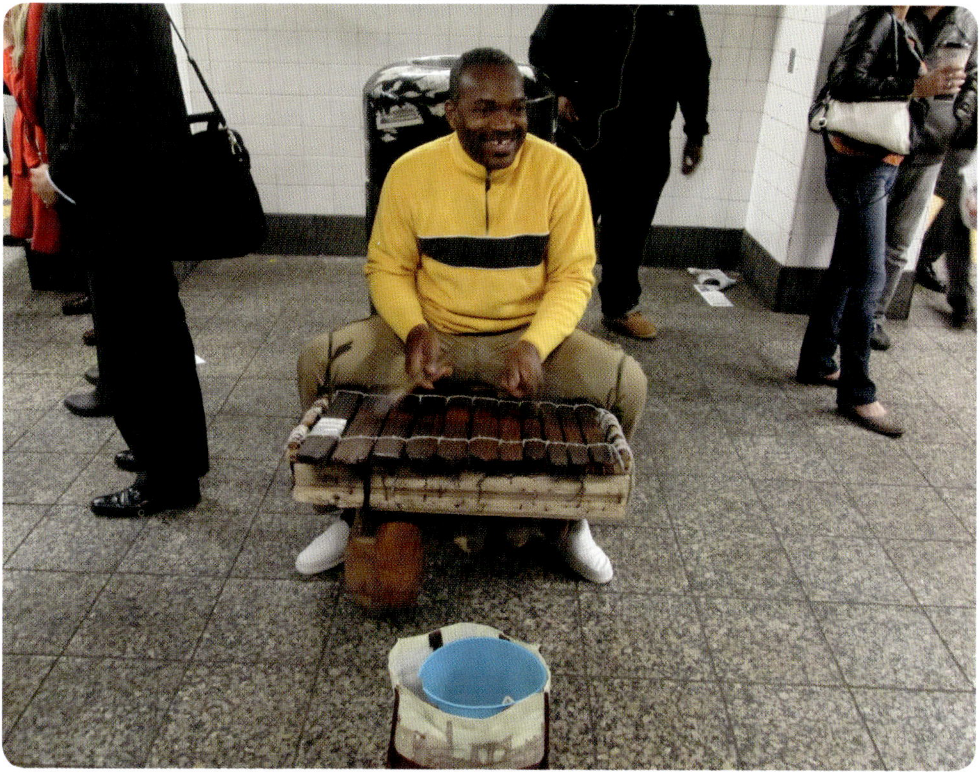

Balophone.

Grand Central Station

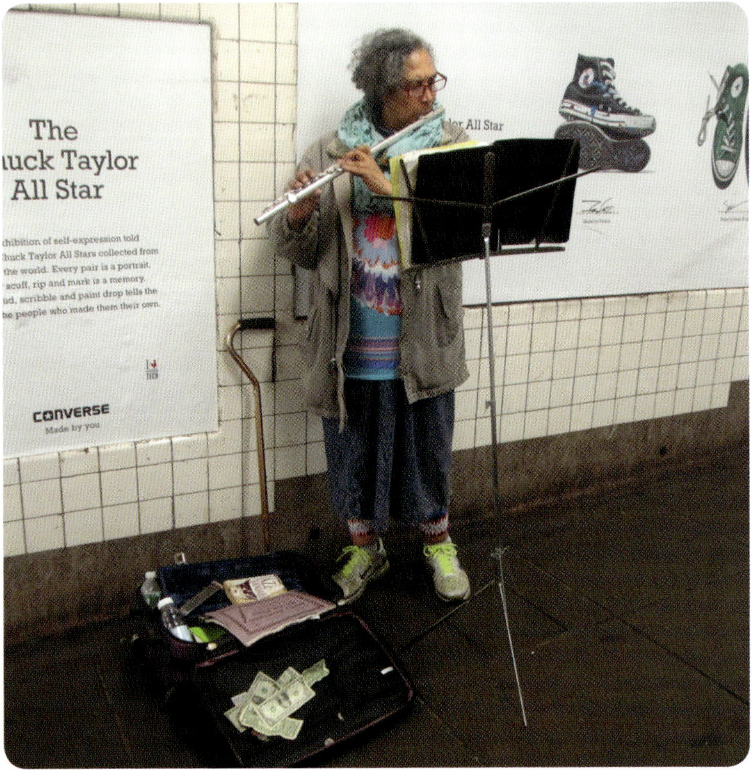

Flute.

West 4th Street Station

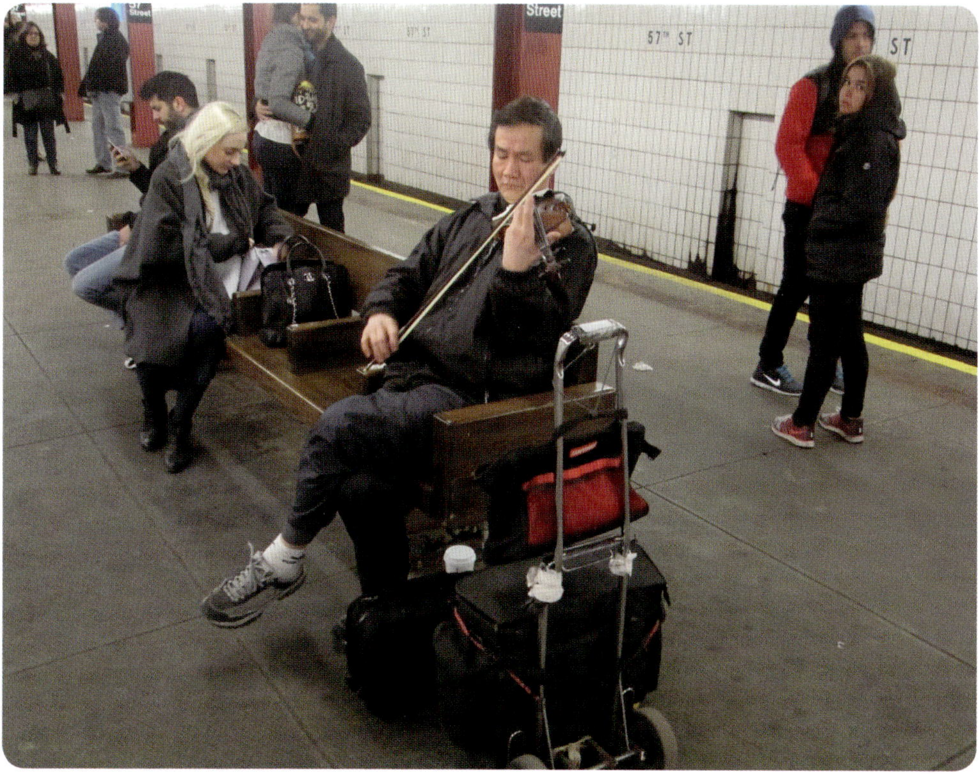

Violin.

57th Street Station

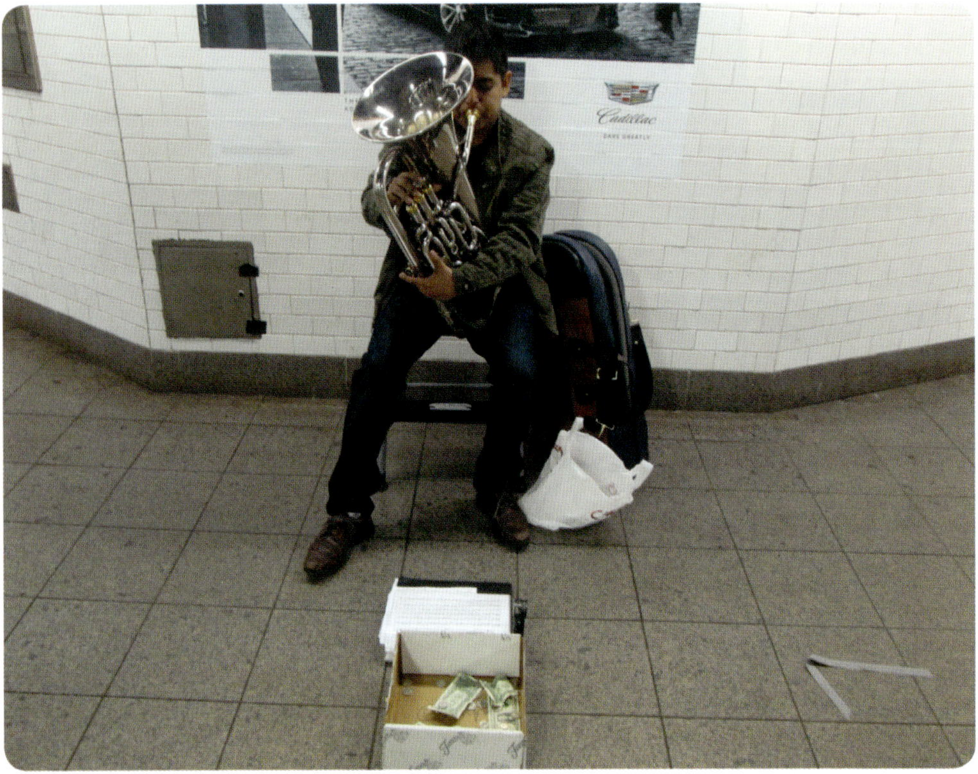

French horn.

59th Street - Lexington Avenue Station

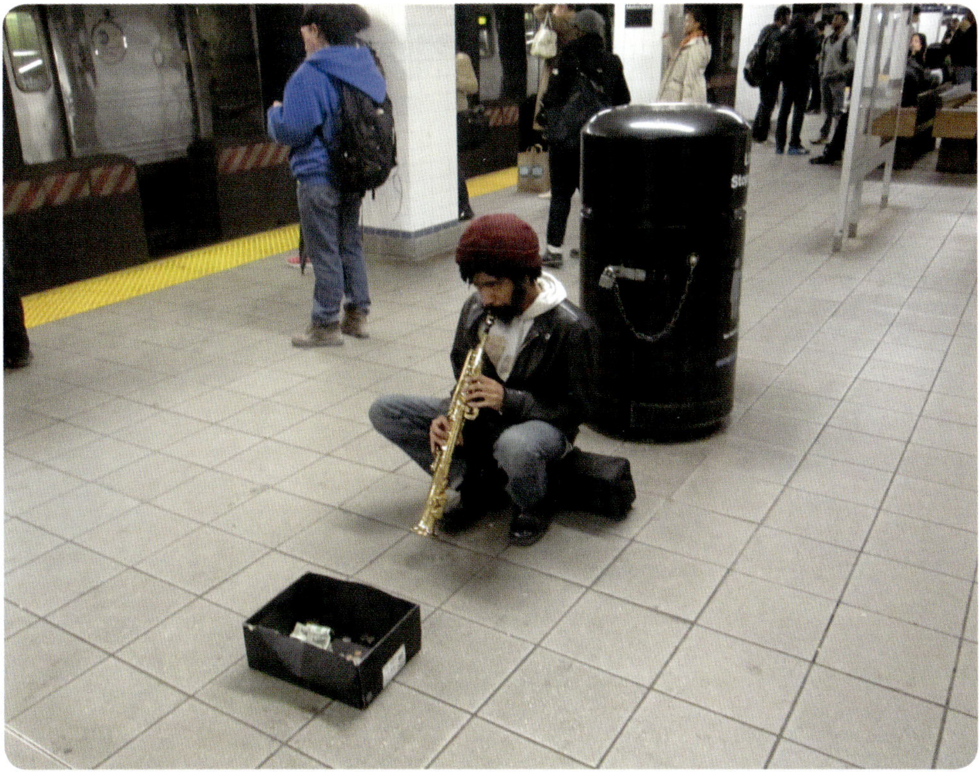

Flute.

Borough Hall Station

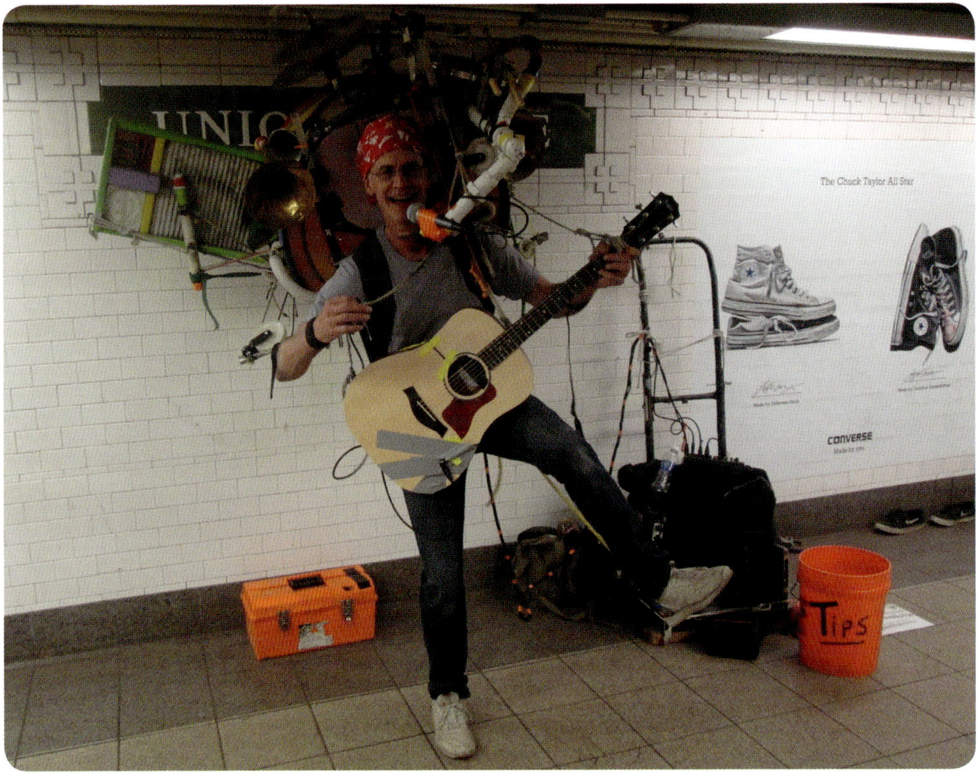

Jeff Masing, one man band.

Union Square Station

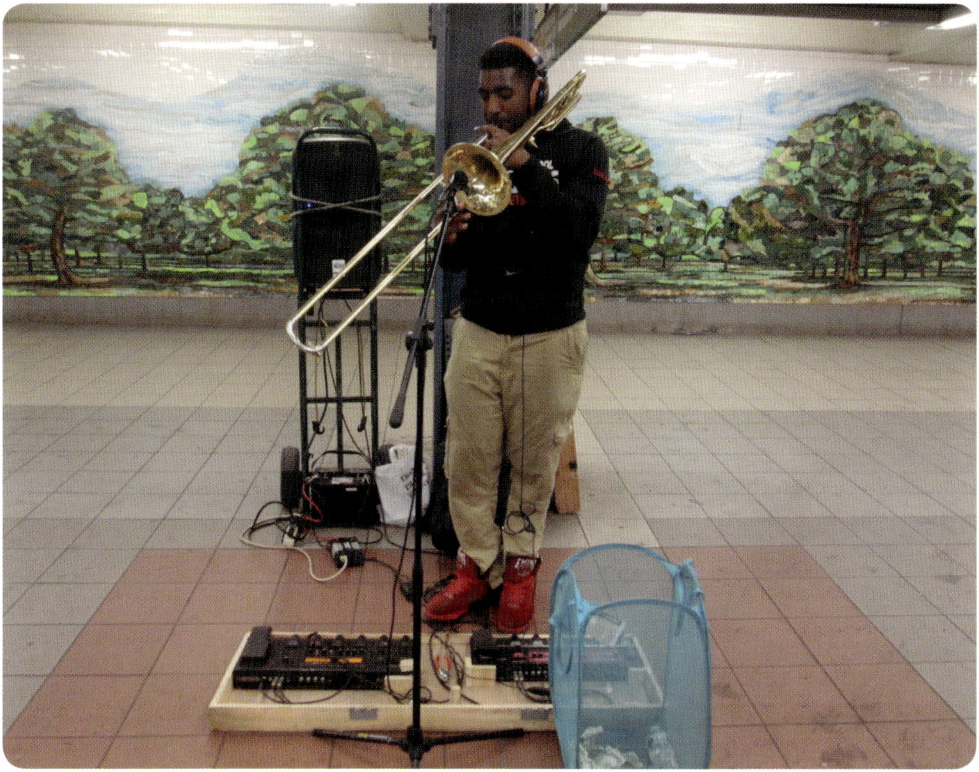

Ebone Underground

Delancey Street Station

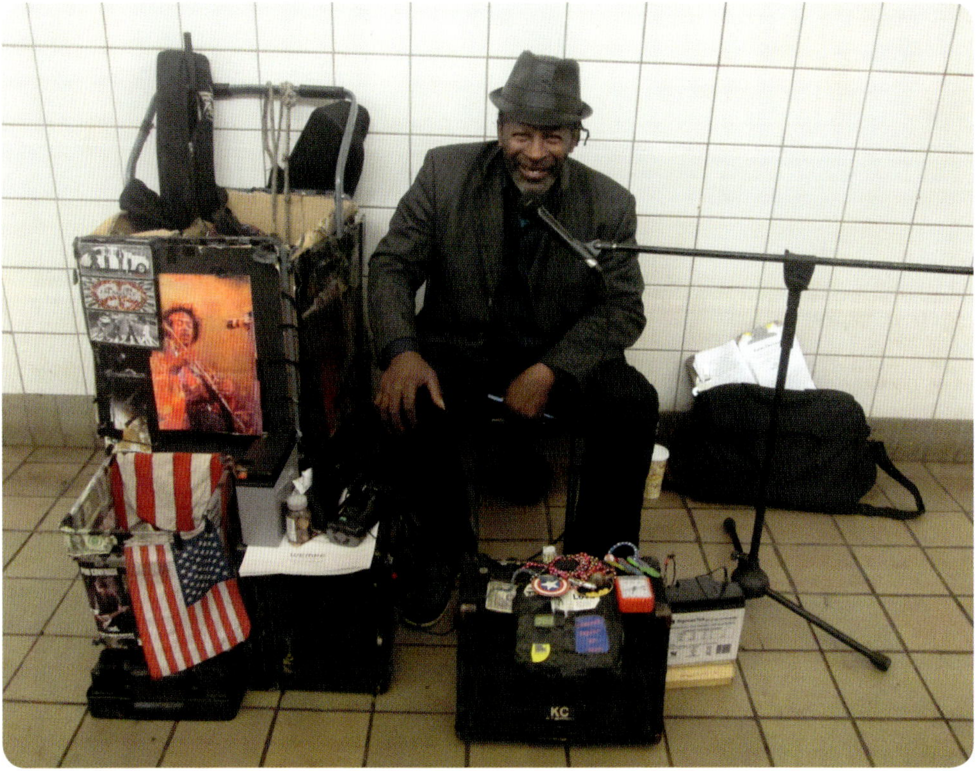

Tyrone Cooper

5th Avenue and 53rd Street Station

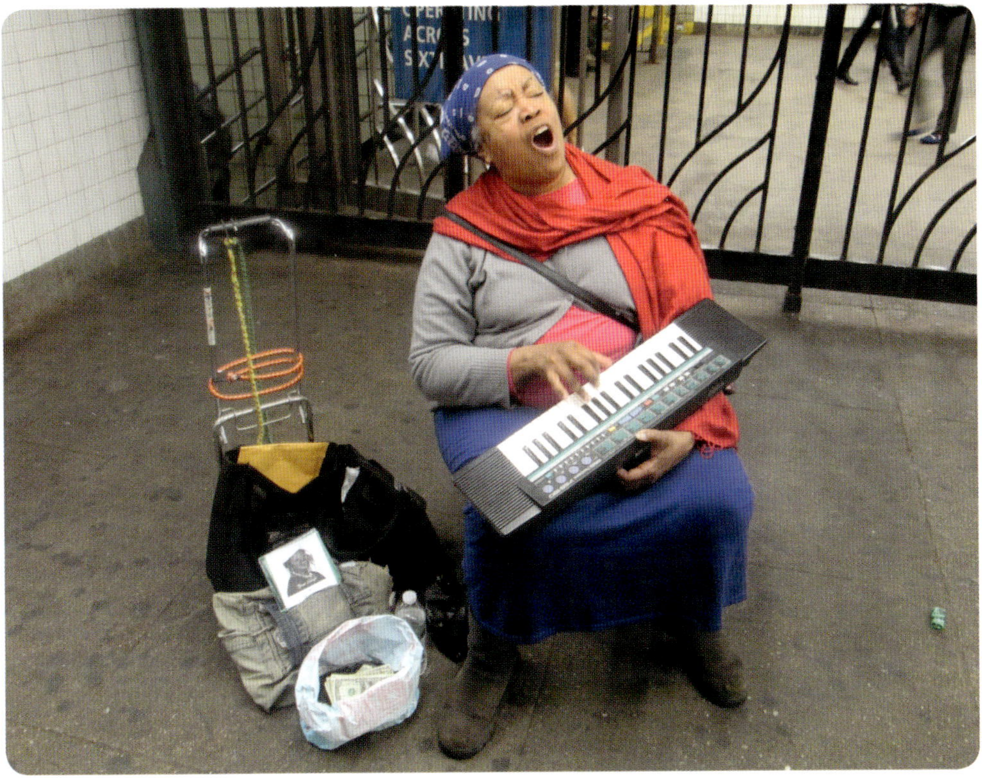

Rosa Teresa

14th Street - 6th Avenue Station

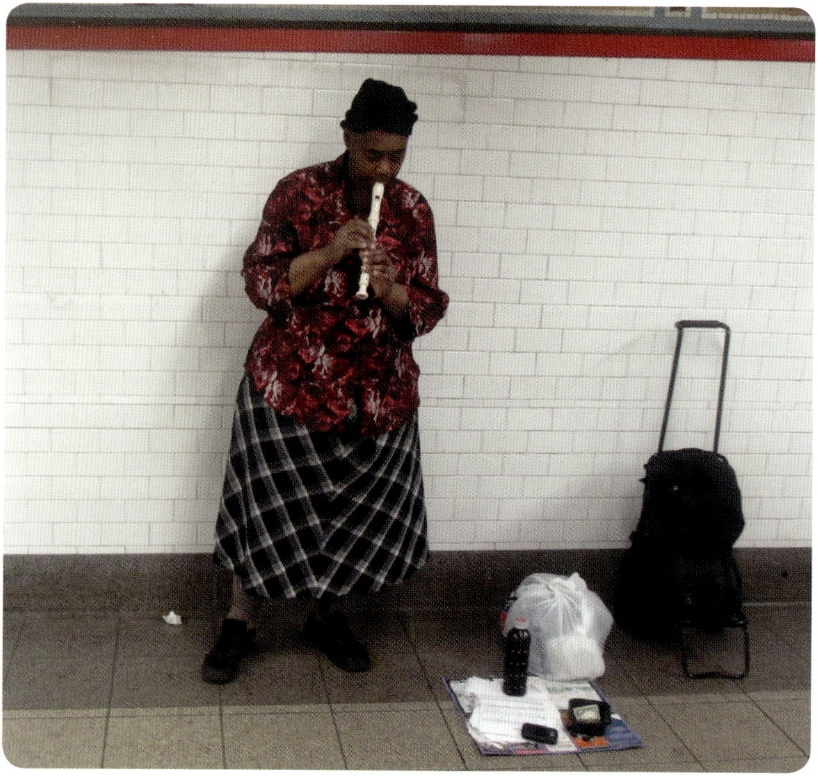

Soprano recorder flute.

Union Square Station

Chamber Street Station

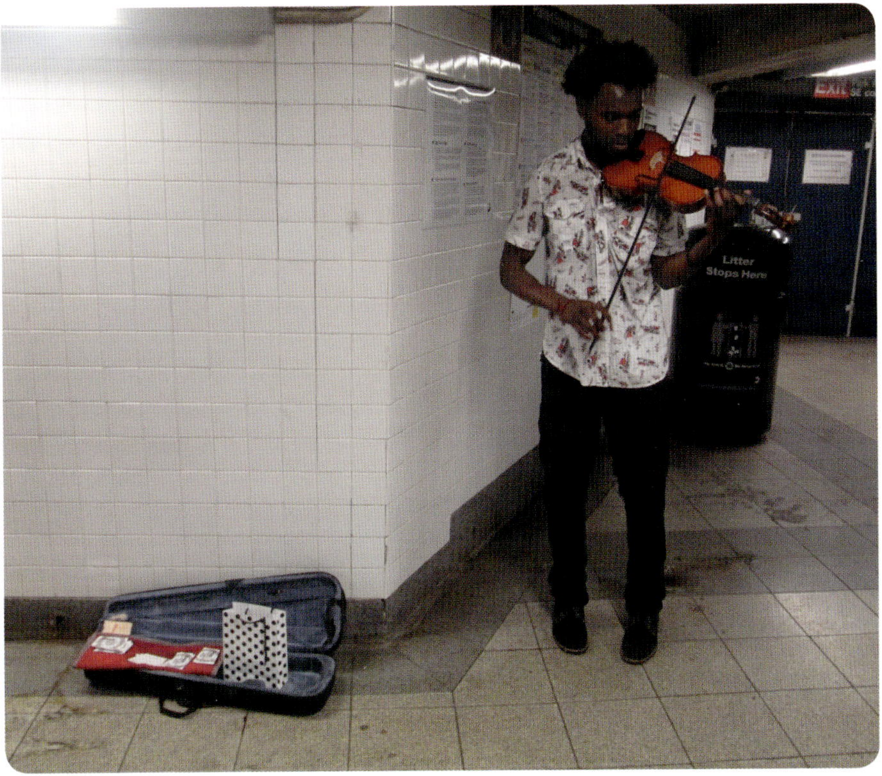

J. Read, violin.

51st Street Station

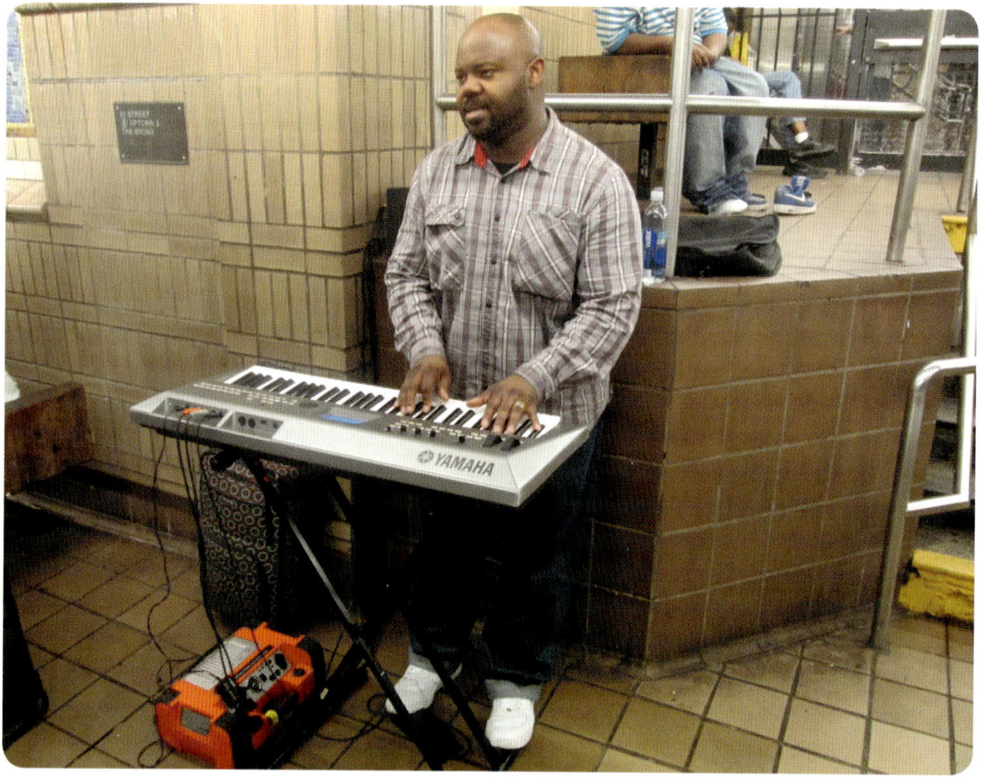

Terrel Q. Lane, electric organ.

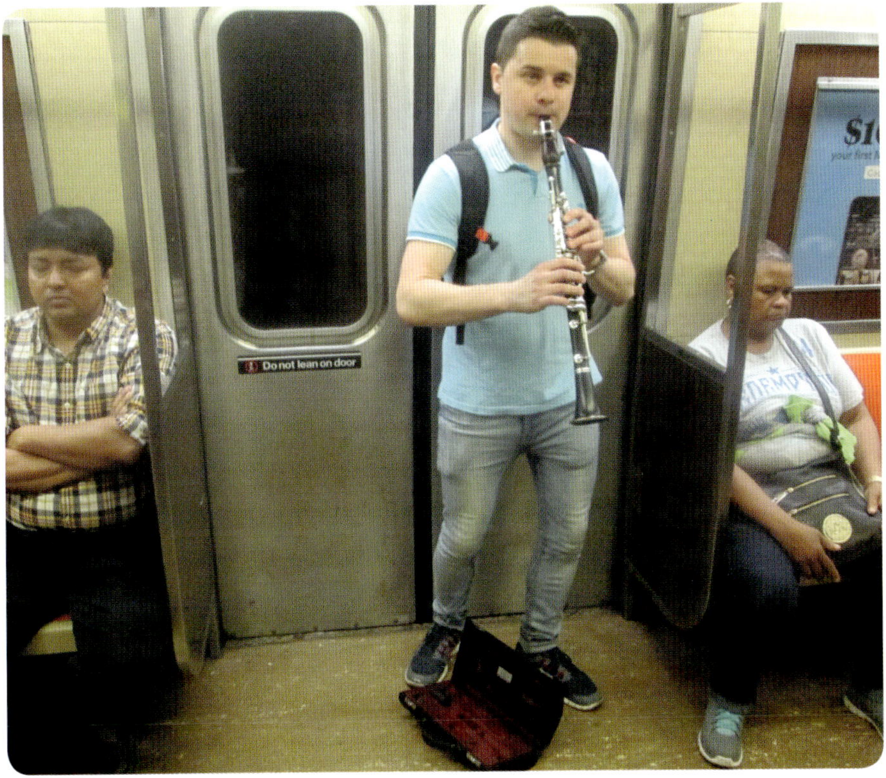

Flute player performing on the train

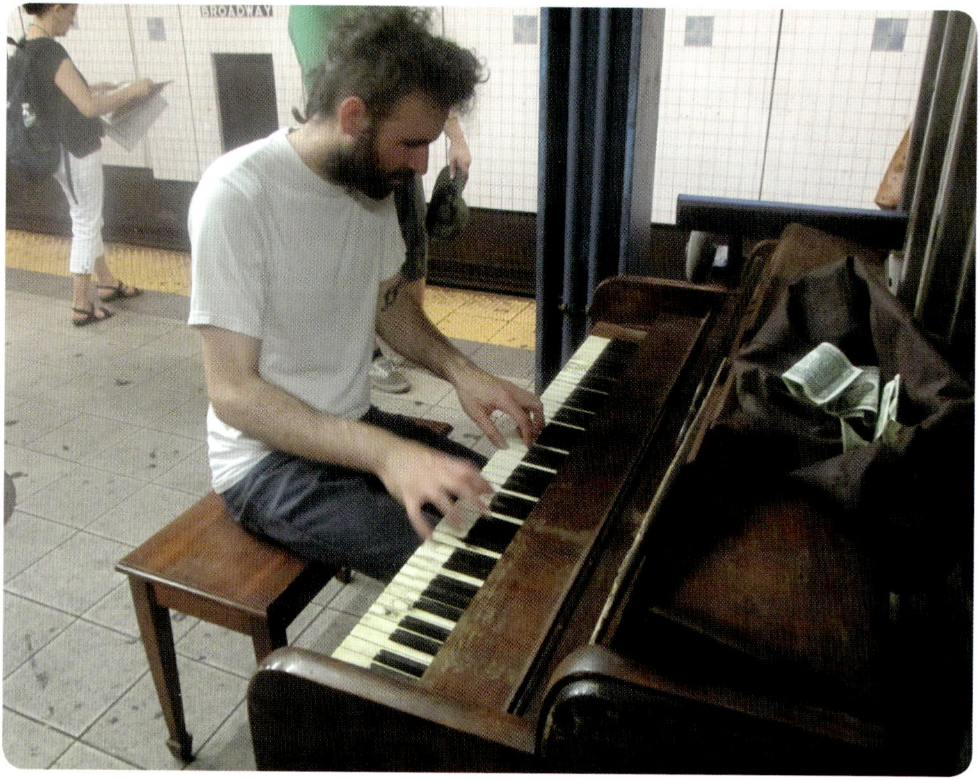

The Andrew Artist, piano.

Broadway-Lafayette Station Platform

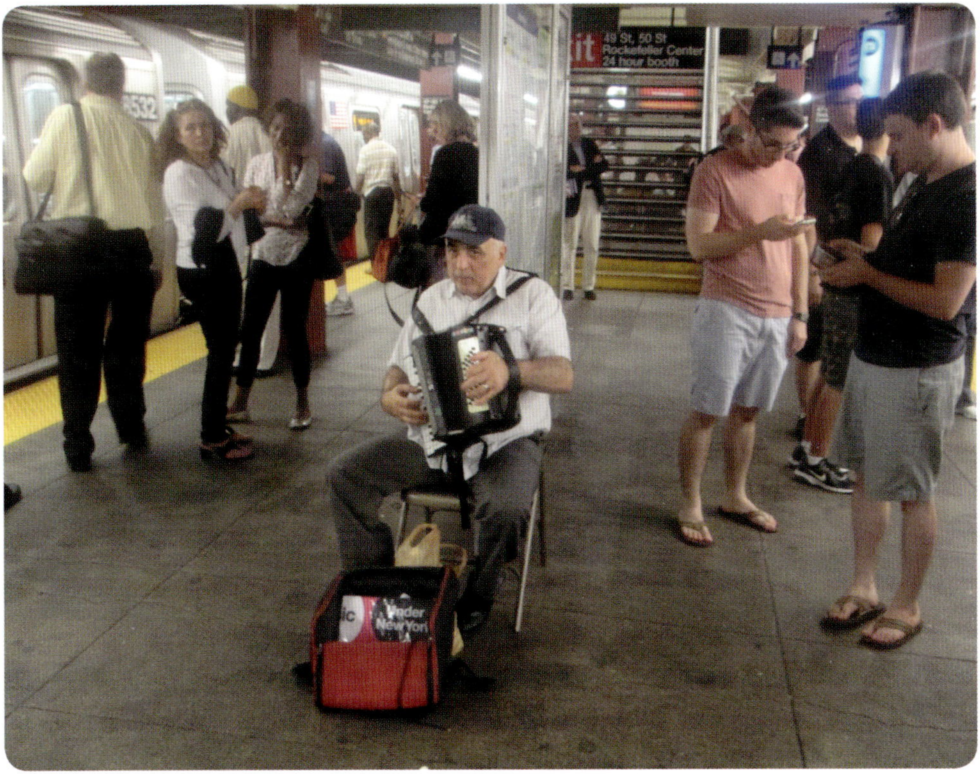

Accordion.

Rockefeller Center Station

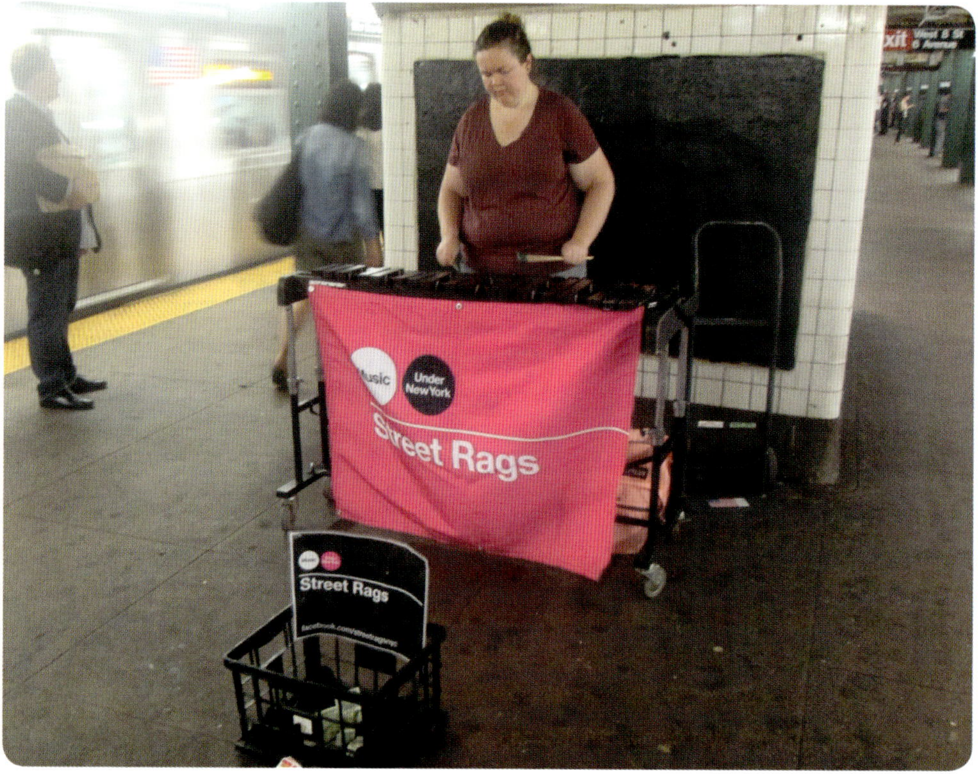

Street Rags

West 4th Street Station

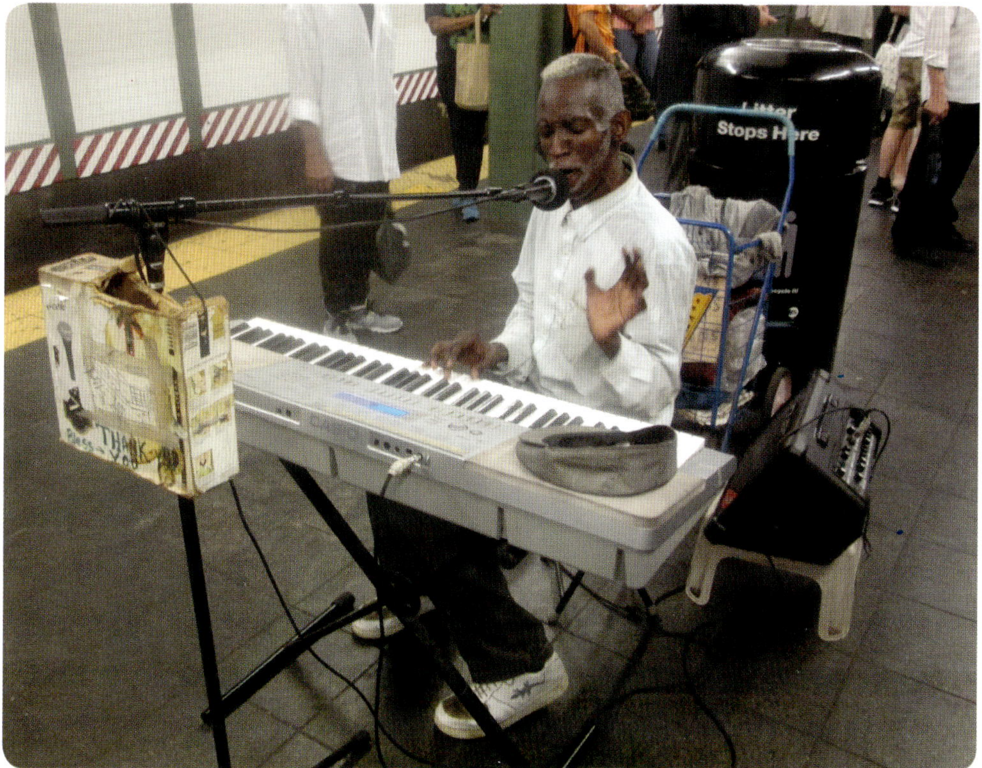

Electric organ.

42nd Street - Times Square Platform

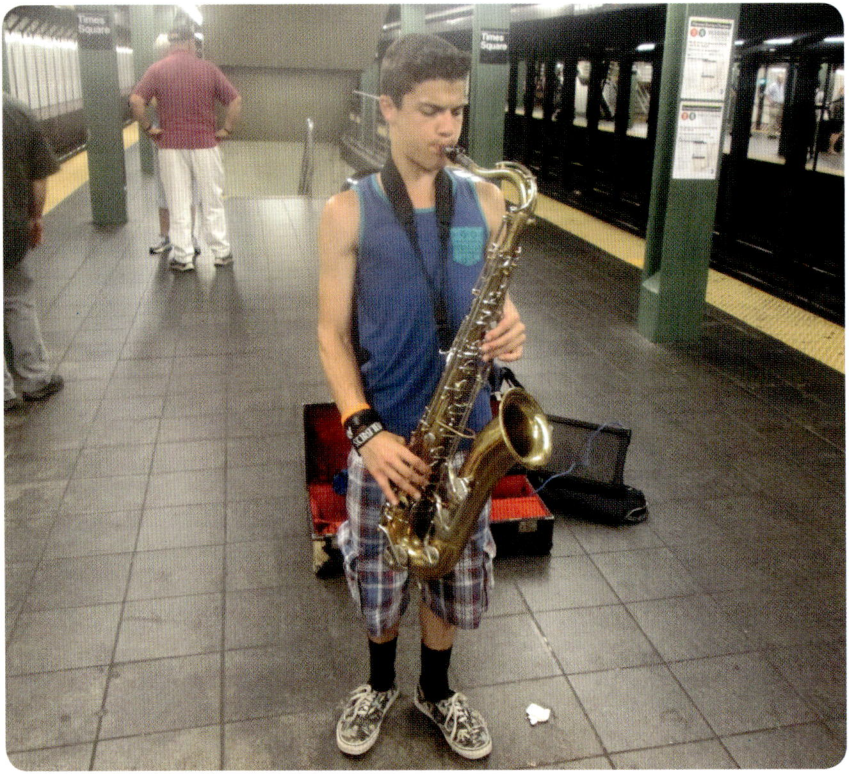

Josh Junglar, saxophone.

42nd Street - Times Square Platform

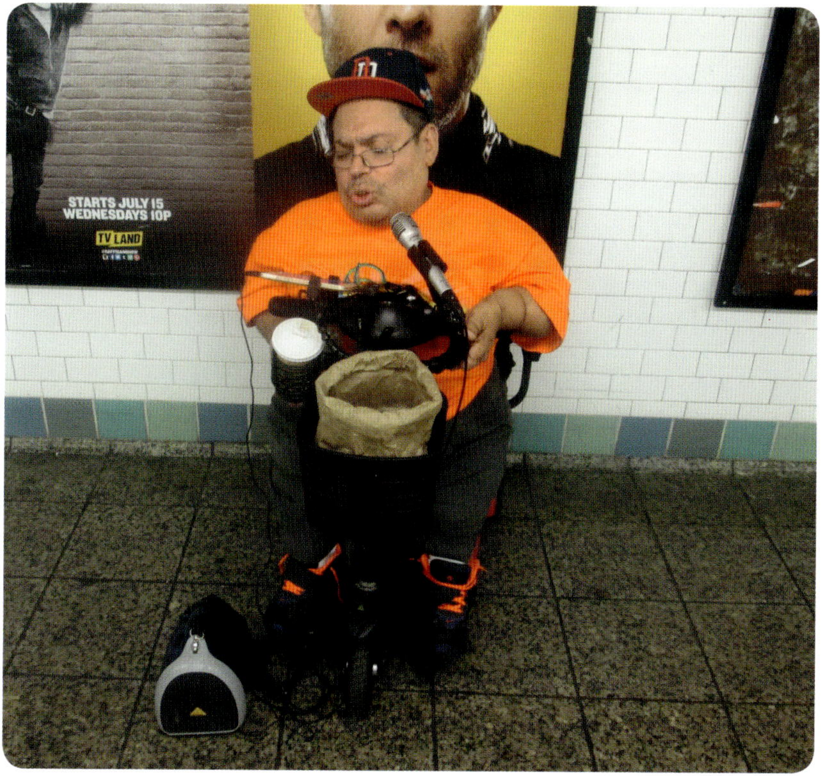

Ramone, singer.

Times Square Station

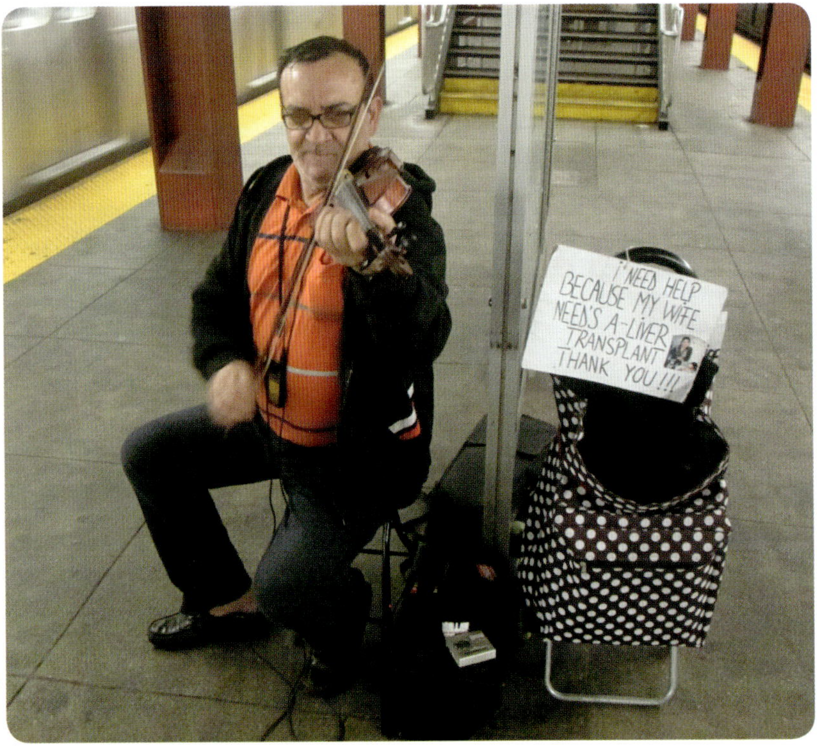

Adrian

Rockefeller Center Station

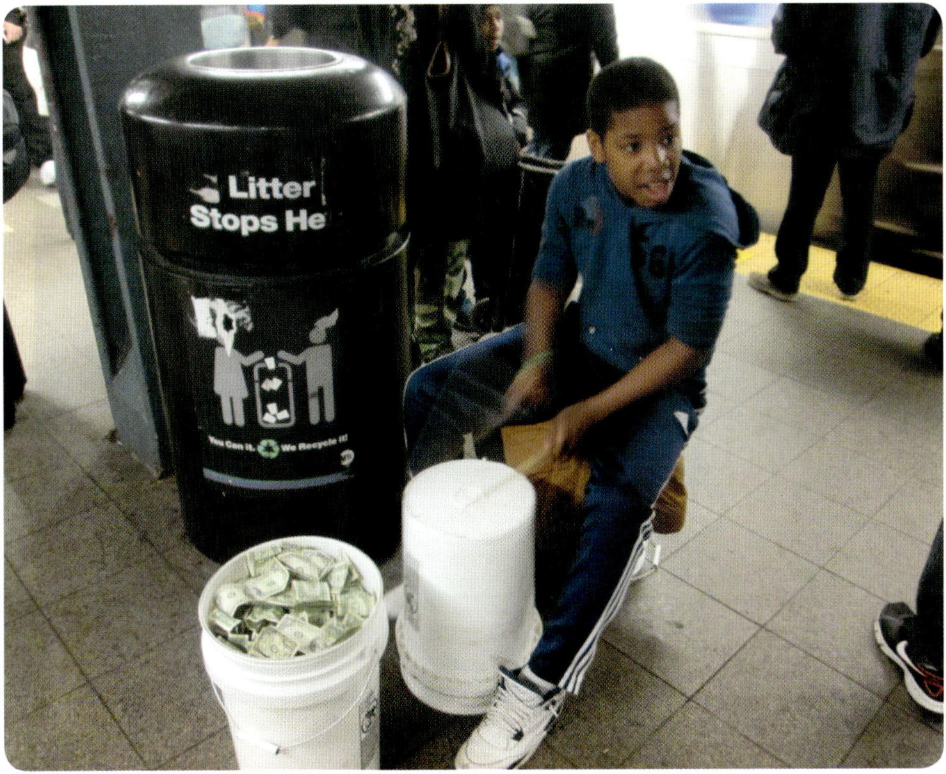

Larry Wright Son, bucket drummer.

Union Square Station

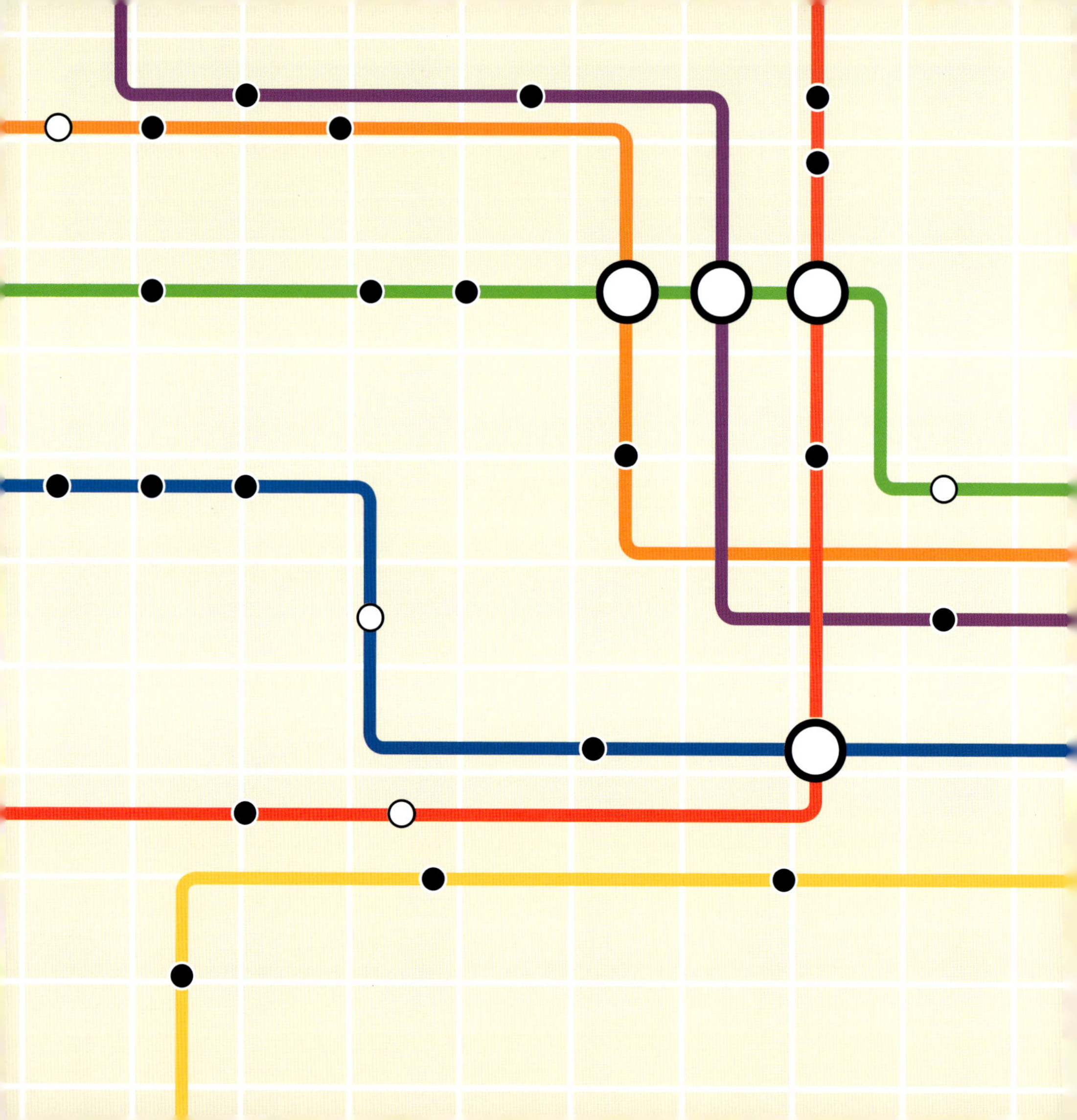

Chapter 4

Snapshots of the Busk NY Festival

Celebrating 30 Years of Subway Music

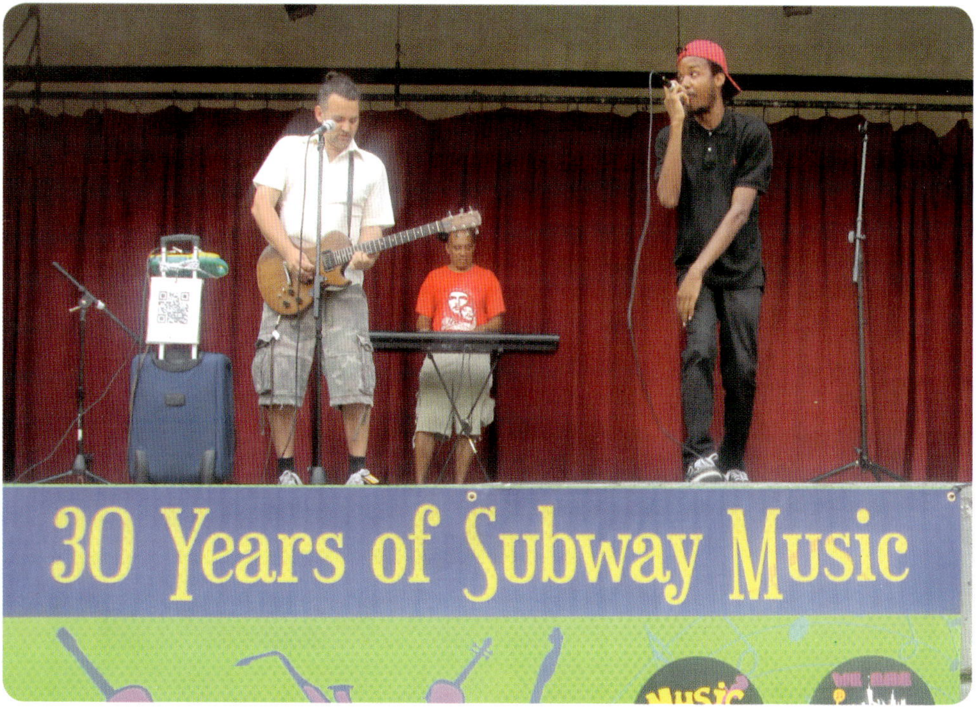

Stories For Days, hip hop band.

Herbert Von King Park

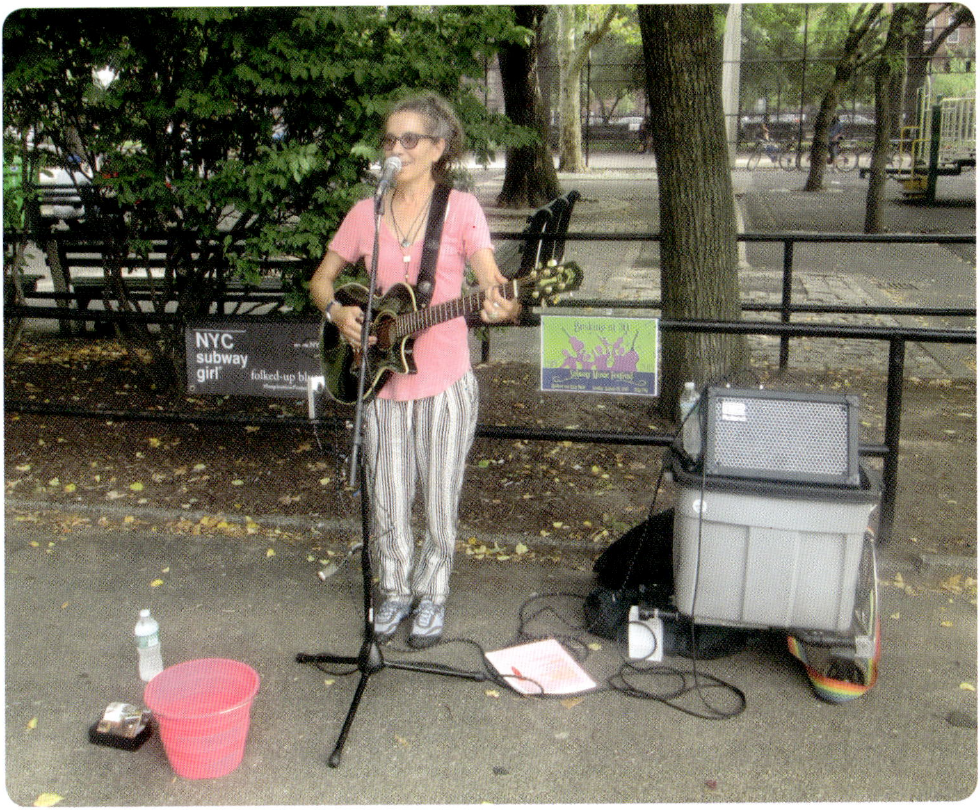

Cathy Grier, NYC subway girl.

Herbert Von King Park

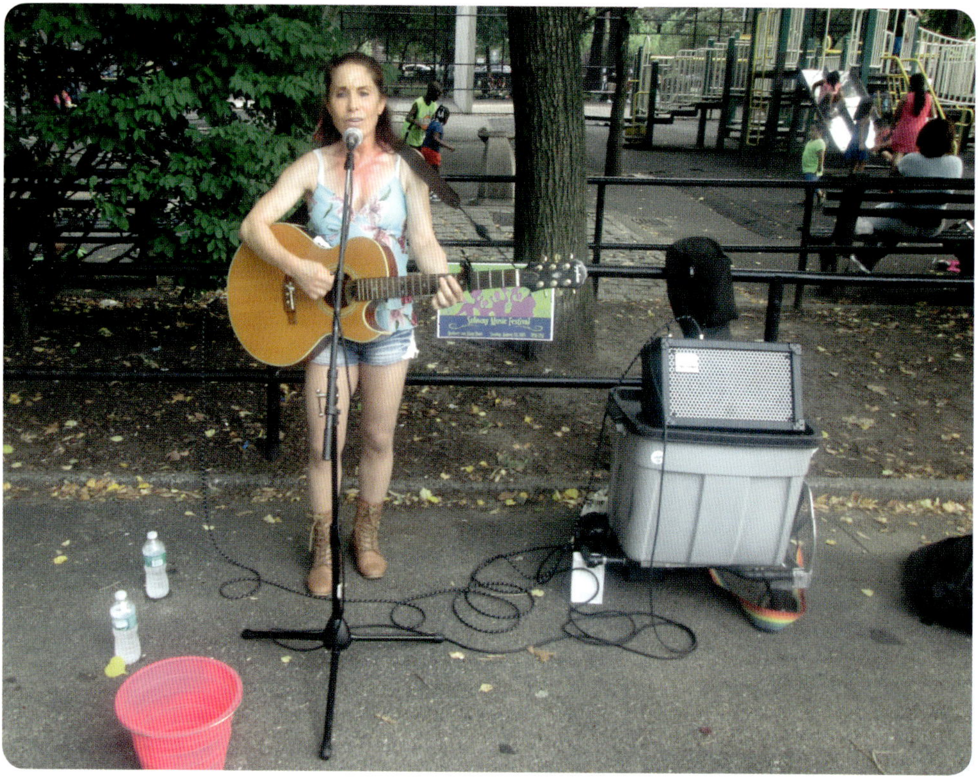

Heidi Kole, folk guitar.

Herbert Von King Park

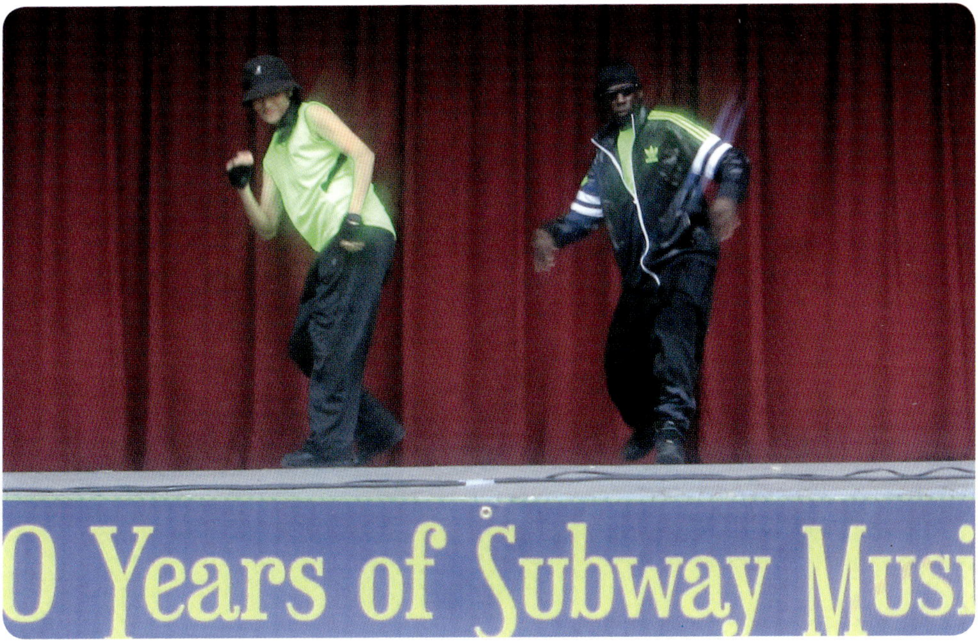

The Float Masters

Herbert Von King Park

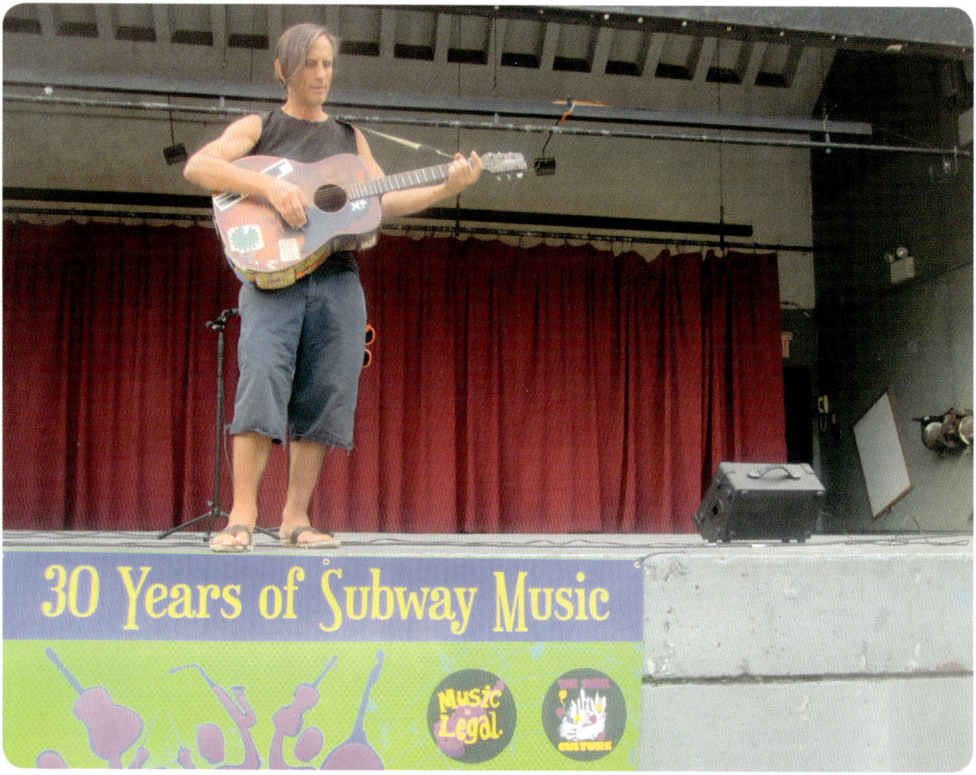

Roger Manning, folk guitar.

Herbert Von King Park

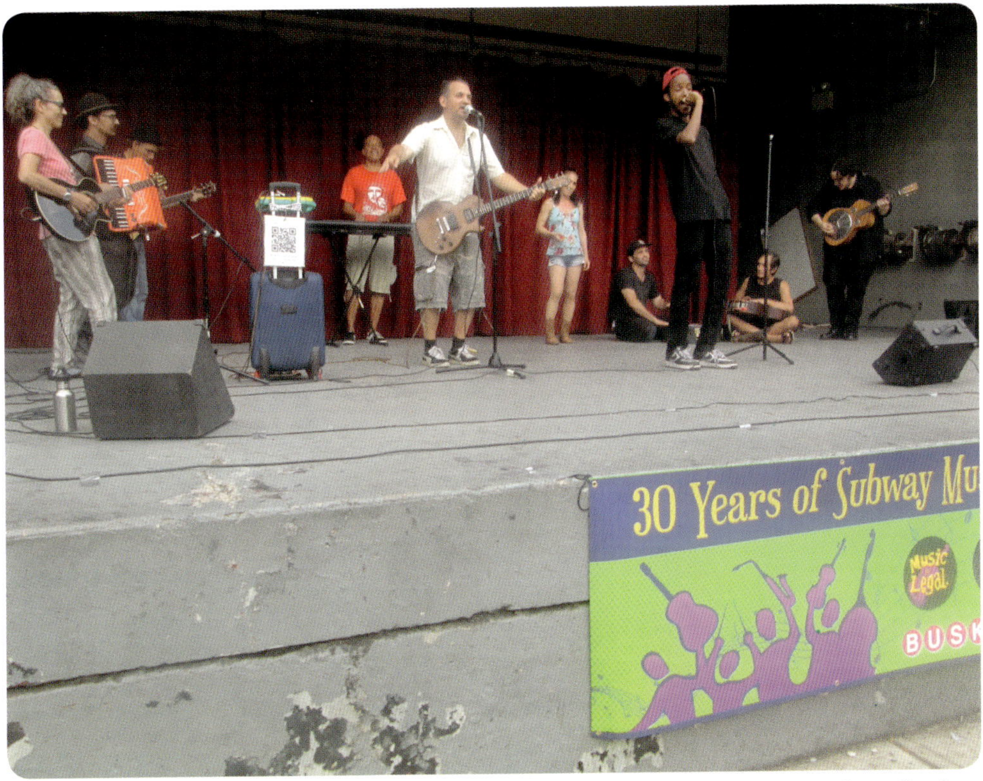

Group Session

Herbert Von King Park

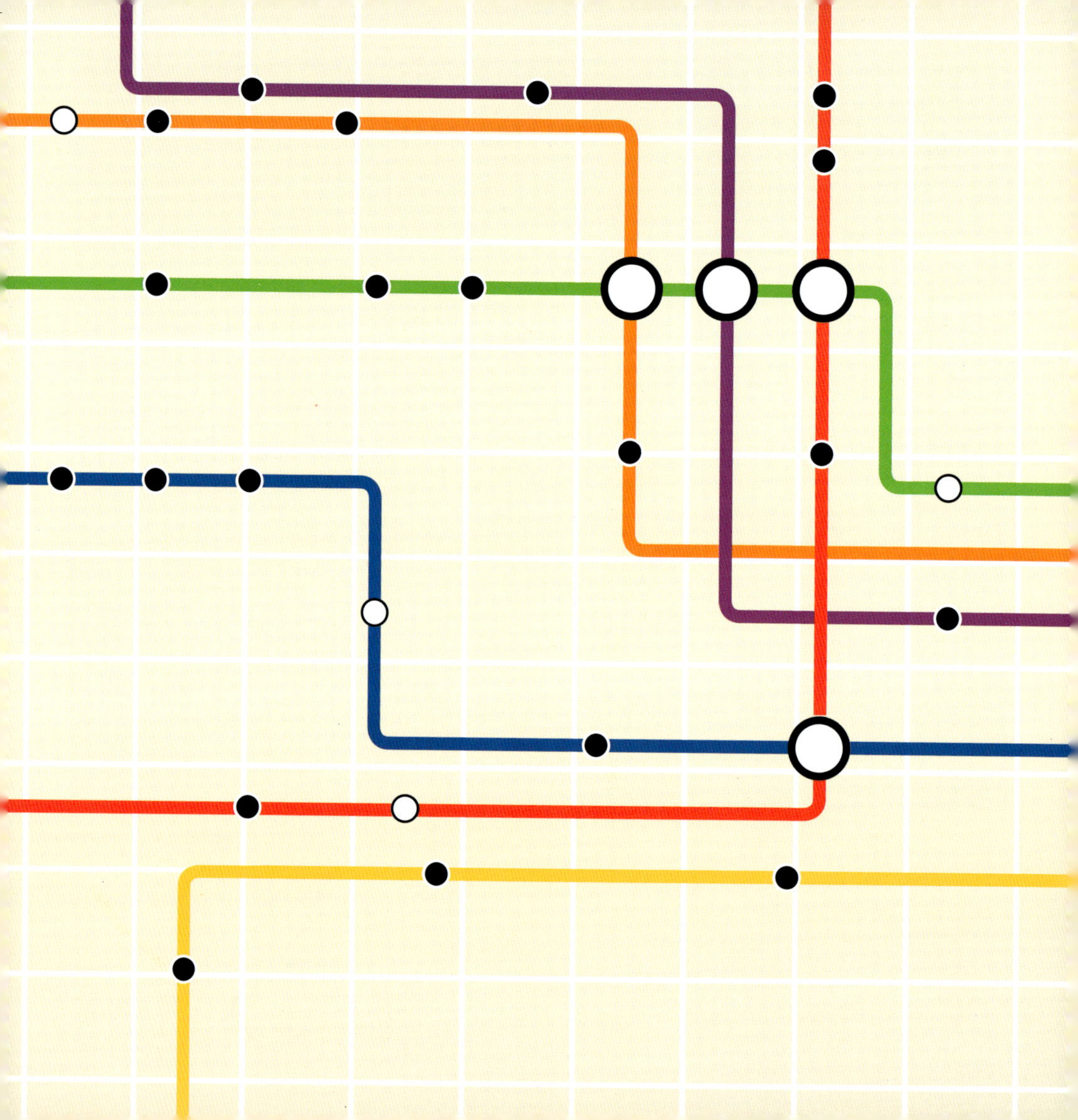

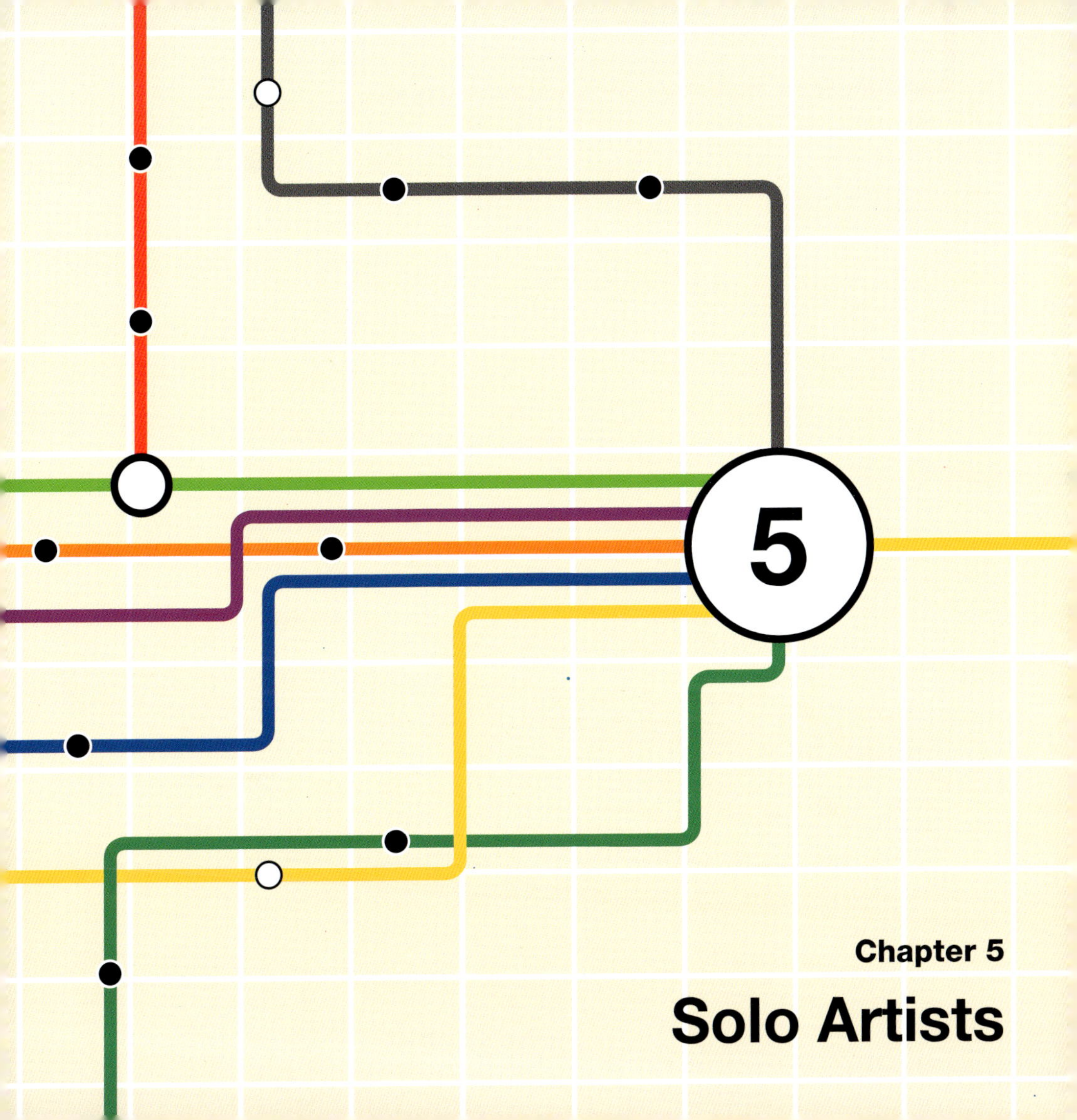

Chapter 5

Solo Artists

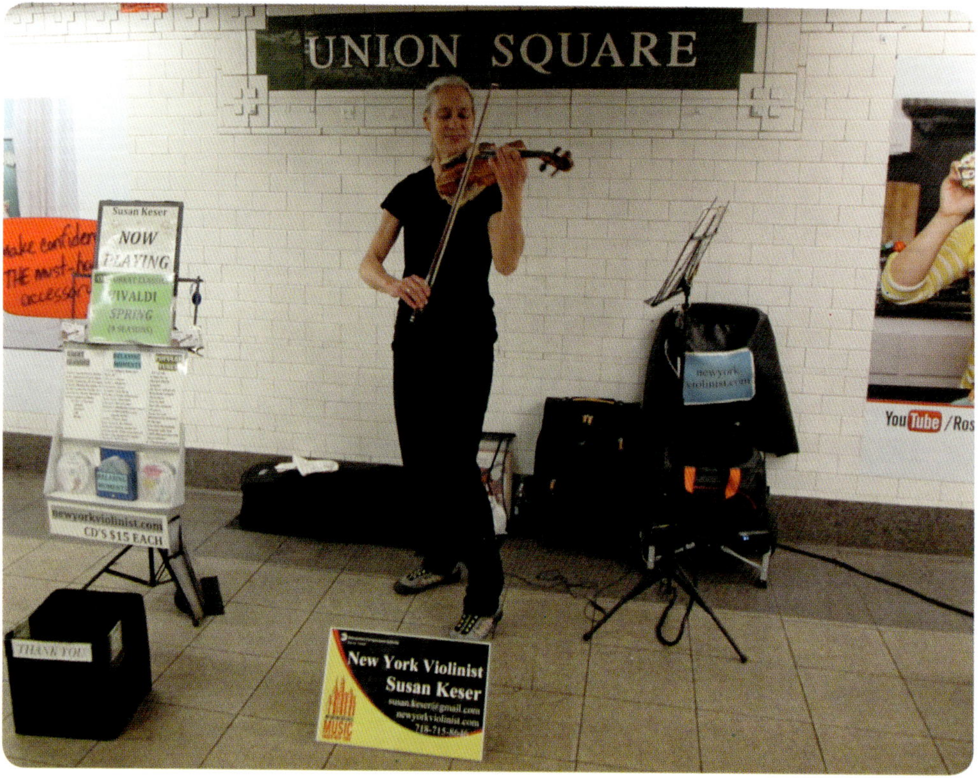

Susan Keser, New York violinist.

Union Square Station

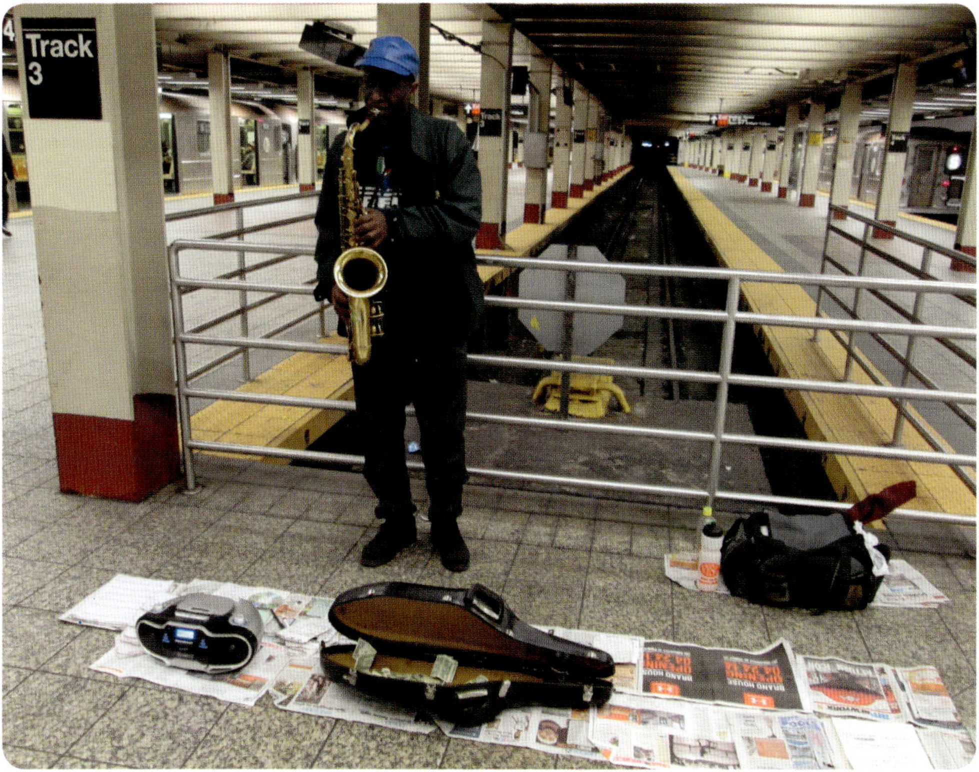

Saxophone.

Grand Central Station Shuttle Platform

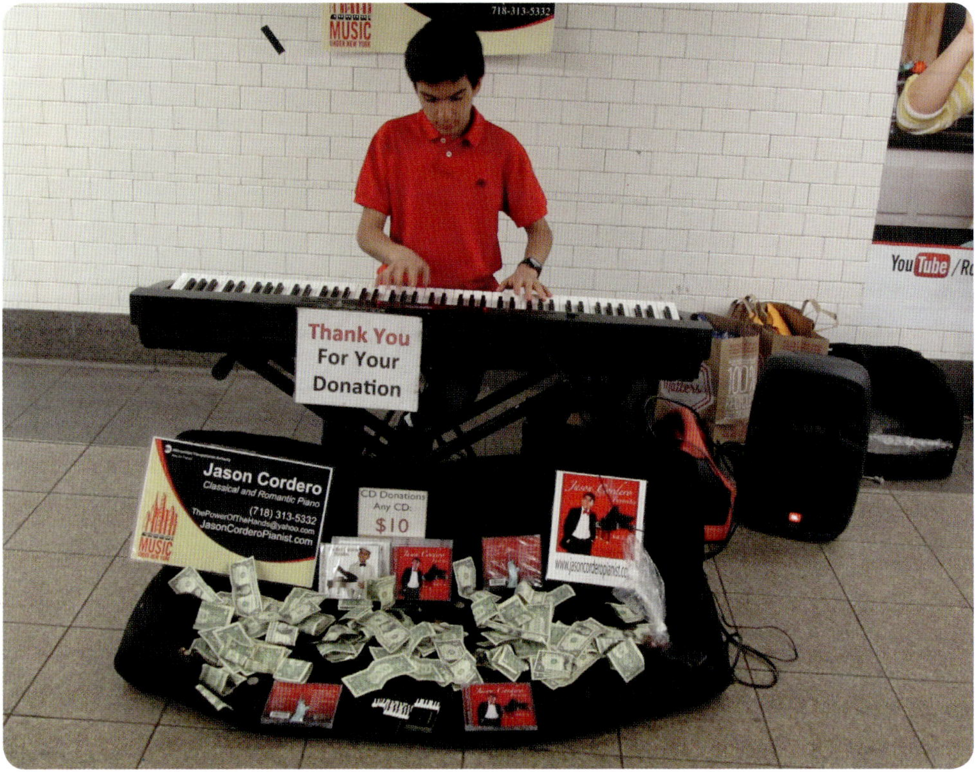

Jason Cordero, classical and romantic piano.

Union Square Station

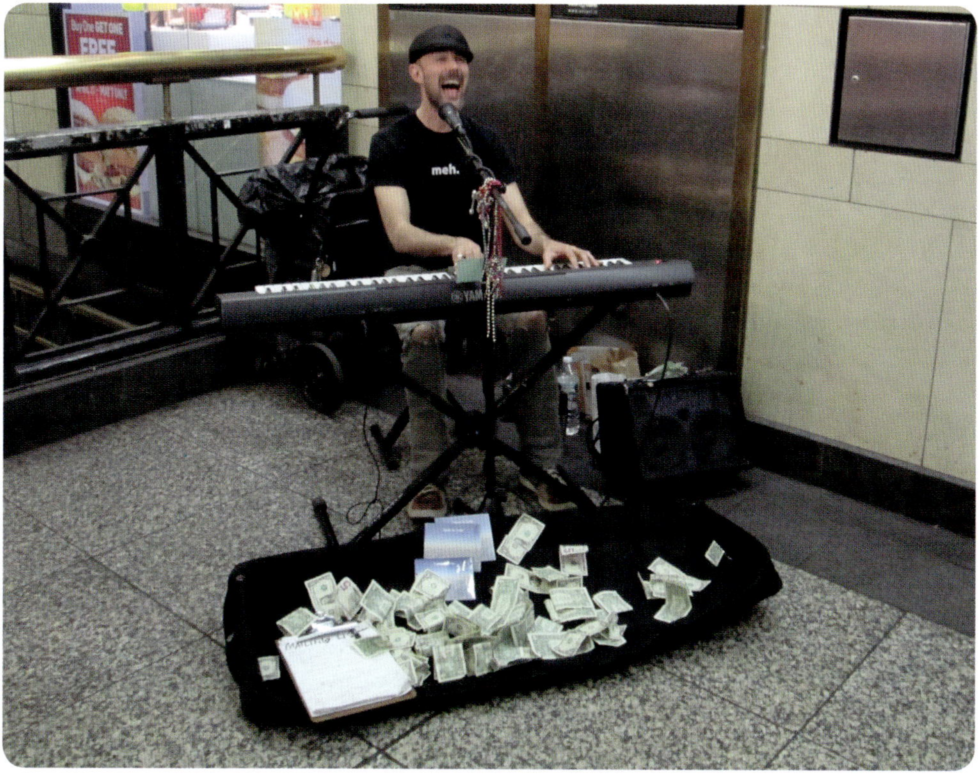

Galdort Gumbo, New Orleans blues piano.

34th Street - Penn Station

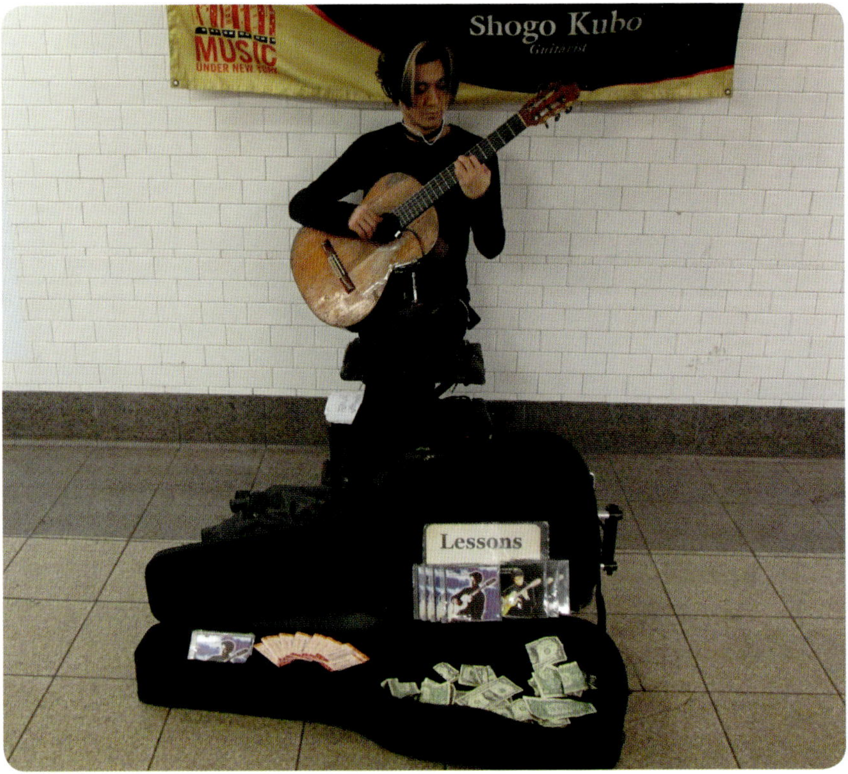

Shugo Kubo, guitarist.

Union Square Station

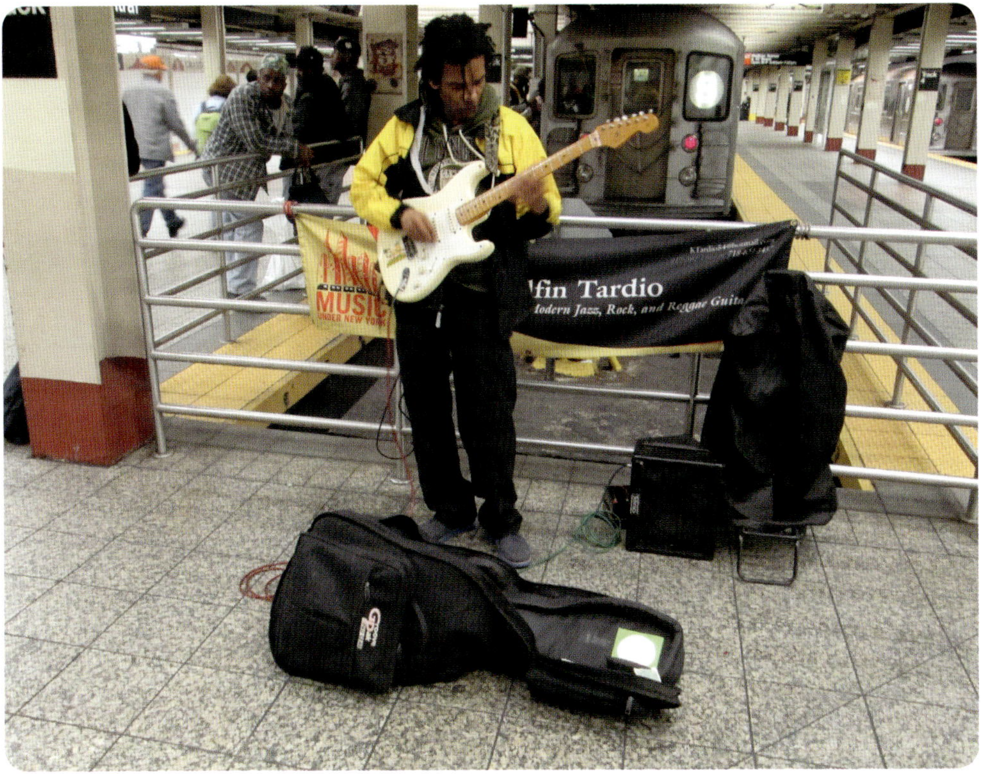

Delfin Tardio, modern jazz, rock, and reggae guitar.

Grand Central Station Shuttle Platform

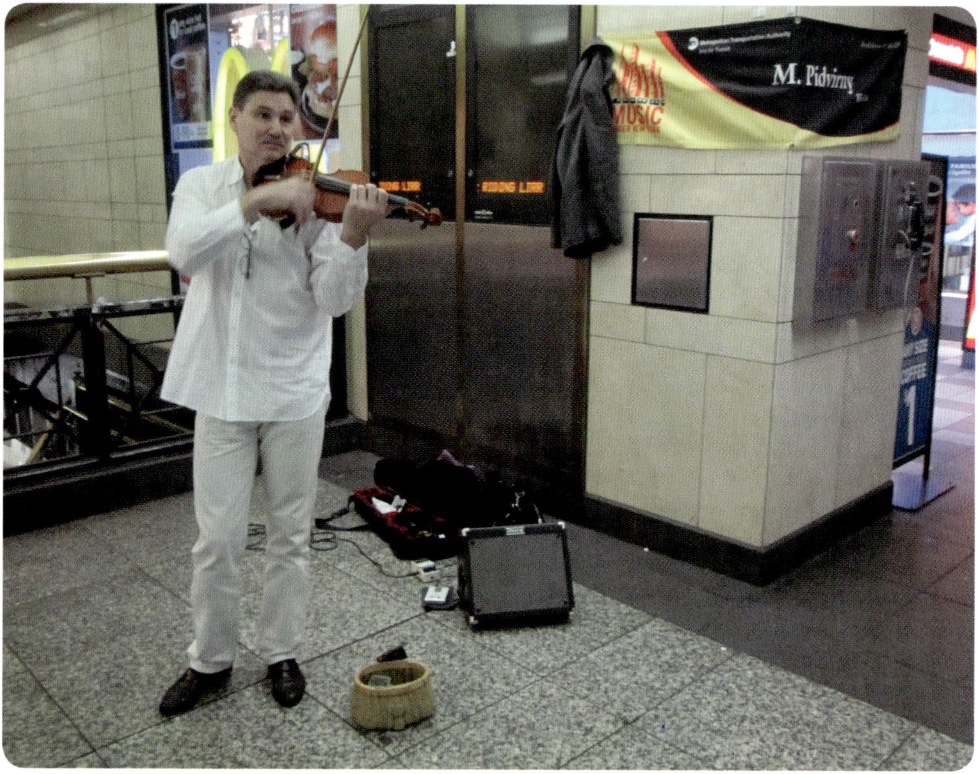

M. Pidvirny, violin.

34th Street - Penn Station

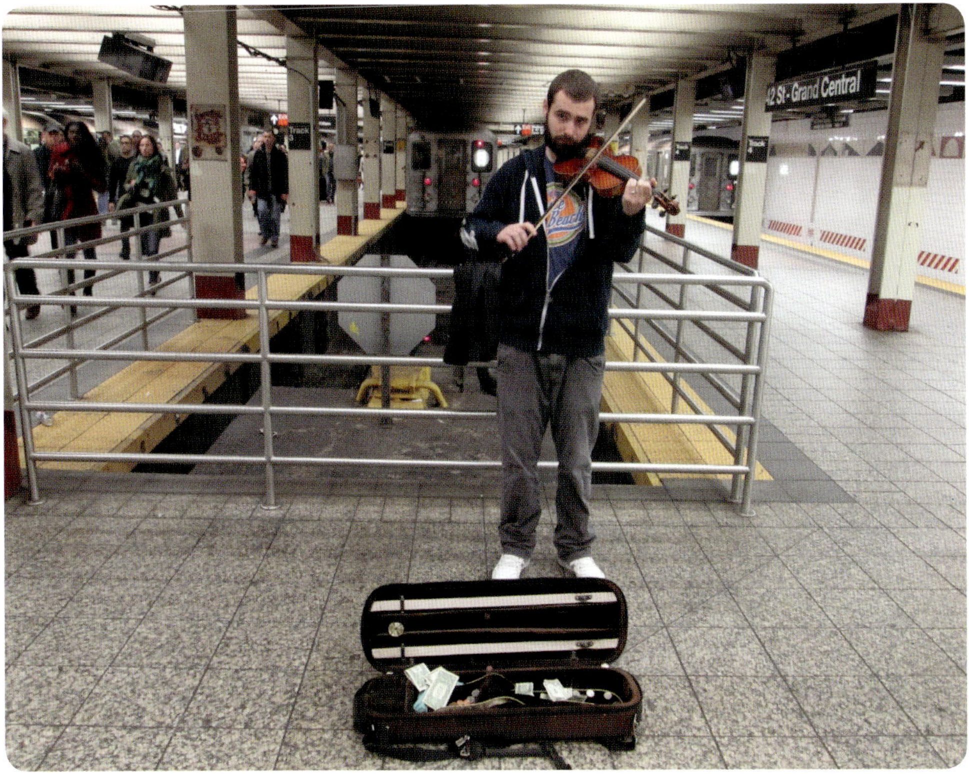

Violin.

Grand Central Station Shuttle Platform

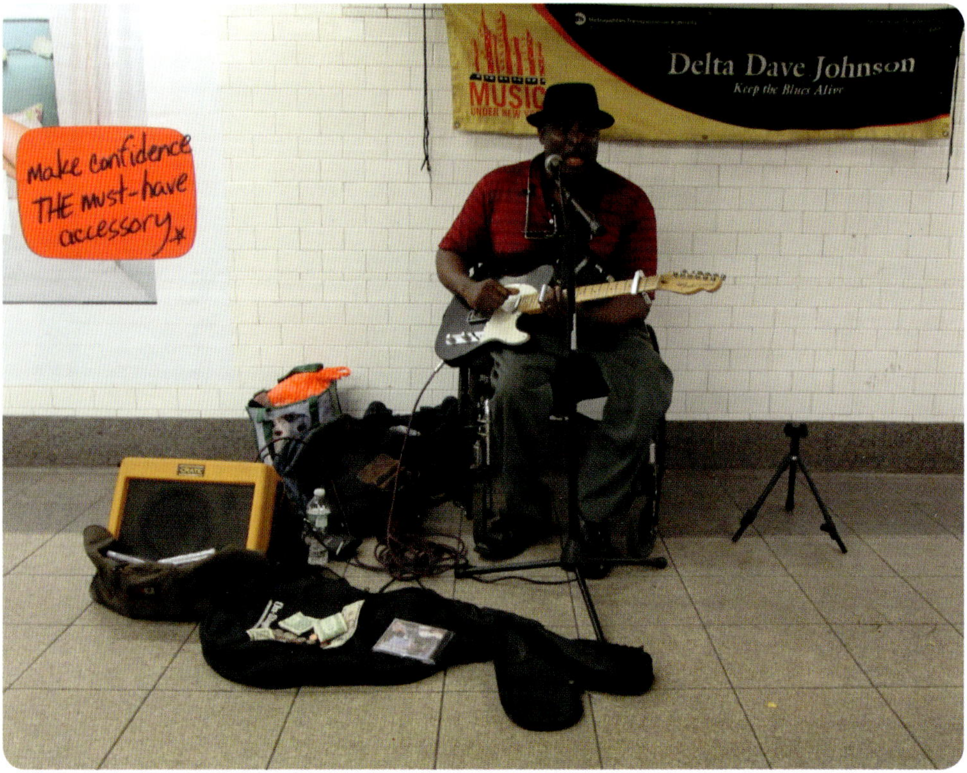

Delta Dave Johnson, blues guitar.

Union Square Station

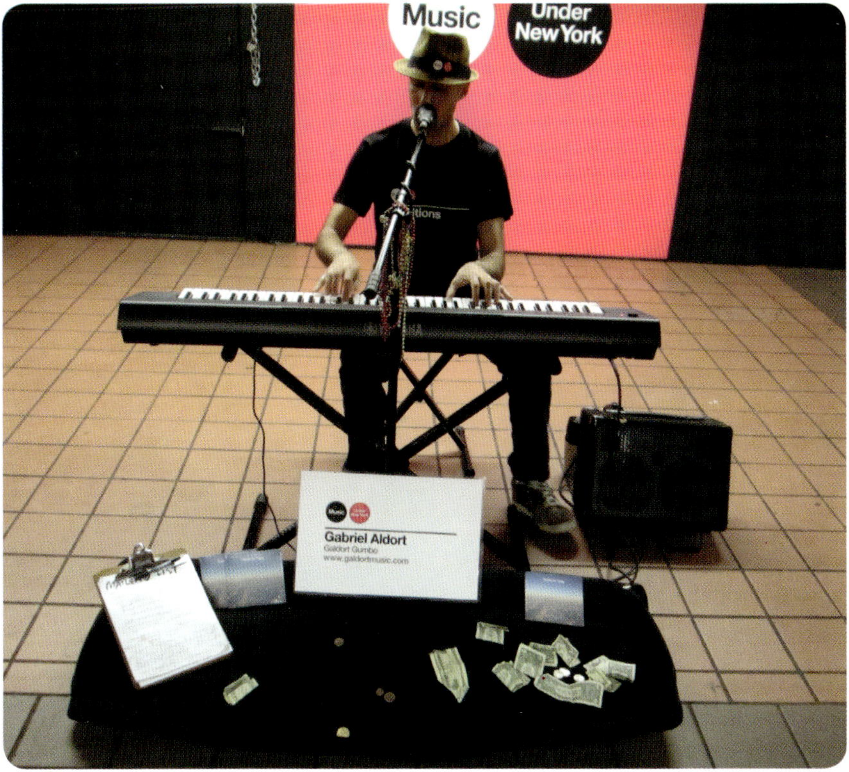

Gabriel Aldort, electric organ.

Grand Central Station

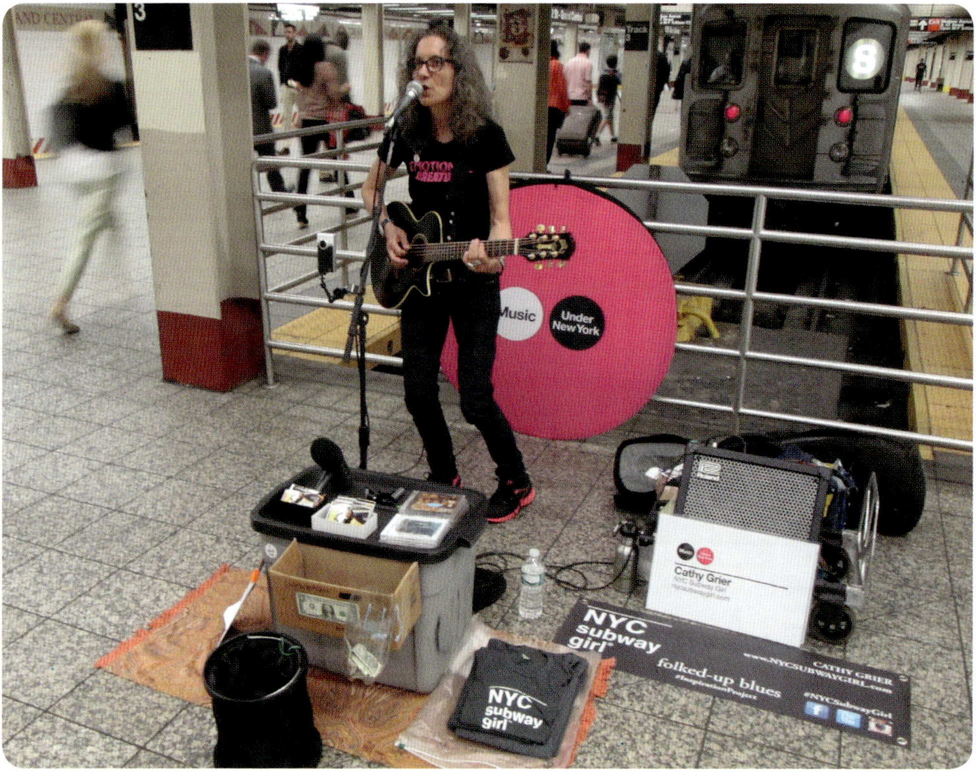

Cathy Grier, folked-up blues - NYC Subway Girl

Grand Central Station Shuttle Platform

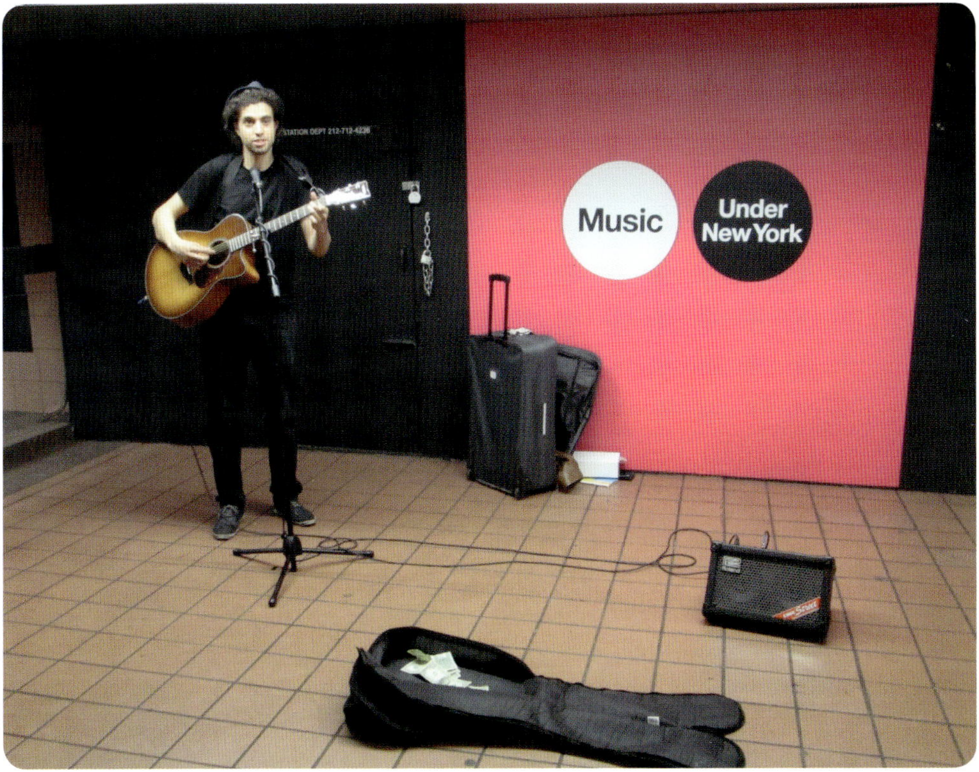

Folk guitar.

Grand Central Station

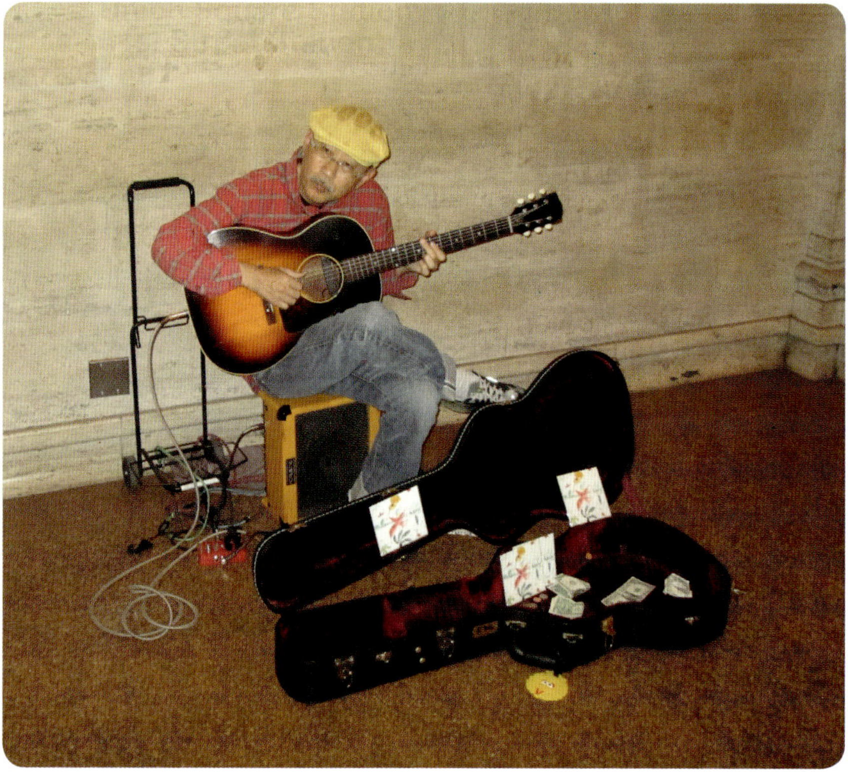

Sound of Kyushu.

Grand Central Terminal

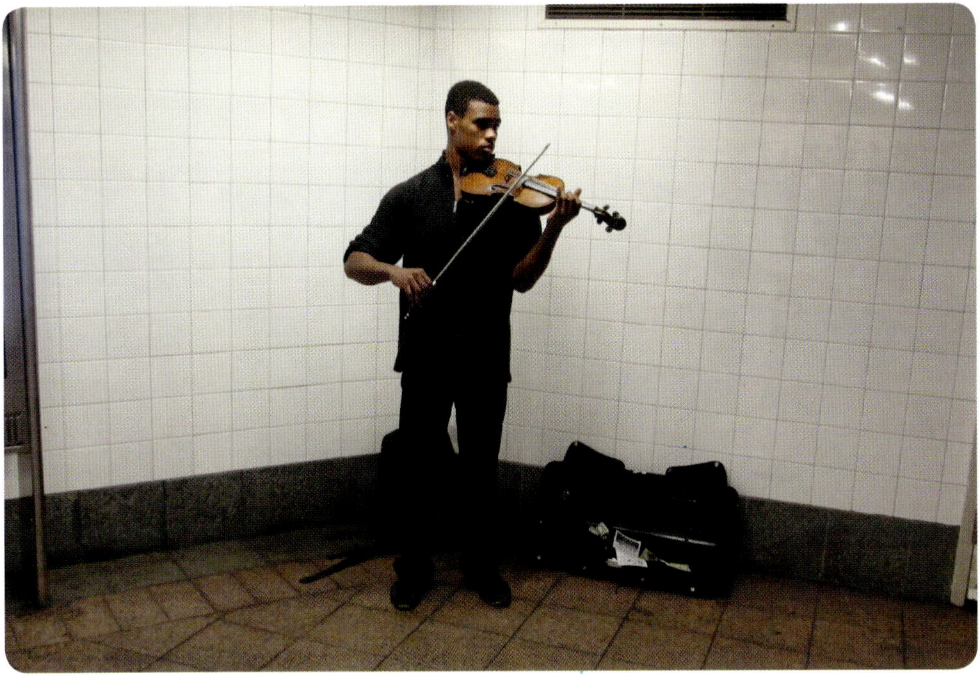

Violin.

Grand Central Station Shuttle Walkway

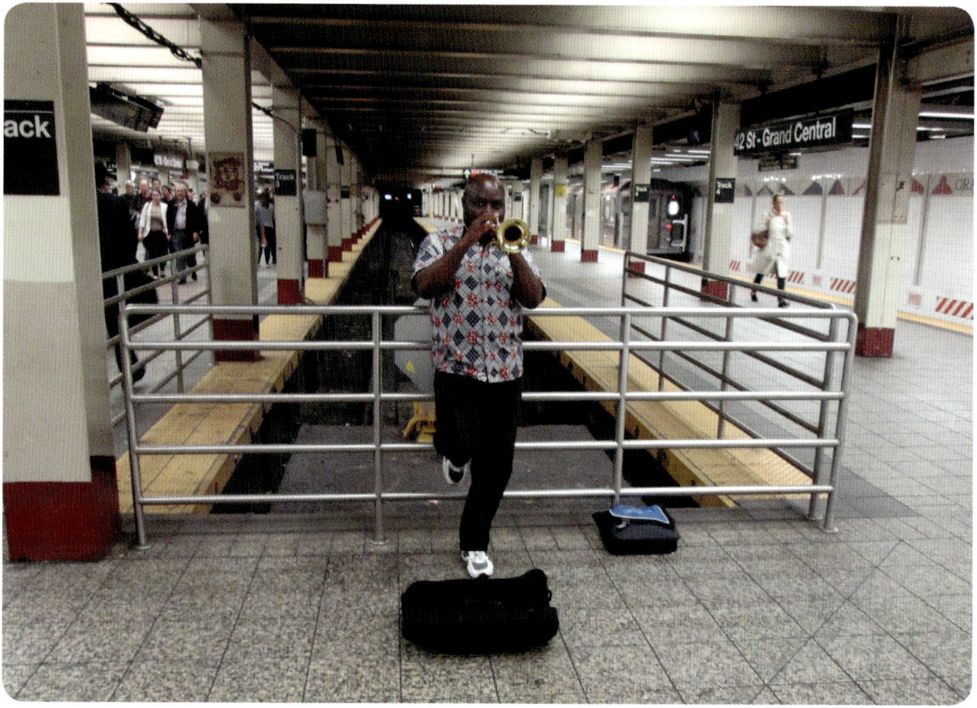

Trumpet.

Grand Central Station Shuttle Platform

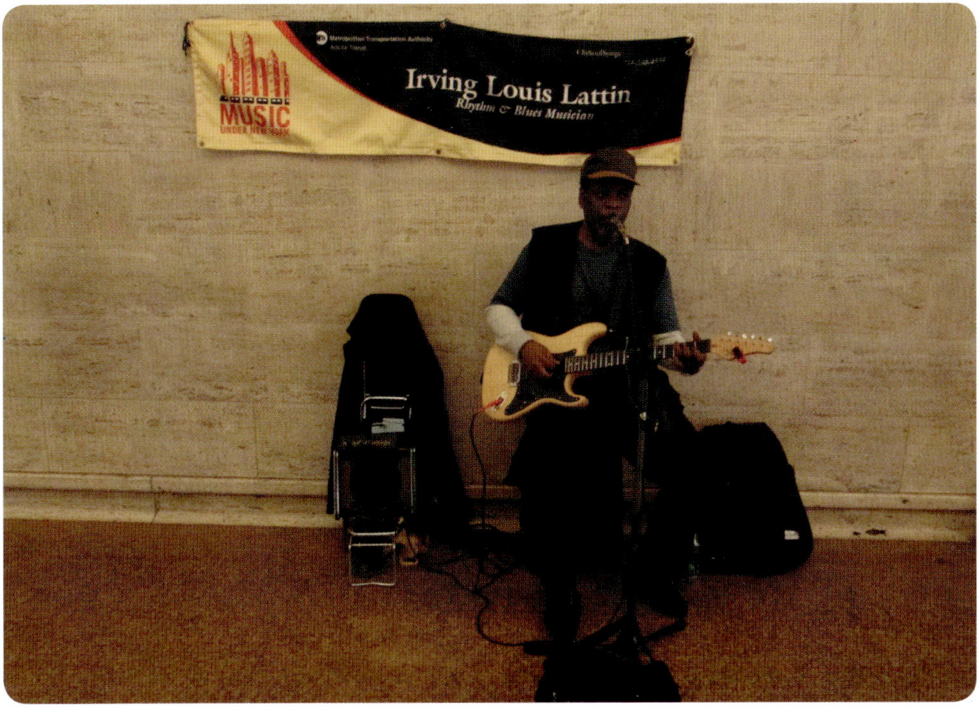

Irving Louis Lattin, rhythm and blues musician.

Grand Central Terminal

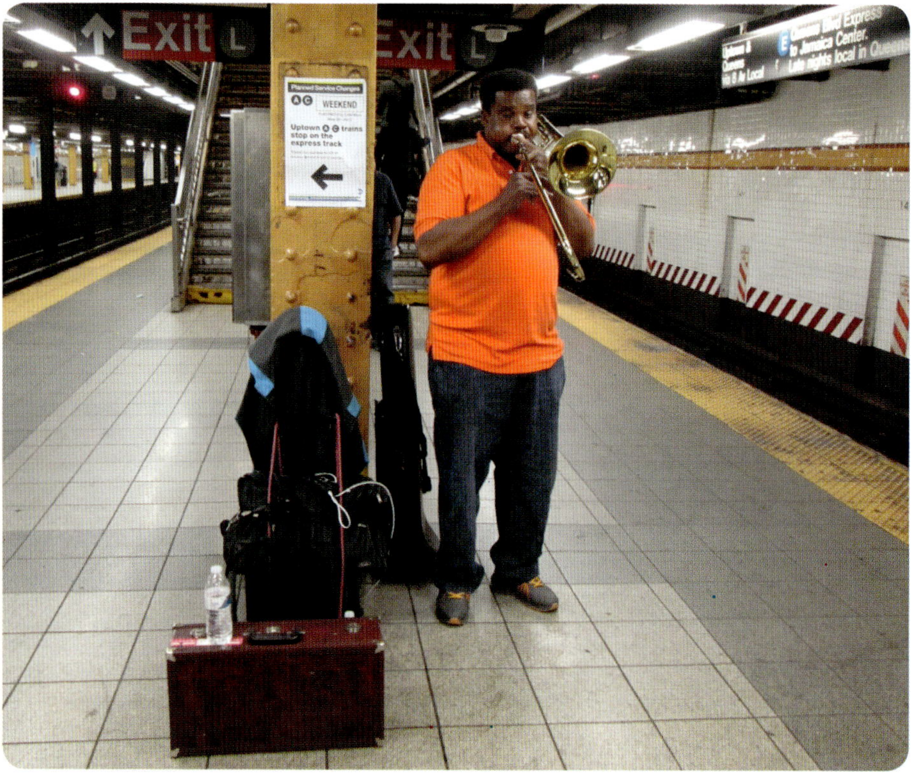

Trombone player, member of the Kenny J. Orchestra.

14th Street and 8th Avenue Station

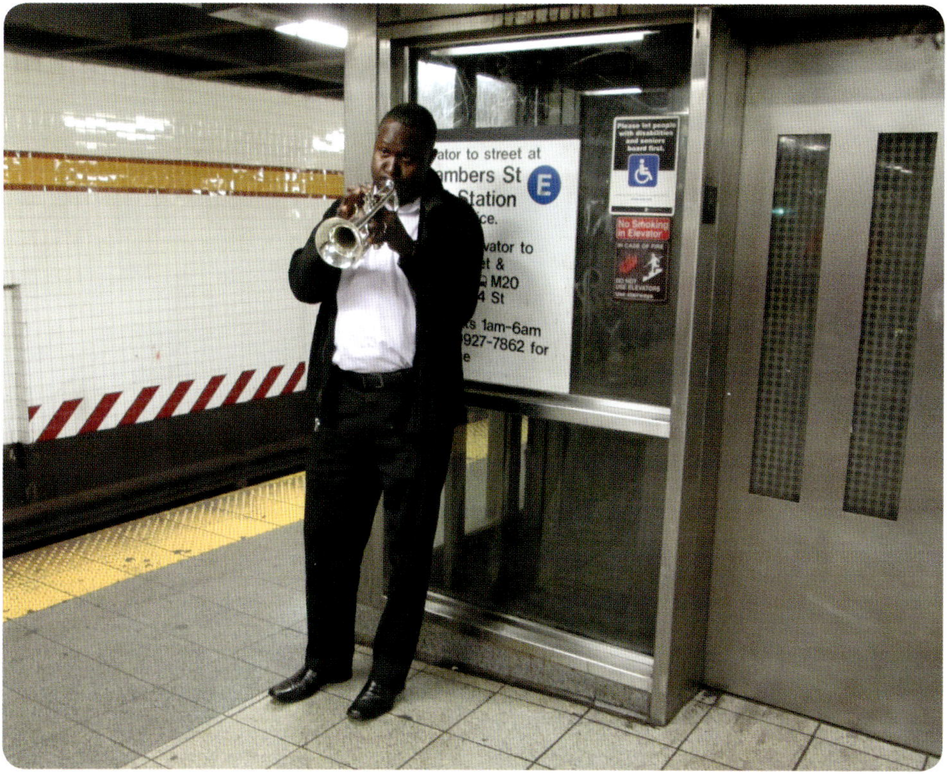

Kenny John, trumpeter, director of the Kenny J. Orchestra.

14th Street and 8th Avenue Station

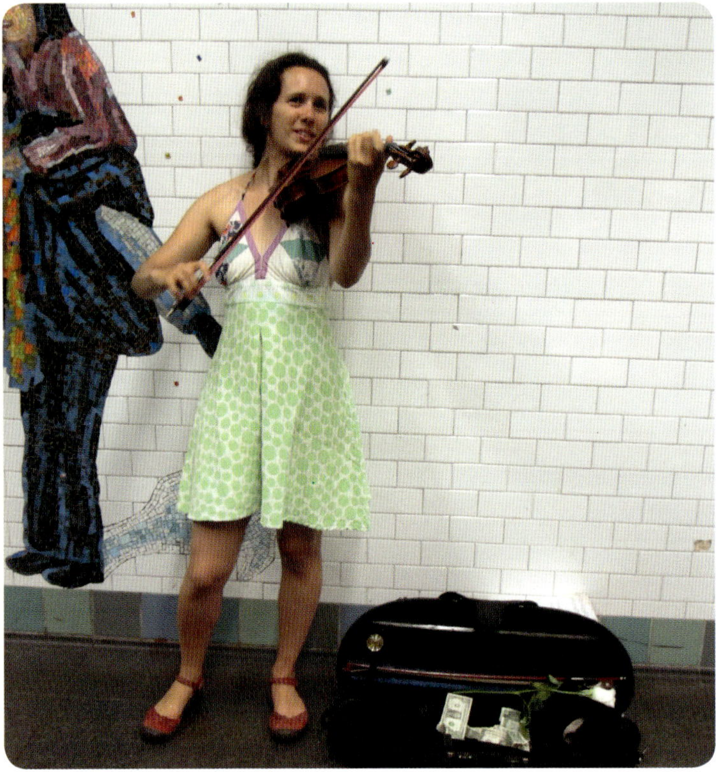

Violin.

42nd Street - Port Authority Station

Union Square Station

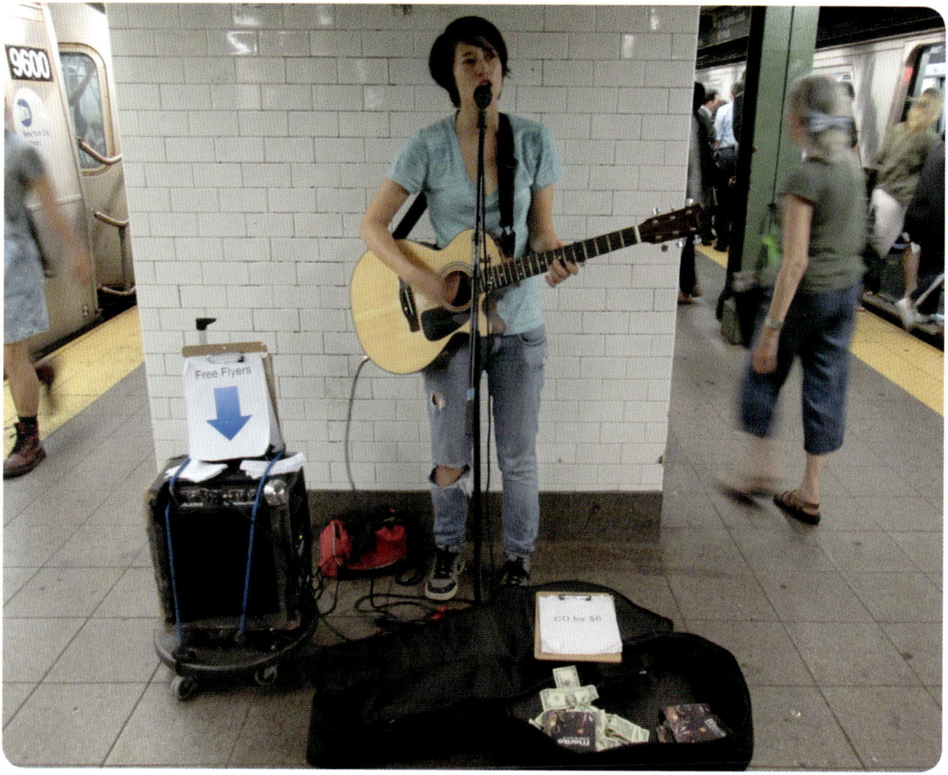

Electric folk guitar player and singer.

34th Street - Penn Station

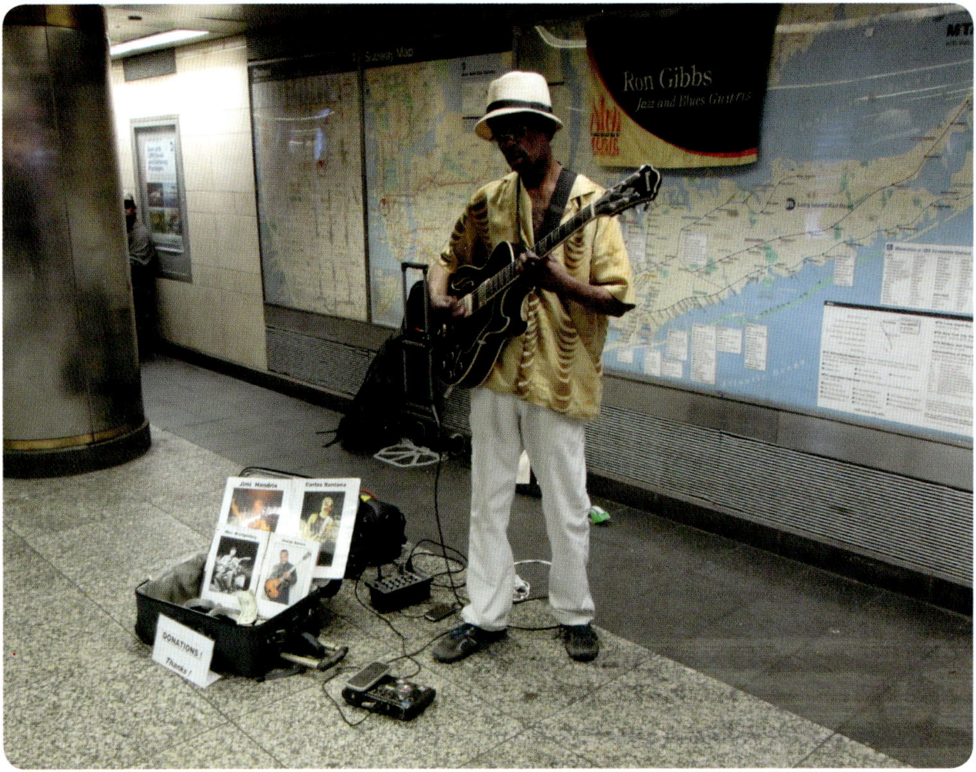

Ron Gibbs, jazz and blues guitarist.

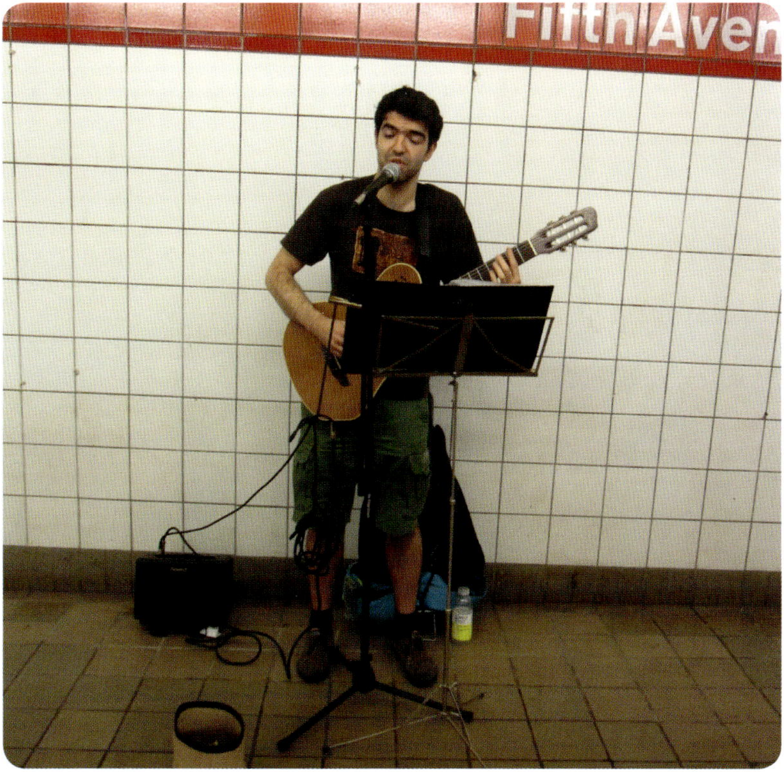

Electric folk guitar player and singer.

53rd Street and 5th Avenue Station

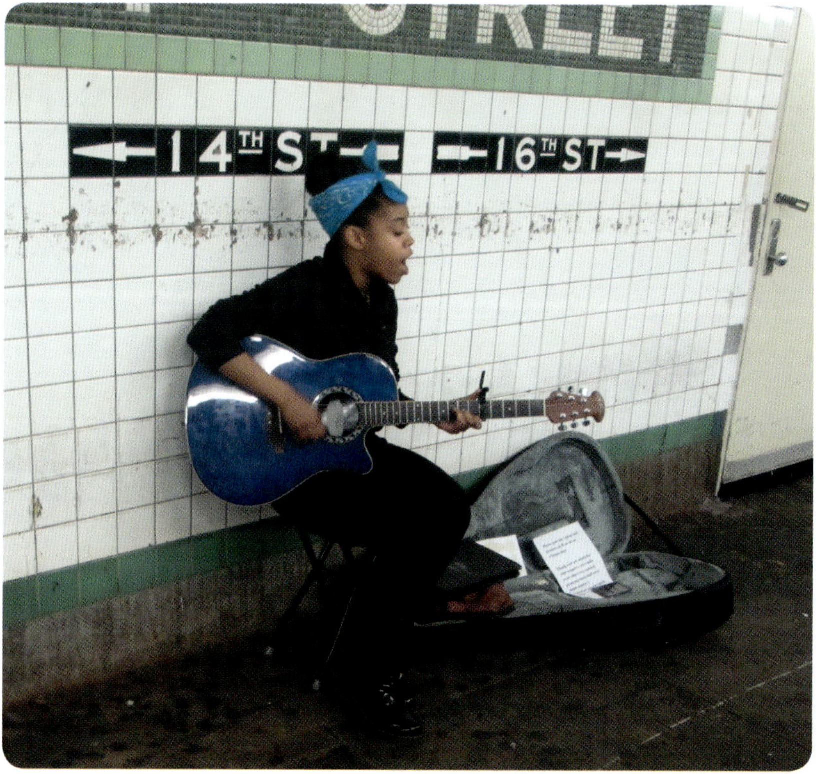

Folk guitar player and singer.

14th Street and Sixth Avenue Station

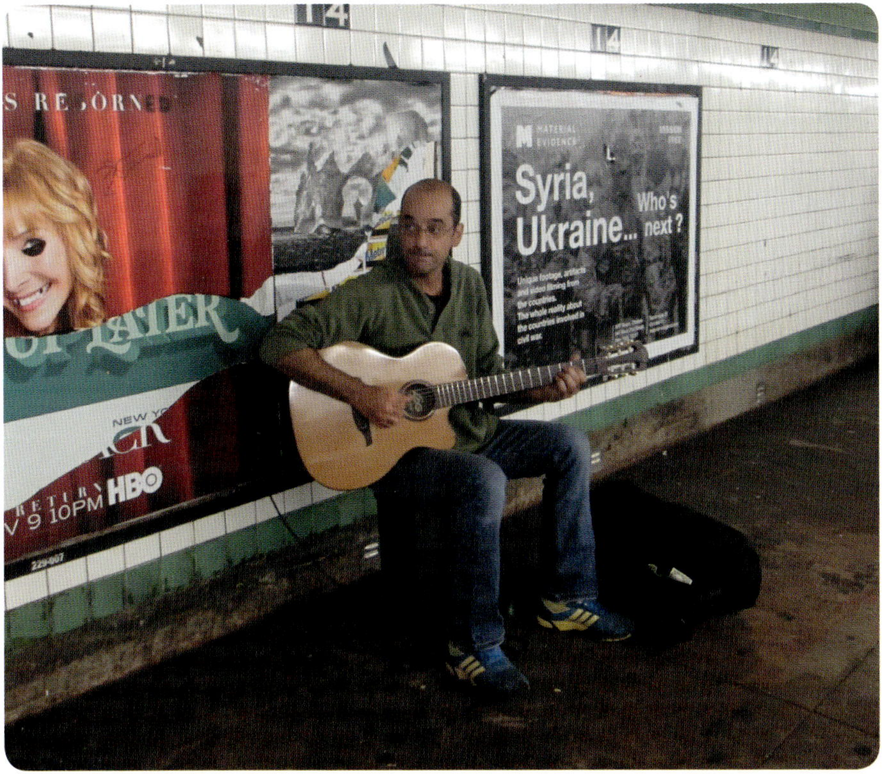

Electric folk guitar player and singer.

14th Street and Sixth Avenue Station

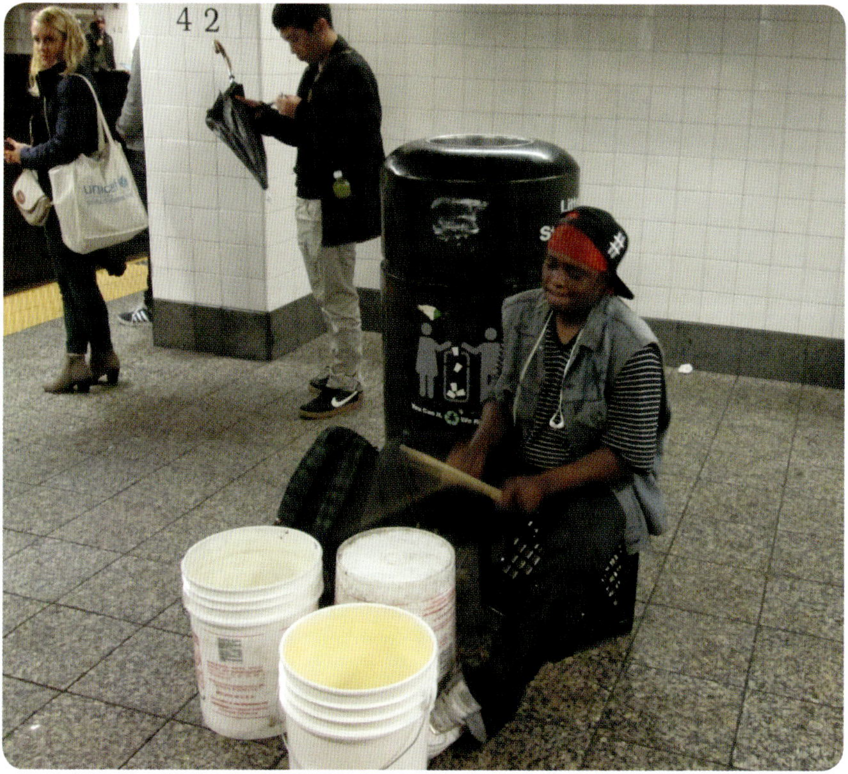

Bucket drummer.

Grand Central Station

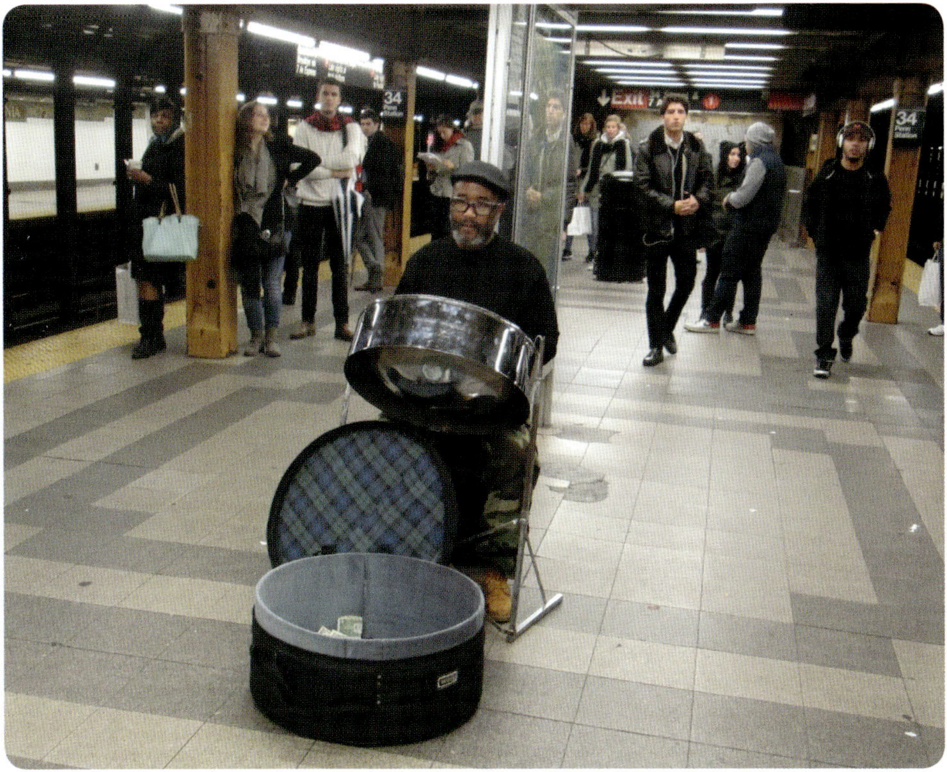

Steel drum.

34th Street - Penn Station

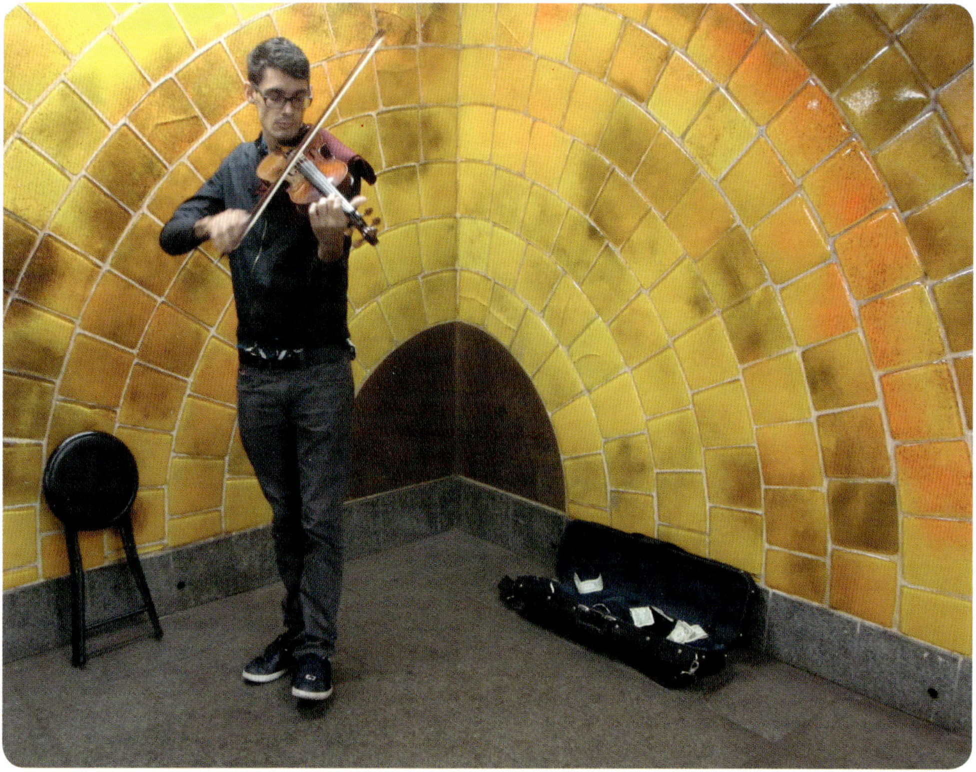

Matthew Christian, violin player, co-founder of Busk NY.

81st Station and Central Park West

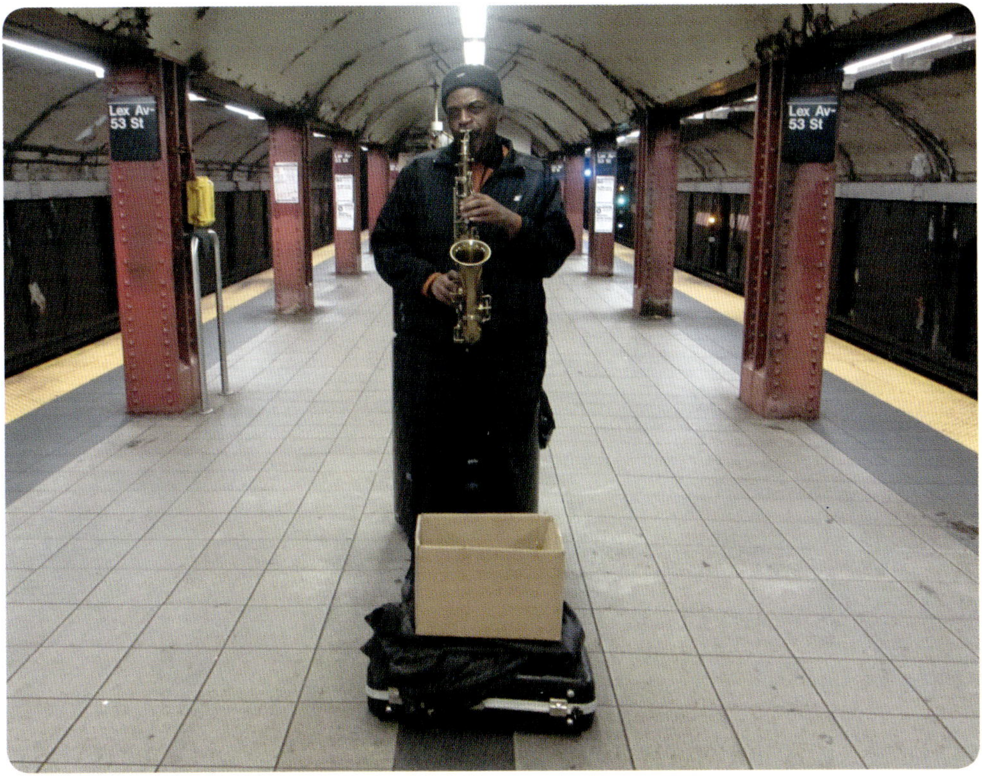

Duke Curry, saxophone.

53rd Street and Lexington Avenue Station

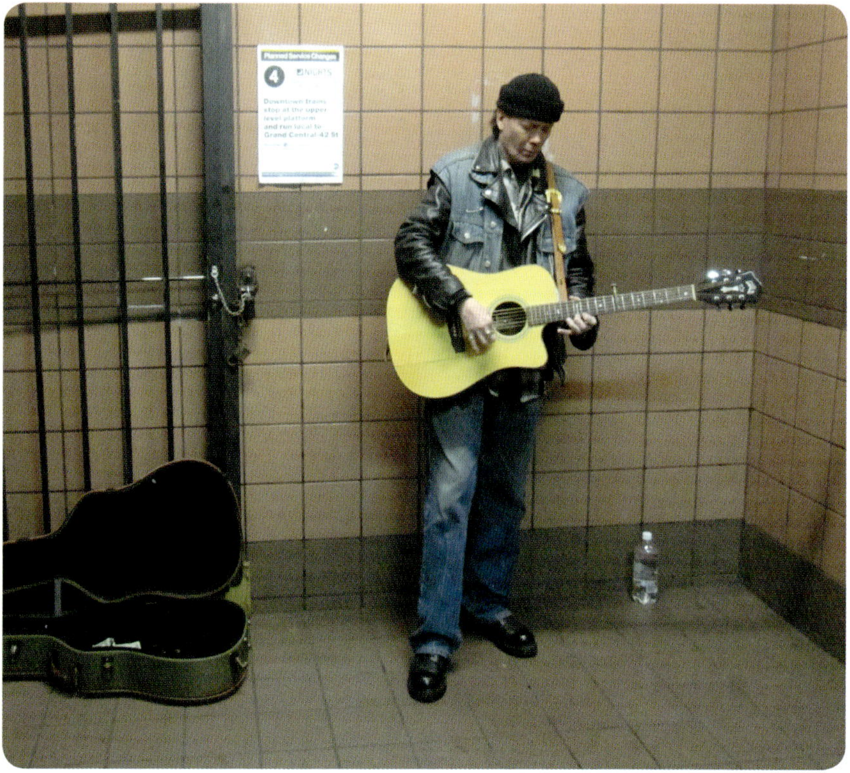

Folk guitar.

59th Street and Lexington Avenue Station

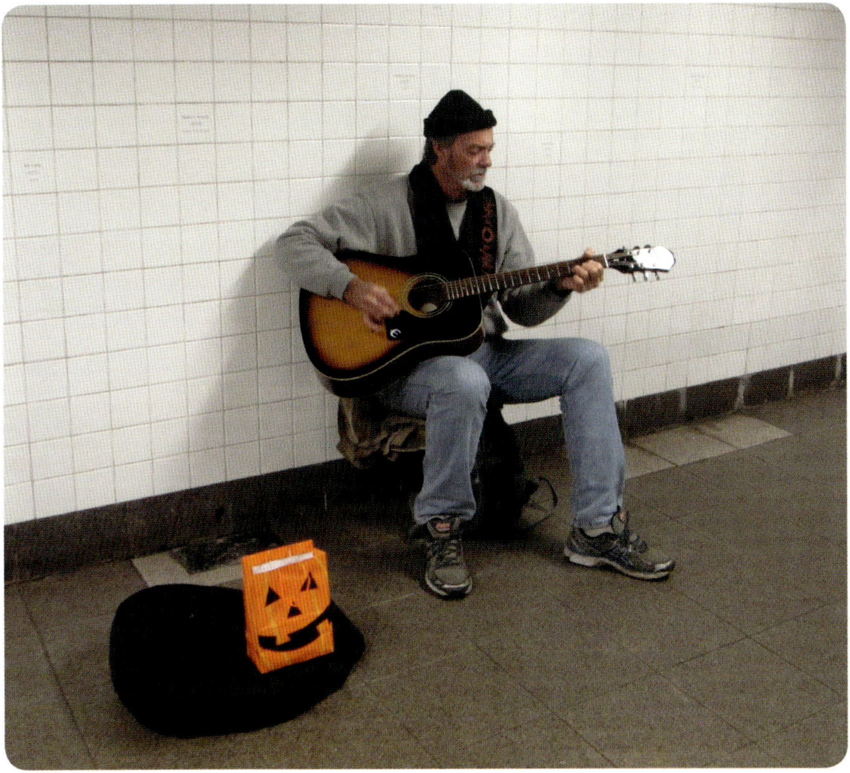

Folk guitar.

59th Street Station/Halloween Donation Bag

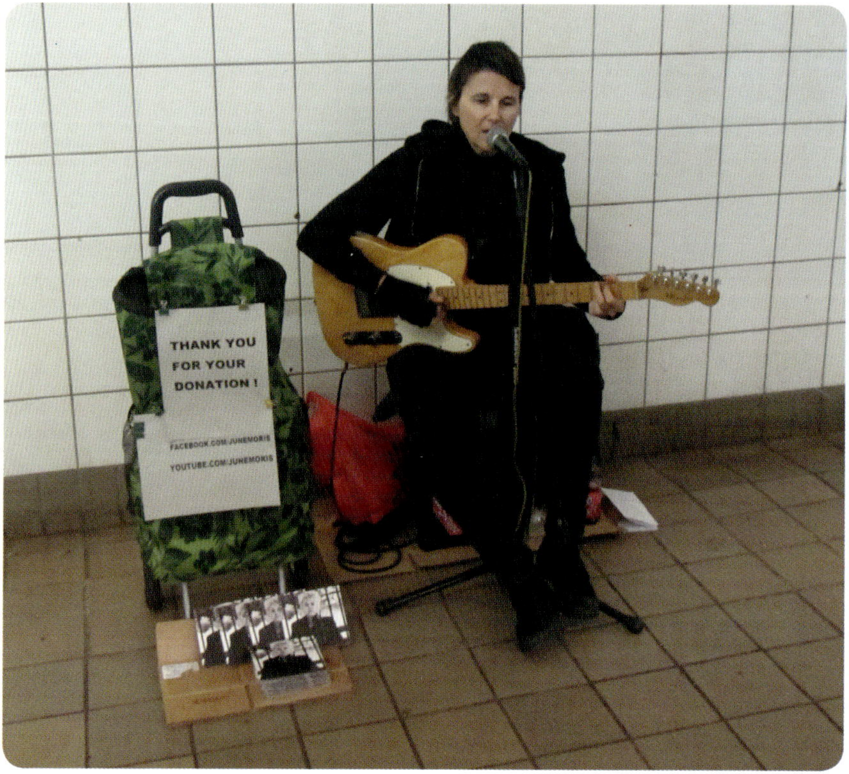

June Morris, singer.

5th Avenue and 53rd Street Station

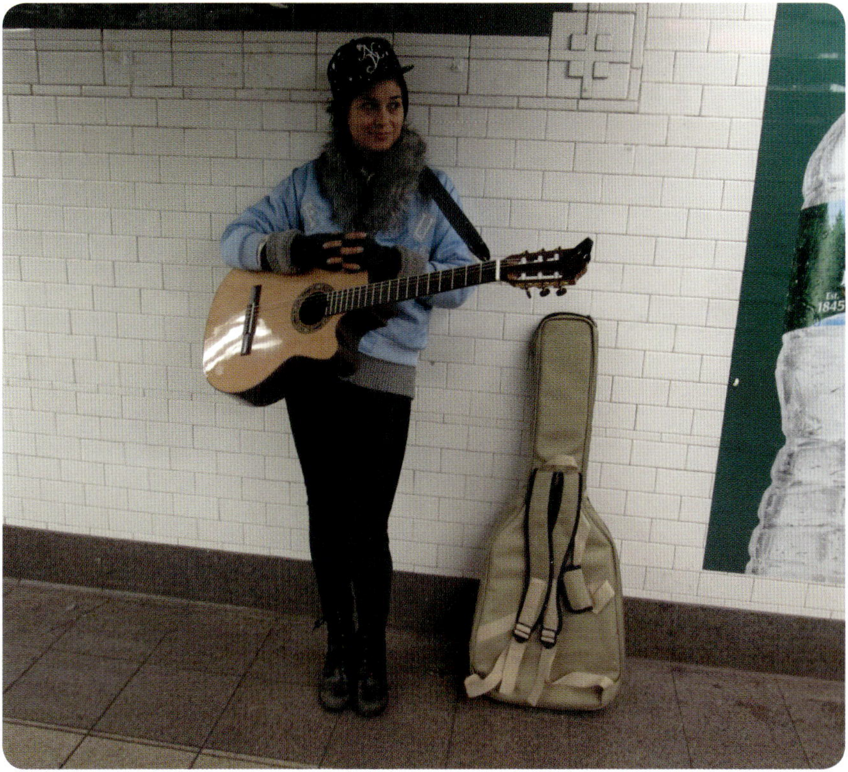

Folk guitar player and singer.

Union Square Station

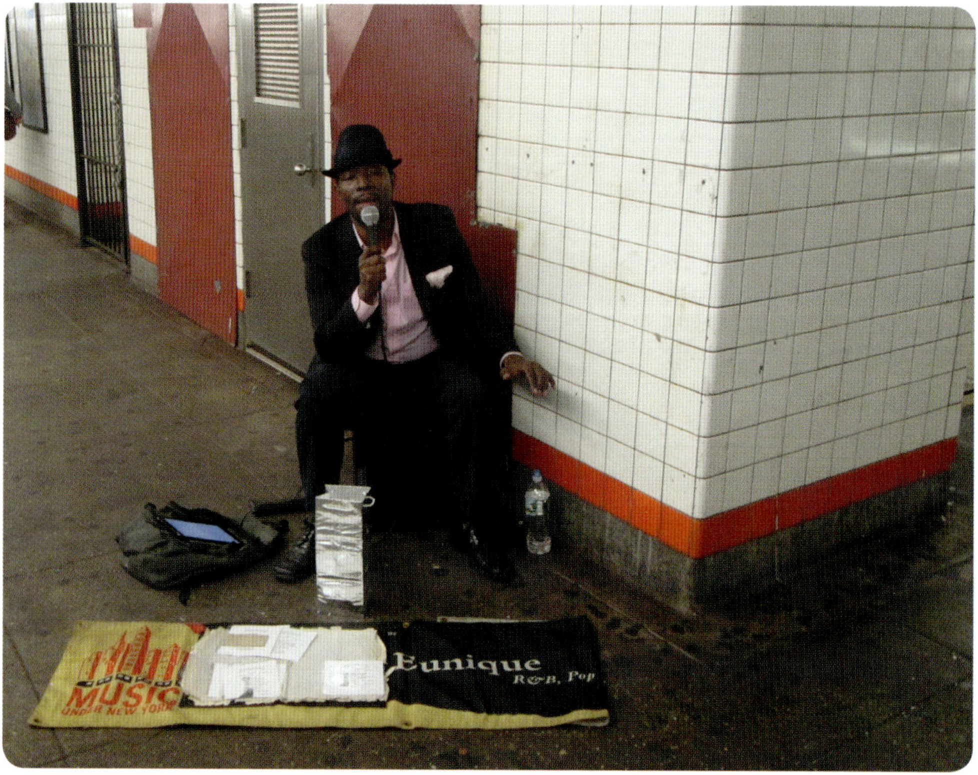

Eunique, R&B pop singer.

Rockefeller Center Station

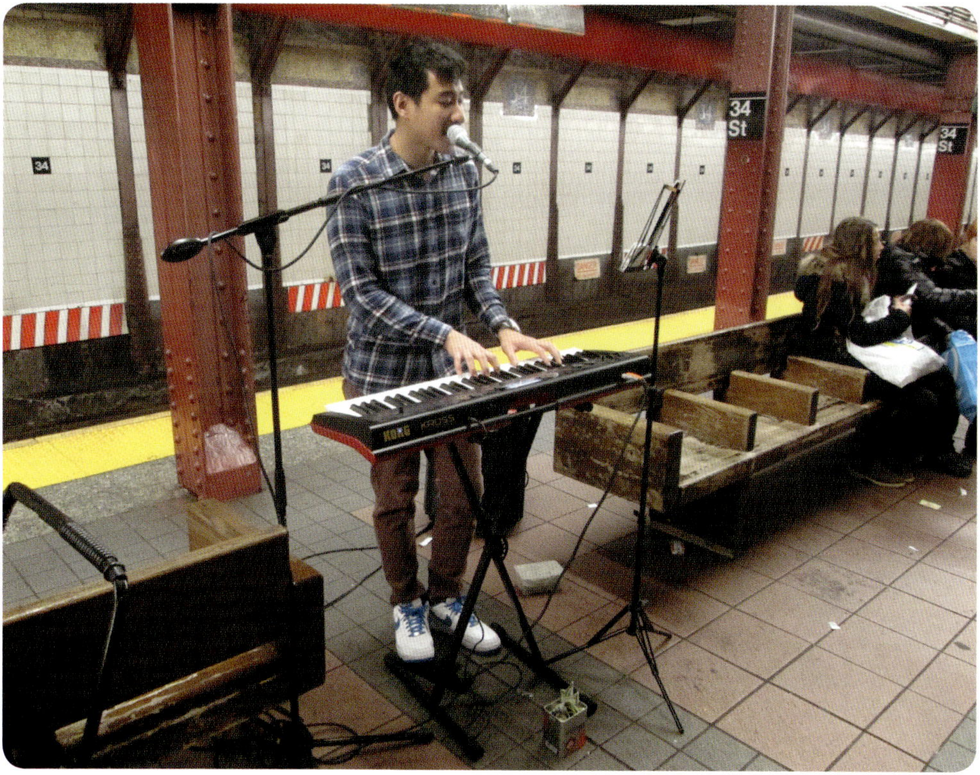

Electric organ.

34th Street and 6th Avenue Station

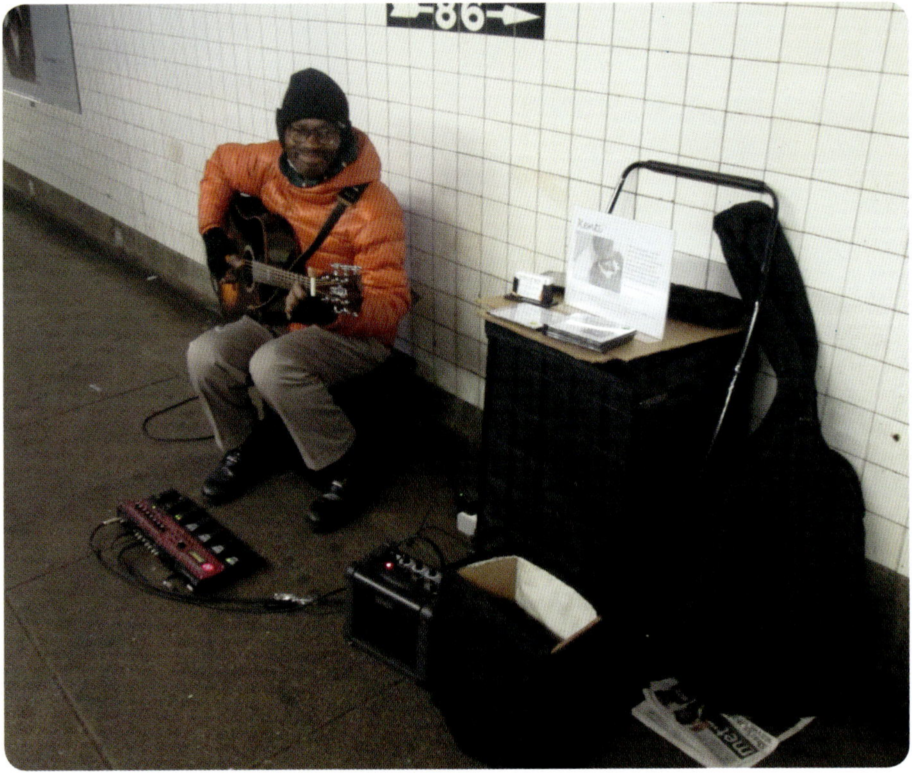

Kenti

86th Street and Central Park West Station

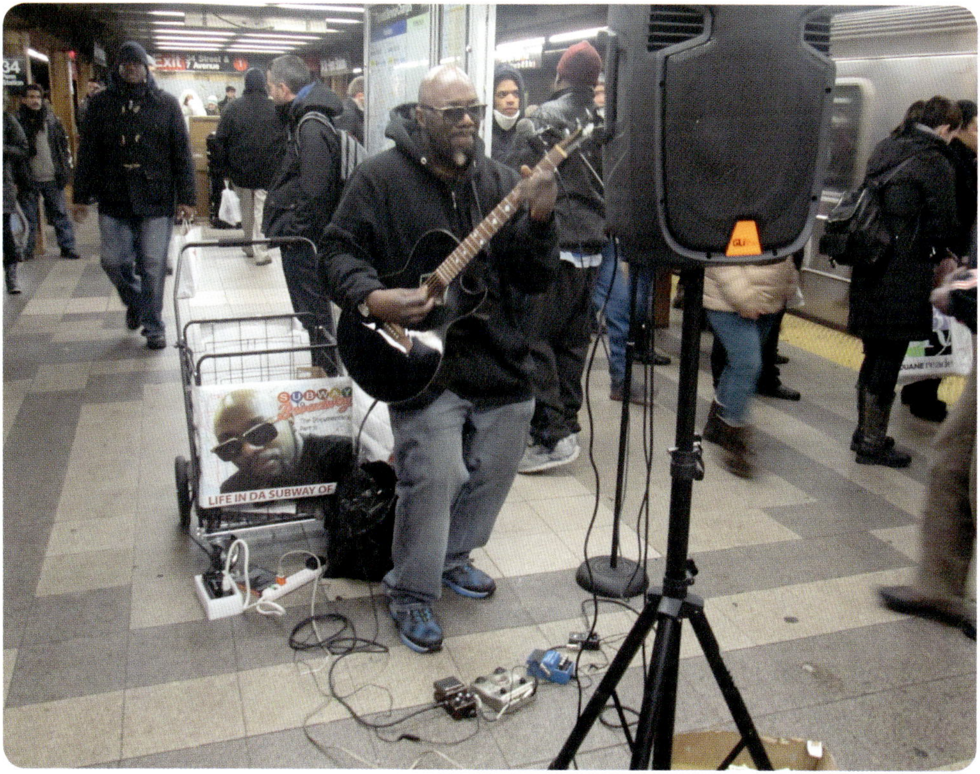

GWY 11, Greg Willis, R&B and jazz.

34th Street - Penn Station

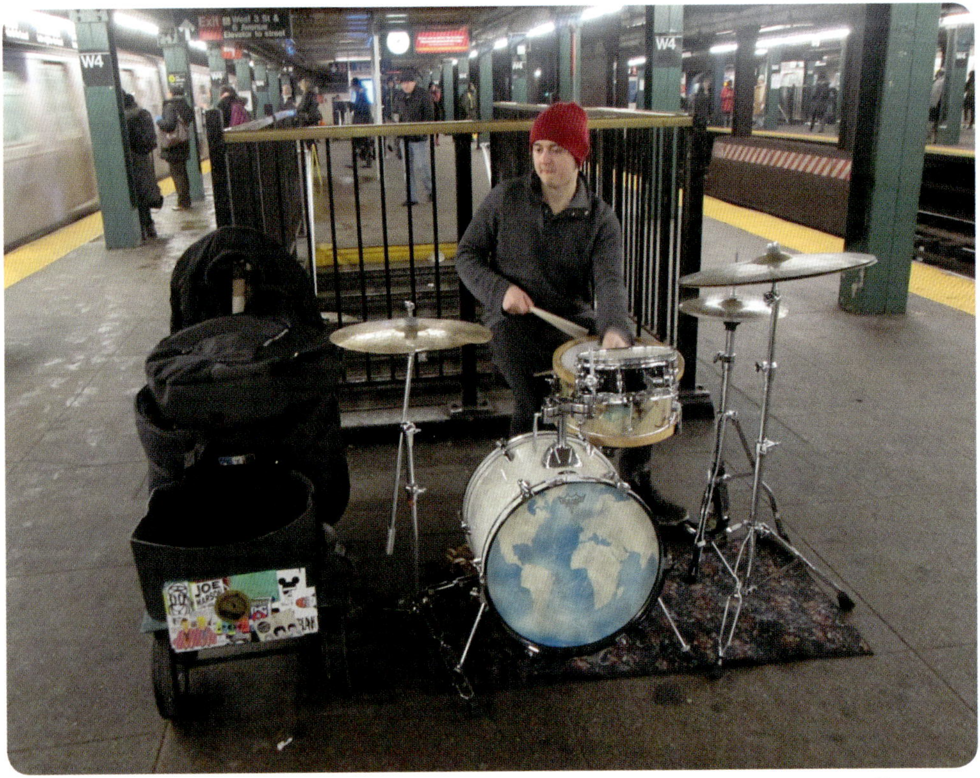

Drummer.

West 4th Street Station

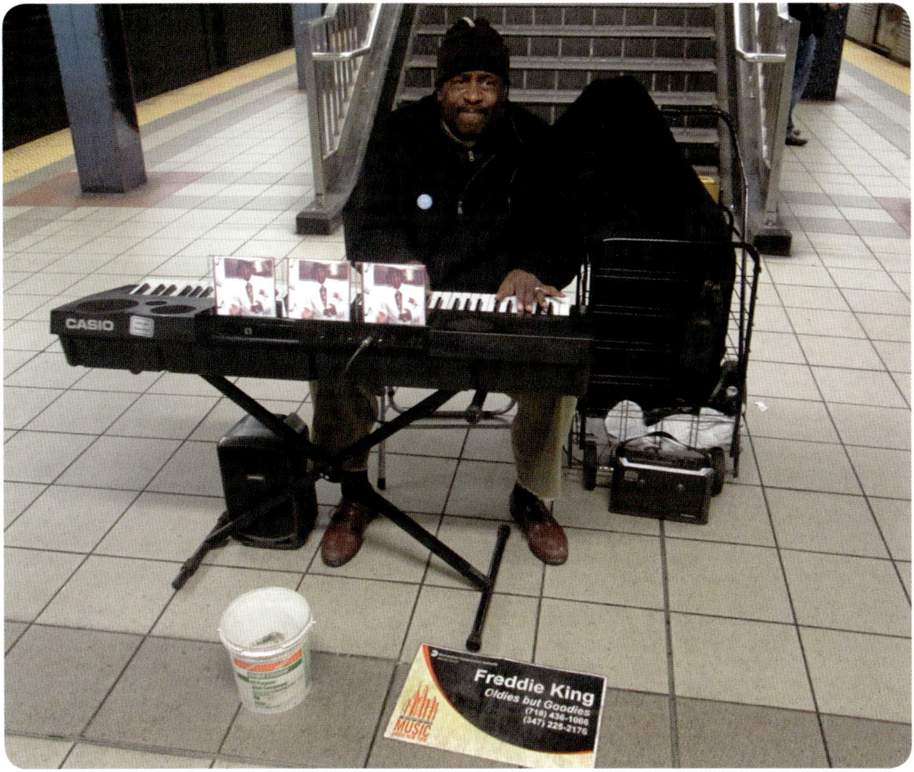

Freddie King, Oldies but Goodies.

42nd Street - Port Authority Station

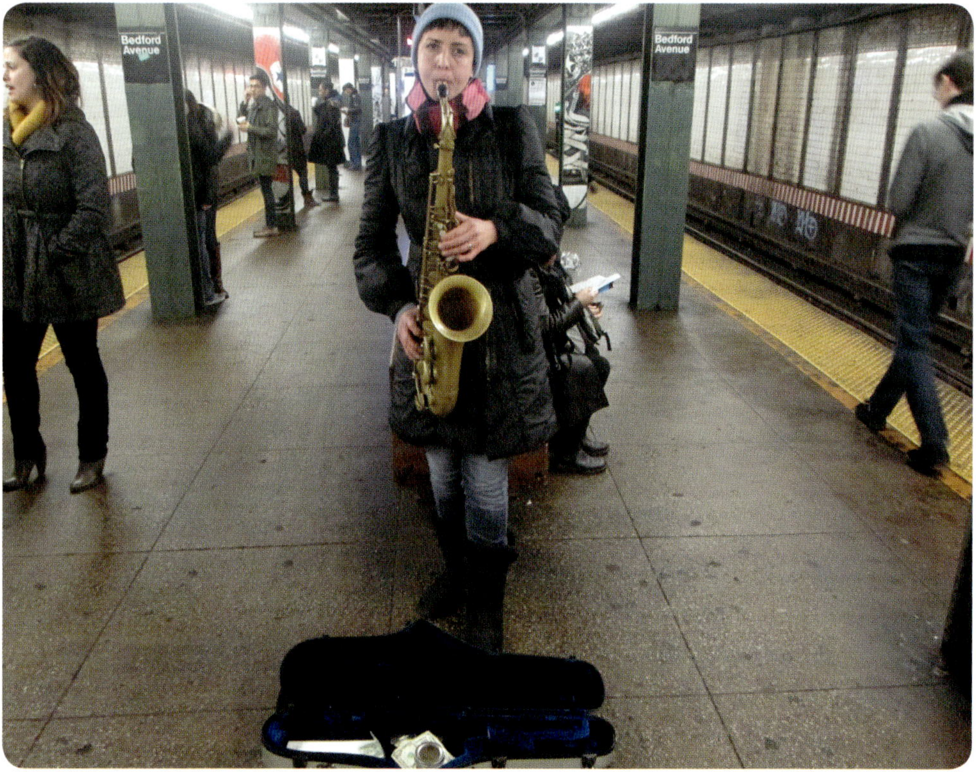

Saxophone.

Bedford Avenue Station

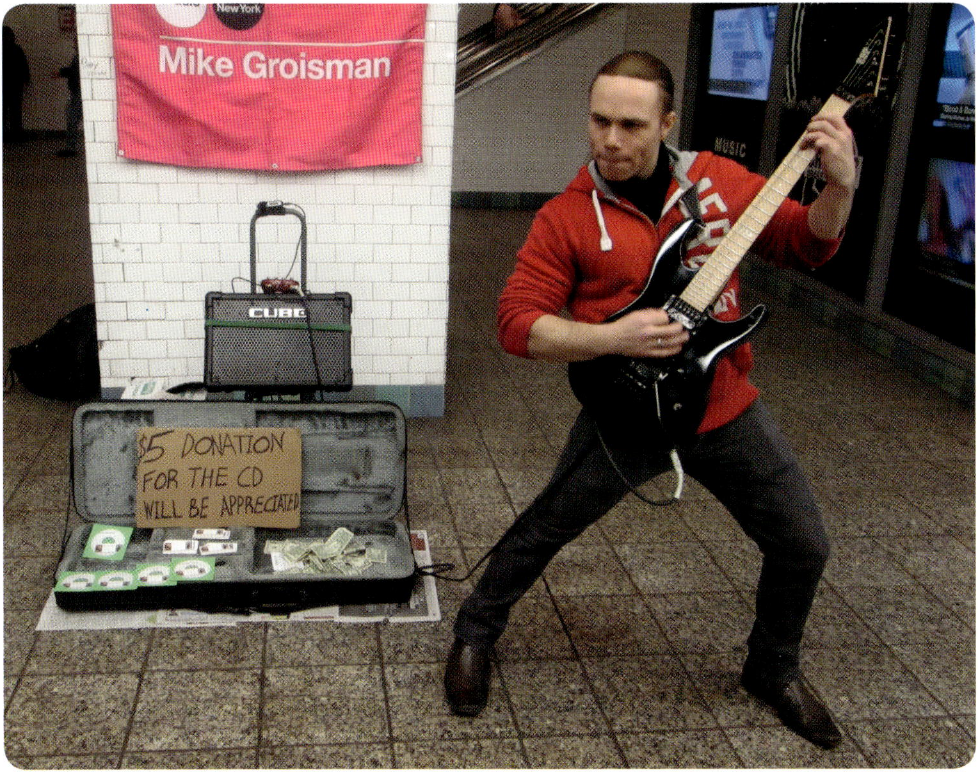

Mike Groisman, electric guitar.

Times Square Station

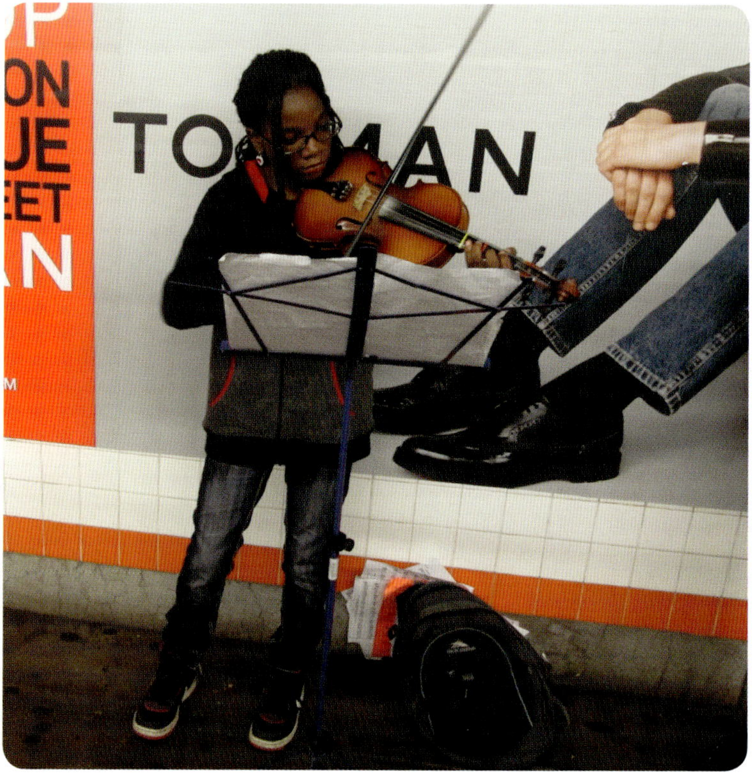

Young violinist.

Grand Central Station Shuttle Walkway

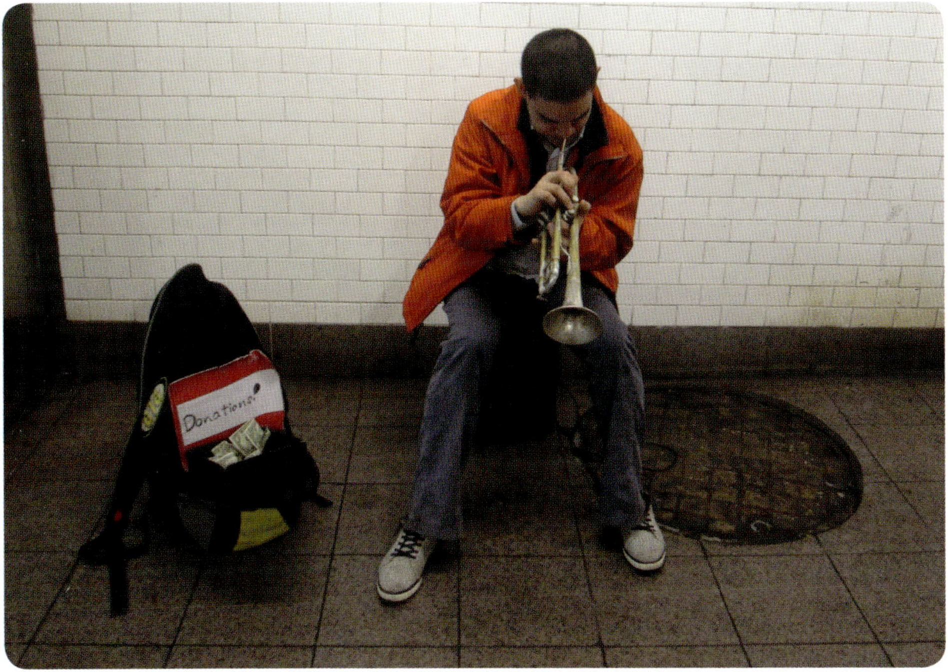

Trumpet.

59th Street and Lexington Avenue

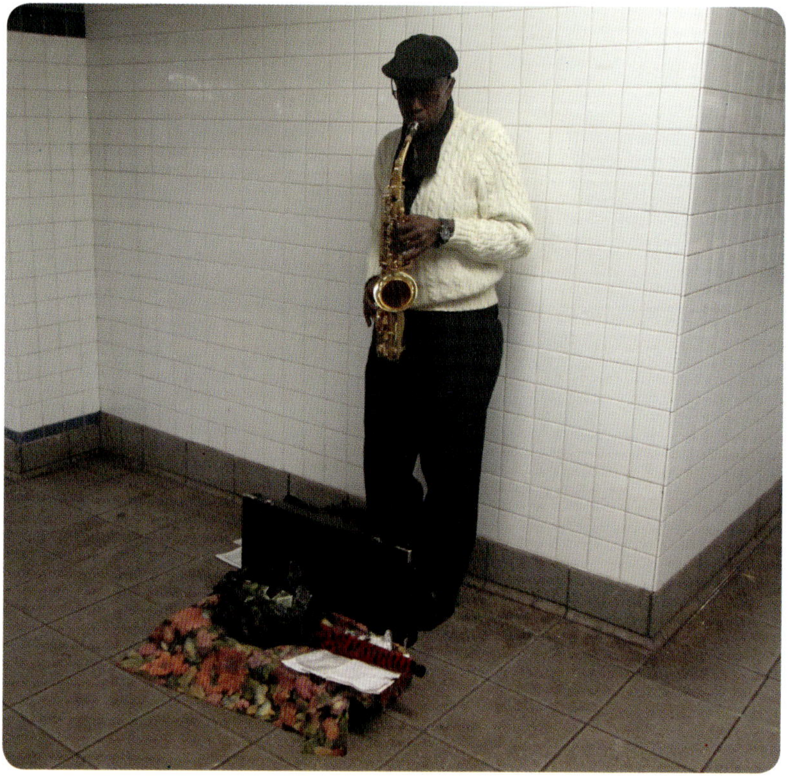

Saxophone.

Boro Hall Station

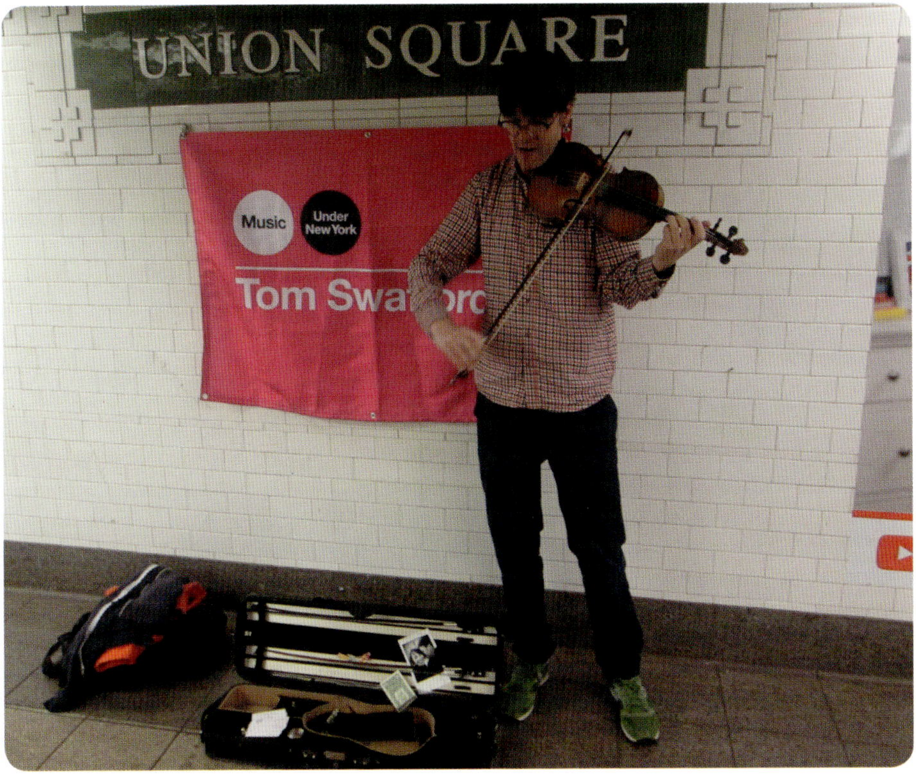

Tom Swafford, electric violin.

Union Square Station

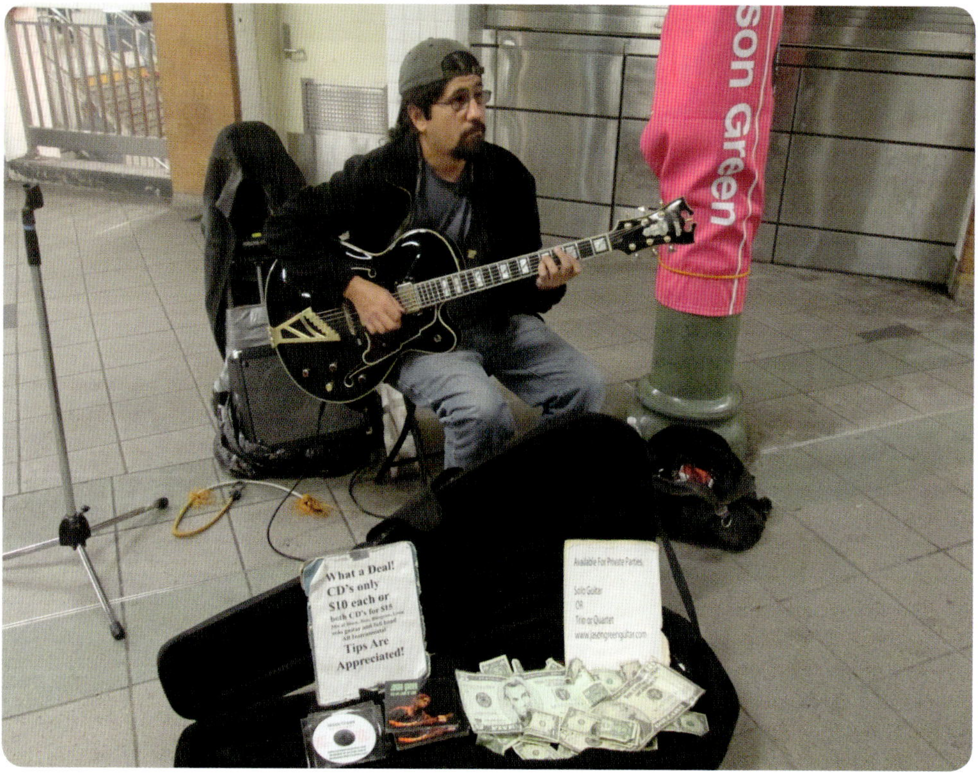

Jason Green, guitar.

59th Street and Columbus Circle

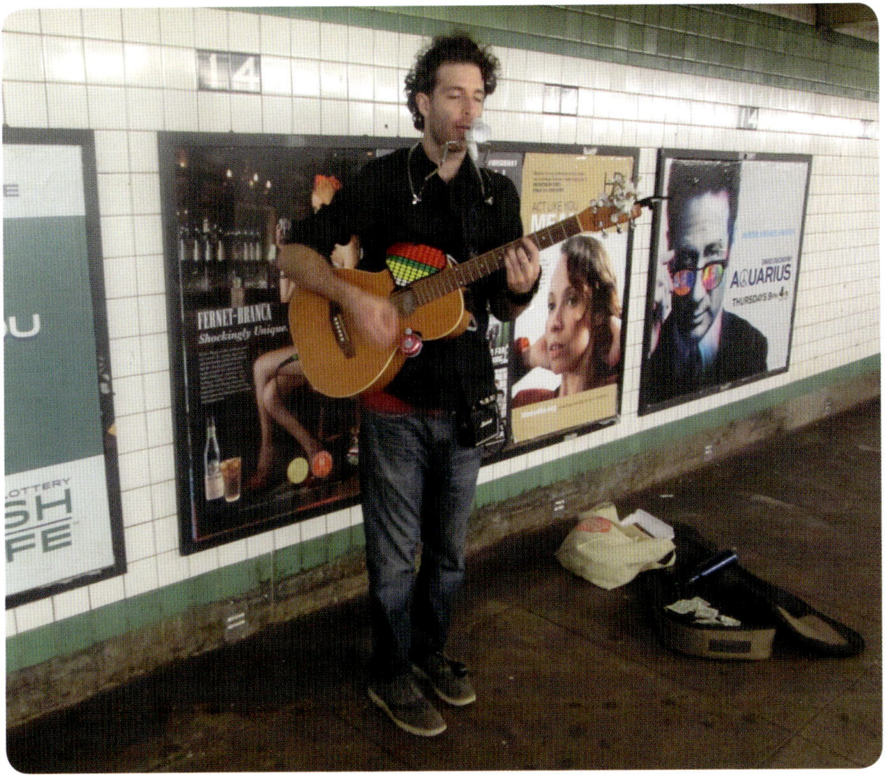

Folk guitar.

14th Street and 6th Avenue Station

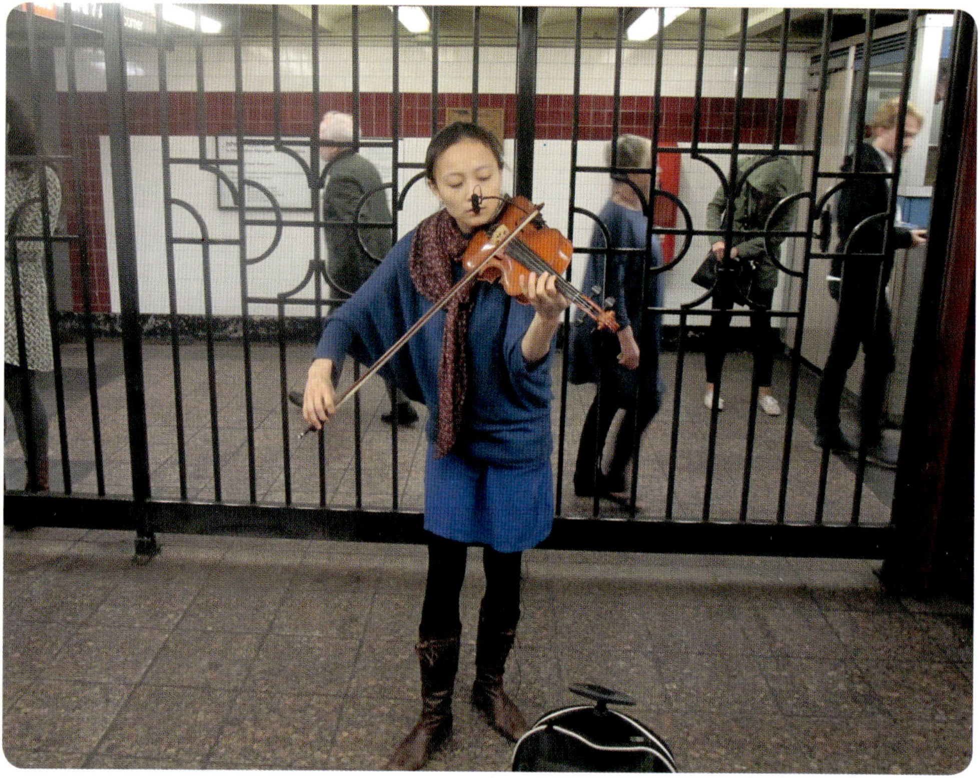

Jia Doughman, violin.

23rd Street and 7th Avenue Station

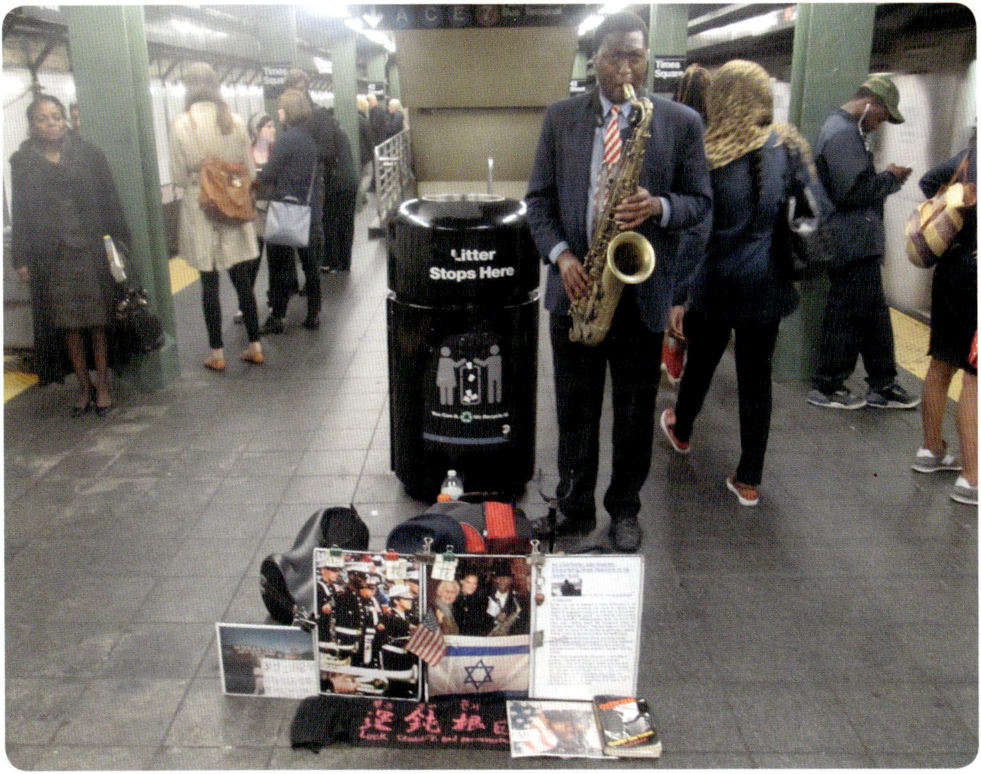

Isaiah Richardson, saxophone.

Times Square Station

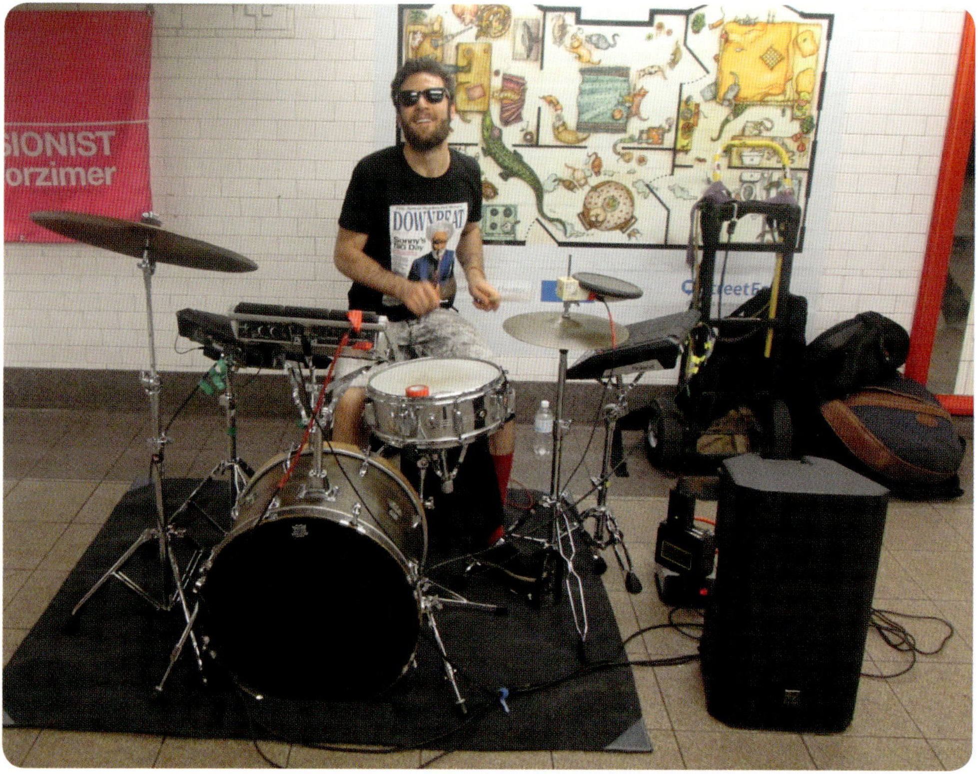

Matt Vorzimer, ecussionist.

Union Square Station

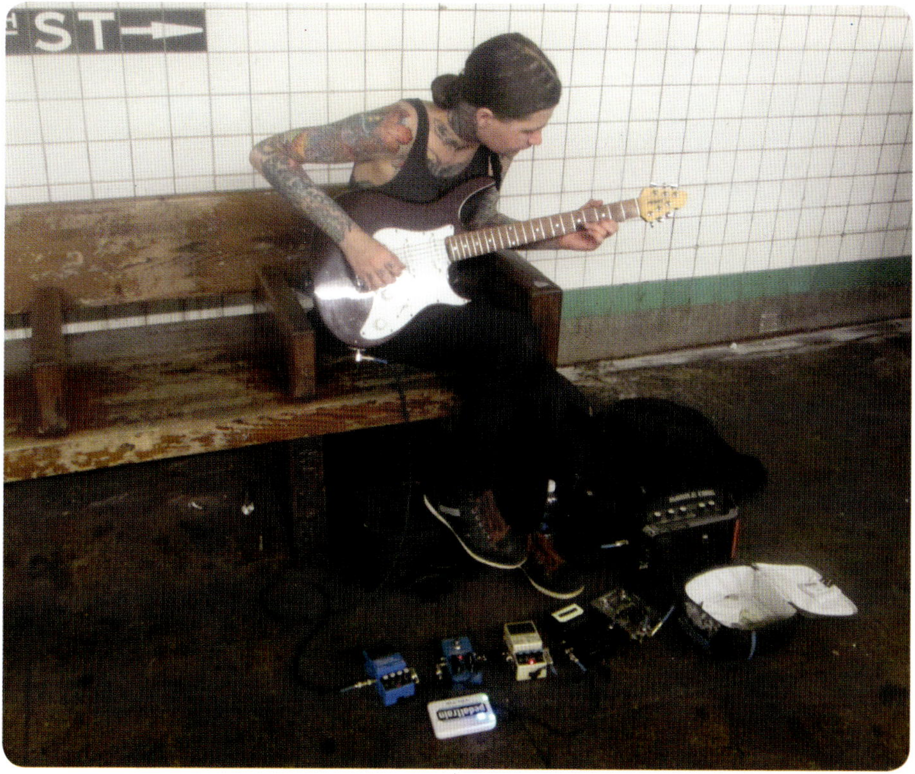

Matti Maranda, electric guitar.

14th Street and 6th Avenue Station

Chamber Street Station

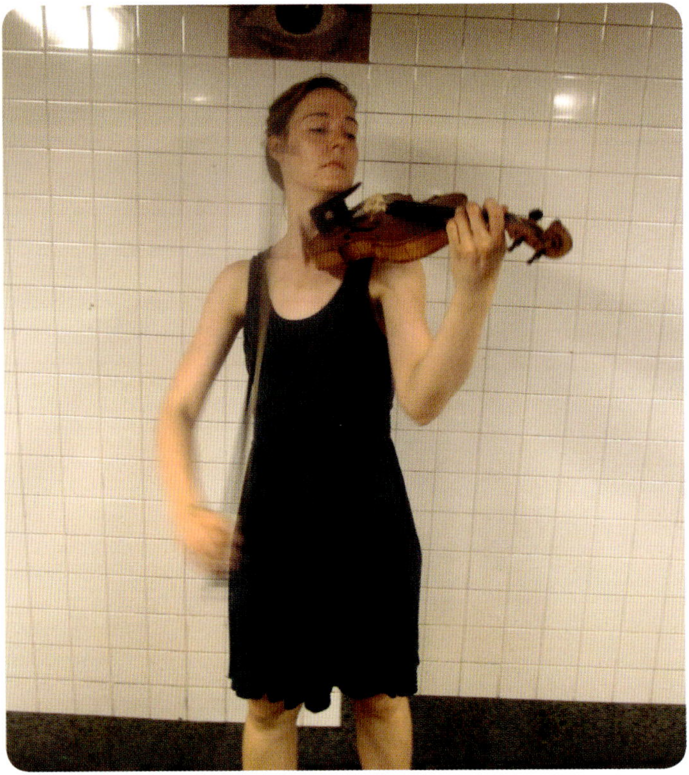

Rebekah Butler, violin.

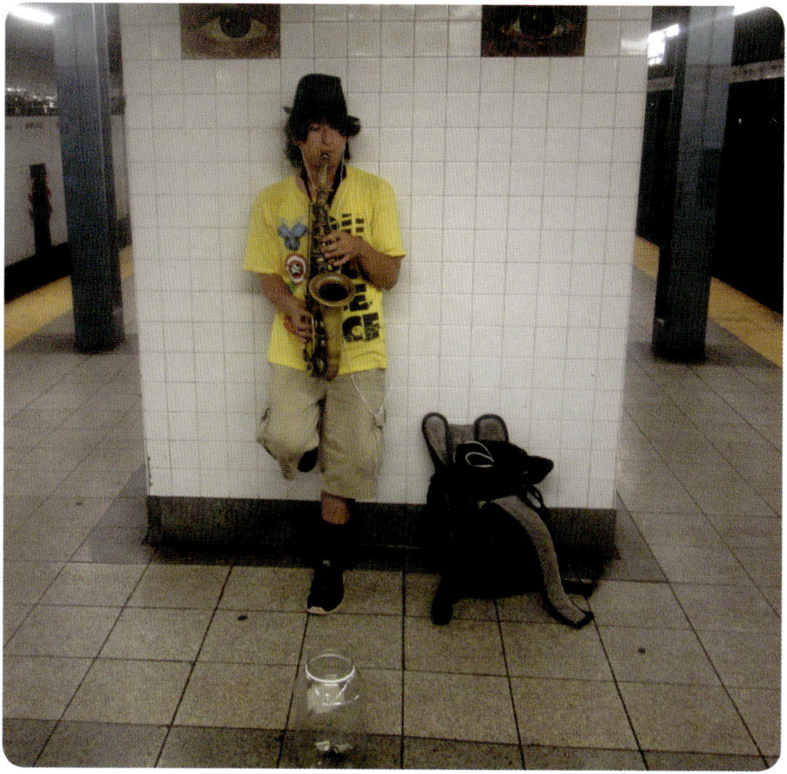

Lucas Perez de la Roca, saxophone.

Chamber Street Station

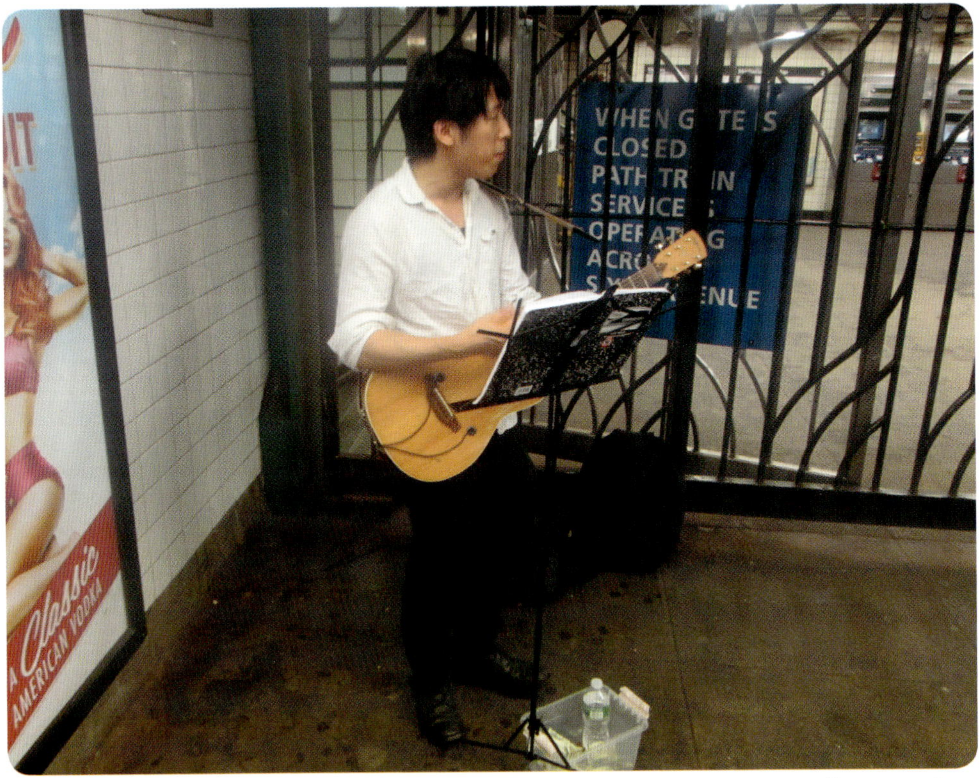

Nozumu, guitar.

23rd Street and Sixth Avenue Station

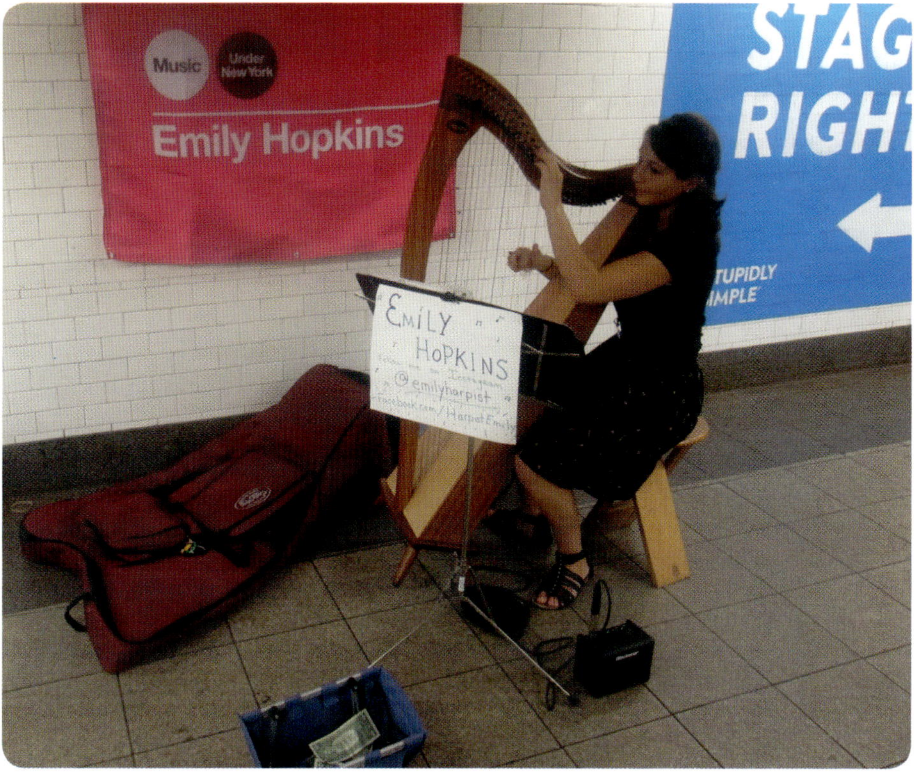

Emily Hopkins, harp.

Union Square Station

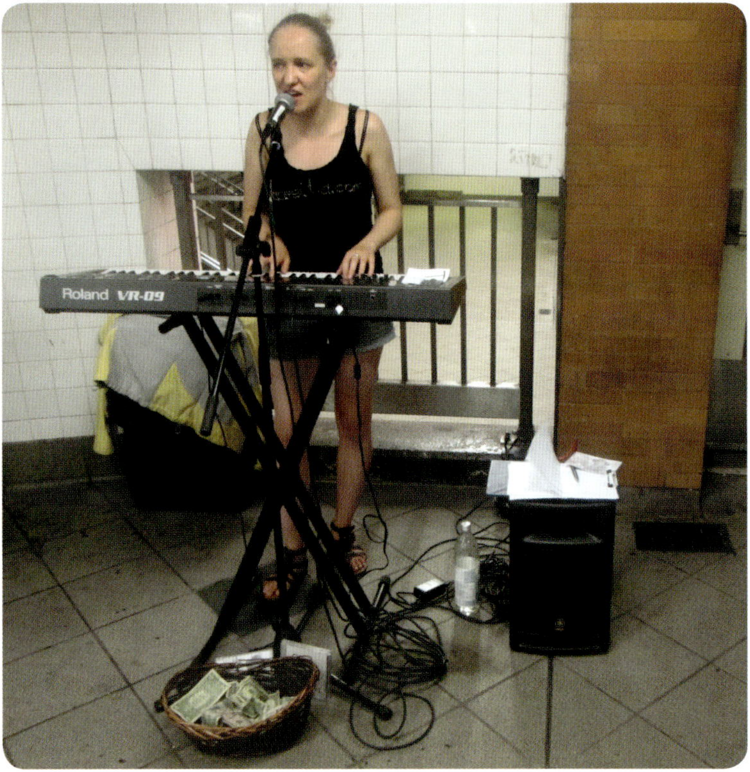

Didi, electric organ and singer.

59th Street and Columbus Circle Station

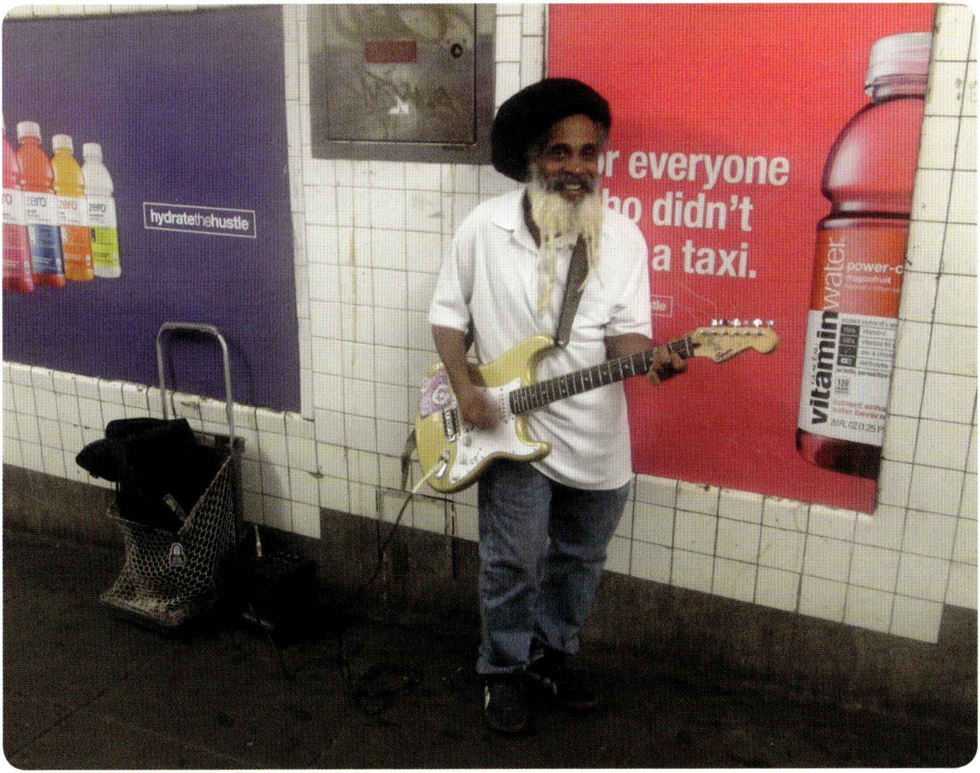

Salvador.

West 4th Street Station

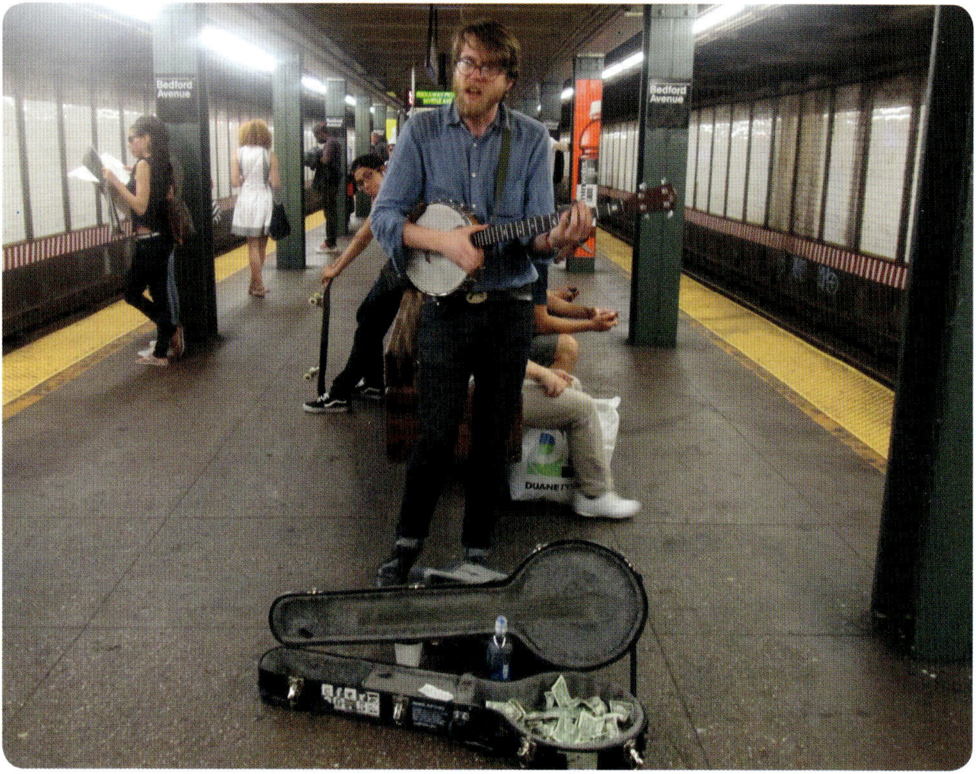

Taylor Ashton.

Bedford Avenue Station

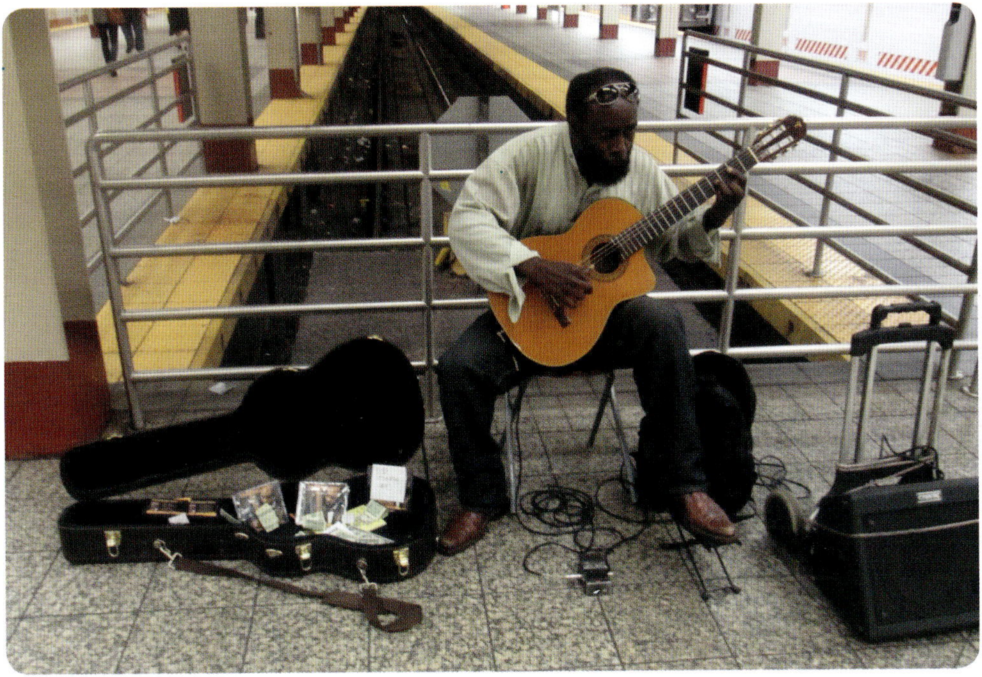

Desmond Ivey.

Grand Central Station Shuttle Platform

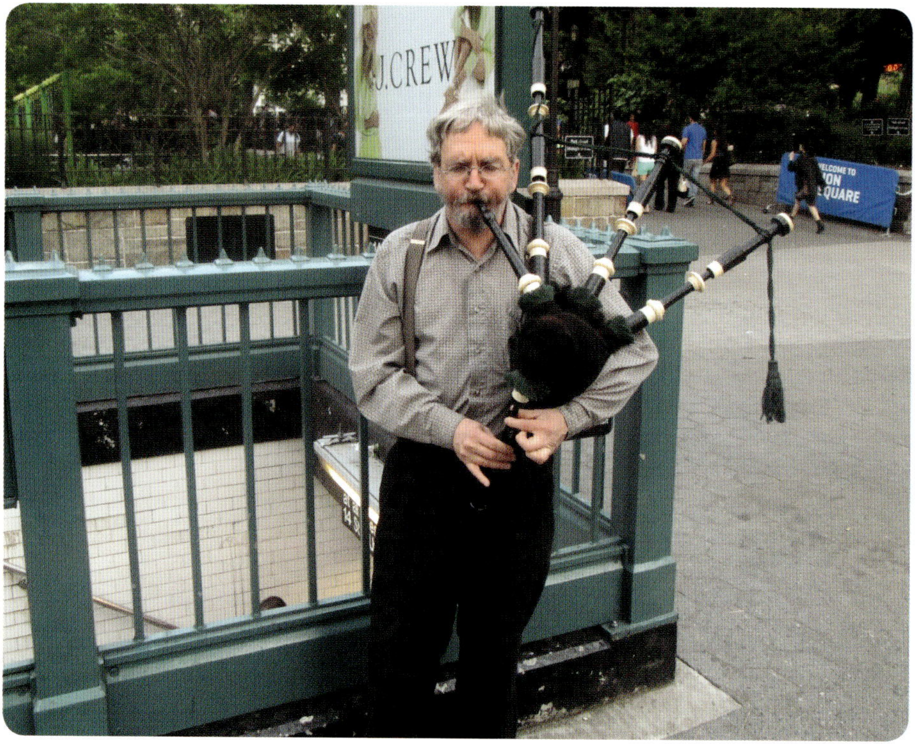

Bagpipe player.

Union Square Station

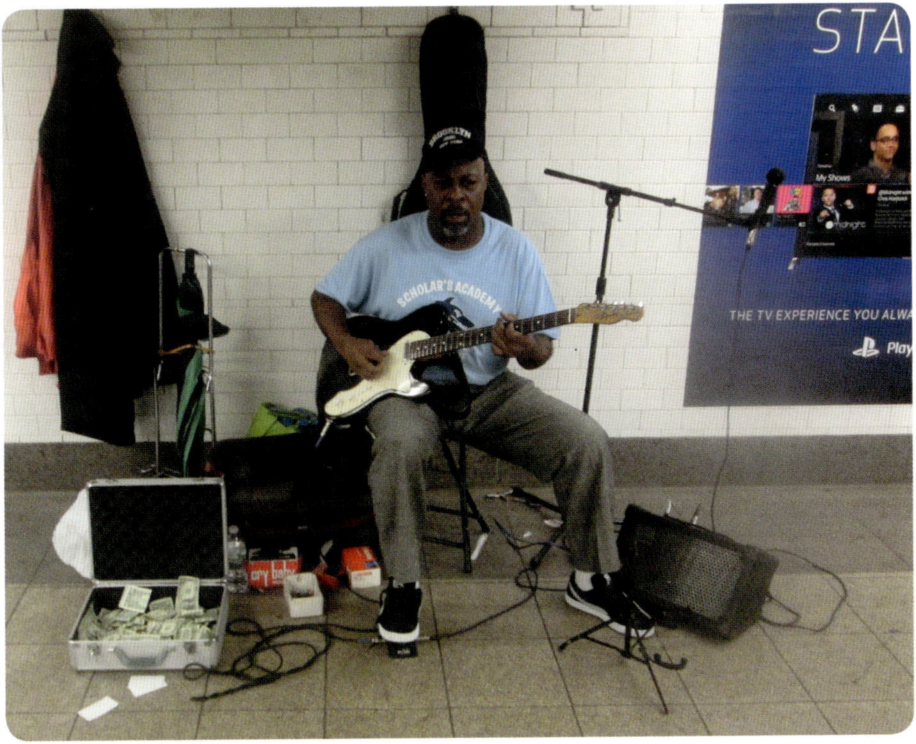

Dee Dee King, electric guitar.

Union Square Station

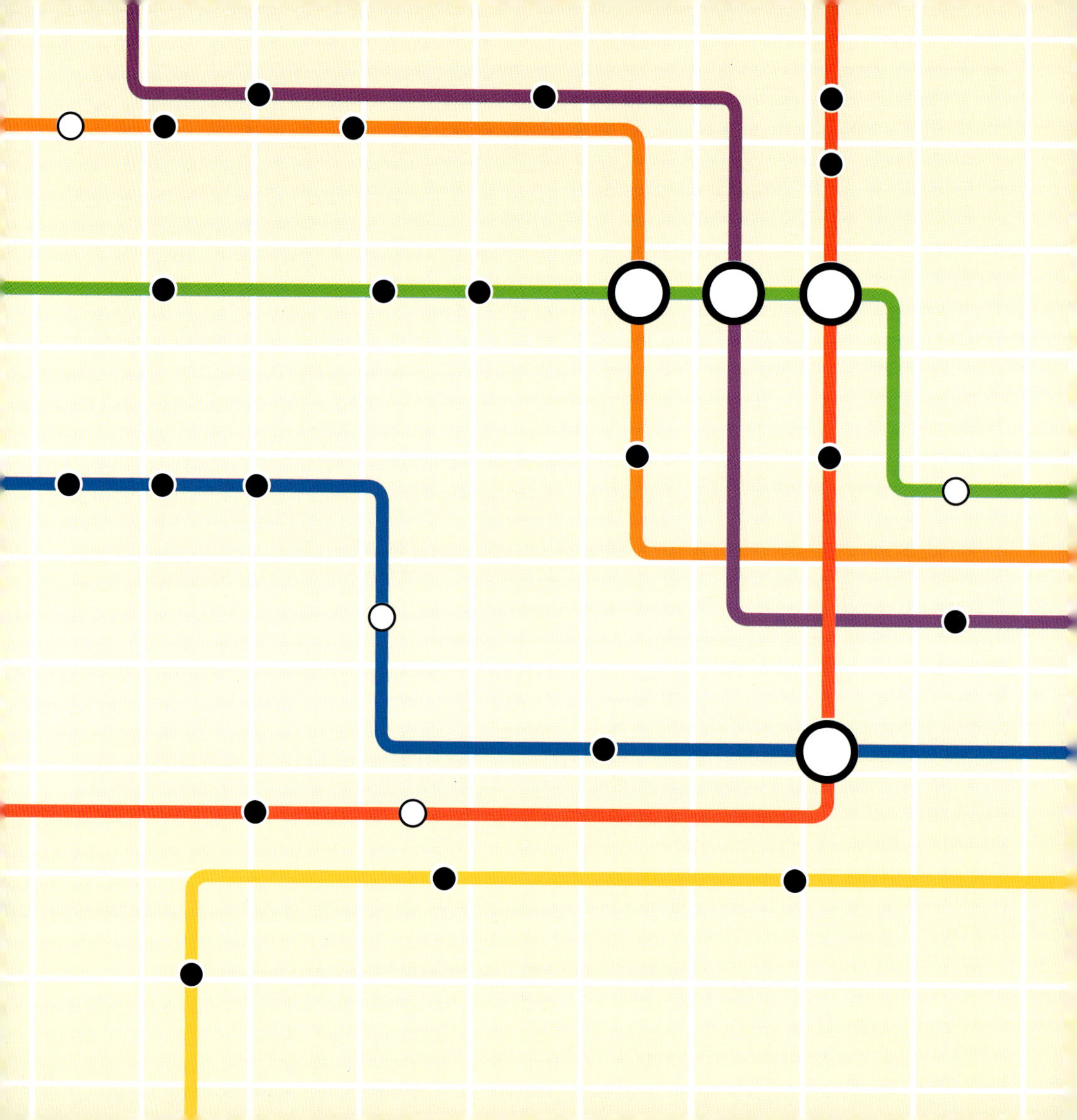

Chapter 6

Bands and Duets

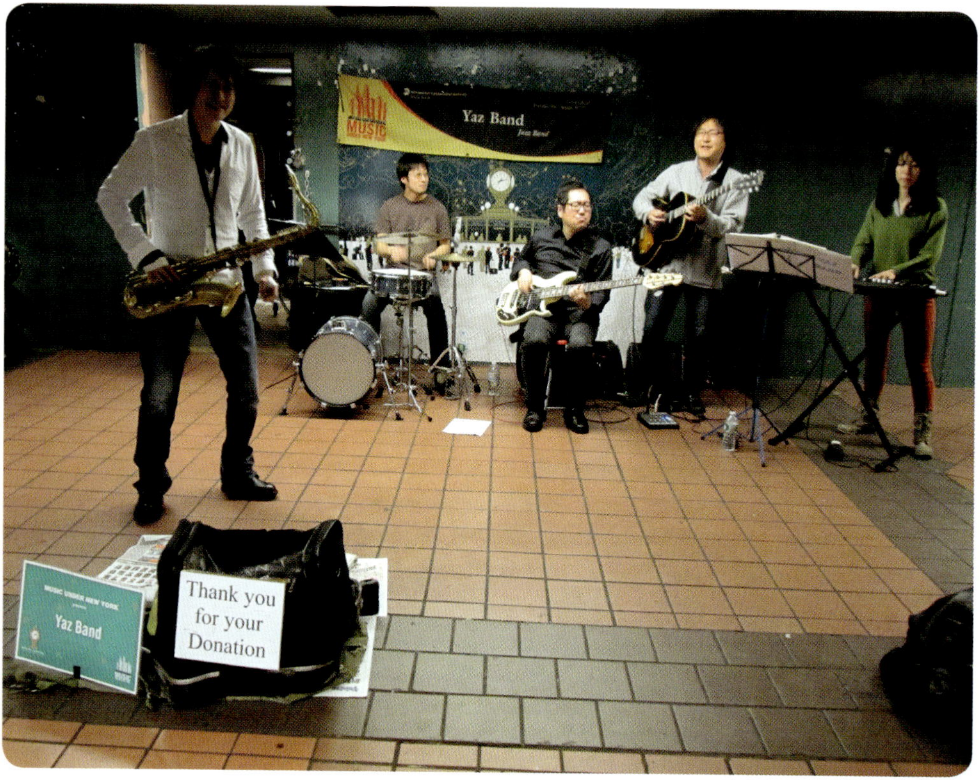

Yaz Band.

Grand Central Station

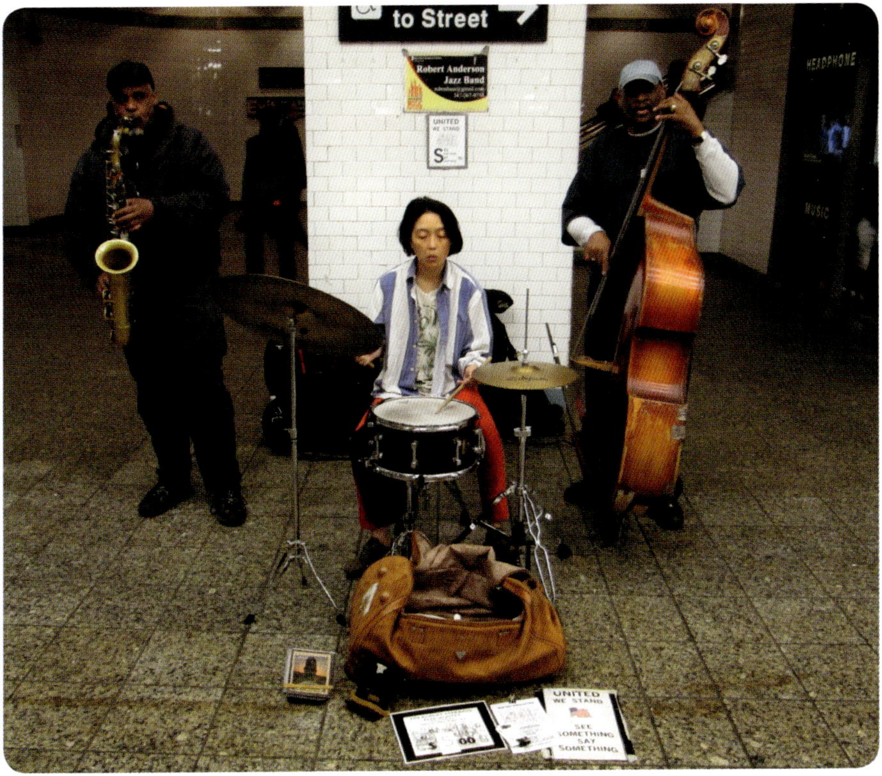

Robert Anderson Jazz Band.

Times Square Station

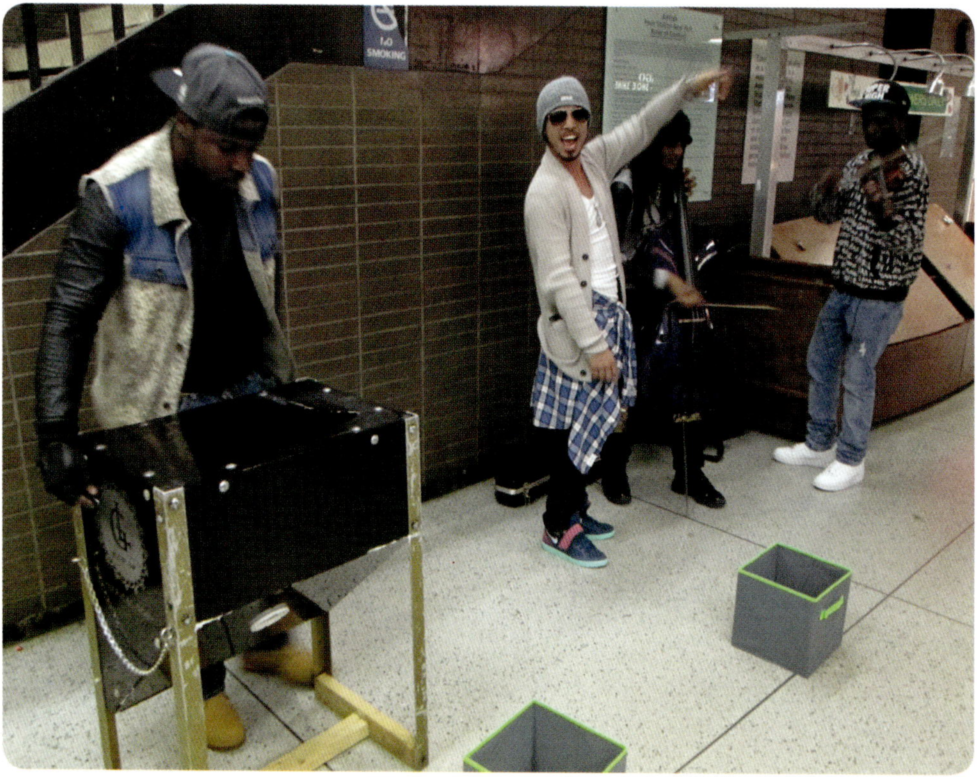

Lyrical Gods.

34th Street - Penn Station

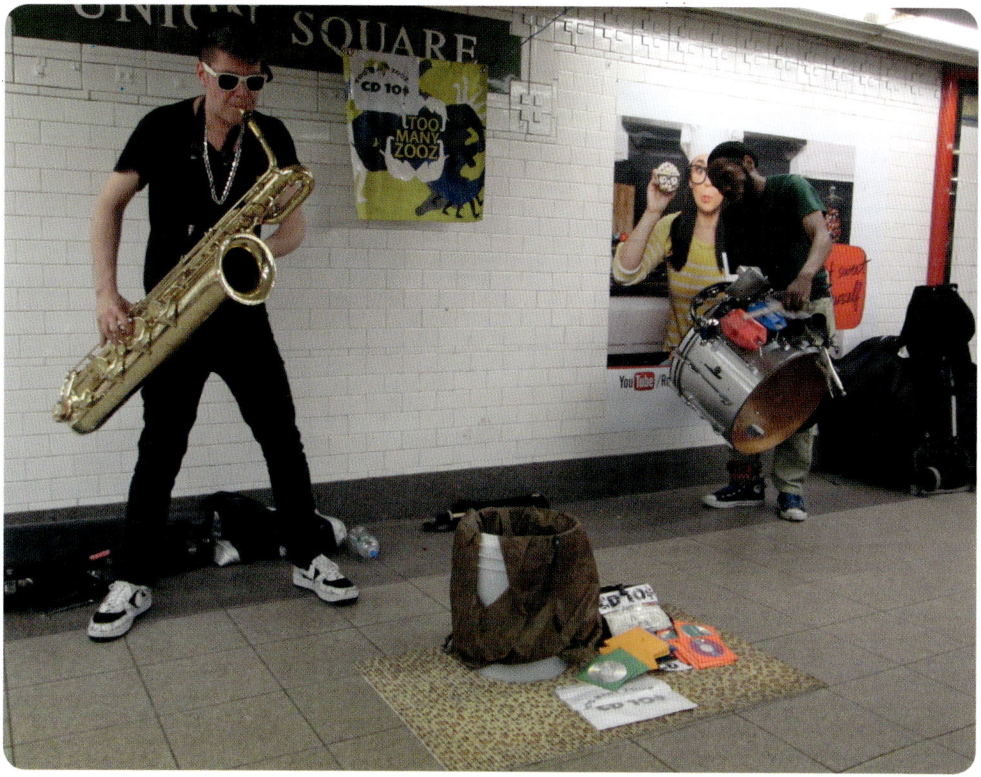

Too Many Zooz.

Union Square Station

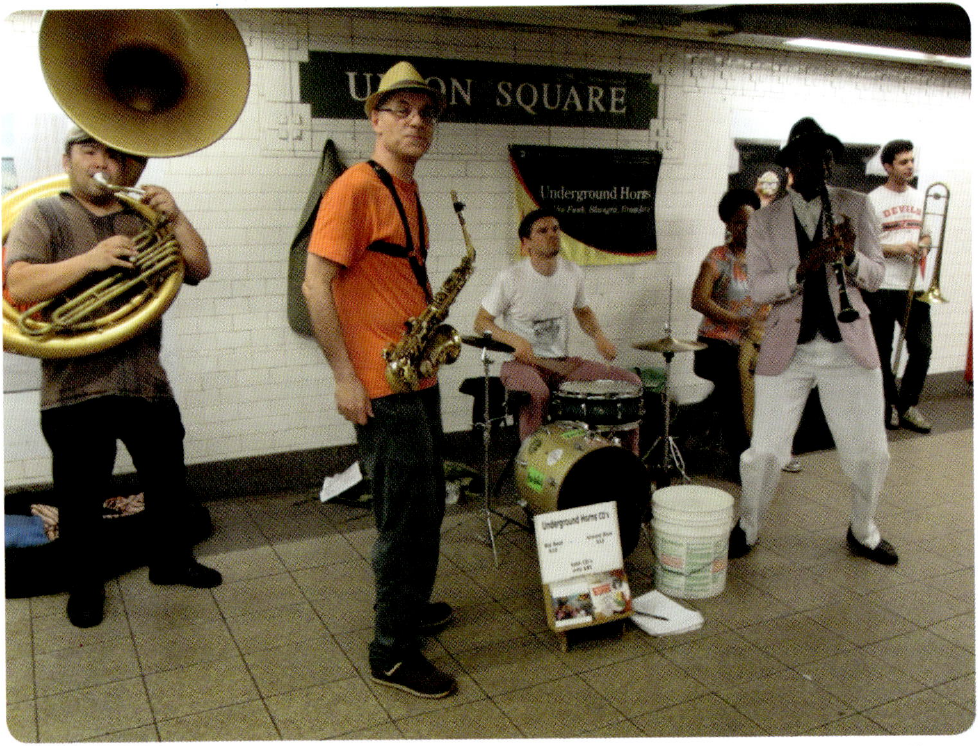

Underground Horns.

Union Square Station

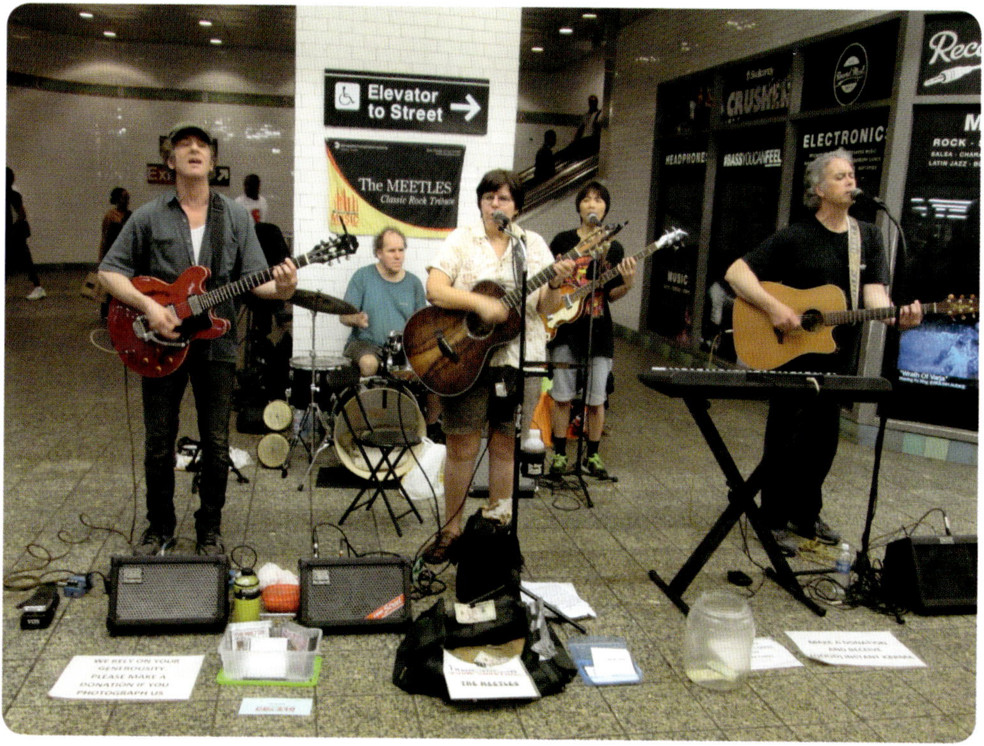

The Meetles, classic rock tribute.

Times Square Station

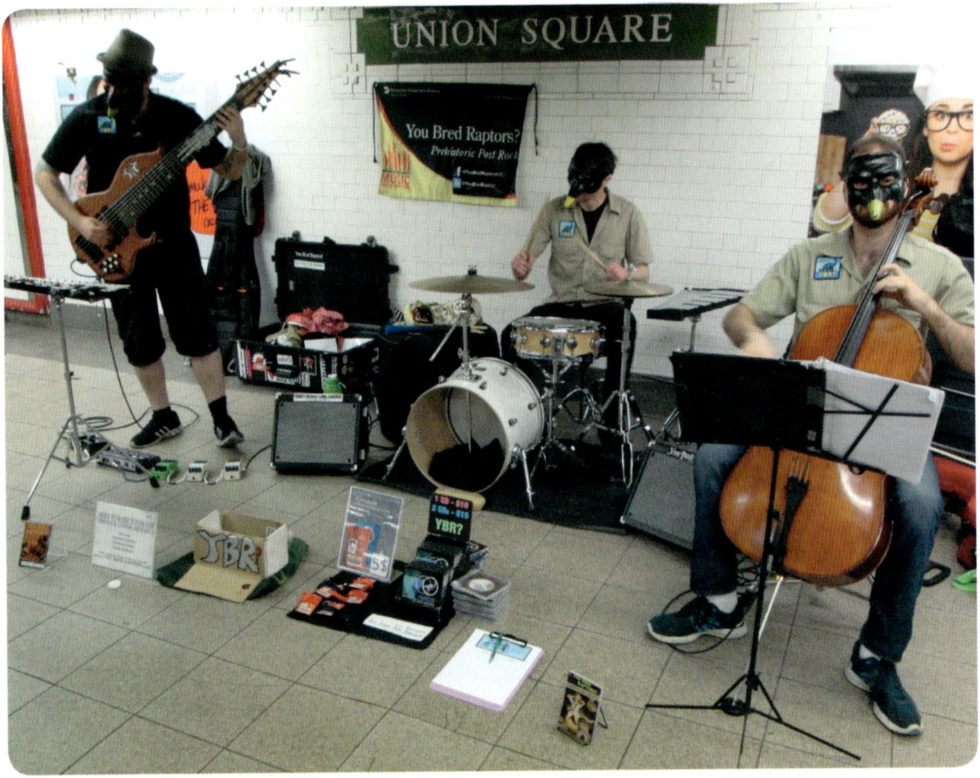

You Bred Raptors?, prehistoric post rock.

Union Square Station

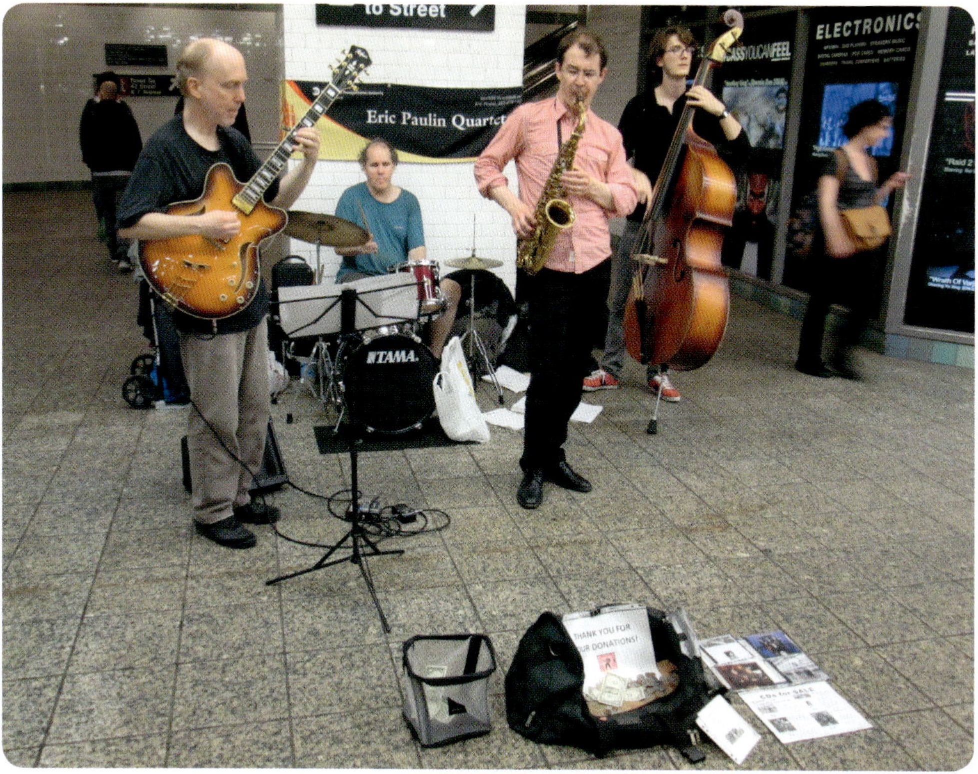

Eric Paulin Quartet.

Times Square Station

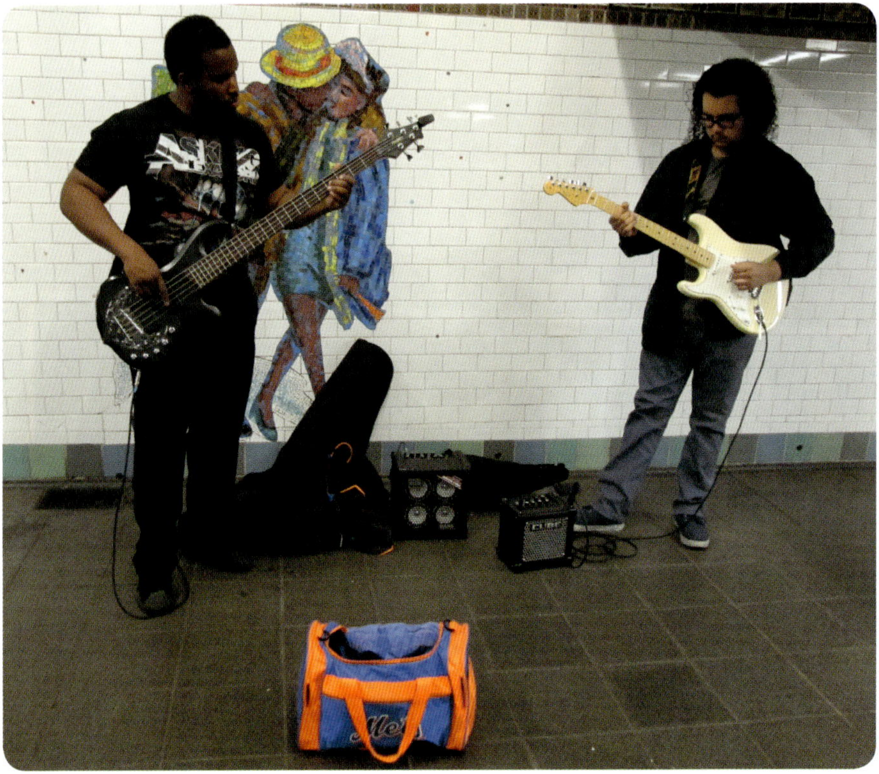

Two guitar players.

42nd Street - Port Authority Station

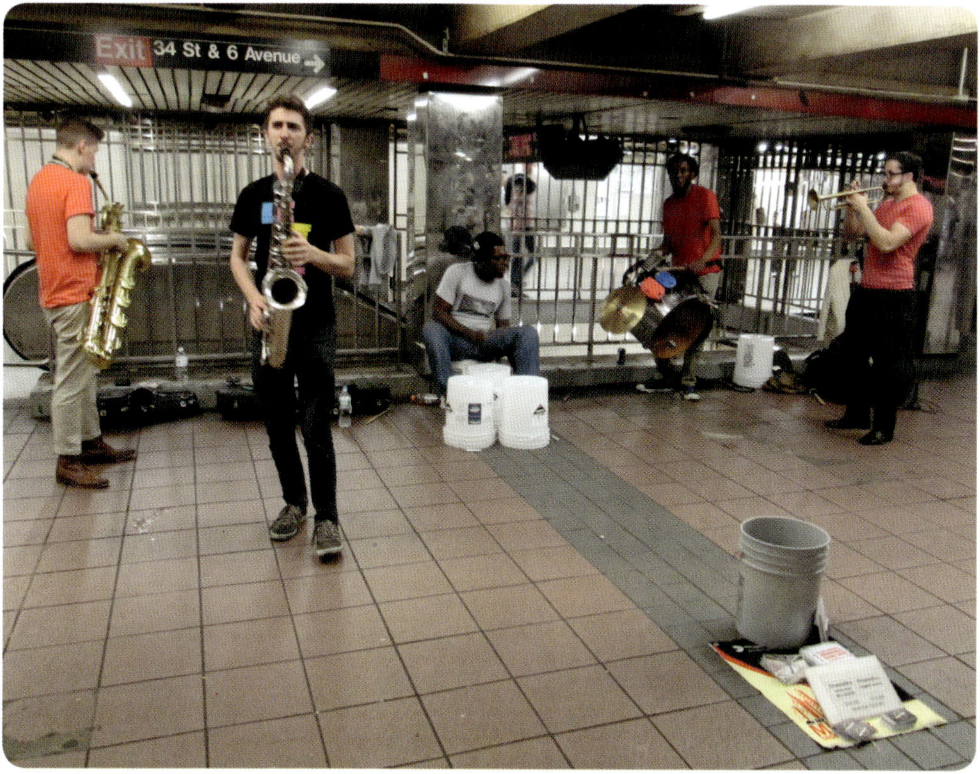

Drumadics.

34th Street - Herald Square Station

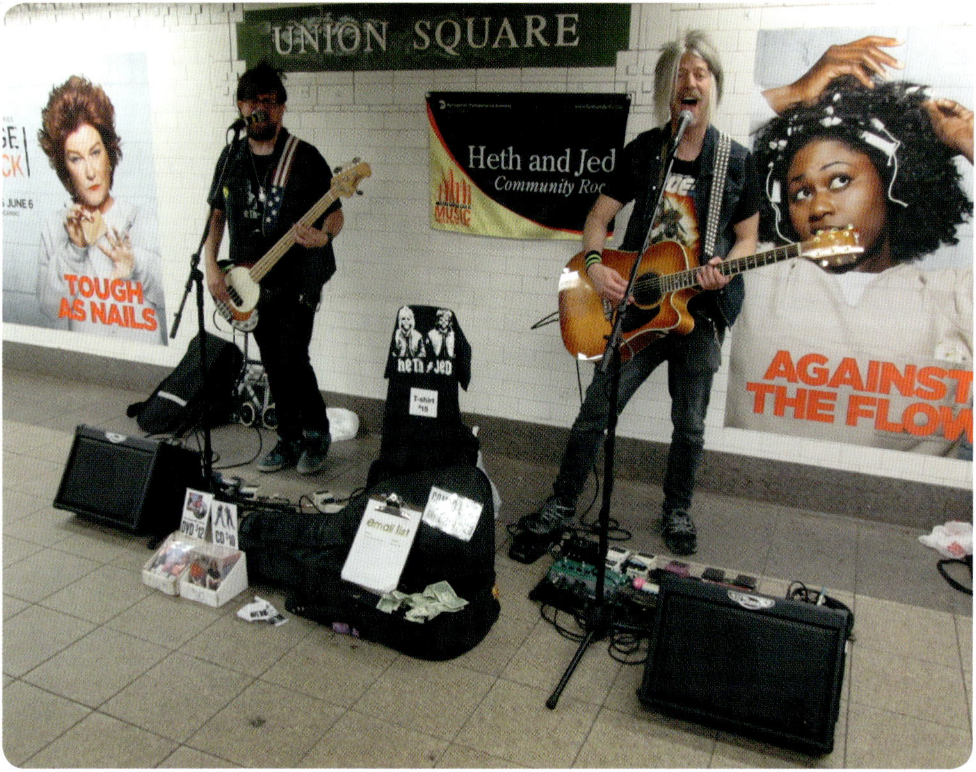

Heth and Jed, community rock.

Union Square Station

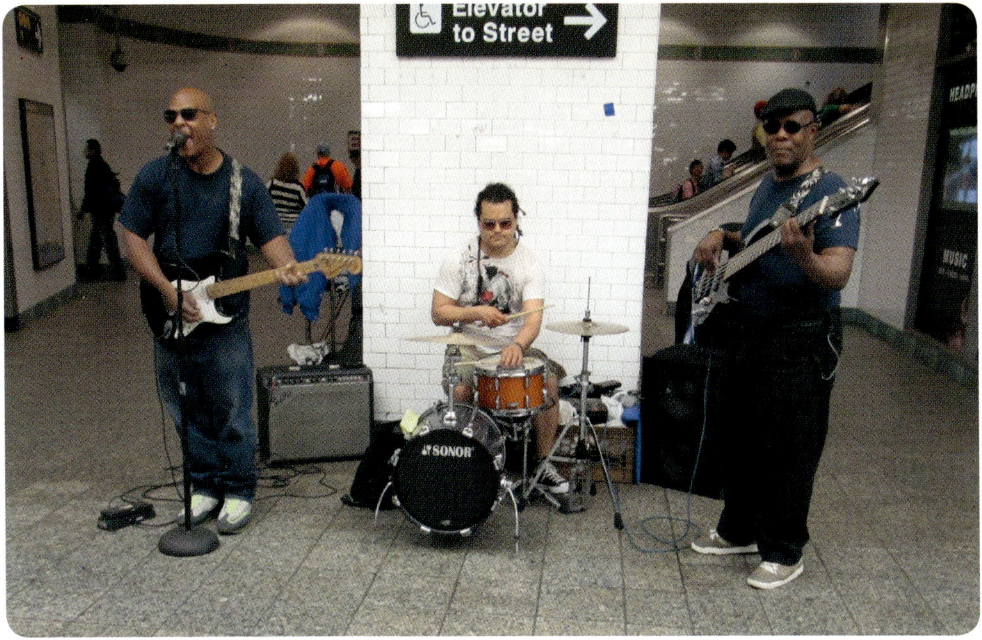

Swann Conaway, R&B, jazz singer, and guitarist.

Times Square Station

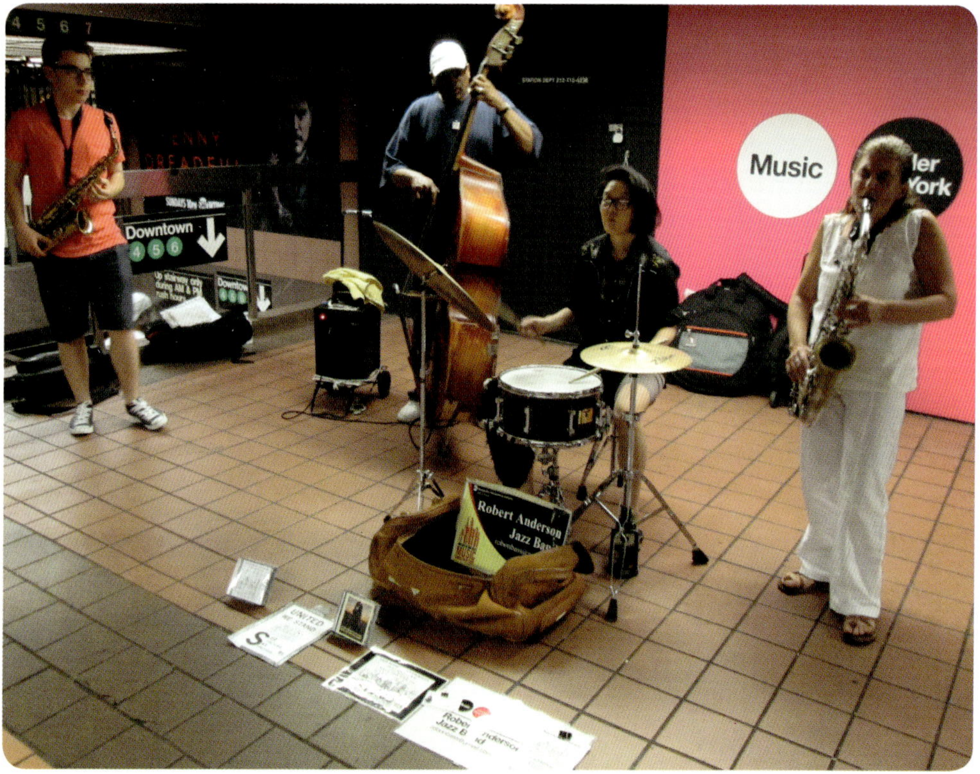

Robert Anderson Jazz Band.

Grand Central Station

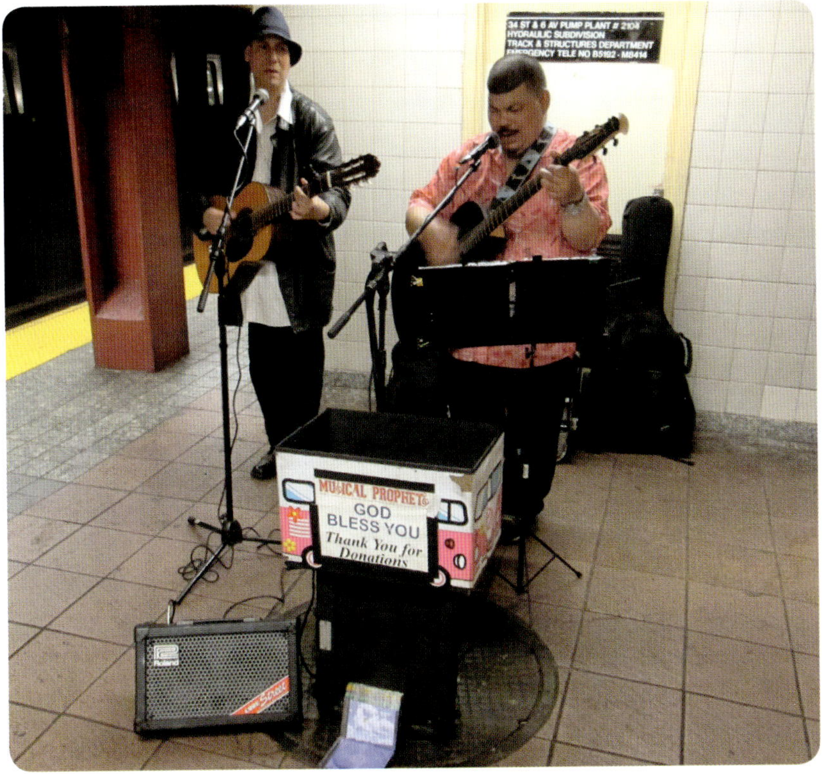

Musical Prophet.

34th Street Station Platform

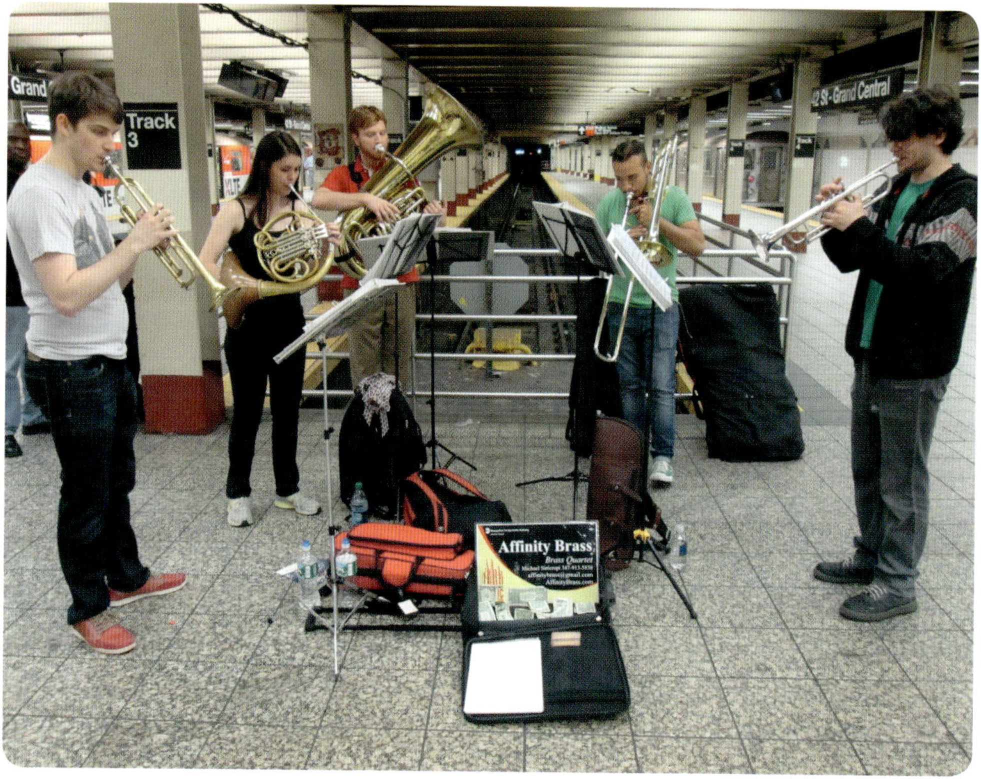

Affinity Brass.

Grand Central Station Shuttle Platform

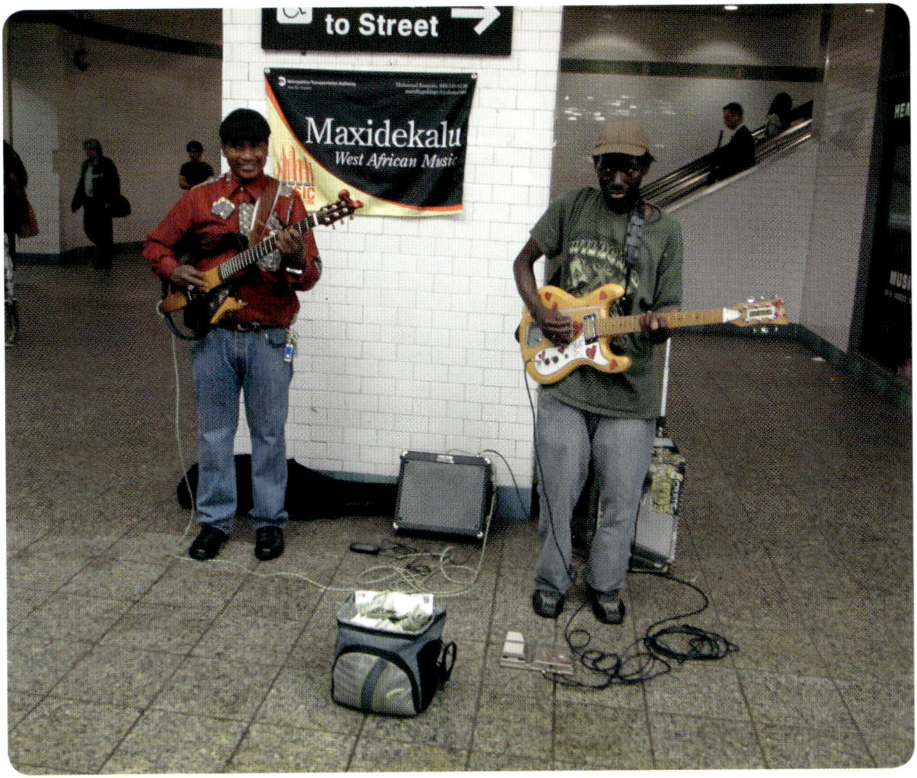

Maxidekalu, West African music.

Times Square Station

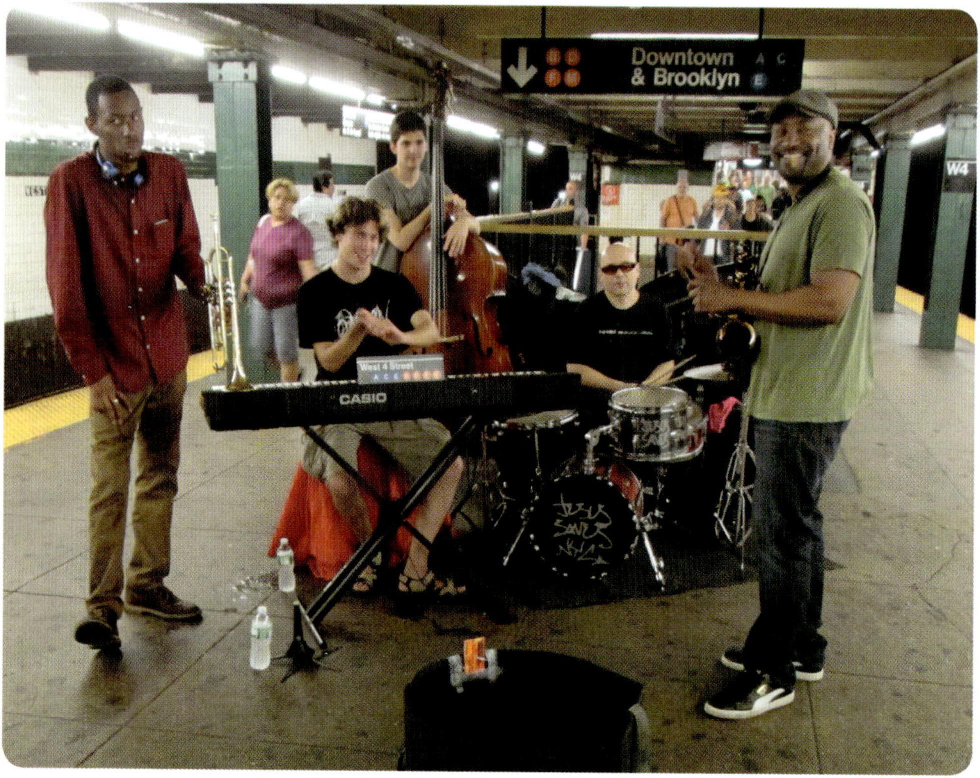

Uros Markovic, Gospel Jazz Music Ministry.

West 4th Street Station

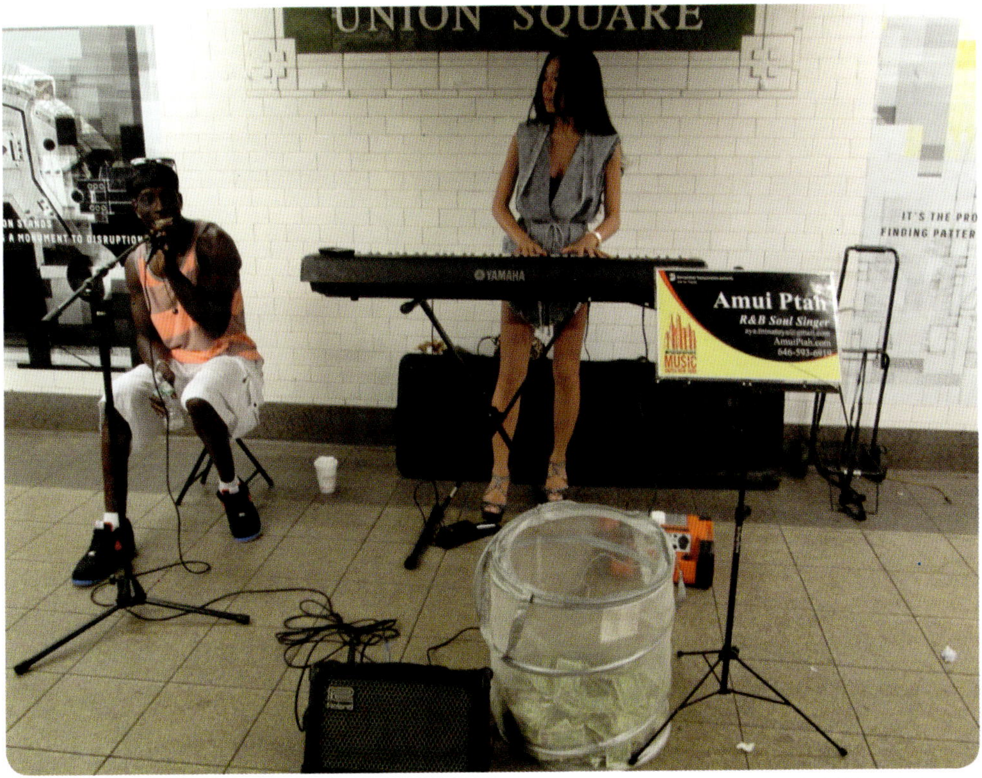

Amui Ptah, R&B soul singer.

Union Square Station

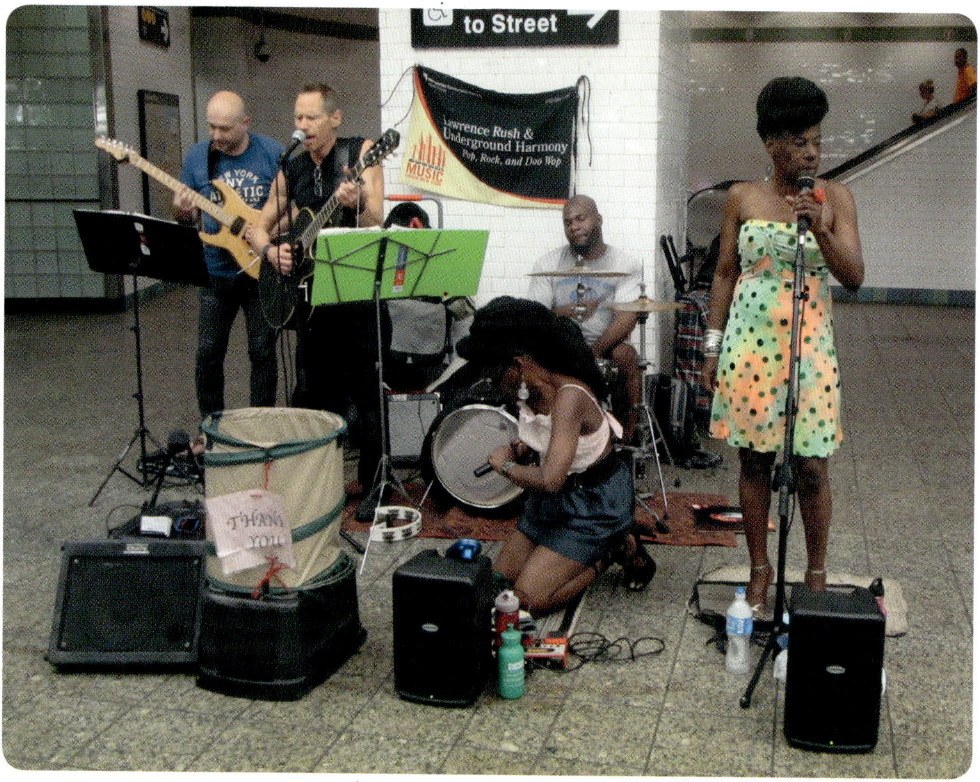

Lawrence Rush and the Underground Harmony, pop, rock, and doo wop.

Times Square Station

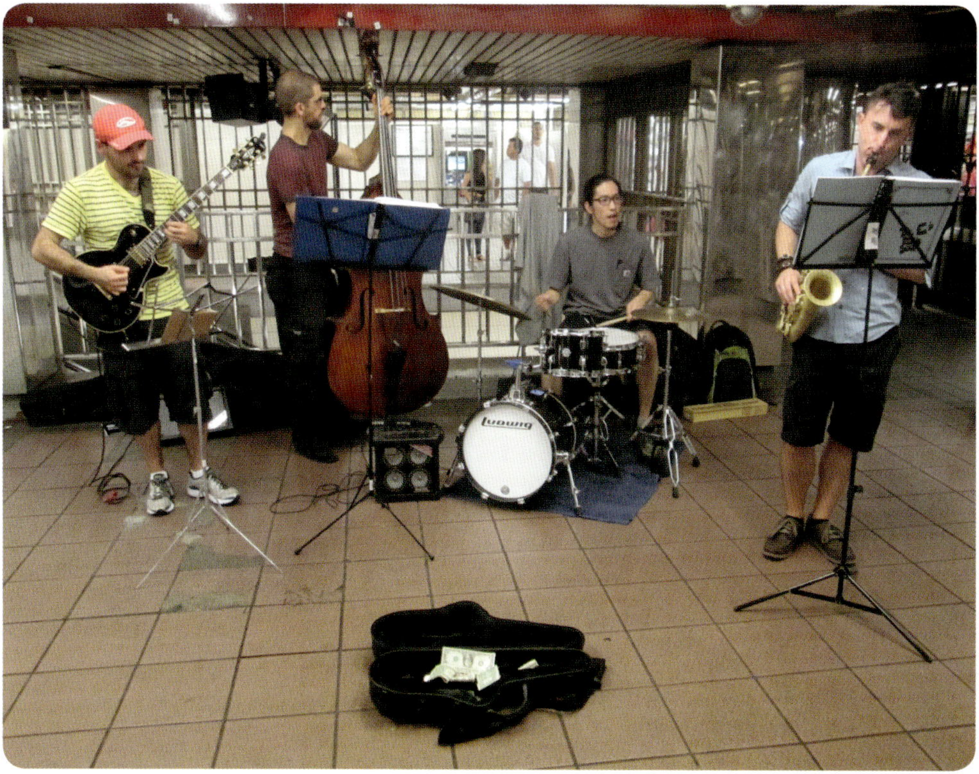

Quartet.

34th Street Station

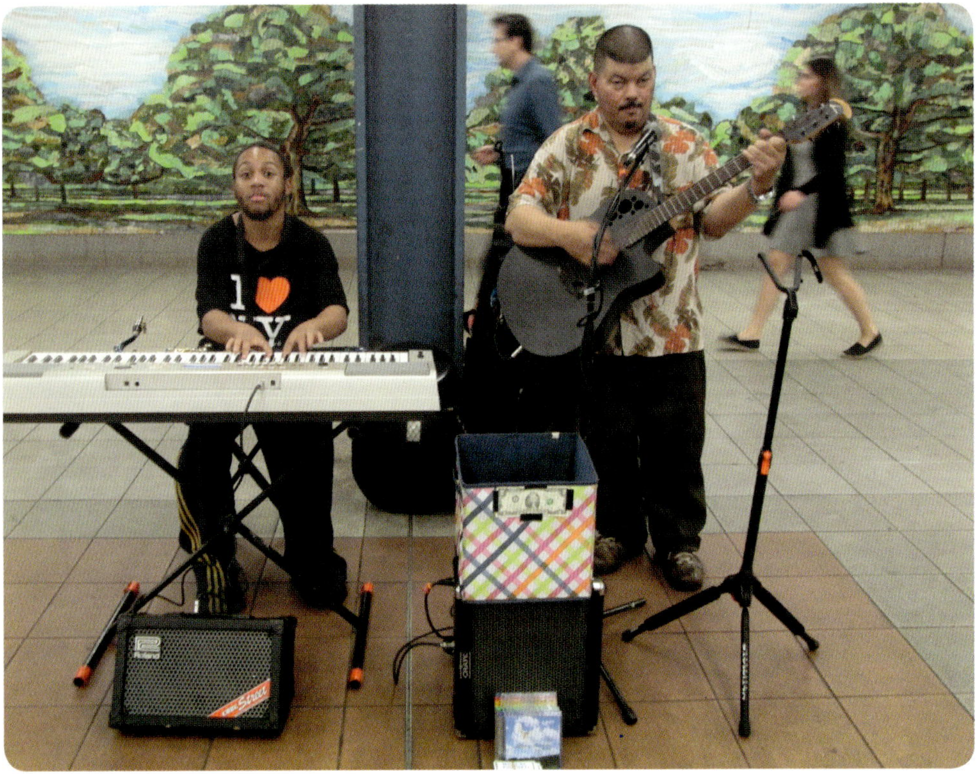

Musical Prophet.

Delancey Street Station

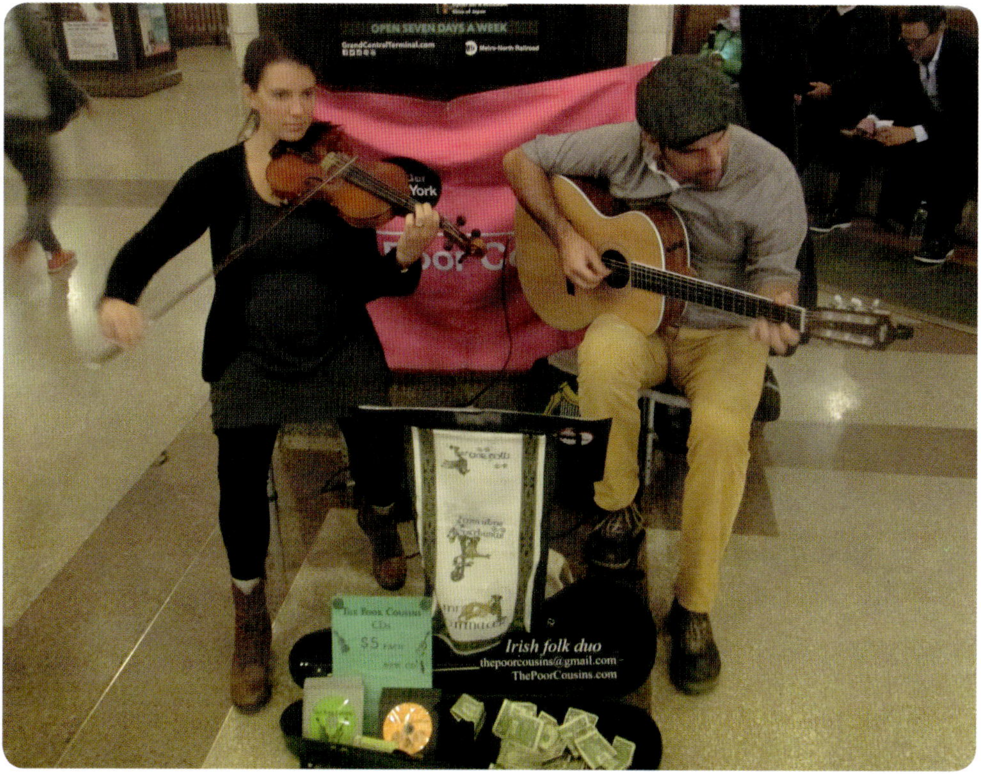

The Poor Cousins.

Grand Central Terminal

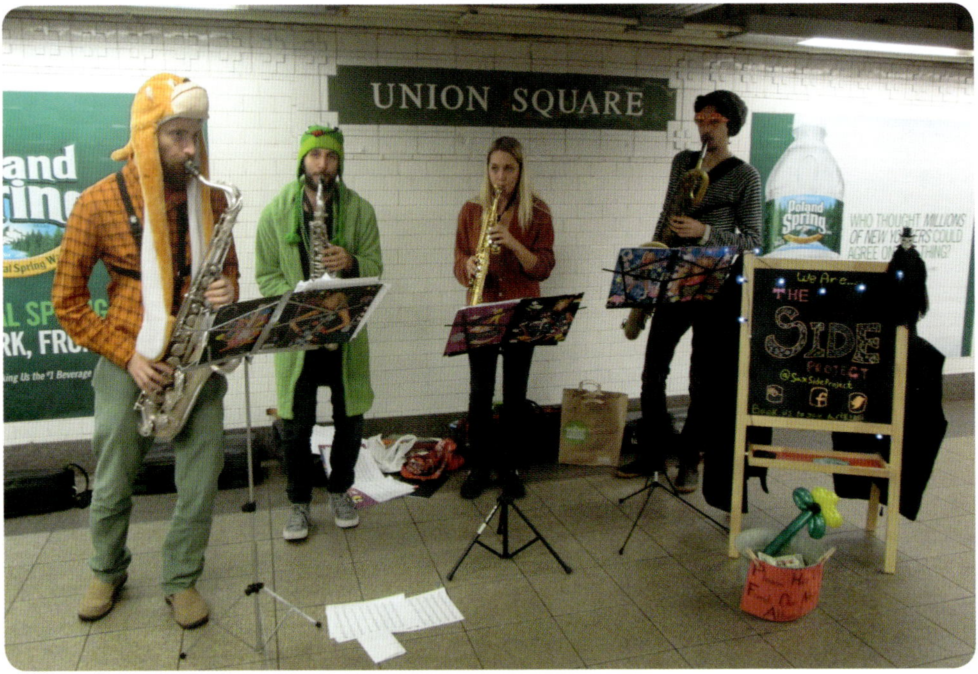

The Side Project, saxophone quartet.

Union Square Station

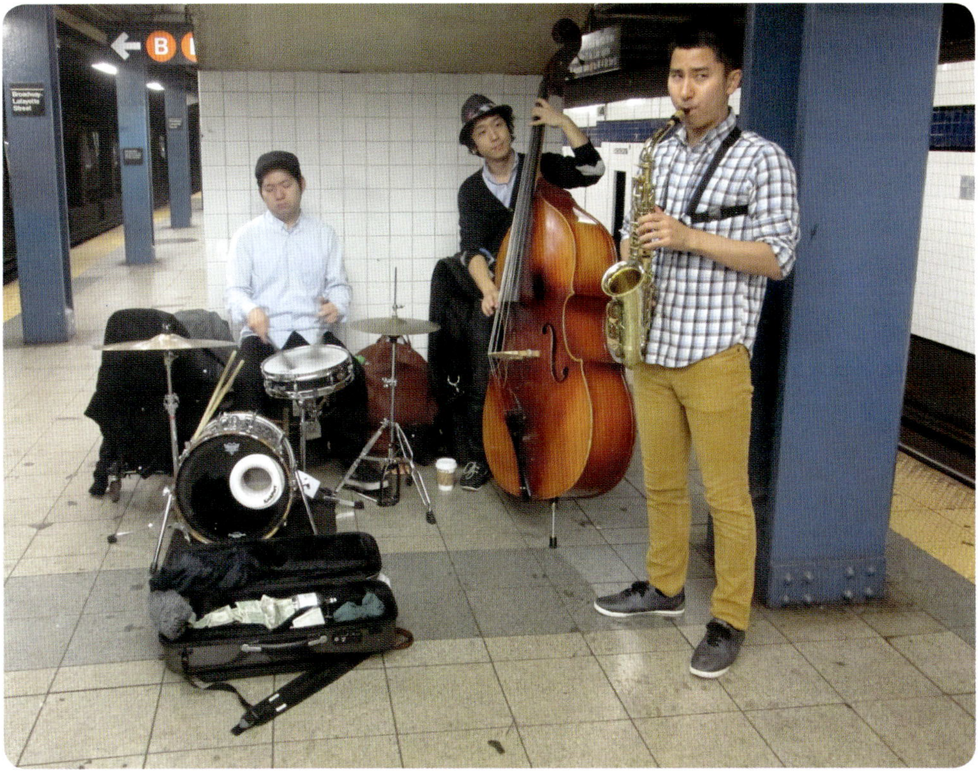

Trio.

Broadway-Lafayette Station

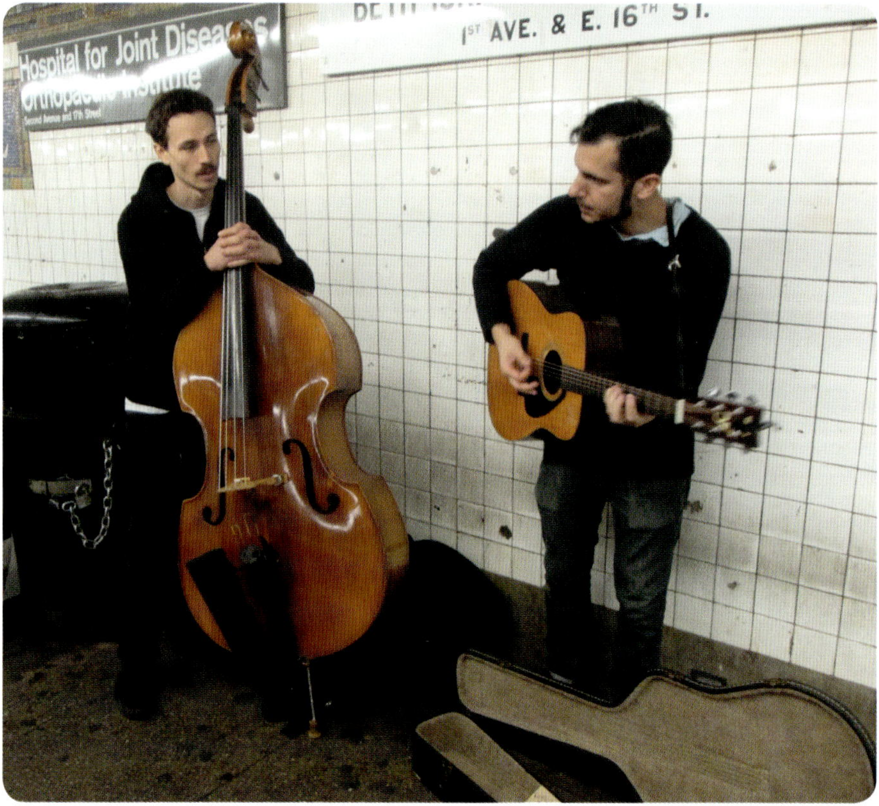

Crooner And Duke.

First Avenue Station

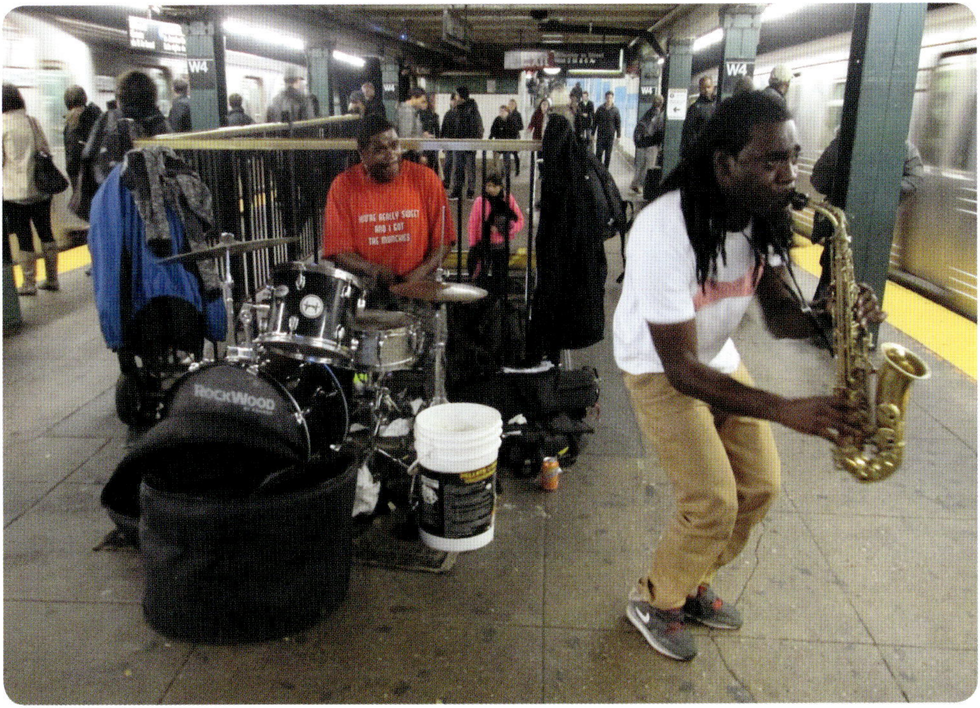

Roger, Blu Funk Orchestra, drummer and saxophonist.

West 4th Street Station

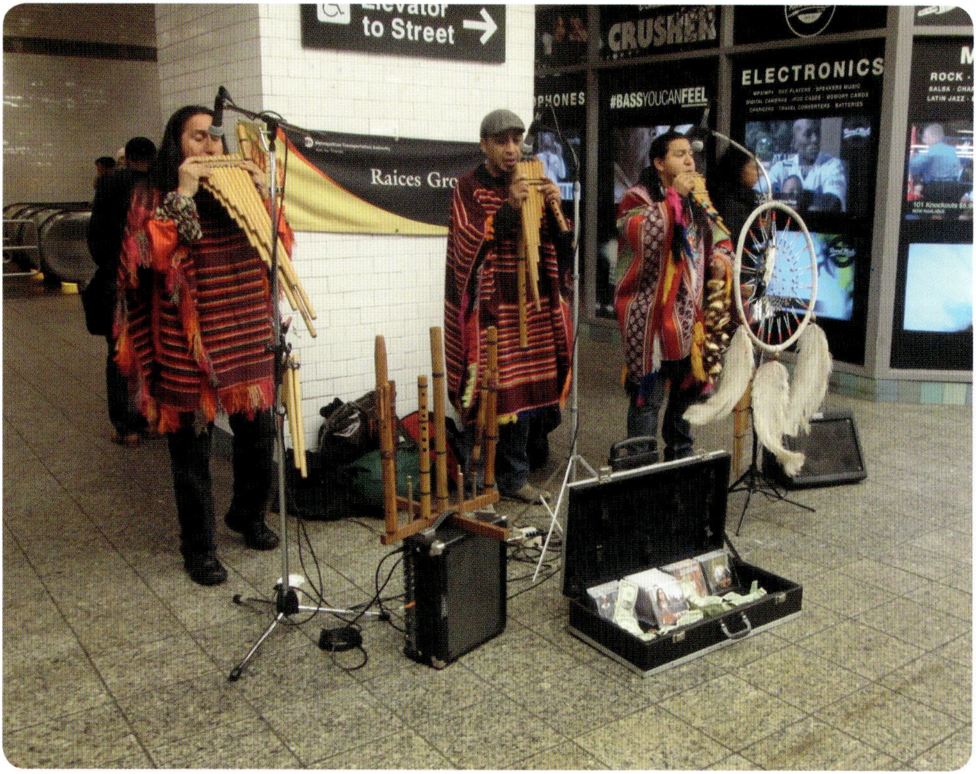

Raices Group.

Times Square Station

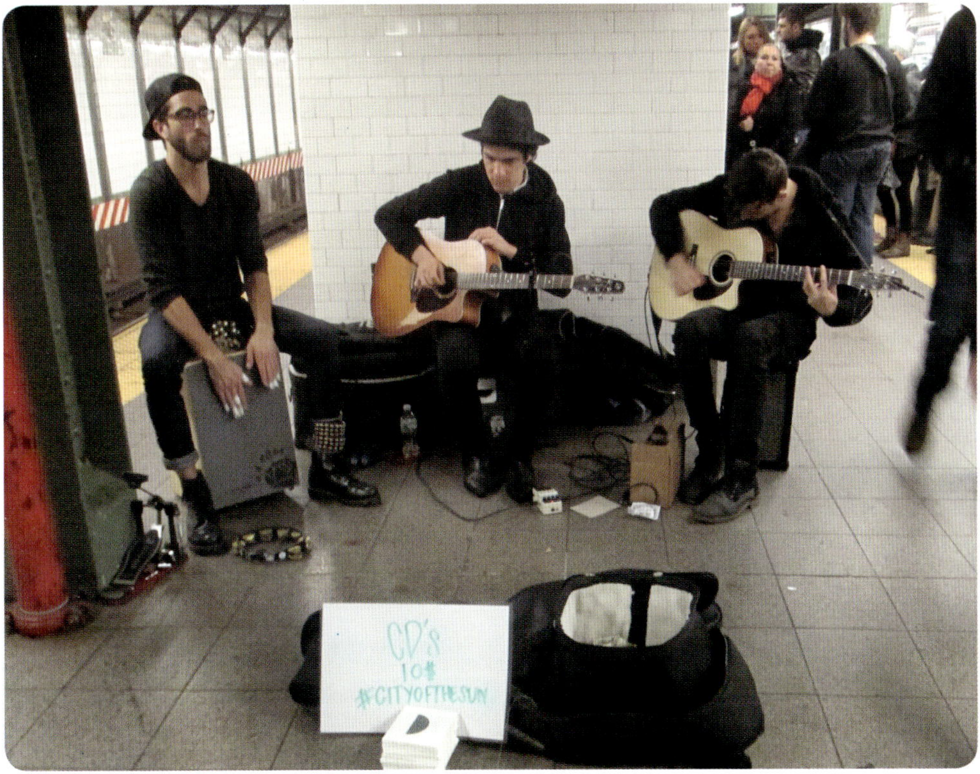

City of the Sun.

Union Square Station

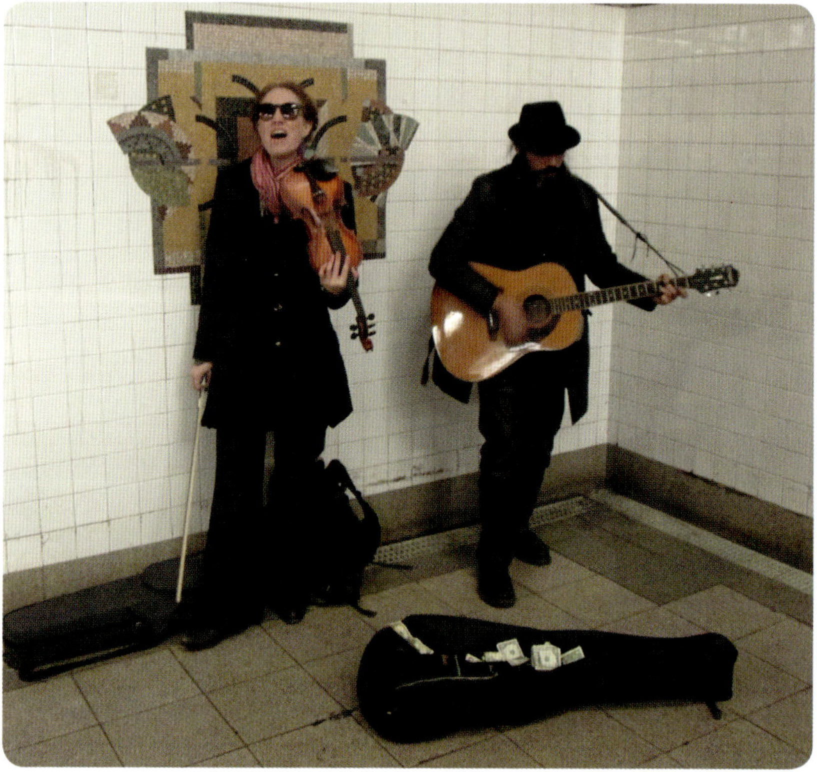

Violin and folk guitar.

96th Street and Lexington Avenue Station

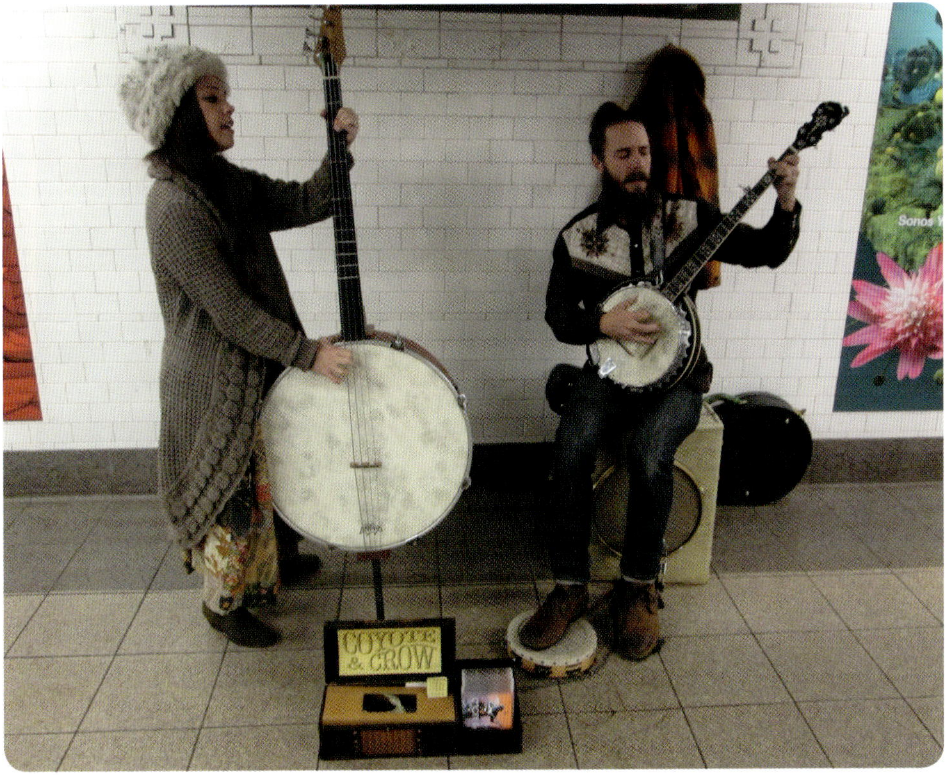

Coyote & Crow.

Union Square Station

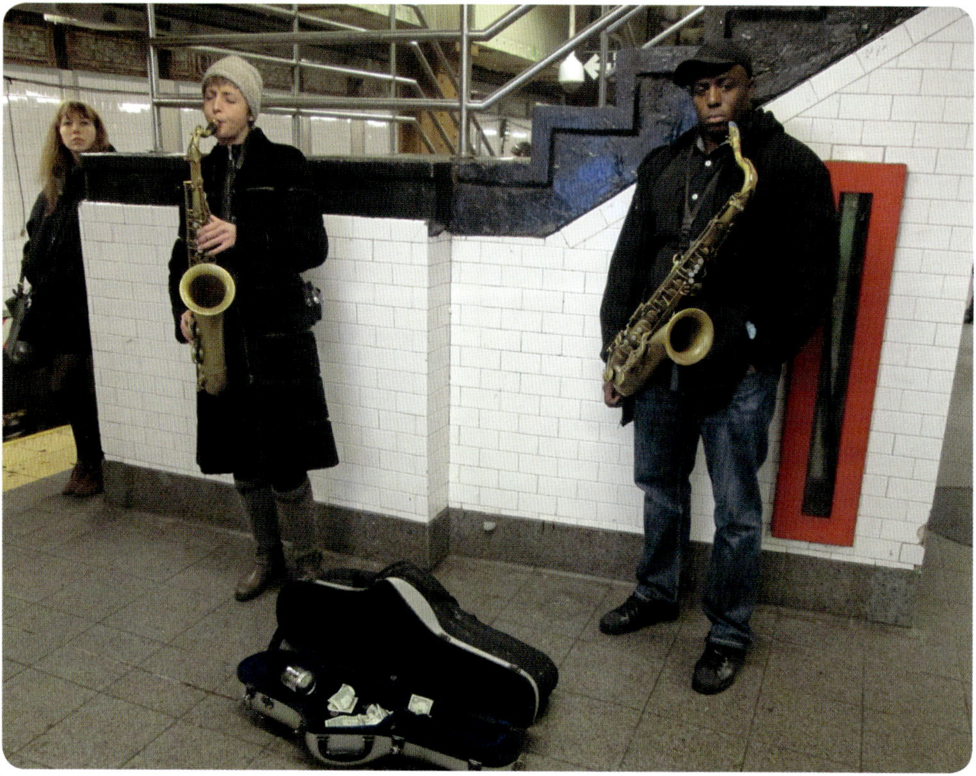

Two saxophonists.

Union Square Station - L Train Platform

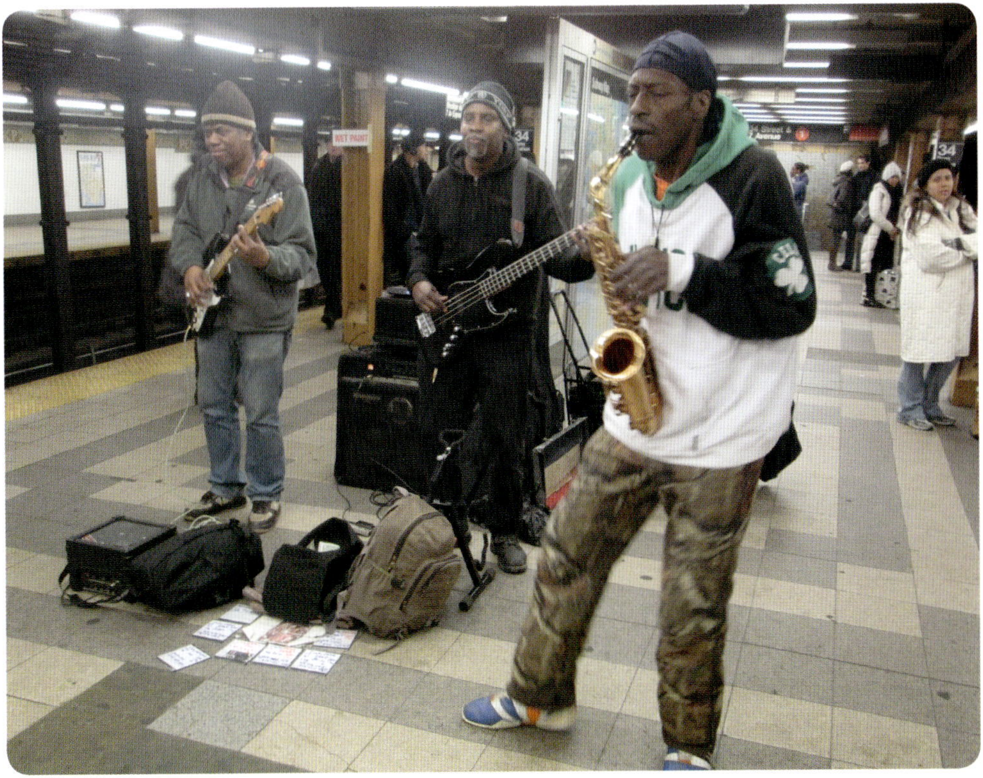

Saxophonist and two guitar players.

34th Street - Penn Station

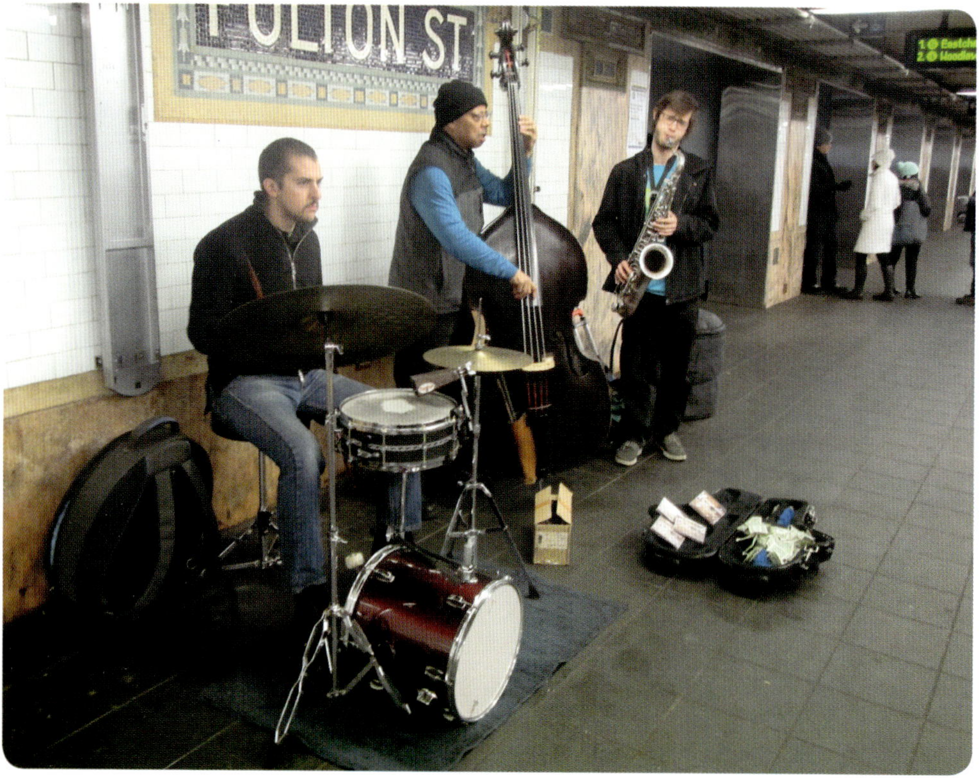

Fernando Garcia Jazz Trio.

Fulton Street Station

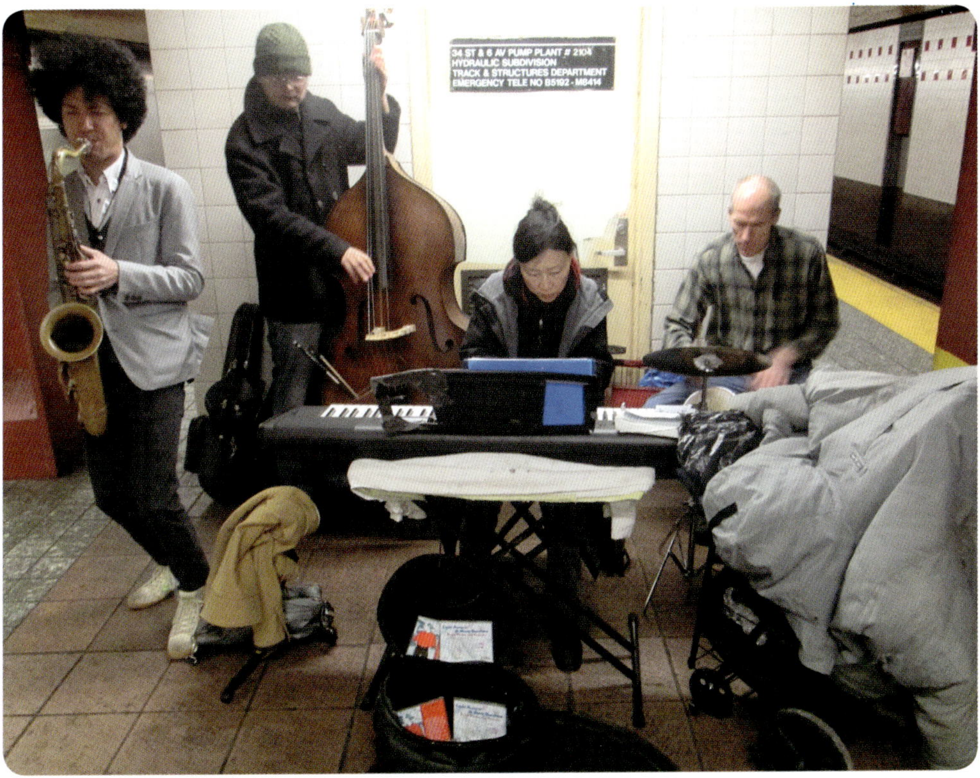

David Picton and Friends.

34th Street Station

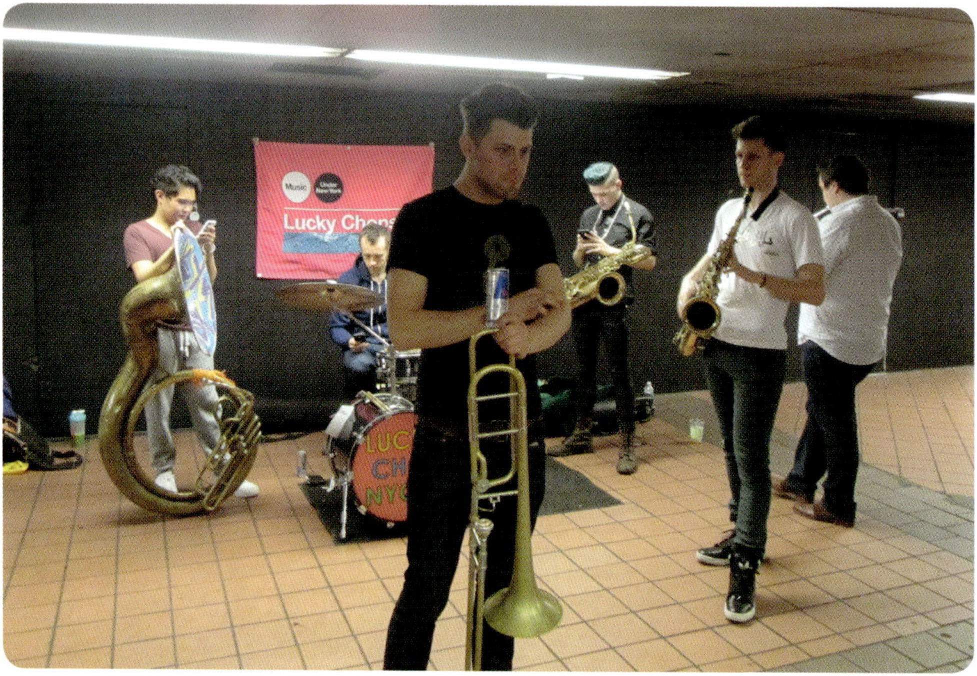

Lucky Chops.

Grand Central Station

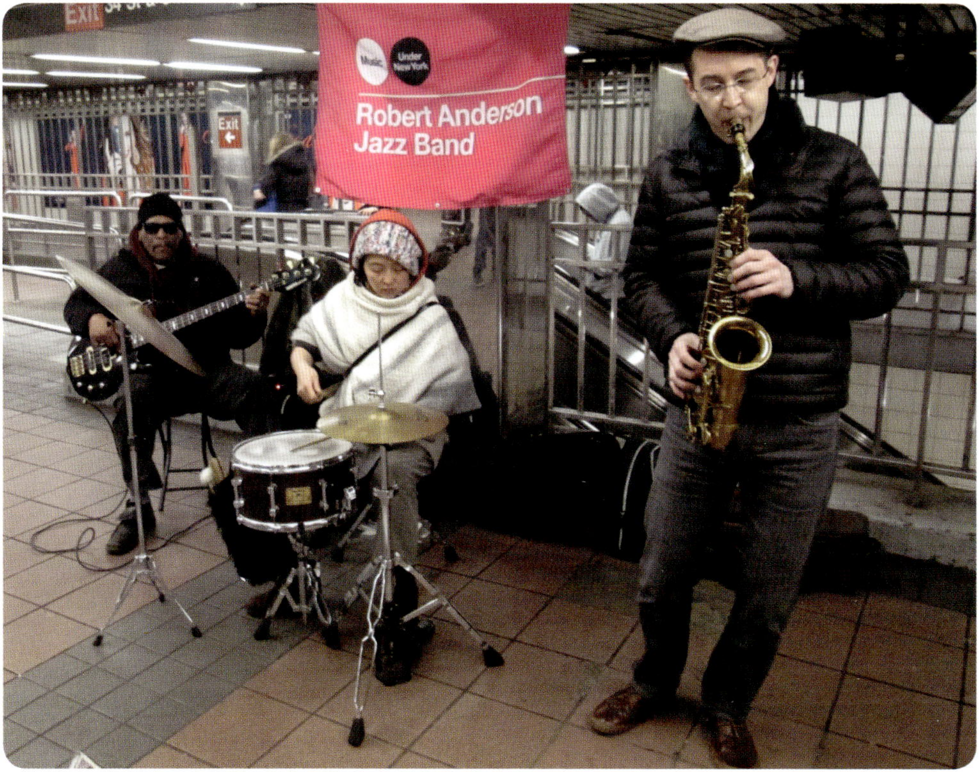

Robert Anderson Jazz Band.

34th Street Station

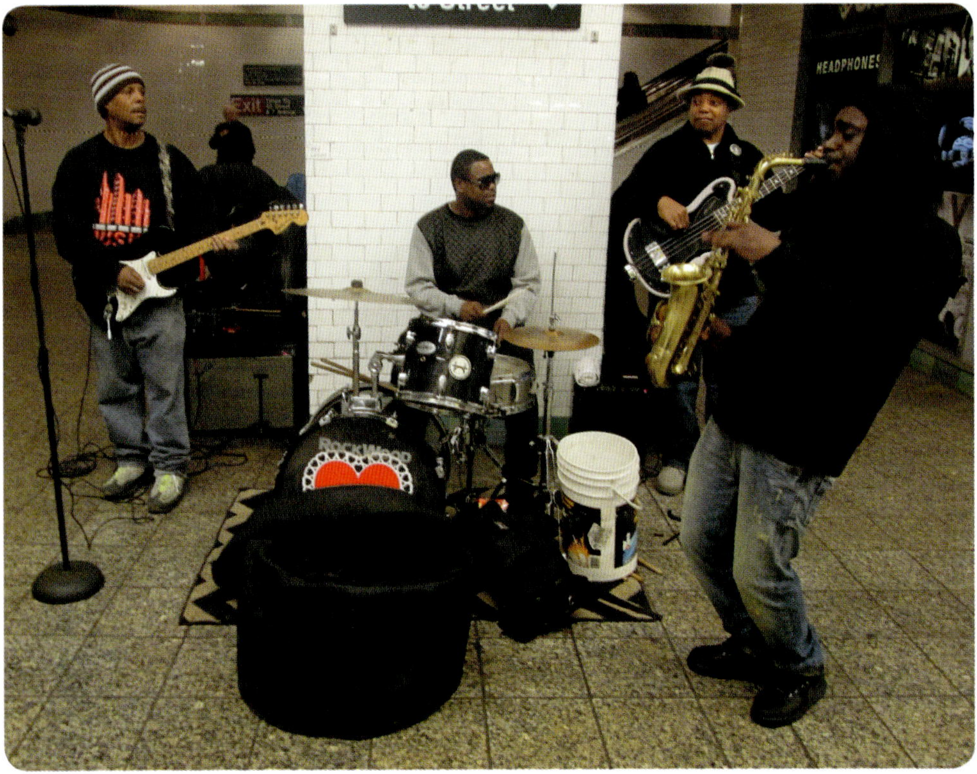

Band at 42nd Street.

Times Square Station

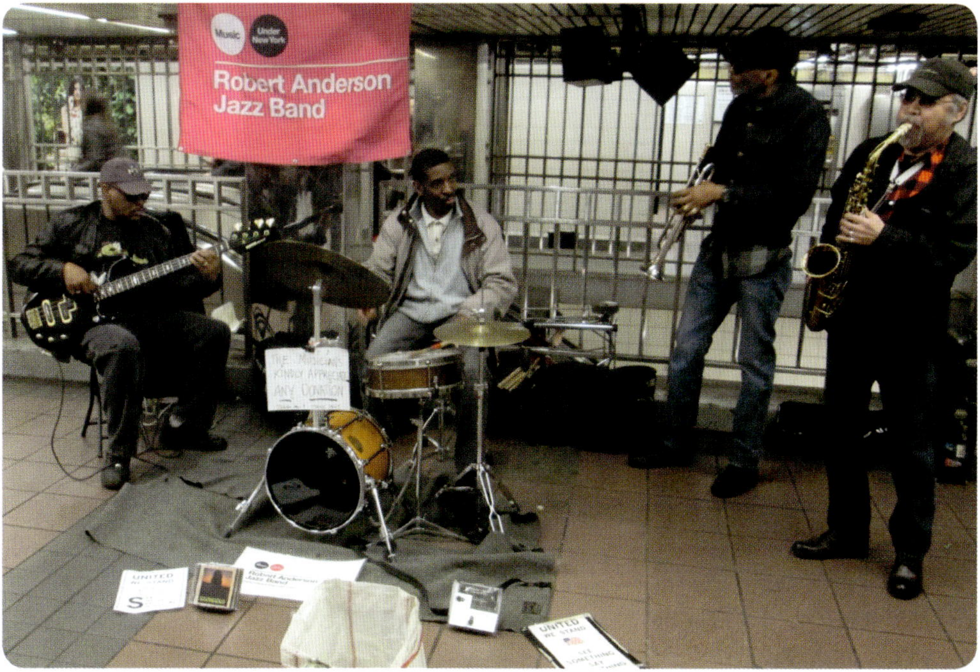

Robert Andersen Jazz Band.

34th Street - Penn Station

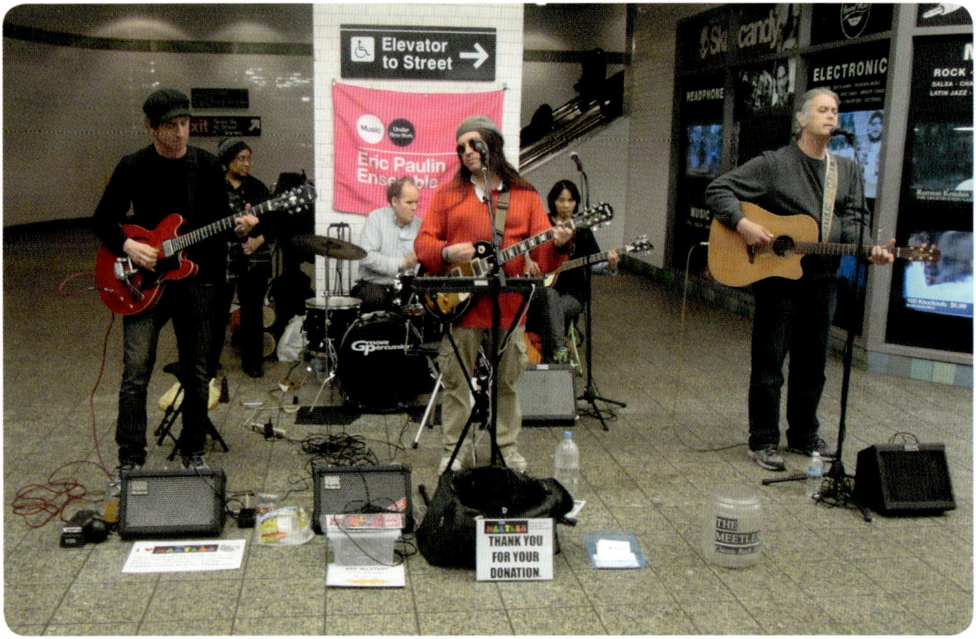

Eric Paulin Ensemble.

Times Square Station

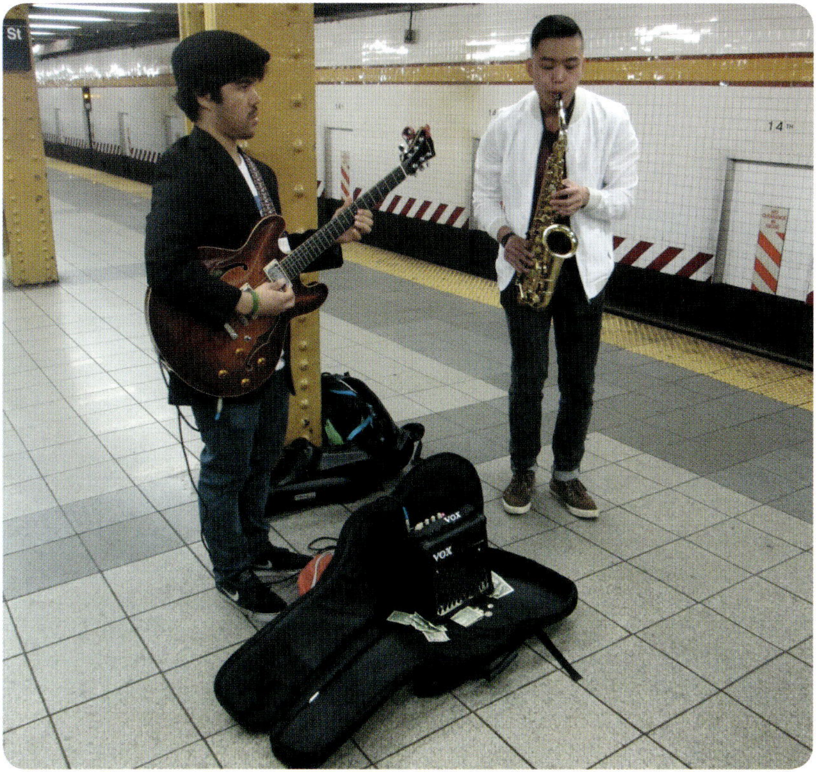

Members of the QNA Band.

14th Street - 8th Avenue Station

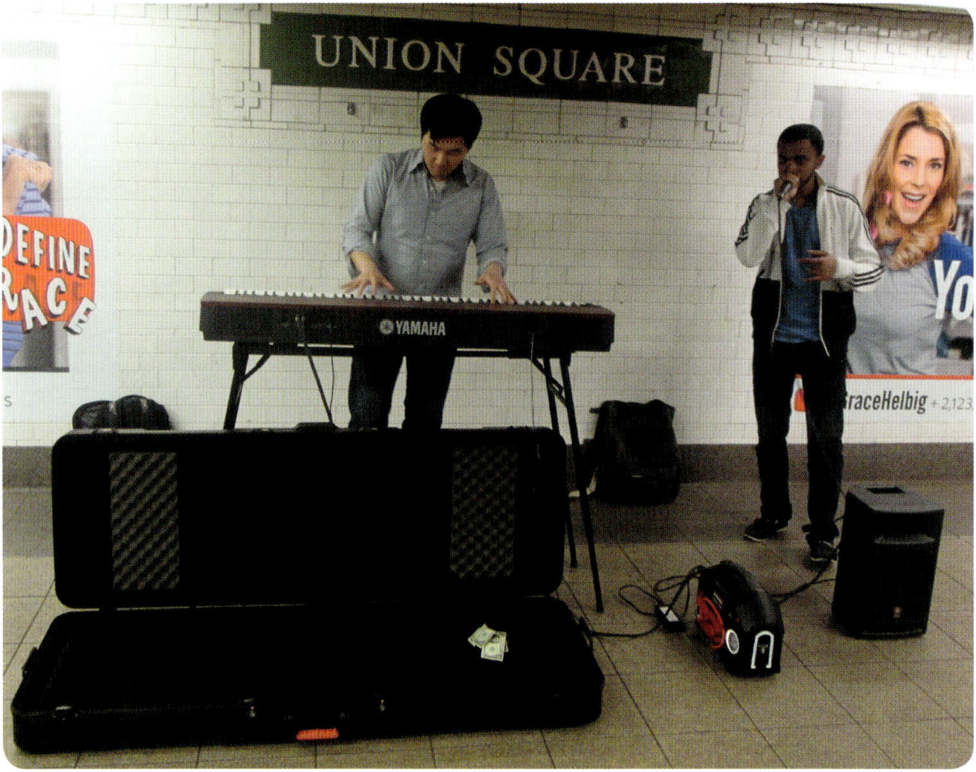

Electric organ player and rapper.

Union Square Station

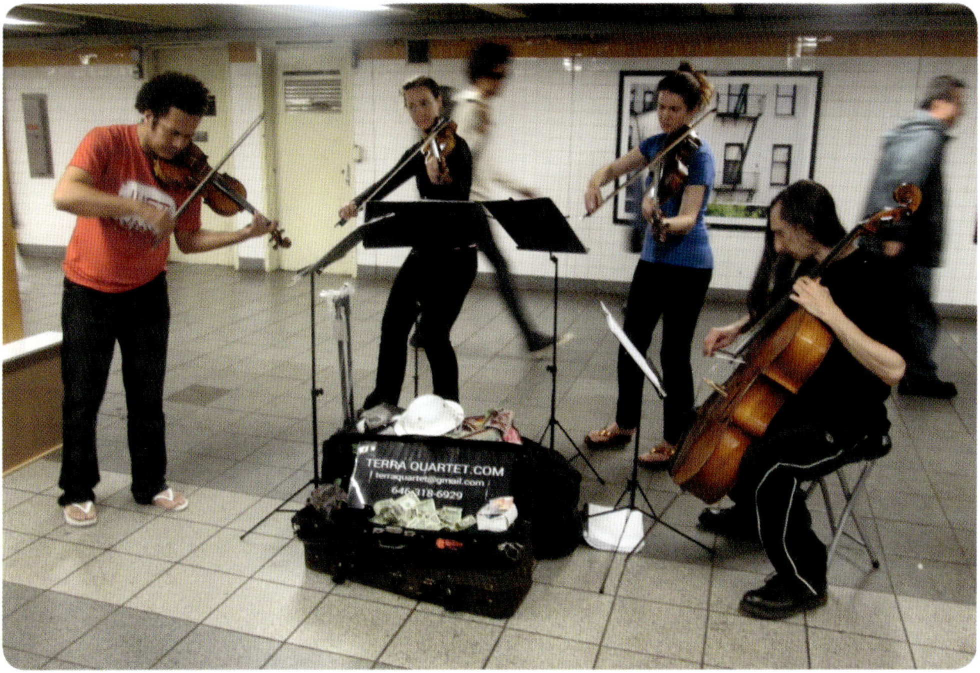

Terra Quartet.

14th Street Station - 8th Avenue

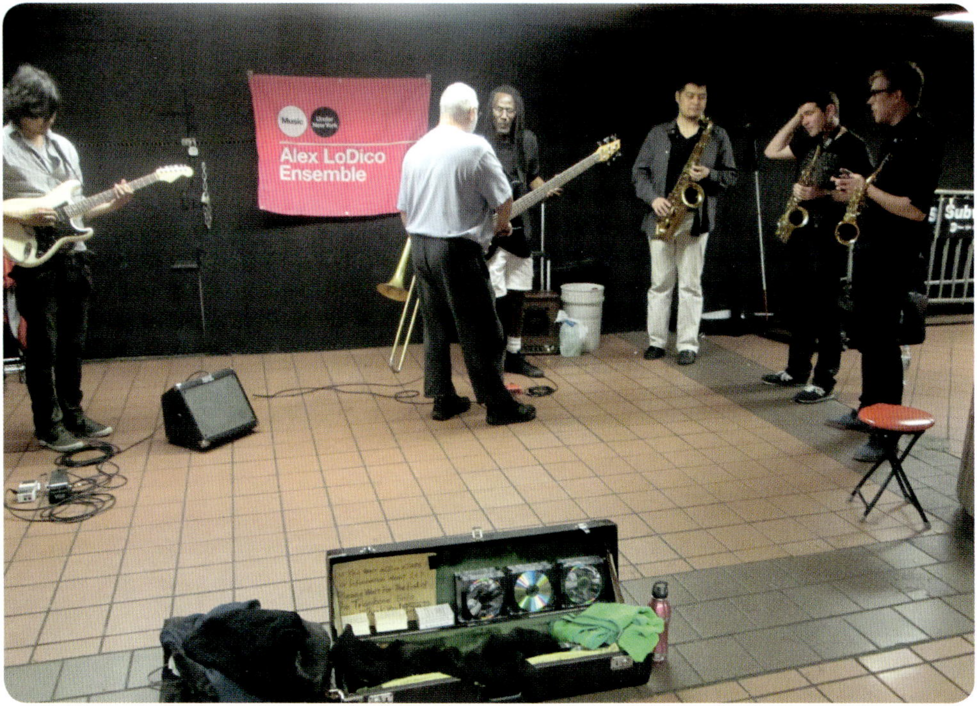

Alex LoDico Ensemble.

Grand Central Station

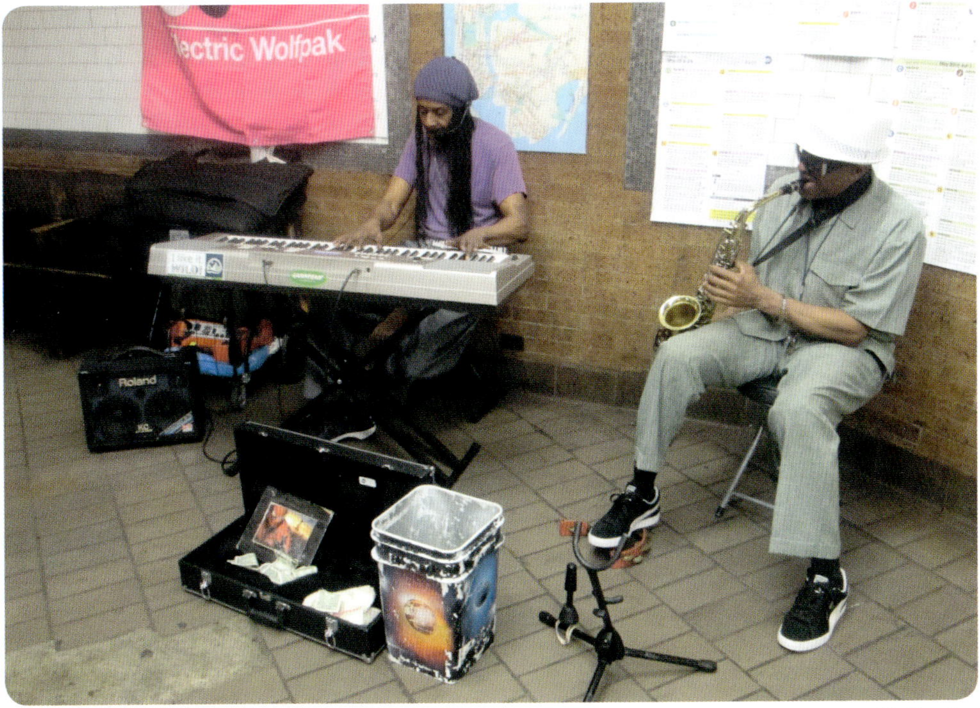

Electric Wolfpack.

Astor Place Station

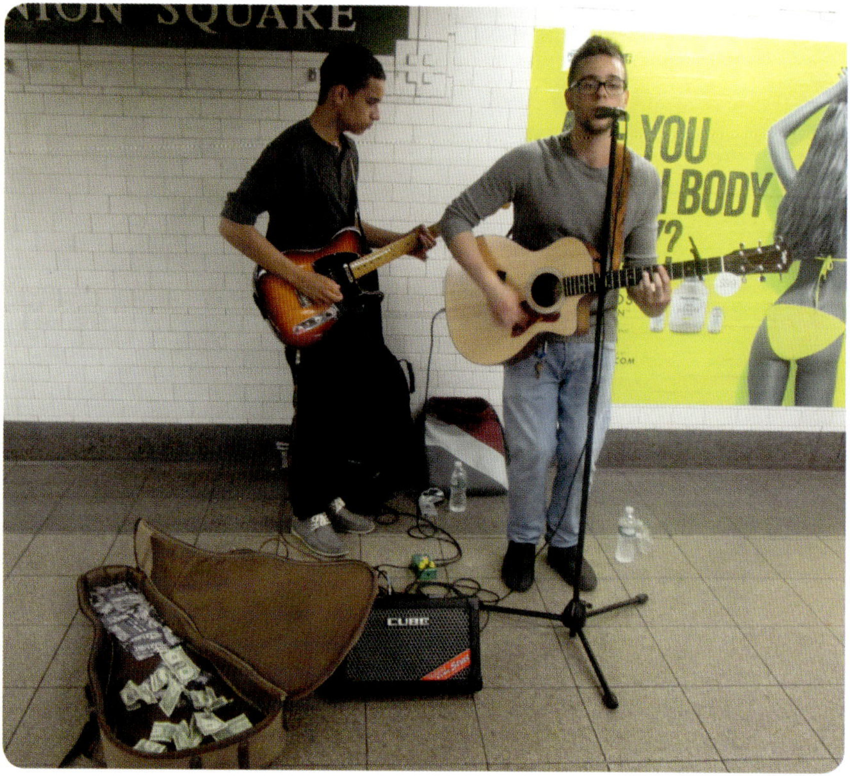

The Art of BKC.

Union Square Station

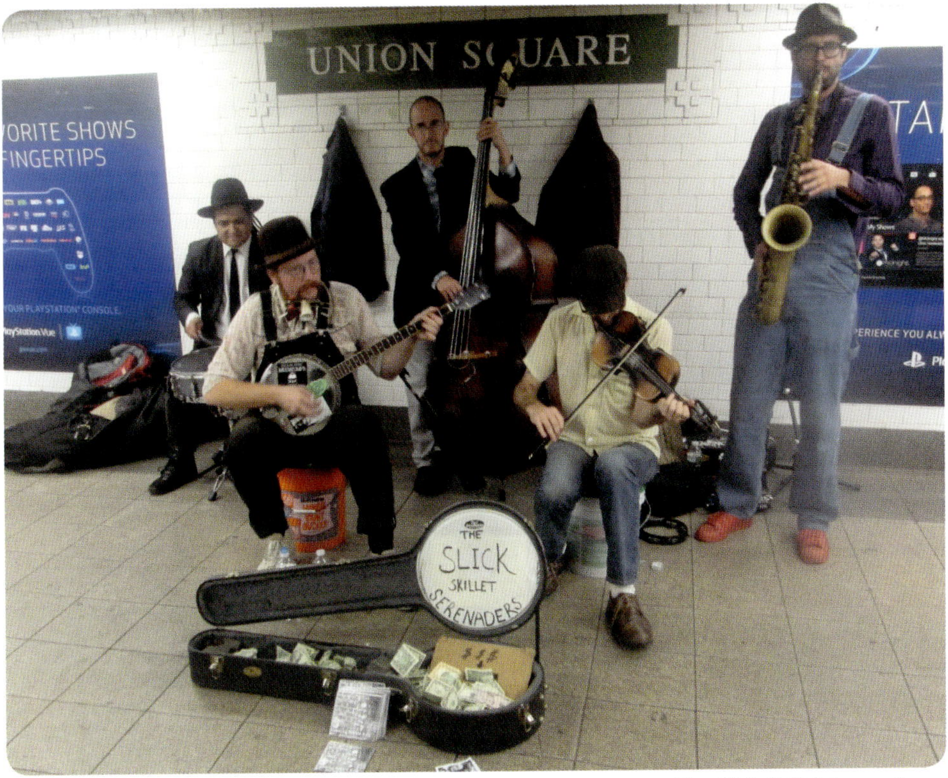

The Slick Skillet Serenaders.

Union Square Station

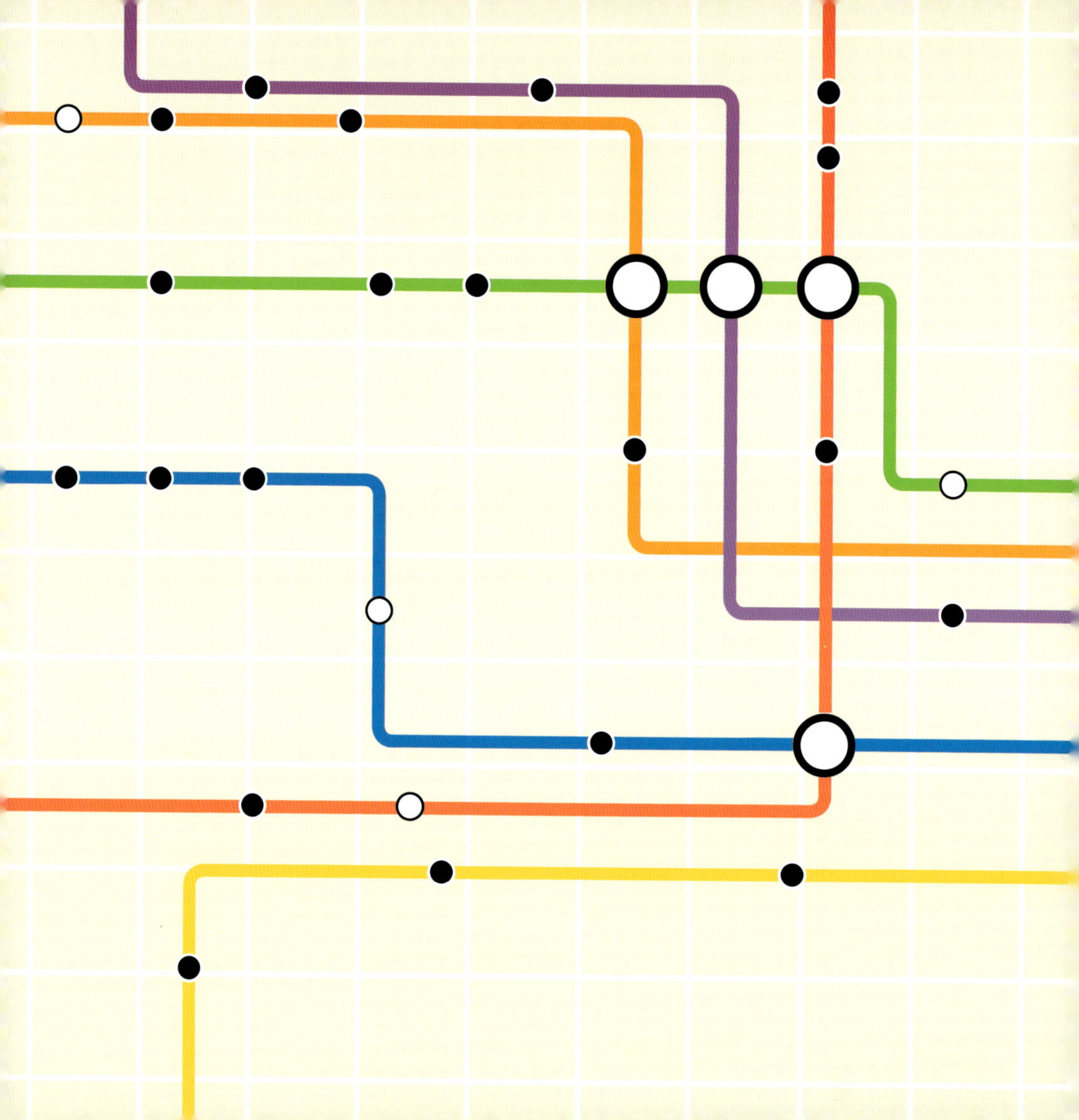

Chapter 7

Singing Groups and Singers

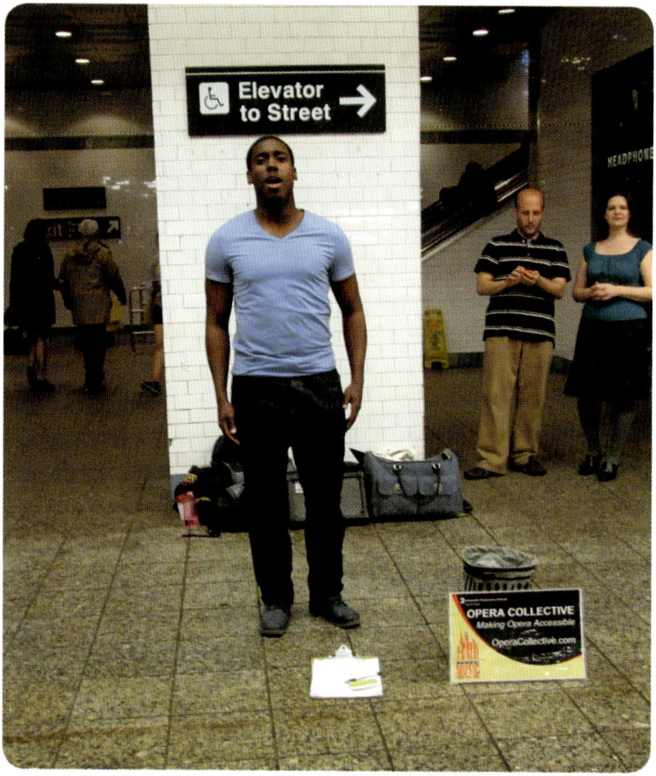

Opera Collective singer.

Times Square Station

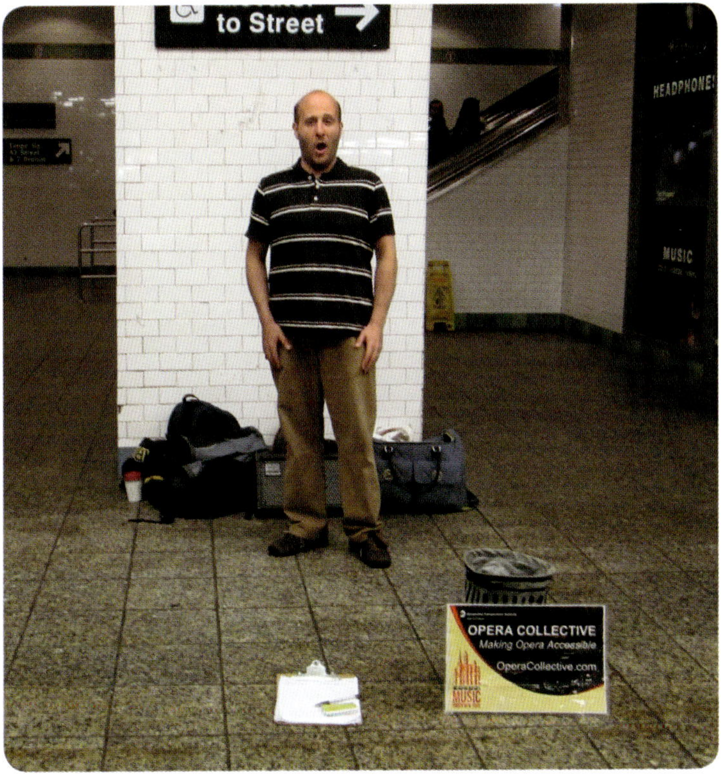

Opera Collective singer.

Grand Central Station Shuttle Walkway

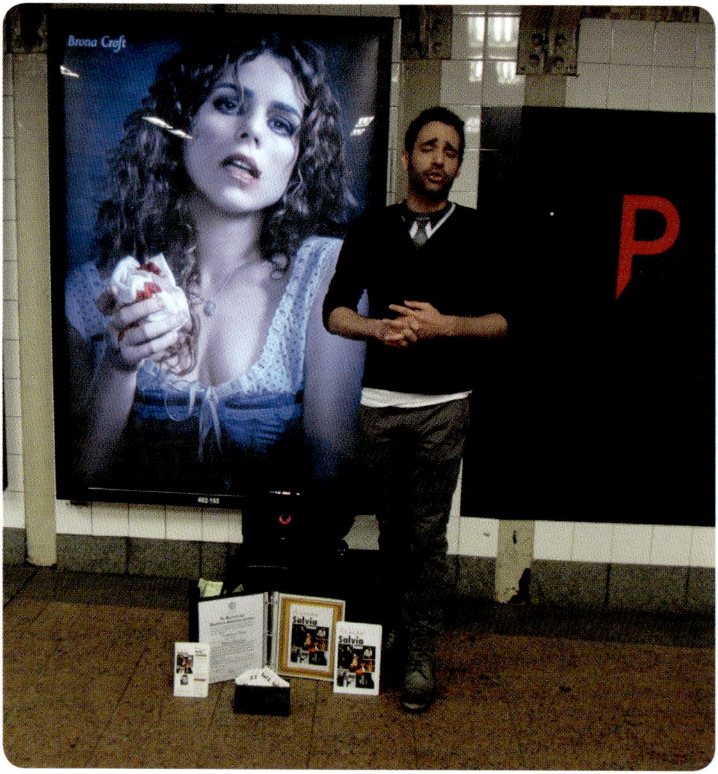

Alejandro Salvia, tenor.

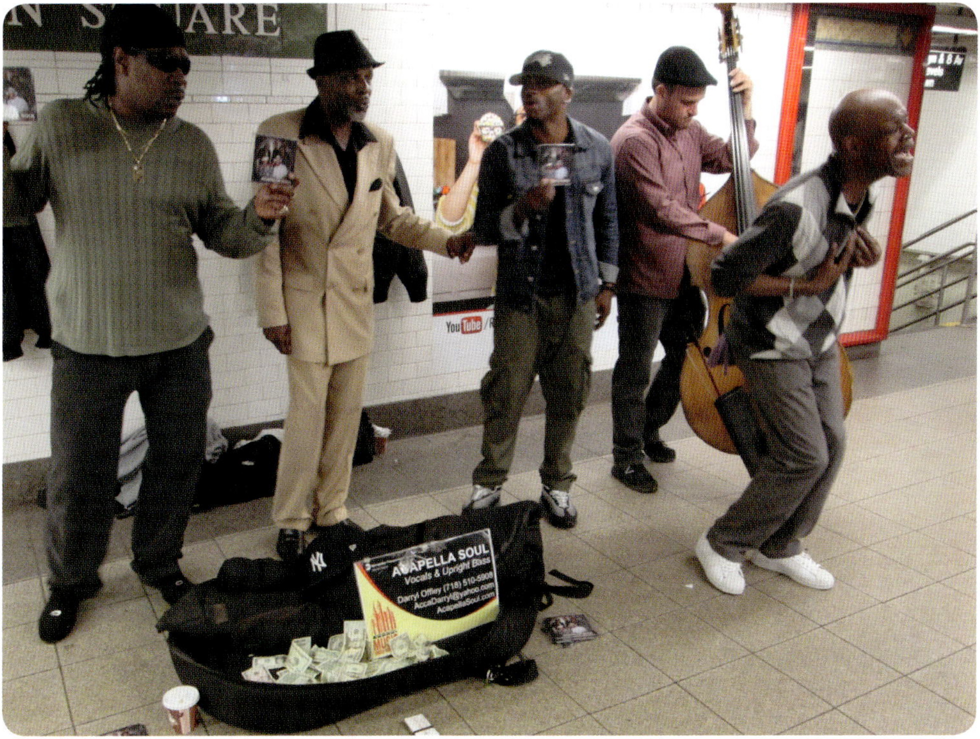

Acapella Soul, vocals and upright bass.

Union Square Station

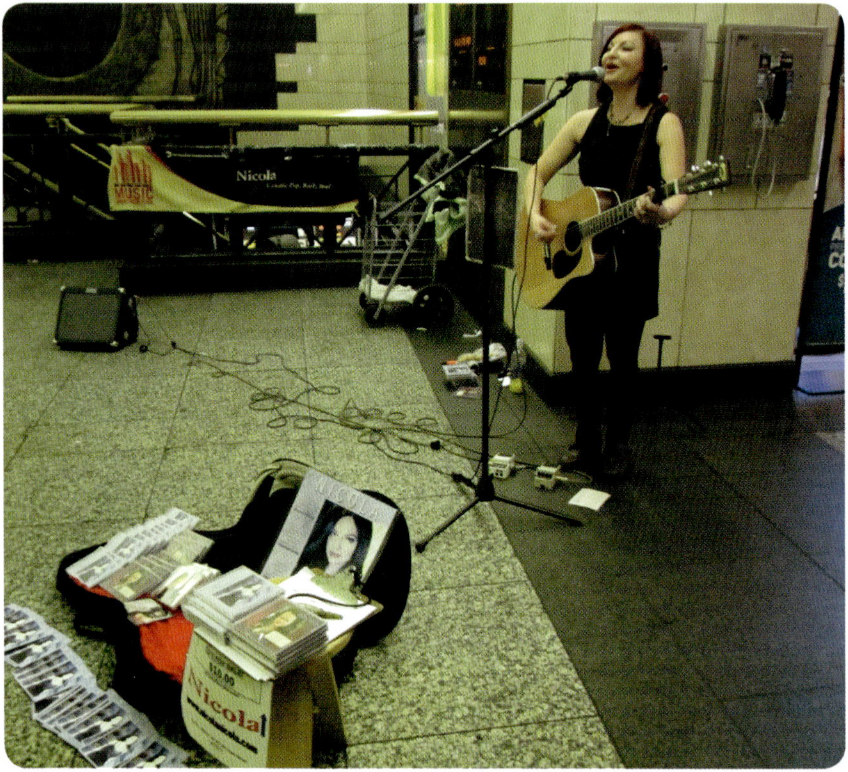

Nicola, acoustic pop, rock, and soul.

34th Street - Penn Station

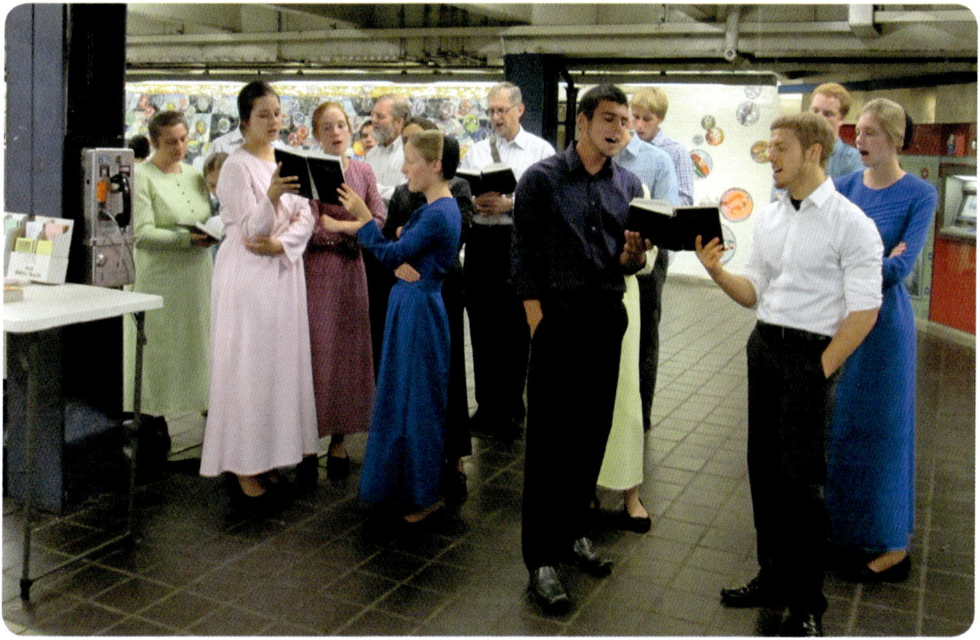

Chorus.

42nd Street - Port Authority Station

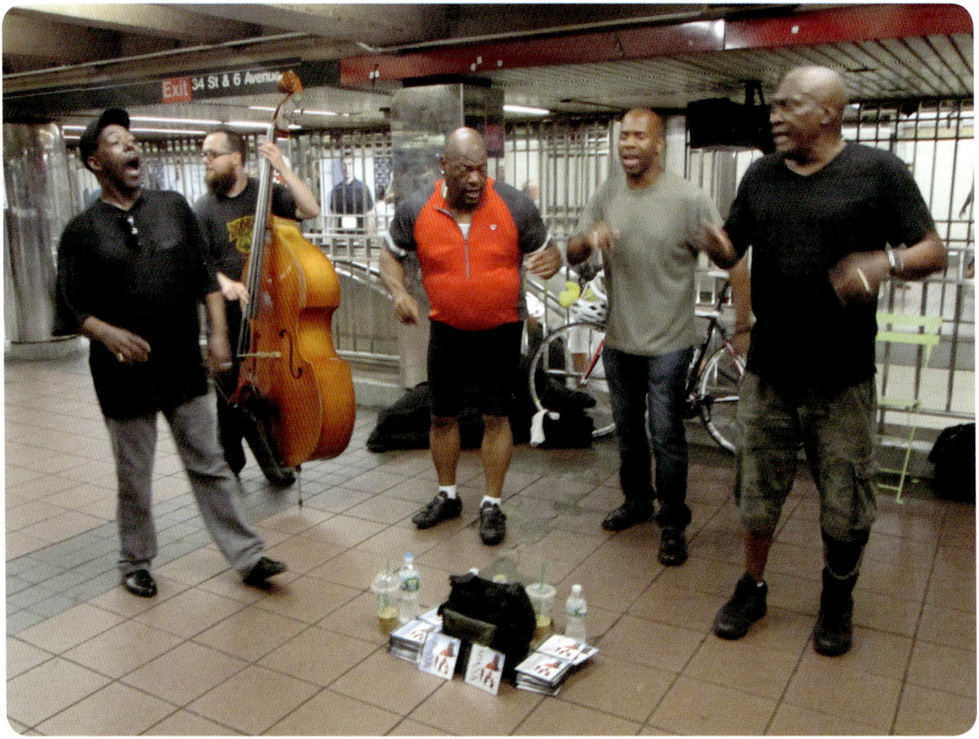

Singing group.

34th Street Station & 6th Avenue

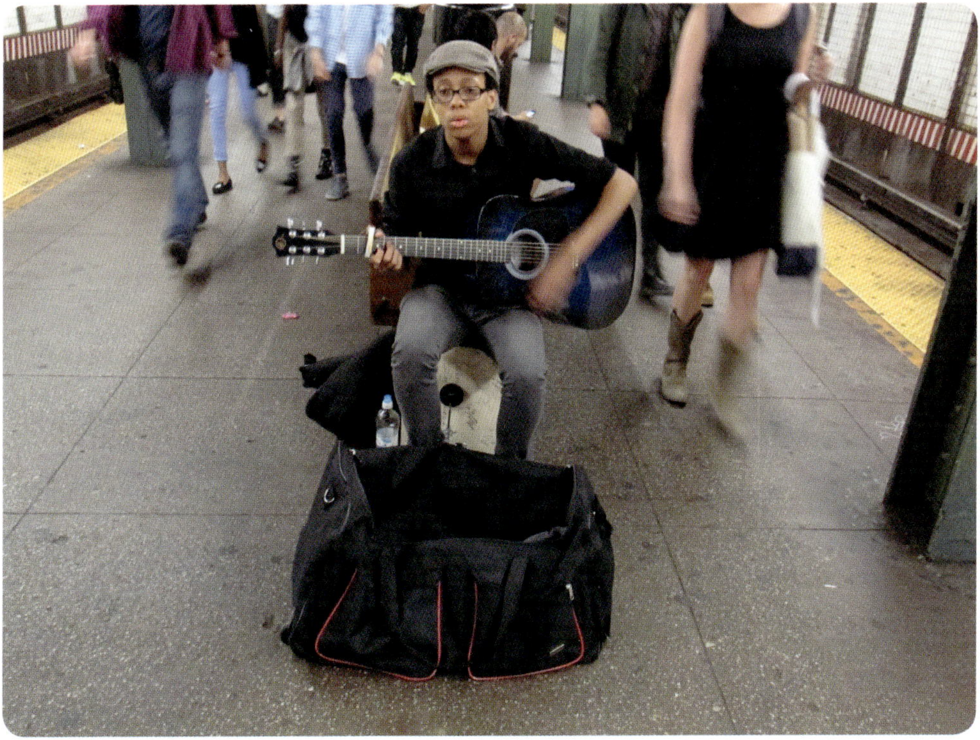

Folk guitar singer.

Bedford Avenue Station

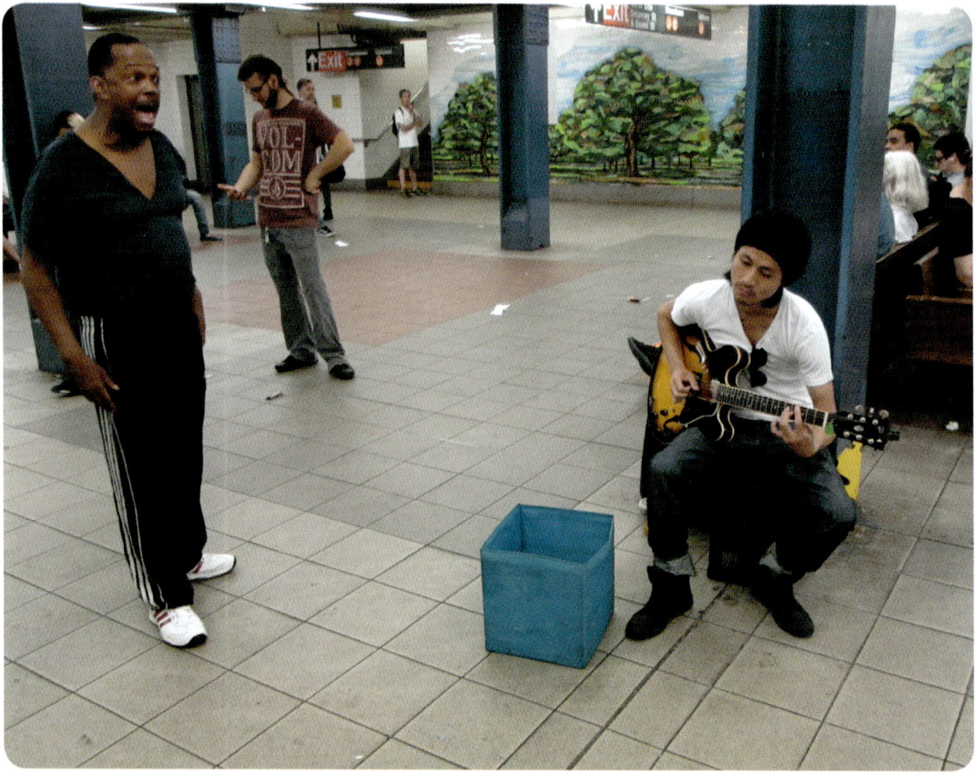

Majestic K. Funk.

Delancey Street

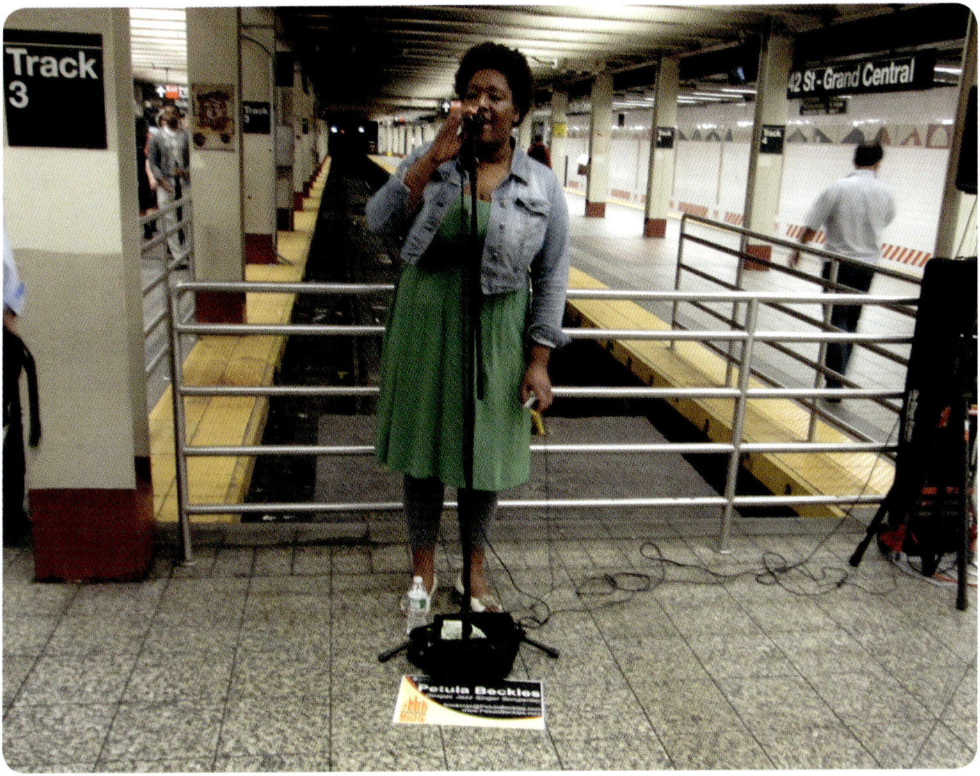

Petula Beckles, gospel and jazz singer.

Grand Central Station Shuttle Platform

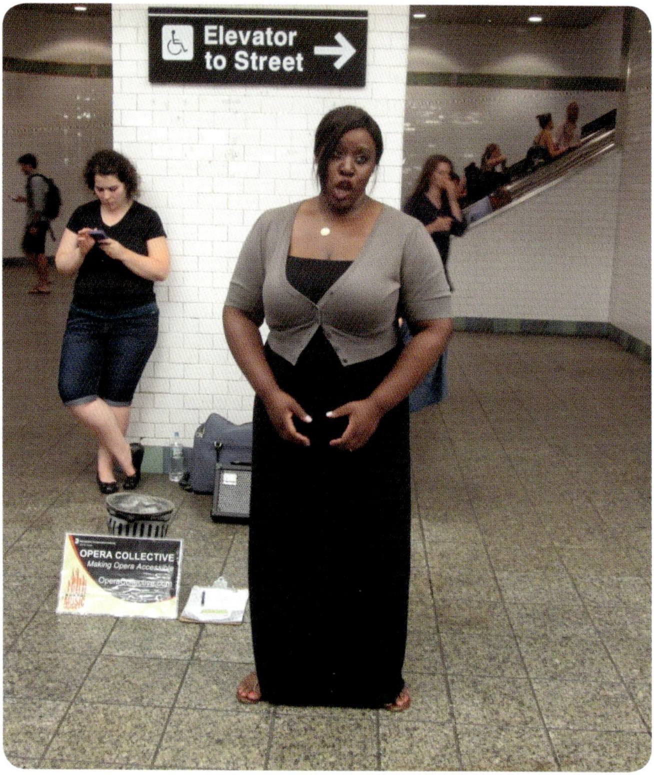

Opera Collective singer.

Times Square Station

42nd Street - Port Authority Station

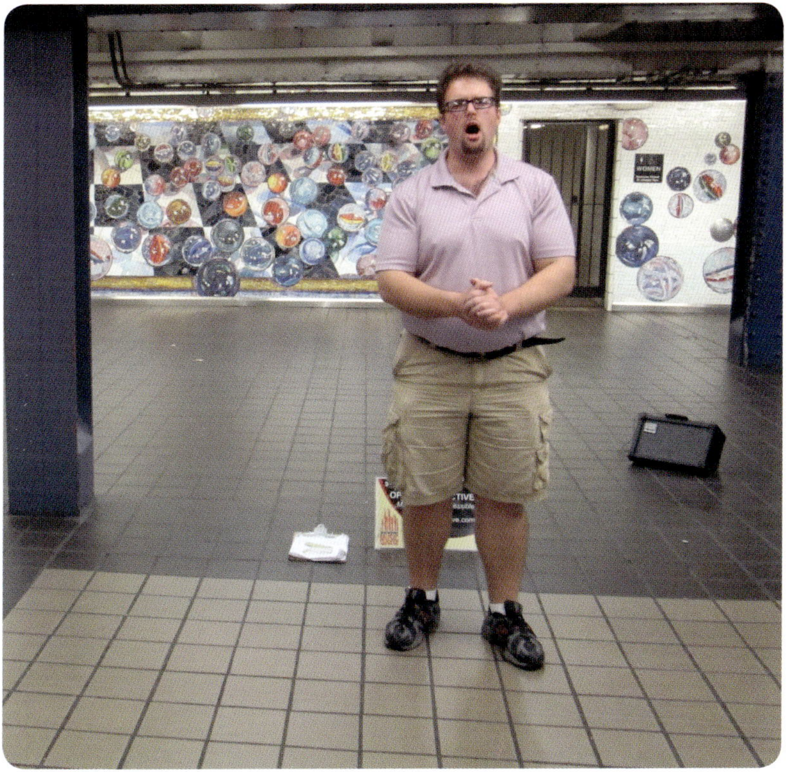

Opera Collective singer.

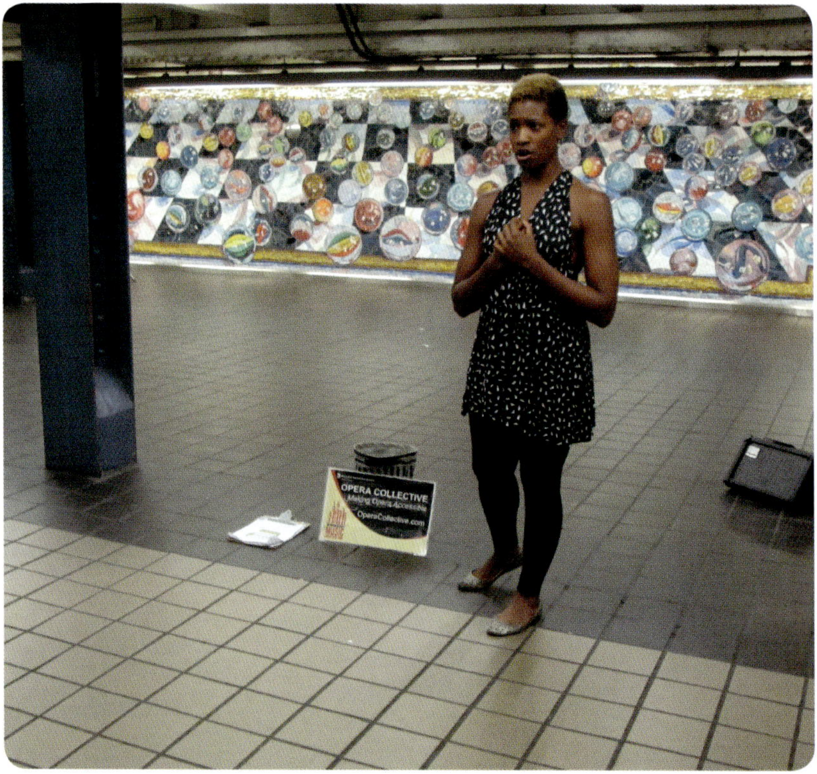

Opera Collective singer.

42nd Street - Port Authority Station

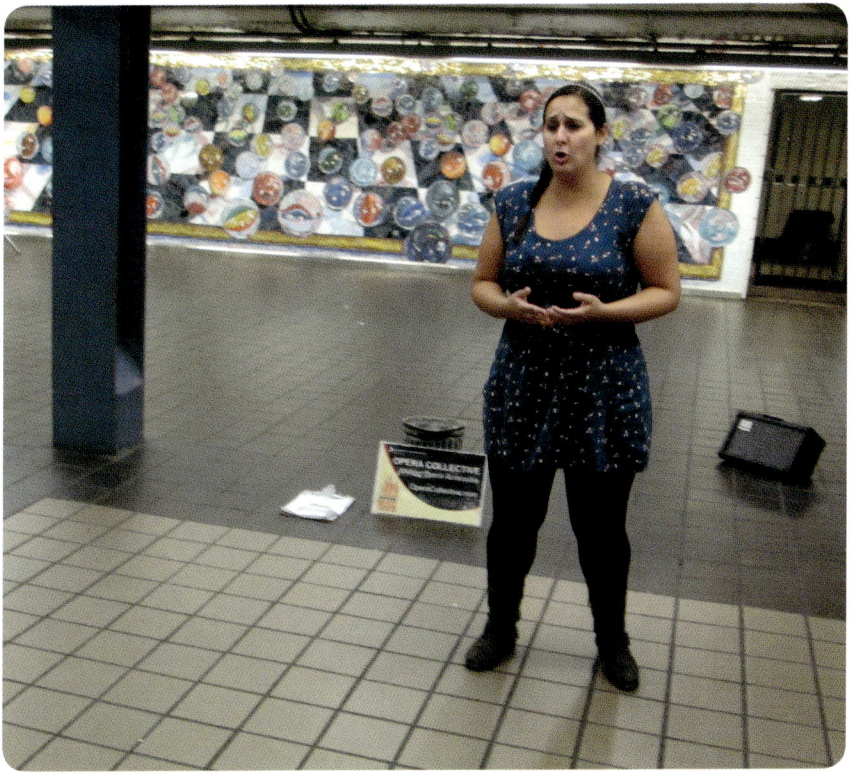

Opera Collective singer.

42nd Street - Port Authority Station

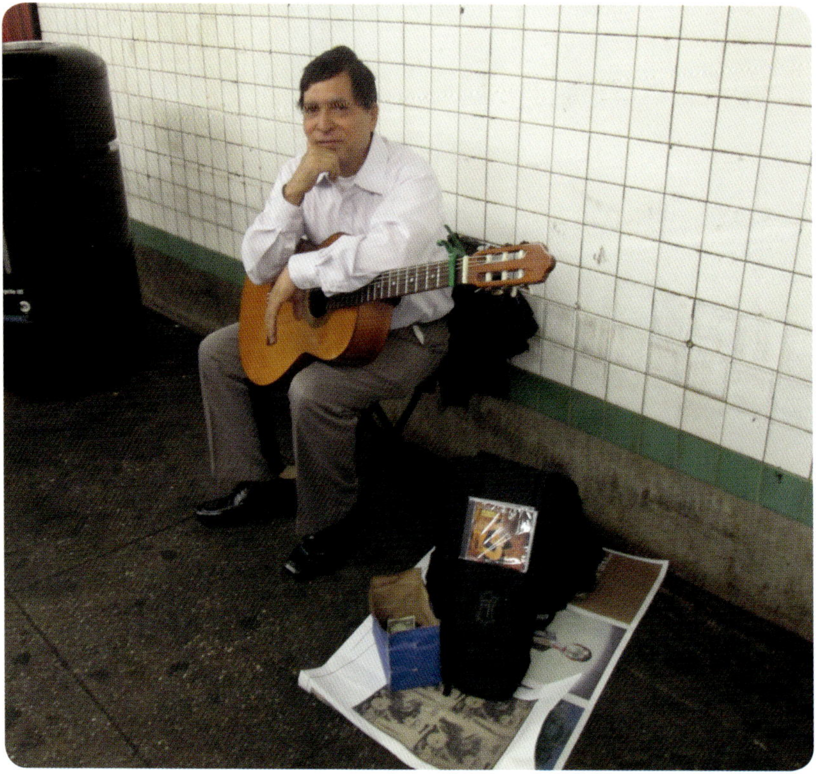

Guitarist.

23rd Street and 6th Avenue Station

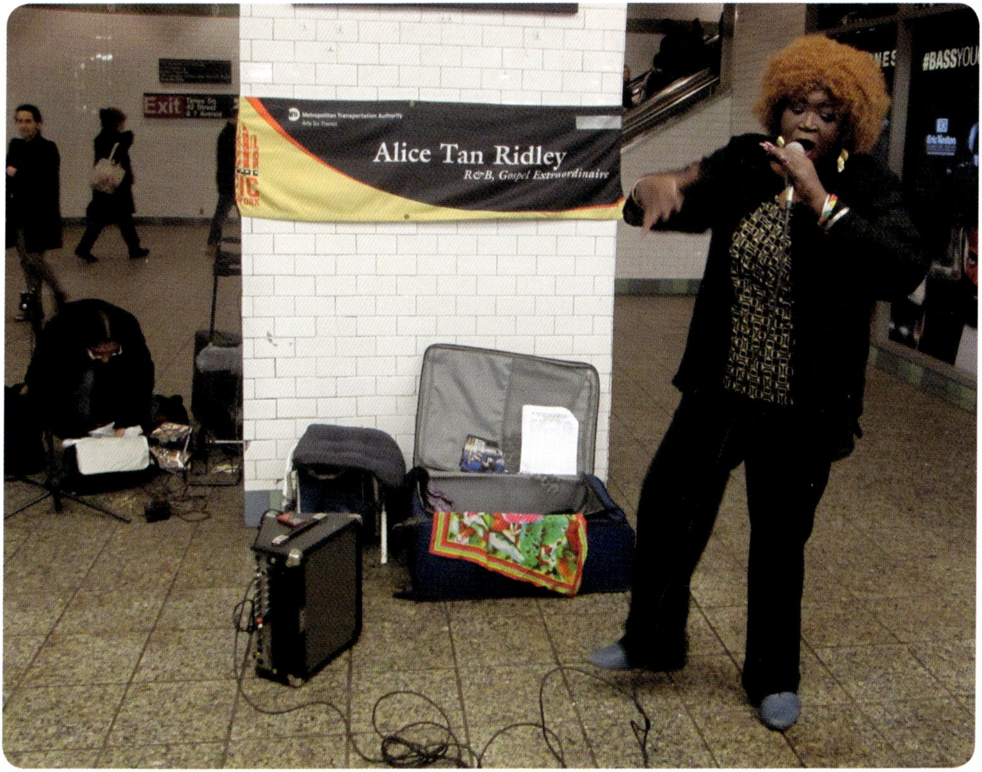

Alice Tan Ridley, R&B and Gospel Extraordinaire.

Times Square Station

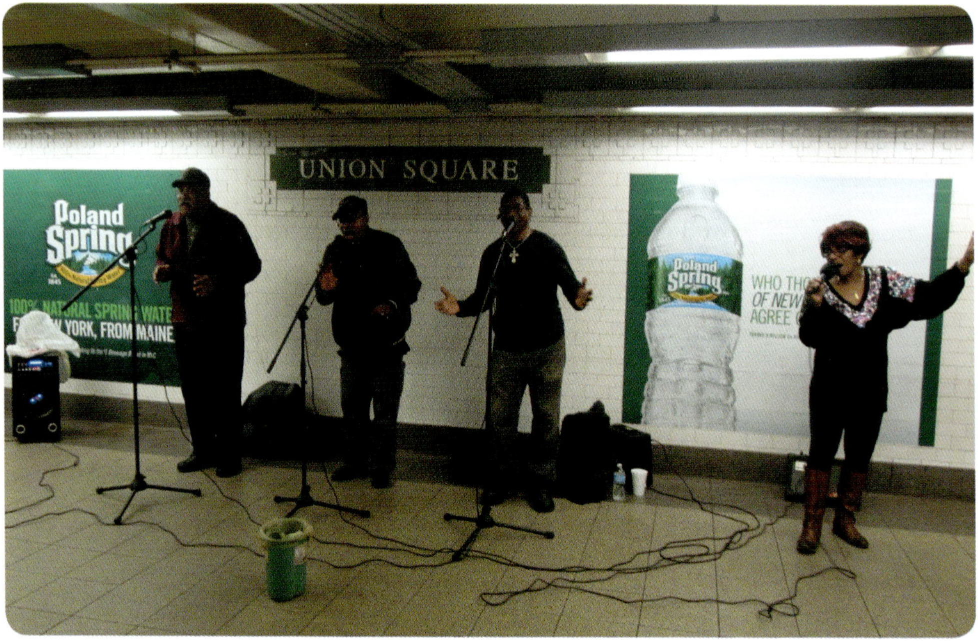

Singing quartet.

Union Square Station

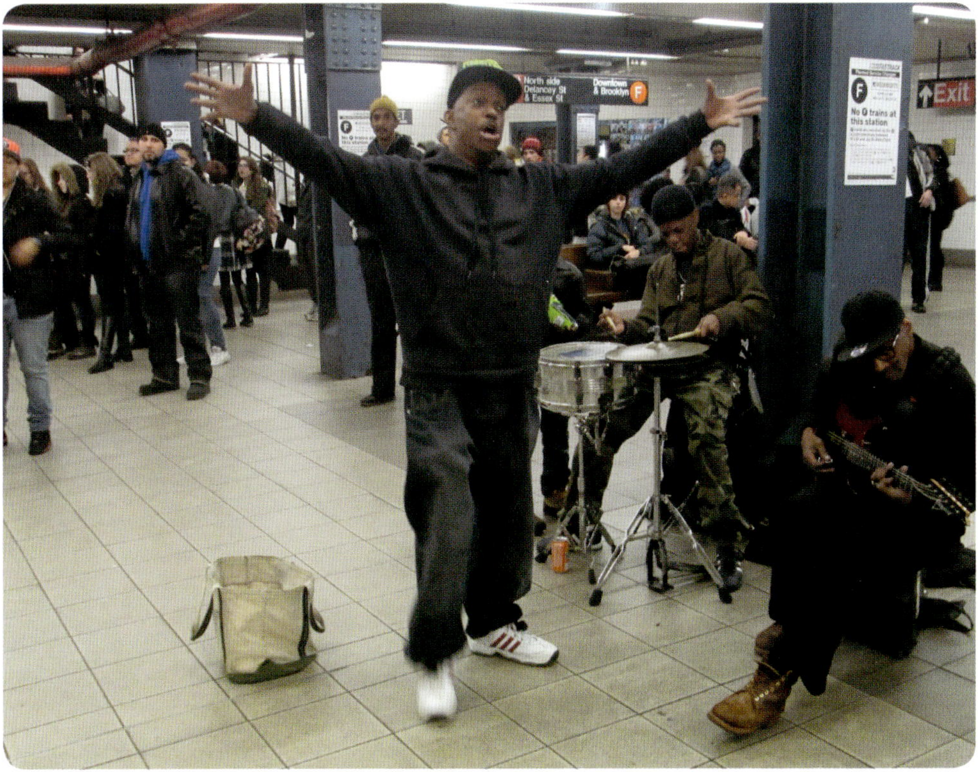

Majestic K. Funk.

Delancey Street Station

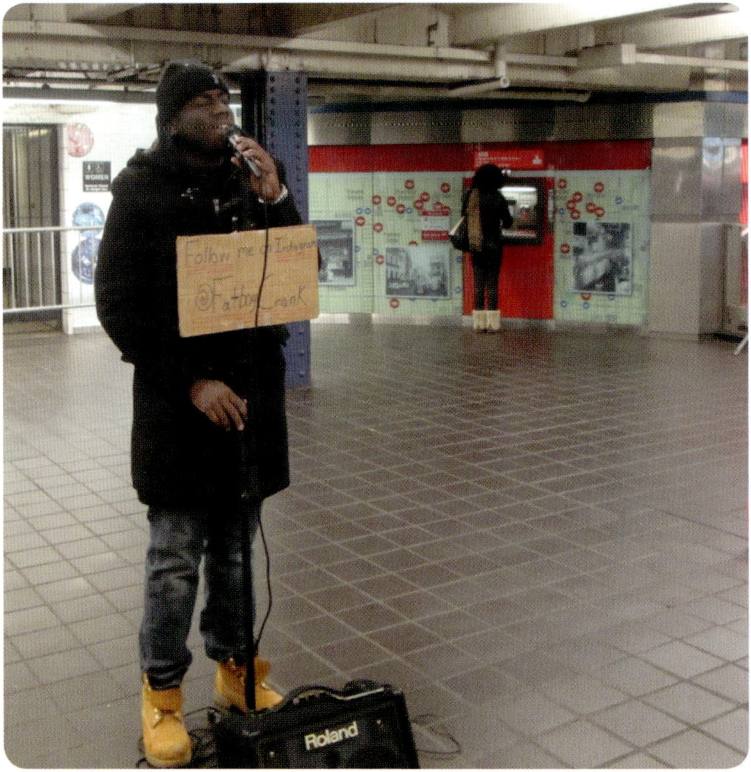

Fat Boy Crank.

42nd Street - Port Authority Station

Union Square Station

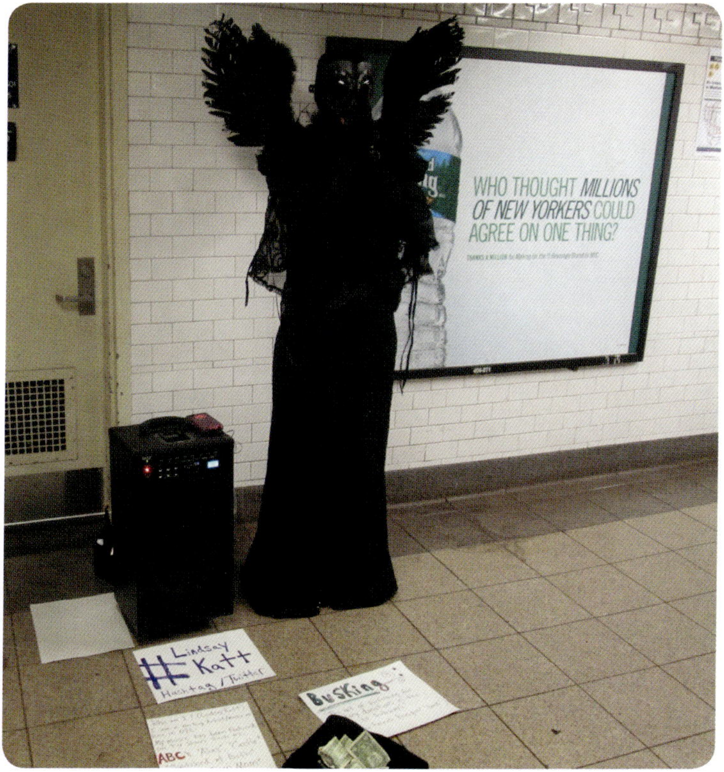

Lindsay Katt.

34th Street - Herald Square Station

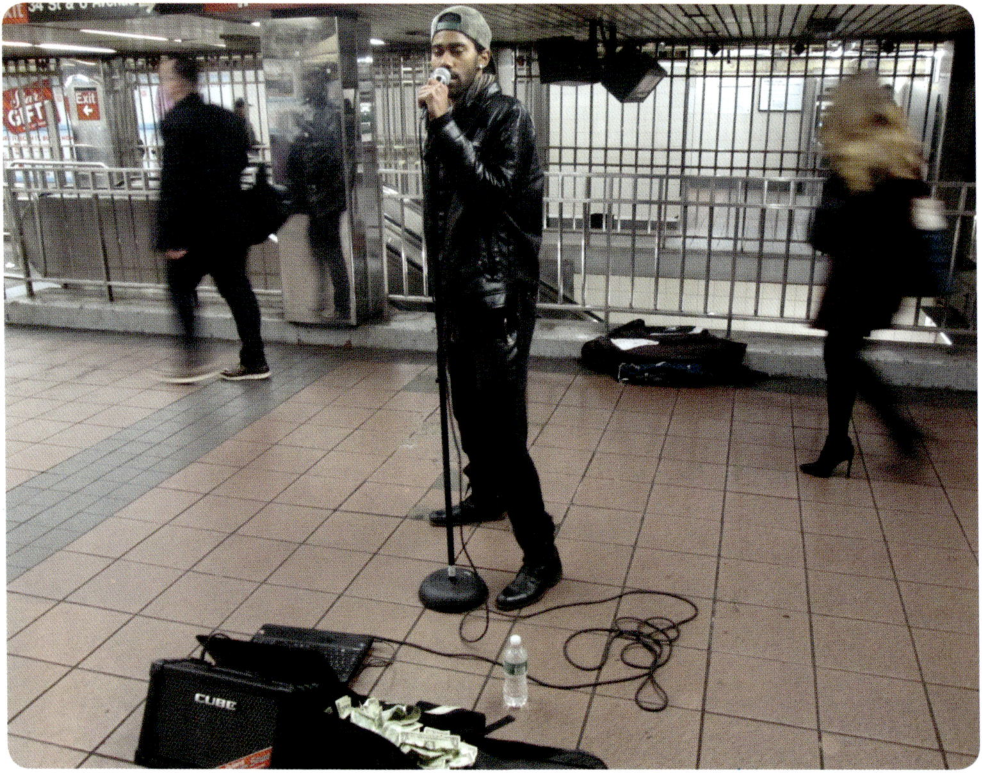

Von Middleton, singer.

7th Avenue Station

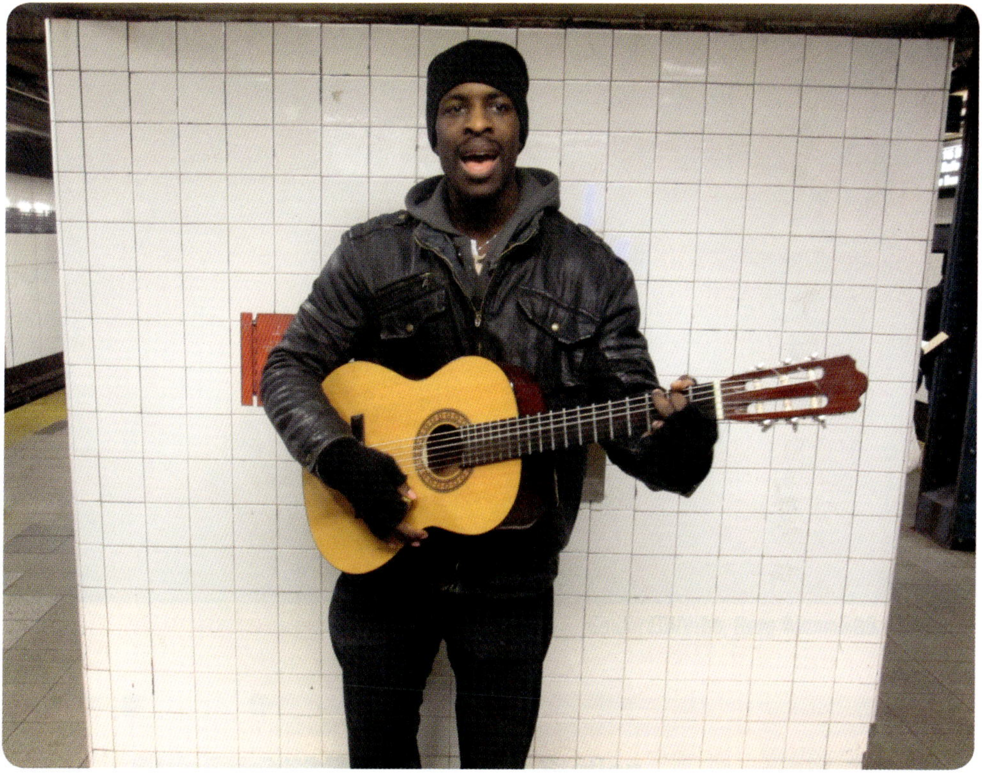

Damiyr, folk guitar.

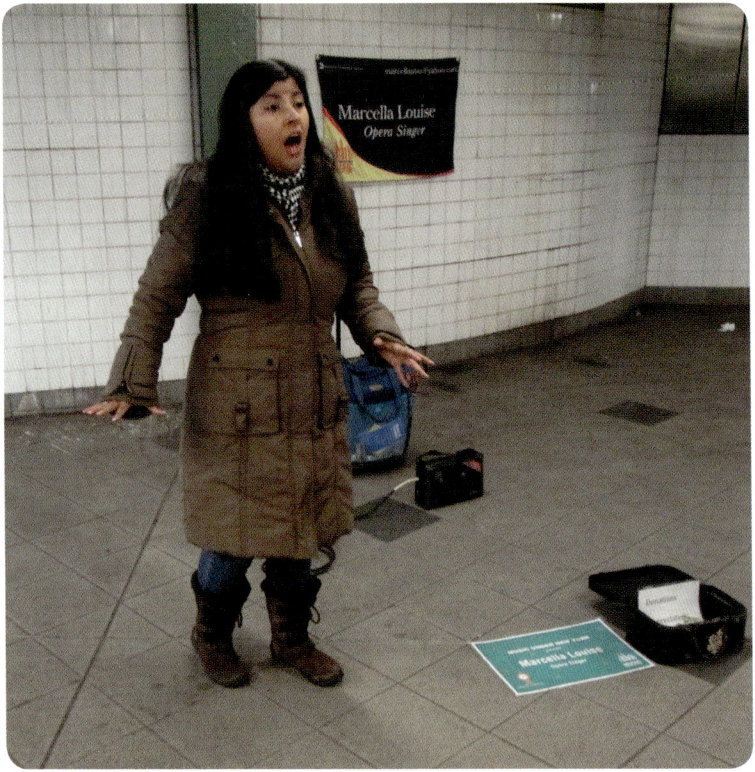

Marcella Louise, opera singer.

59th Street and Columbus Circle Station

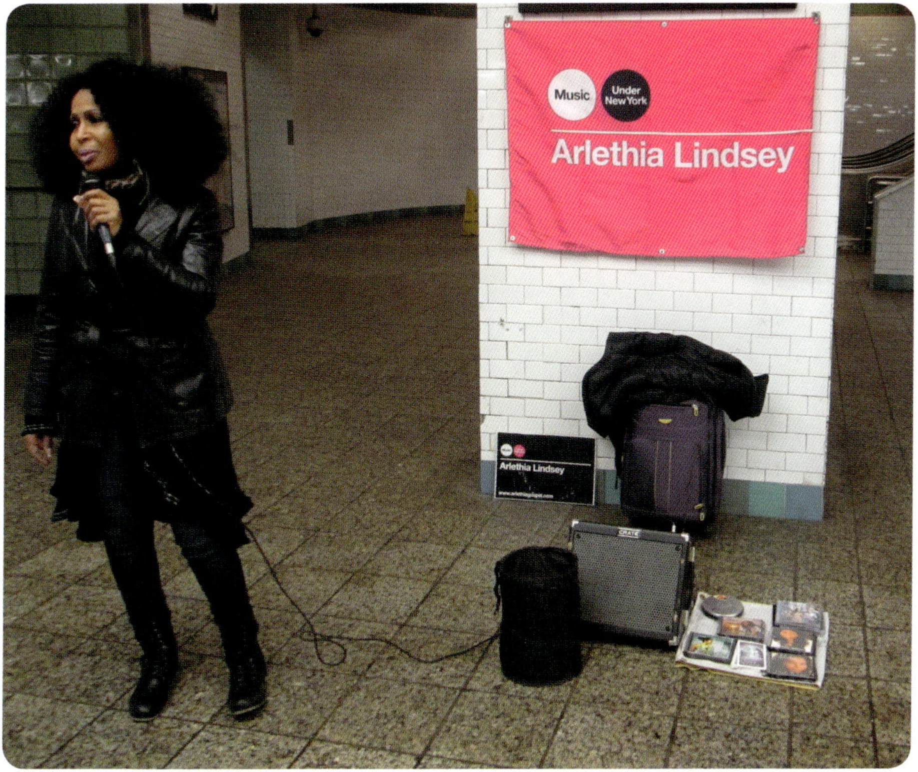

Arlethia Lindsey.

Times Square Station

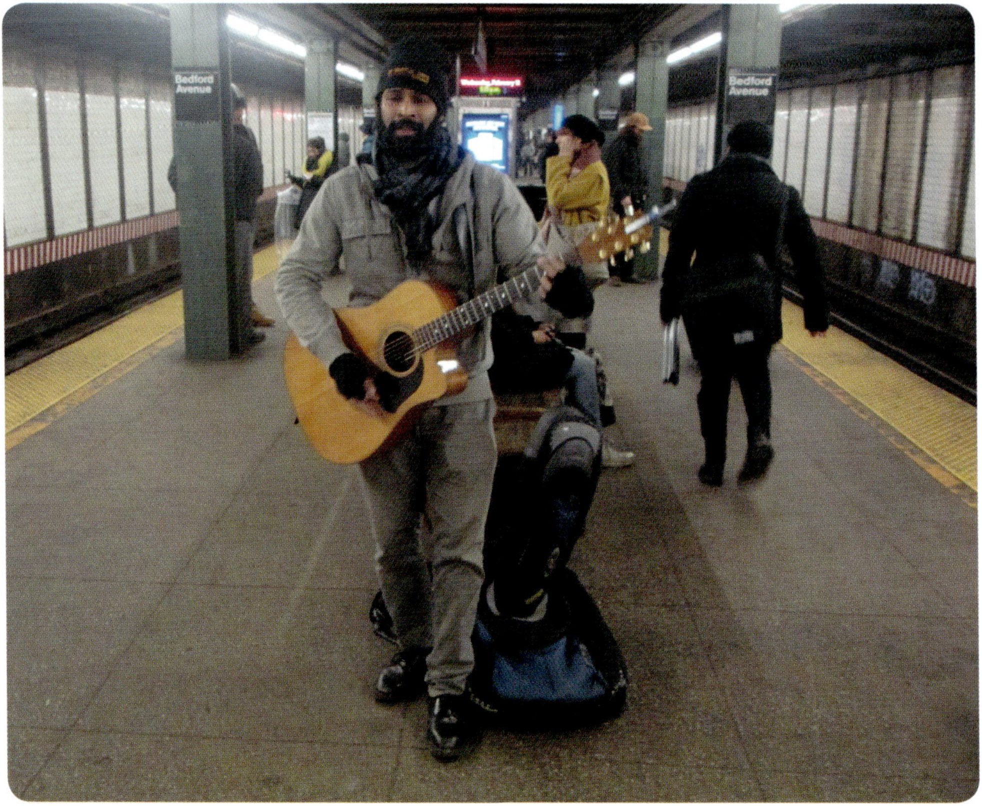

Folk guitarist.

Bedford Avenue Station

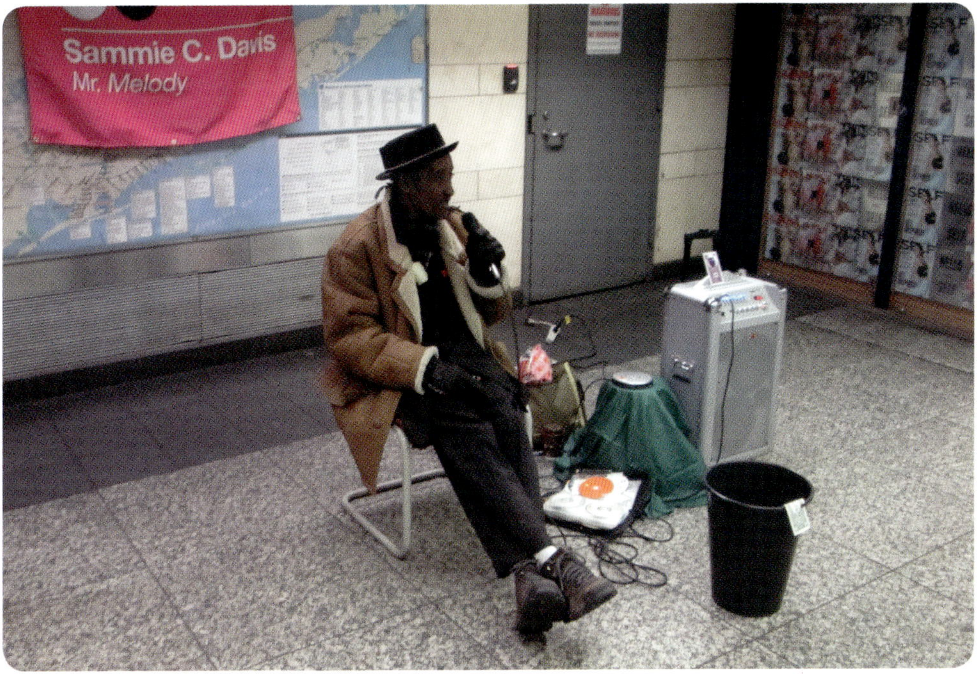

Sammie C. Davis, Mr. Melody.

34th Street - Penn Station

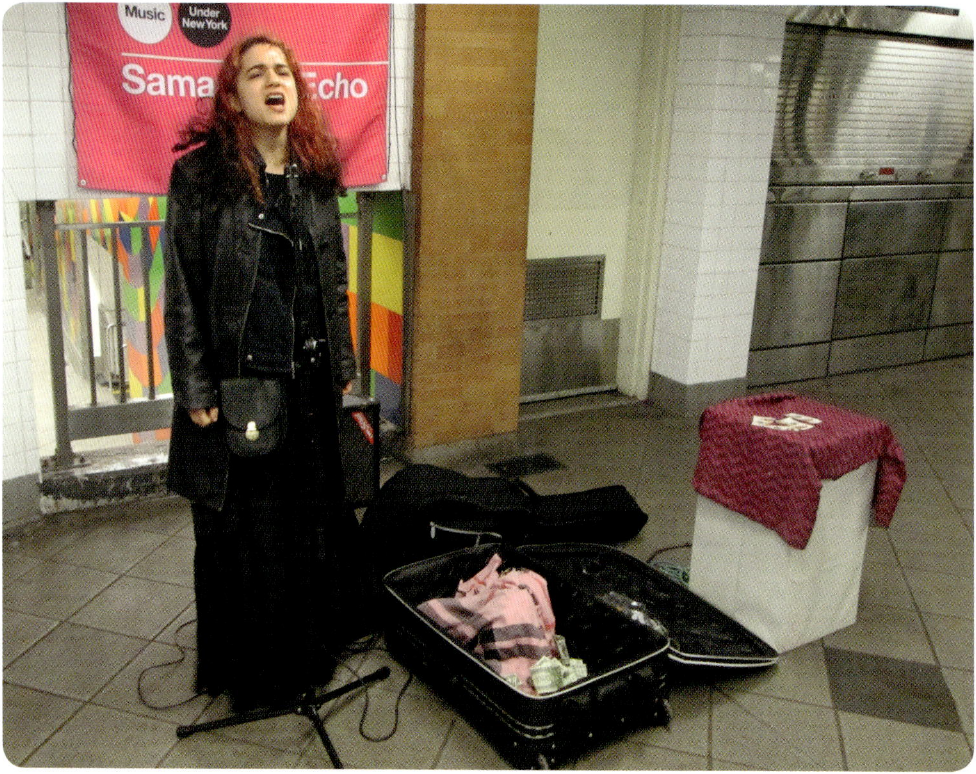

Samantha Echo.

59th Street and Columbus Circle Station

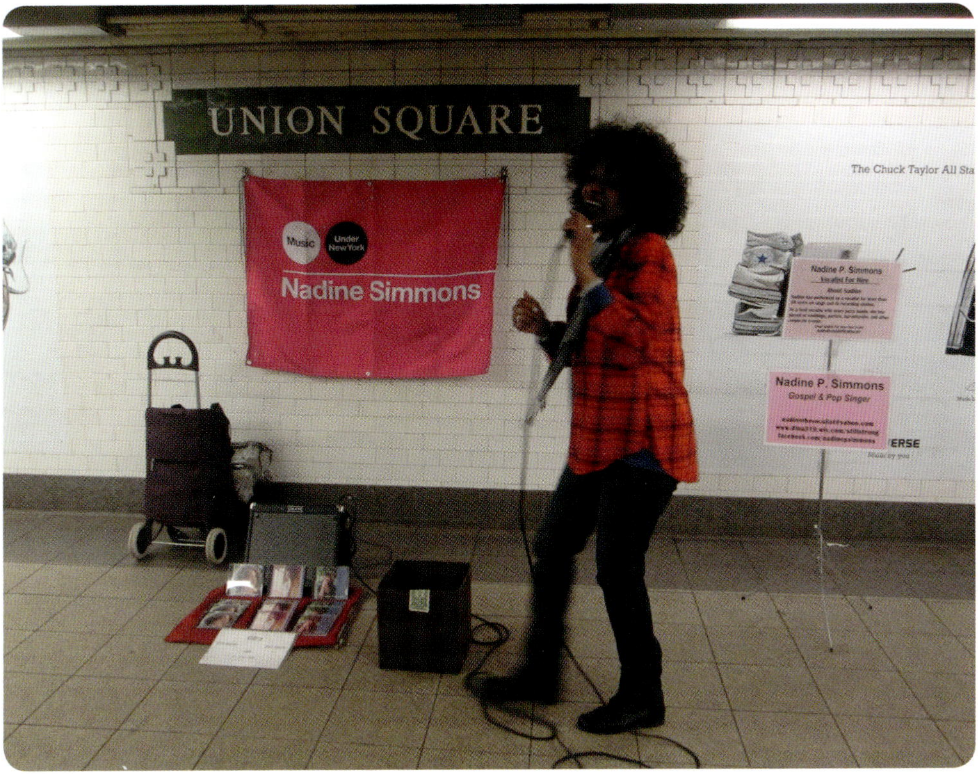

Nadine Simmons, gospel and pop singer.

Union Square Station

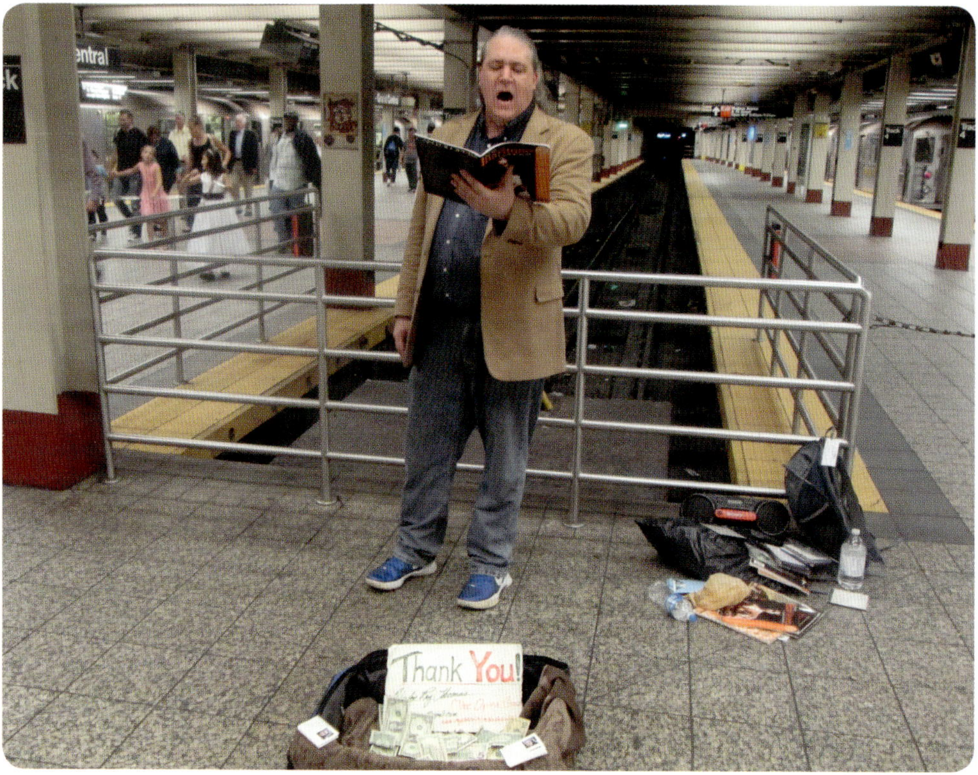

Wesley Ray Thomas, baritone.

Grand Central Station Shuttle Platform

Union Square Station

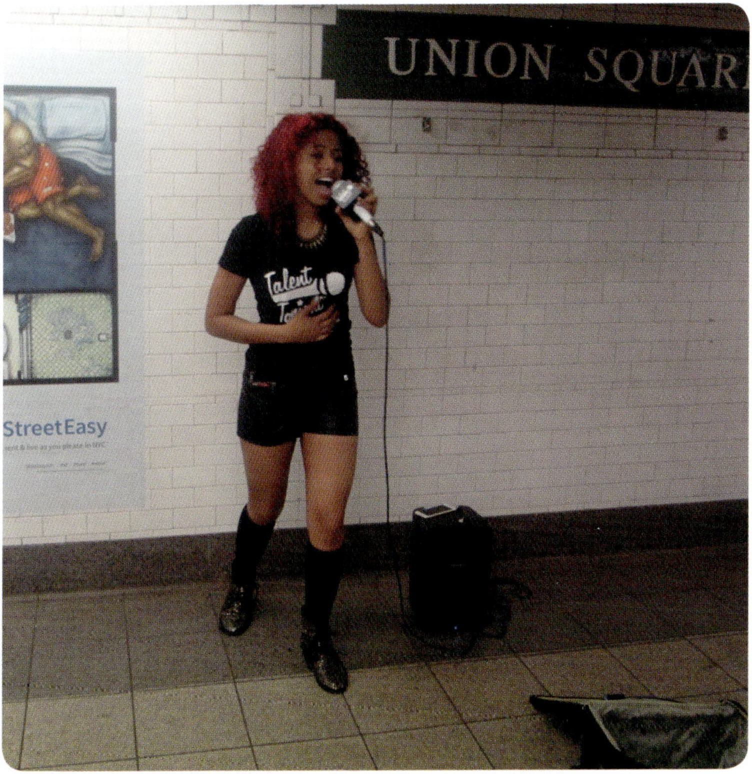

Talent Tonight singer.

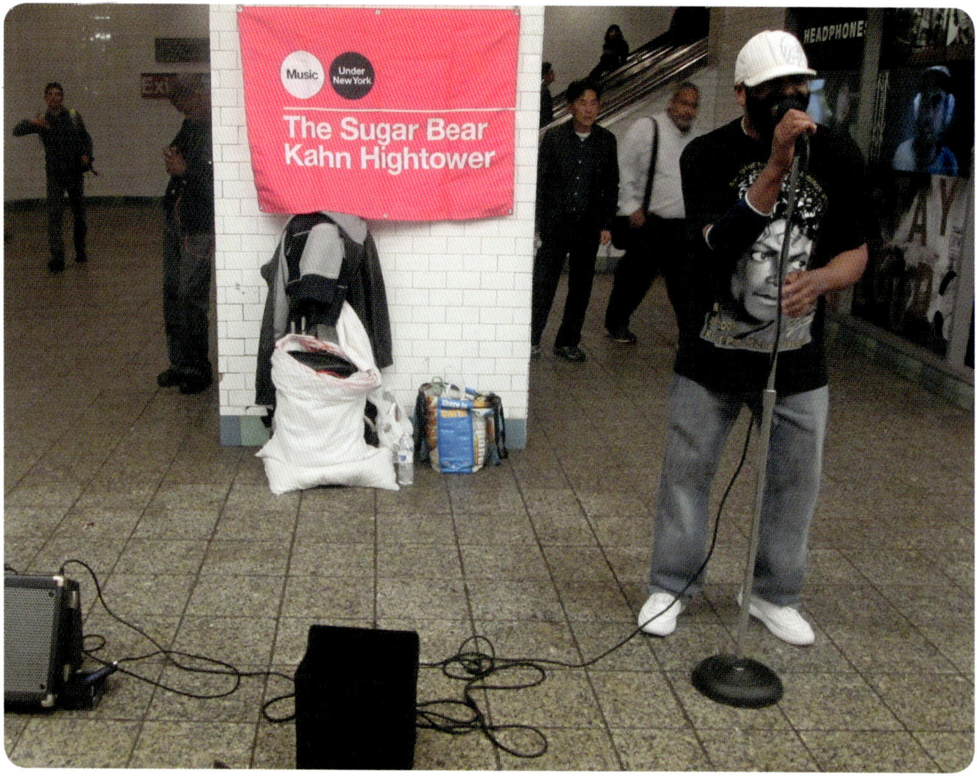

Kahn Hightower - The Sugar Bear.

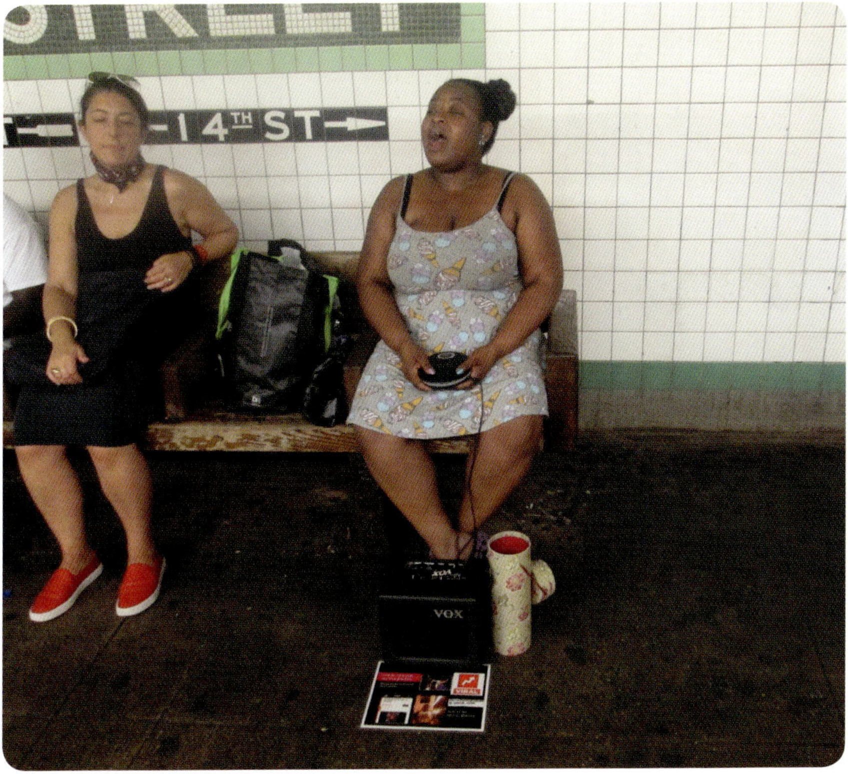

Silvia Jhony, viral singer.

14th Street and 6th Avenue Station

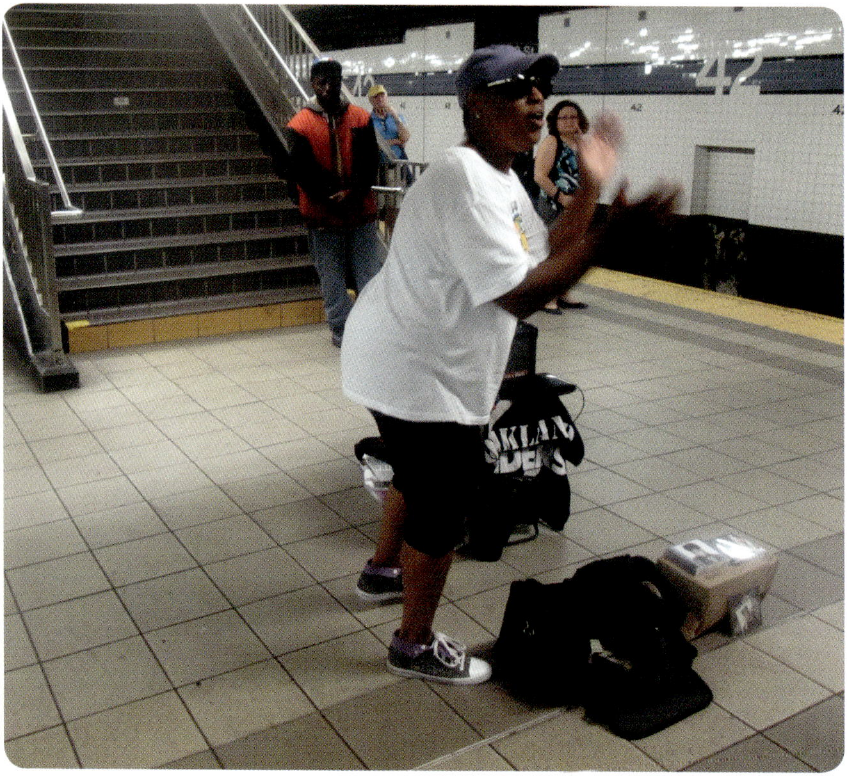

Annette Taylor.

42nd Street - Port Authority Station

42nd Street - Port Authority Station

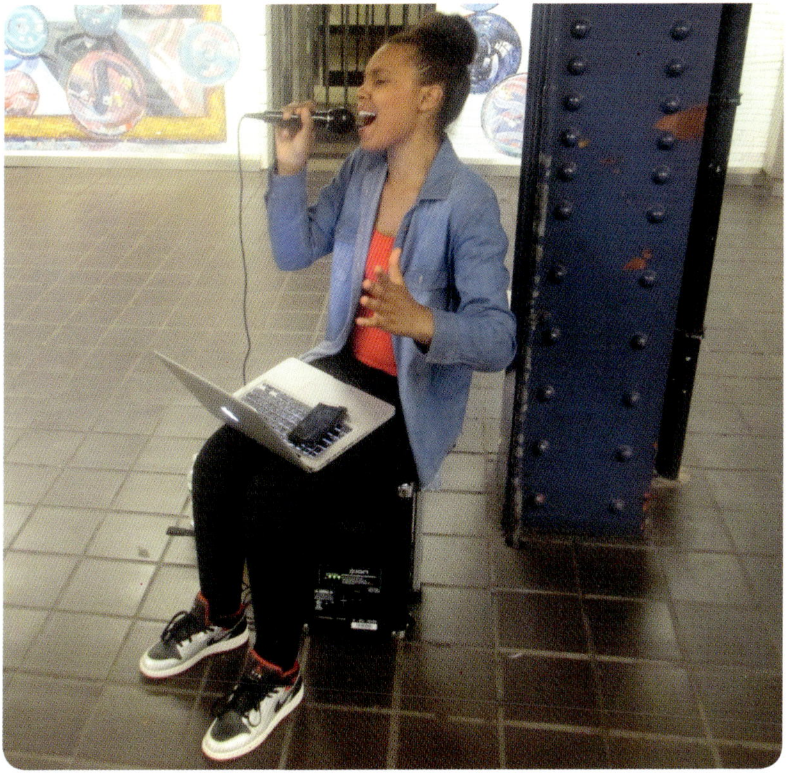

Ayanna Joni, singer, songwriter, and performer.

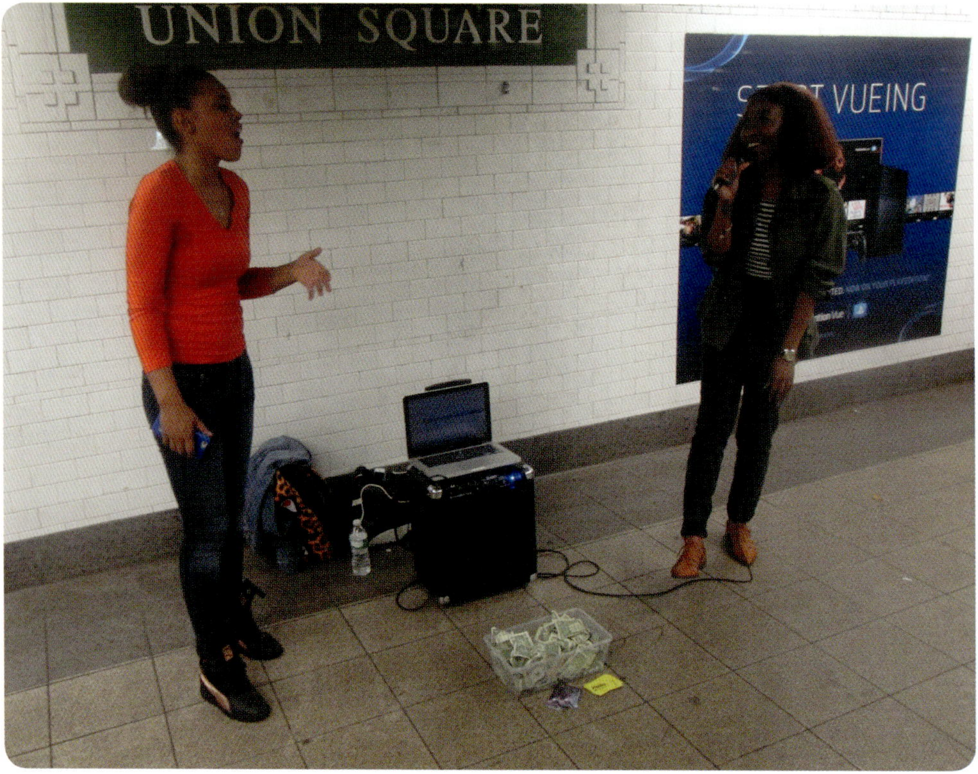

Ayanna Joni and Kamil Sahar.

Union Square Station

Times Square Station

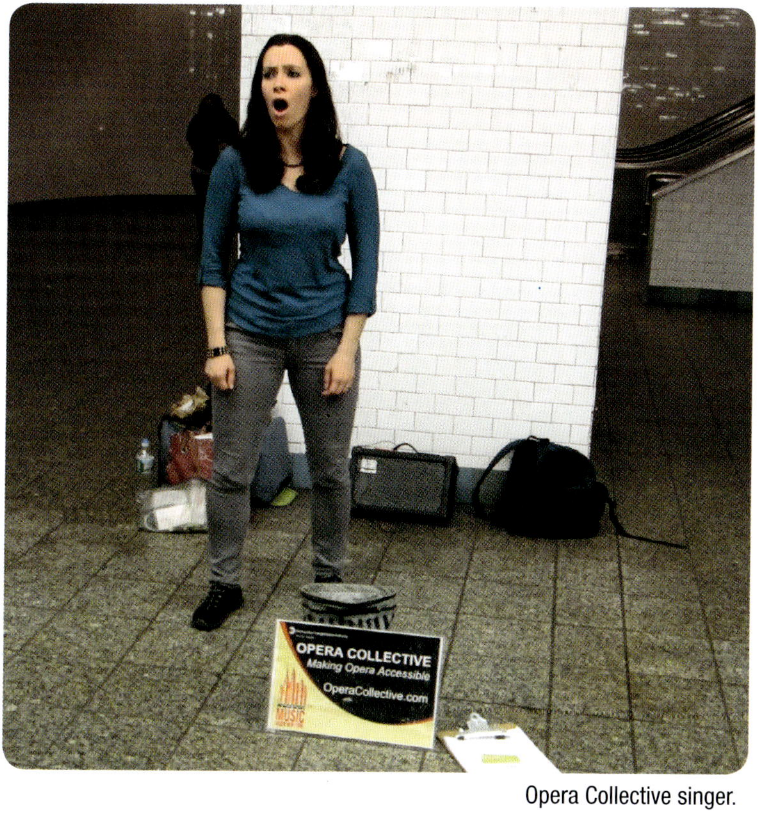

Opera Collective singer.

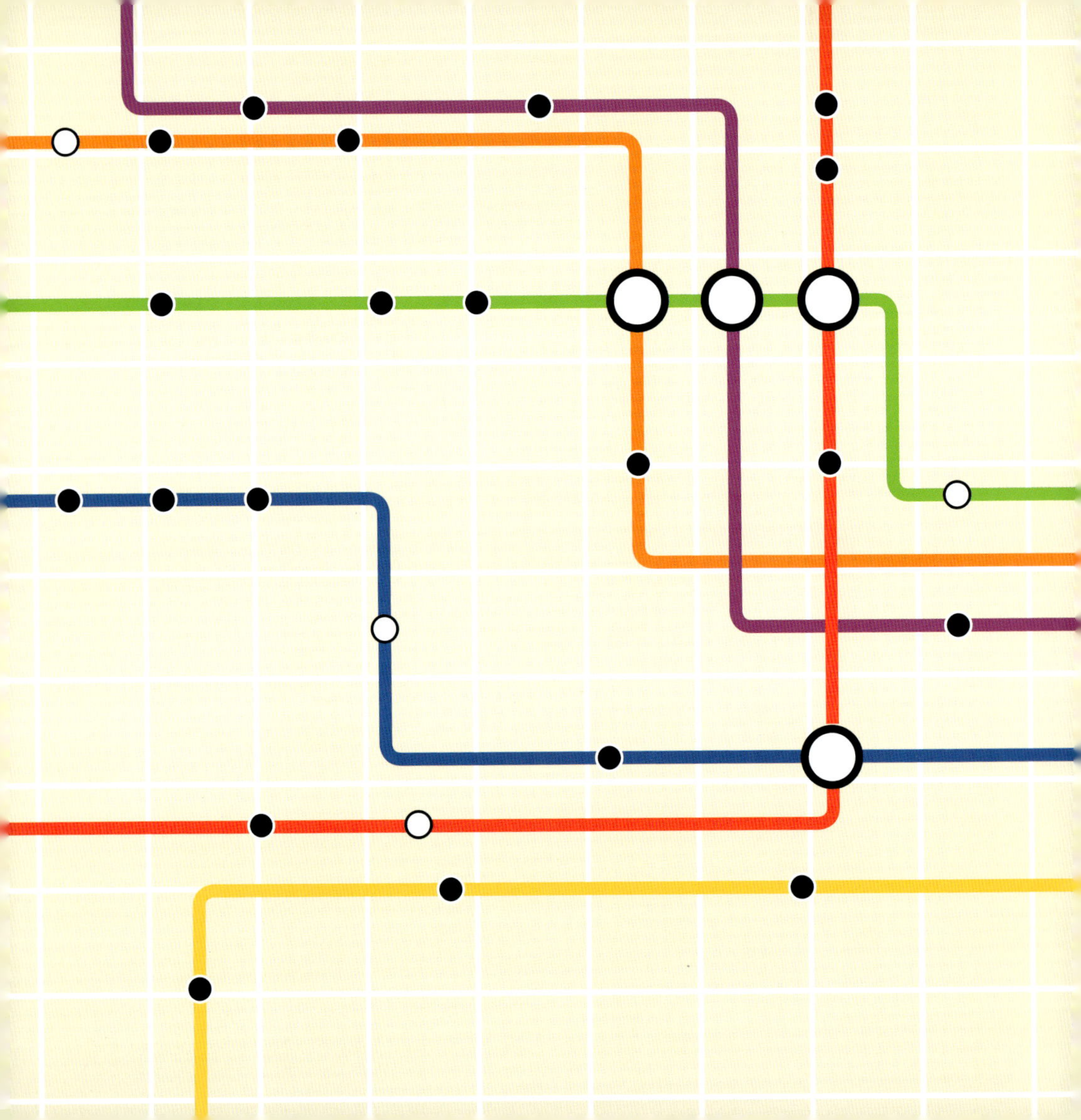

Chapter 8

Interviews

Matthew Christian

(Director of Busk NY)

Q: *What is Busk New York?*

A: It's an organization that advocates for subway performers.

Q: *What is a busker?*

A: A busker is someone who performs in public and accepts donations for it.

Q: *What are the goals of Busk NY in the next couple of years?*

A: We are looking to promote the interests of subway performers and help New York City recognize the contributions subway musicians make to the cultural fabric of the city.

Q: *From your estimate how many buskers are active in New York?*

A: It's tough to know a total. I think in the subway there are at least 300 people who perform regularly.

Q: *What is the significance of the celebration you have today and the case* People vs. Manning*?*

A: We are just recognizing that it's been thirty years since the case that first allowed subway musicians to perform legally. It was a very important moment for New York City that the people got right. We wanted to give it a good recognition at thirty years.

Roger Manning

(Former subway performer and Subject of *People vs. Manning)*

Q: *How long have you been a subway performer?*

A: I haven't sung in the subways for a number of years now, but I started around 1983 and continued until the late 1990s, singing on the subways.

Q: *What was that like?*

A: It was a good thing. It gave me a place where I could develop, develop my craft, and sometimes support yourself, and not have to be under the control of the music industry. You don't have to wait for a club owner to book you or anything like that. You go and play and just do it, as they say. It's real important to be able to do that.

Q: *You are known for a particular court case against NYC. Tell me about that?*

A: The case was against me. It was called *People (New York) vs. Manning.* There is a copy of it on the Busk New York website. It was about a law called "Entertaining Passengers: no one shall entertain passengers by singing or dancing or do anything in or about the subway in MTA." It was found to be unconstitutional regarding the first amendment, because they consider New York City subway platforms an actual public thoroughfare. So it's kind of like a sidewalk. Even though the MTA is technically

(Roger Manning interview continued)

a private area, it's a public thoroughfare and you have the right to perform there, provided it's within certain safety considerations and that kind of thing. The court ruled in my favor that I could constitutionally perform in the subway.

So, okay, we got that. Then after that they harassed us for other things: now you're doing this or that, or soliciting. There were other people after me who have been getting into court and challenging things, and that added to what my case achieved. Which bring us to where we are now.

Q: *What instruments do you play?*

A: When I was subway performing, I played the guitar and sang, then I branched out to the clarinet and played with a radical marching band in Brooklyn.

Q: *Have you recorded any albums?*

A: I have four albums and I'm in the process of reissuing old ones on the Internet.

Cathy Grier

(NYC subway performer and stage performer, member of the MTA Music program)

Q: *How did you become a subway performer?*

A: I became a subway performer because I was a stage performer for a very long time, probably twenty years. I thought of myself as a singer-songwriter, and that my career would be performing on stages. I have lived in places like Key West, Florida, and Paris, France, where I performed in a lot of different clubs. When I moved to New York City at the end of the 1990s, I just found the club scene was really not inspiring me. I wanted to play, and I thought this [subway performance] would be a great opportunity to keep playing and be part of the city, so I started busking. And then I understood what it meant to perform in public spaces and the importance of art, music, and dance in public spaces—they're just incredibly important.

Q: *What's it like to be a busker?*

A: It's a great question, because as a stage performer you expect people to come in, sit, and listen to you. You're the show. But in street performing or subway performing you're not the show. You are a sidebar—you're something along the way. A passage you happen to be in, this wonderful little thing somebody comes across. Any musician that goes into street performing and expects people to stop what they're doing to form a crowd and hang out and listen... well, that happens infrequently, or maybe just for a song or two, but not for a whole show like you do on stage. It's just this constant sound, like we are part of a soundtrack. Whether it's people's feet in the turnstile or screeching trains or sirens above ground, it's not a perfect setting. So that's what is different about it. You have to integrate into that, include it in the show. It's almost like learning a whole new way of walking, a whole new way of performance.

Q: *Donations are part of the experience. How do you as a performer look at the donations as part of being a busker?*

A: The donations are our contract. I've just given you something. It could be a smile as a donation. Money is always good. We love to get paid for what we do. We love to think in today's world, in 2015, that people will actually be paid for art. Unfortunately, we live in a time where people pay $3 ATM fees for using their bankcard but they won't pay for music. I think by being a busker and having a tip bag or something you are saying to somebody, "I am going to perform for you. Feel free to contribute to this lovely experience, but you don't have to." Somebody can give me a penny, a smile, $100, or a gig.

Q: *So there is opportunity from busking?*

A: Yes, totally. People walk by and say, "Would you play at my wedding?" "Would you play at my club?" "Do you have your music online?" "How do I find your music?"

Q: *How many years have you been busking?*

A: I have busked since 1999. I have been performing since 1978.

Q: *What is it like being in the* MTA Music *program versus not being in the program?*

A: The only difference is for artists like myself coming out of stage performing. I wanted the structure of a schedule, to be able to call in every two weeks and say, "These are locations I would like to play. These are the times I would like to play." I like that feeling of a little structure, that I could set up at this location and I wouldn't be pushing some other artist out of the way or some artist wouldn't be trying to push me out of the way later, and that I have my three-hour set. I think it's really important the transit authority has a program like this. But in terms of what we call freelancing—just going out and performing—that's a lot of what today is about. [We are] celebrating thirty years of busking in part because Roger Manning made that happen.

Q: *What is the future of busking in New York?*

A: I don't know what the future of busking is in New York, but if police keep arresting musicians for performing on a platform or for other violations we're in trouble. I think the future needs to have an integrated cultural understanding that it is perfectly legal and acceptable for live music to be played in parks and in the subways.

Heidi Kole

(Author of *The Subway Diaries* and a subway performer)

Q: *When did you start busking?*

A: I started busking about ten or eleven years ago. I am a stunt person as well. I had an accident and I ended up with a concussion and whiplash. I couldn't stand up for that long while I was healing, sometimes just an hour or two, so I didn't have a way to support myself. One day I decided to go straight from physical therapy down to the train station. I brought my guitar to physical therapy. I went straight underground and I was so scared. It was February and it was freezing, and I didn't understand the whole busking thing at all. Some guy told me about the spot at 59th Street and I went to that spot, wherever it was. I sang and lasted about twelve minutes before my voice got hoarse, but in that short time something left me and what remained left me with this feeling of complete abandonment and bliss.

Until I finished my book *The Subway Diaries* I couldn't really figure out what it was that left me, but then I realized what it was: ego. I ended up with this feeling like when you are singing in the shower. You are not trying to impress anyone, you don't care what people think, you don't care what people are saying or doing. And that was what brought me back to the subways. It wasn't the $13 or whatever I had made. It was the feeling of complete and utter abandonment, and having the chance every day to lose your ego and lose yourself in something that's completely selfless.

Over the next bunch of years and decades I guess the subways have given me back so much more than I have given. I have given my heart and soul, but the subways have given me back ten times more. They have allowed me to grow as an artist and find my true voice. I was trained classically in opera and musical theatre, and I didn't really know anything outside of what I was exposed to, but the subways have allowed me to find the style, the music, the flow, and the rhythm that really moves me. And the subways have given me the space, this non-judgmental space to try something new every day I go down there.

And the community; the reason I wrote the book is because of this community of artists. This underground community is the closest thing I have to family on this planet, honestly. It means the world to me. I will protect their right to make art if it's the last thing I do. I feel so strongly about the ability to have continuous, non-corporate sanctioned art and creativity. The community down there is so supportive and amazing.

I love how it works. I love how without any rules written down we all know how to make it work. There is a lot of unspoken etiquette that you learn. It's a learning curve. It took [me] two to three years to learn how the whole thing works. No one will sit you down and share it with you; you have to absorb it through trial and error. People say, "Why are you in New York?" They ask me that all the time. It's hard here sometimes. My answer is always *the subways*.

Q: *What are your most popular stations?*

A: Most of the work takes place uptown A, C, E, and the Times Square-Port Authority station. It's closest to my house. It happens to be one of the best spots in the city. That's always my first choice, because it's less of a commute. It's a good spot, a lot of locals and tourists. It's always busy — sometimes a little too busy. But it's a good spot for me. There are always A and B spots on a platform, but the A spot of uptown A and C is my favorite.

But I have busked everywhere. When I first started I busked tunnels. I busked the Bryant Park tunnels, the ones at 34th Street. I tried platforms all over the city—mostly in the city; I can't say I have gone too far outside. Although about three years ago it was really hot and it was getting very crowded on the platforms, so I decided to try the cars. I love the cars because it's very intermittent. The pressure is on more in the cars. You have to grab people's attention in the first three seconds on that car. You have to be spot on all the time.

For all the times when I busk it's an energy exchange. I go down there to raise the vibration. That's why I go into the trains. The planet is so much in a hole, in such a big way. There's really a lot of dark energy. People on the train—commuters are not a happy lot, for the most part, except for the buskers, so I go down there to change the vibration, even if it's just for three minutes. The most rewarding part for me is to see people coming down there. You know they are just hating life—hate the subways, hate their job—and then they hear a song they recognize and it takes to them to a place that was happy and their whole face changes. All the cares go away. They smile, they get softer, and for a moment they have forgotten what they were upset about and to me, *that's it*. That just makes my day. I know I have done my job.

Q: *In a week for a regular busker, how many hours would a busker perform?*

A: For me, since I am a vocalist, I can last for three hours before my voice gives out. I usually go every other day.

Q: *What will readers learn from your book?*

A: The thing I hear from every single person that reads it is, "I had no idea this world existed. And I will never look at New York City subways the same again, ever." That was one of the reasons I wrote it, because people think we are disconnected down there. And really we're not—we're family. It's a high-energy, connected family, because we all have been through the trenches down there. We all deal with the NYPD, we all deal with the elements, we all deal with no bathroom, no heat, no water, no air conditioning—we deal with it. Anyone who is down there for any extended period of time—meaning years—you end up with some kind of respect from the other performers.

List of Artists

Kurt Boone is a native New Yorker, freelance writer, and poet. He has written for *Narratively*, *PBS Metro Focus* and *Urban Velo* magazine. His numerous other books include *Asphalt Warrior*, *Messenger Poet*, *The Skyscraper Shuffle*, and *Chicago CMWC: The World's Fastest Bicycle Messengers*. For videos, blogs, and more information, visit his websites at www.kurtboonebooks.com and www.subwaybeats.com.